Muirhead Library of Philosophy

CONTEMPORARY BRITISH PHILOSOPHY

MUIRHEAD

Muirhead Library of Philosophy

20TH CENTURY PHILOSOPHY

In 22 Volumes

I	Contemporary American Philosophy (Vol I)	*Adams & Montague*
II	Contemporary American Philosophy (Vol II)	*Adams & Montague*
III	G E Moore	*Ambrose & Lazerowitz*
IV	Ludwig Wittgenstein	*Ambrose & Lazerowitz*
V	Philosophy in America	*Black*
VI	Contemporary Philosophy in Australia	*Brown & Rollins*
VII	A History of Philosophy (Vol I)	*Erdmann*
VIII	A History of Philosophy (Vol II)	*Erdmann*
IX	A History of Philosophy (Vol III)	*Erdmann*
X	Ideas	*Husserl*
XI	The Development of Bertrand Russell's Philosophy	*Jager*
XII	Contemporary British Philosophy (Vol III)	*Lewis*
XIII	Contemporary British Philosophy (Vol IV)	*Lewis*
XIV	A Hundred Years of British Philosophy	*Metz*
XV	Lectures on Philosophy	*Moore*
XVI	Commonplace Book	*Moore*
XVII	Philosophical Papers	*Moore*
XVIII	Some Main Problems of Philosophy	*Moore*
XIX	Bernard Bosanquet and His Friends	*Muirhead*
XX	Contemporary British Philosophy (Vol I)	*Muirhead*
XXI	Contemporary British Philosophy (Vol II)	*Muirhead*
XXII	Bertrand Russell Memorial Volume	*Roberts*

CONTEMPORARY BRITISH PHILOSOPHY

Personal Statements

Volume IV

EDITED BY H D LEWIS

Routledge
Taylor & Francis Group
LONDON AND NEW YORK

First published 1976 by
George Allen & Unwin Ltd

Published 2013 by Routledge
2 Park Square, Milton Park, Abingdon, Oxfordshire OX14 4RN
711 Third Avenue, New York, NY 10017

First issued in paperback 2014

Routledge is an imprint of the Taylor and Francis Group, an informa business

British Library Cataloguing in Publication Data
A CIP catalogue record for this book
is available from the British Library

Contemporary British Philosophy (Vol IV)

20th Century Philosophy: 22 Volumes
ISBN 0-415-29526-2
Muirhead Library of Philosophy: 95 Volumes
ISBN 0-415-27897-X

ISBN 13: 978-1-138-88416-8 (pbk)
ISBN 13: 978-0-415-29547-5 (hbk)

MUIRHEAD LIBRARY OF PHILOSOPHY

An admirable statement of the aims of the Library of Philosophy was provided by the first editor, the late Professor J. H. Muirhead, in his description of the original programme printed in Erdmann's *History of Philosophy* under the date 1890. This was slightly modified in subsequent volumes to take the form of the following statement:

'The Muirhead Library of Philosophy was designed as a contribution to the History of Modern Philosophy under the heads: first of Different Schools of Thought—Sensationalist, Realist, Idealist, Intuitivist; secondly of different Subjects—Psychology, Ethics, Aesthetics, Political Philosophy, Theology. While much had been done in England in tracing the course of evolution in nature, history, economics, morals and religion, little had been done in tracing the development of thought on these subjects. Yet the "evolution of opinion is part of the whole evolution".

'By the co-operation of different writers in carrying out this plan it was hoped that a thoroughness and completeness of treatment, otherwise unattainable, might be secured. It was believed also that from writers mainly British and American fuller consideration of English Philosophy than it had hitherto received might be looked for. In the earlier series of books containing, among others, Bosanquet's *History of Aesthetic*, Pfleiderer's *Rational Theology since Kant*, Albee's *History of English Utilitarianism*, Bonar's *Philosophy and Political Economy*, Brett's *History of Psychology*, Ritchie's *Natural Rights*, these objects were to a large extent effected.

'In the meantime original work of a high order was being produced both in England and America by such writers as Bradley, Stout, Bertrand Russell, Baldwin, Urban, Montague, and others, and a new interest in foreign works, German, French and Italian, which had either become classical or were attracting public attention, had developed. The scope of the Library thus became extended into something more international, and it is entering on the fifth decade of its existence in the hope that it may contribute to that mutual understanding between countries which is so pressing a need of the present time.'

The need which Professor Muirhead stressed is no less pressing today, and few will deny that philosophy has much to do with enabling us to meet it, although no one, least of all Muirhead himself, would regard that as the sole, or even the main, object of philosophy. As Professor Muirhead continues to lend the distinction of his name to the Library of Philosophy it seemed not inappropriate to allow him to recall us to these aims in his own words. The emphasis on the history of thought also seemed to me very timely: and the number of important works promised for the Library in the very near future augur well for the continued fulfilment, in this and other ways, of the expectations of the original editor.

H. D. LEWIS

CONTEMPORARY BRITISH PHILOSOPHY

Personal Statements

FOURTH SERIES

G. E. M. ANSCOMBE
RENFORD BAMBROUGH
MICHAEL DUMMETT
ANTONY FLEW
PETER GEACH
D. W. HAMLYN
R. M. HARE
JONATHAN HARRISON
R. W. HEPBURN
STEPHAN KÖRNER
P. F. STRAWSON
RICHARD SWINBURNE
J. O. URMSON
GODFREY VESEY
W. H. WALSH
GEOFFREY WARNOCK
BERNARD WILLIAMS
PETER WINCH

EDITED BY
H. D. LEWIS

LONDON: GEORGE ALLEN & UNWIN LTD

HUMANITIES PRESS INC.
ATLANTIC HIGHLANDS, N.J.

First published in Great Britain in 1976

ISBN 0–391–00716–5

Library of Congress Cataloging in Publication Data (Revised)

Main entry under title:

Contemporary British philosophy

(Library of Philosophy)
First-second ser. edited by J. H. Muirhead; third- ser. edited by H. D. Lewis.
Third- ser. have series title: The Muirhead library of philosophy.
Vol. 4 has imprint: London, Allen & Unwin; Atlantic Highlands, N.J., Humanities Press.
Includes bibliographies.
1. Philosophy, English—20th century—Addresses, essays, lectures. I. Muirhead, John Henry, 1855–1940,

Library of Congress Cataloging in Publication Data

ed. II. Lewis, Hywel David, ed.
B1615.C6 192 24-26491

Printed in Great Britain
in 11 point Baskerville type
by Clarke, Doble & Brendon Ltd
Plymouth and London

EDITOR'S PREFACE

This book is the fourth in the series started by my predecessor as editor of the Library of Philosophy which, by a happy thought of his friend and admirer Sir Stanley Unwin, has in recent years been named in his honour the Muirhead Library of Philosophy. Muirhead edited two volumes in the present series in 1924 and 1925, and these continue to be in demand and much in use. I edited a further volume in 1956. In my directions to the contributors at that time I quoted the request of the first editor to his team, namely that they should indicate 'what they regard as the main problem of philosophy and what they have endeavoured to make central in their own speculation upon it'. I was also aware of the considerable changes in the philosophical scene since the early part of the century and reminded readers as well as contributors that philosophers were no longer much inclined to single out one problem as the main or crucial one. Nor was Muirhead himself in the least unmindful of the close inter-relations of philosophical questions. The best course seemed to be to invite contributors to write about some particular topic in a way which illustrated some of the things they considered most important at the time and in their own work. This seemed most likely to ensure that we had lively and original papers which did not stay too much with generalities about the course of philosophy and what it ought to be. I have sought to give body to the present volume by adopting substantially the same policy. For the same reason I did not insist on a biographical part of the papers themselves, providing instead a short, fairly formal, note about the contributors at the end and leaving it to them to determine how best to exhibit their own stance and concern in the subject. They seem to me to have done this very skilfully and I am grateful to them.

As in the previous volumes there are some regrettable omissions, mainly due to factors which could not have been anticipated at the start. I also decided, in view of the limitations imposed by the exigencies of publishing today, to reduce my list by not approaching those who have been working mainly in the borderland of philosophy and other subjects or in the history of philosophy. This will be corrected if it proves feasible to have a further volume without the long gap between the present volume and the earlier ones. That will also enable the picture to be completed in some other ways, notably by the inclusion of thinkers who have only lately made their impact.

My final word must be to those who allowed me to consult them, especially at the early stages of preparing this volume. They will know already how grateful I feel to them. I must also thank the contributors for their promptness and courtesy at every stage. The proofs for this volume reached me close to the time of my departure for an extended visit abroad and I am very grateful to Dr D. A. Rees, of Jesus College, Oxford, for making the Index of proper names.

H. D. LEWIS

CONTENTS

MEMORY, 'EXPERIENCE' AND CAUSATION

by

G. E. M. Anscombe

Professor of Philosophy, University of Cambridge

In the *Theaetetus* of Plato, Socrates disputes the definition of knowledge as perception with the objection: If I see, and then shut my eyes and remember what I saw, I still know it, but am not perceiving it. Therefore knowledge is not the same thing as perception. Later, putting a defence for phenomenalism into the mouth of Protagoras, he counters this argument with: 'Do you suppose anyone will agree that in remembering what he has experienced, a man is having the same sort of experience (*pathos*) as he had when he was experiencing what he now remembers?'

The only certain implication of this defence is that memory is not knowledge of the remembered thing. There is a strong suggestion, however, that memory *is* knowledge of the 'experience' that it itself is. No more is said, because Socrates has a weapon to attack phenomenalism more easily. Our interest in *expectation* is concerned with the actual event when it happens (or fails to happen). It would be too patently absurd to construct an analogue to the argument about memory, saying: expectation cannot be the same experience as one has when one observes the expected thing happen, it just is a different one, and therefore expectation cannot be mistaken! Nor does Plato suggest any such argument for Protagoras.

The sentence I quoted about memory is, I think, the first appearance in the literature of the peculiar philosophical concept of 'experience'. In essence this involves an assimilation of memory to sensation. This makes the content of memory present, not past.

Now consider saying, 'I don't know if I remember this, or if

I was told it.' If someone said this about having had a headache that very day, we might look for some extraordinary circumstances to explain his words; lacking any, we should be puzzled to understand him. But when Goethe says at the beginning of his autobiography that he is going to tell of things belonging to his childhood, of which he does not know whether he remembers them or was told them, there is nothing extraordinary about it. It seems familiar and intelligible. Nevertheless, it can raise a puzzle, and it is worth investigating.

In philosophy we sometimes meet, and sometimes may feel inclined to use, the expression 'If I remember or ostensibly remember' or 'If I at least ostensibly remember.' (To the question 'ostensibly to whom?' the answer is clearly 'to myself'.) Now we might formulate the puzzlement that Goethe's remark may elicit by saying: Surely he either 'at least ostensibly remembered' or definitely did not 'at least ostensibly remember': how could he be in doubt about *that*?

But can I say, can I give expression to an experience by saying, 'I at least ostensibly remember'? It would not be at all the same as 'I seem to remember.' The purpose of this last utterance is rather to say 'I remember' somewhat doubtfully, and the theme of doubt is the past, not the present: or, so far as the doubt relates to the present, it concerns one's capacity to tell what happened. Or again, I may say, for example, 'Even though I know you didn't have a beard, I keep on remembering you as bearded.' But this too does not capture the intent of 'I at least ostensibly remember.' Nor does 'I keep on feeling as if I remembered seeing that happen, though I wasn't there.' For if anyone judged that his own memory was false, he *would not say* that he '*ostensibly* remembered'; and correspondingly in the other case. And yet the content of the hypothetical 'If I at least ostensibly remember' is supposed to be the hypothesis *merely* that I am experiencing what anyone experiences inasmuch as he is remembering – it being left open whether what I 'at least ostensibly remember' happened or not.

Well, if there is such an experience, let me coin a verb for it. Ought it not to have a direct verbal expression? I will coin the verb 'REMBER' for this.

'I REMBER' will express a *cogitatio*, in Descartes' sense. With 'REMBER' I mean to isolate the central experience of memory from the further implications which are components of the sense of 'remember'; and with 'I REMBER' I mean to abstract from any judgement whatever about the past. I then propose as analysis: 'He remembers' is a complex idea: 'he REMBERS, and the thing happened, and he witnessed it.' 'I keep on remembering it as it wasn't' will be a complex of 'I REMBER that it was . . .' and 'It wasn't. . . .' 'I keep on seeming to remember, though I wasn't there' will be explicable as: 'I REMBER, and I wasn't there.'

Now, can I fail to know whether I am REMBERING or not? Let us return to Goethe's remark: 'I do not know if I remember the things I shall relate or was told them.' Does this mean: 'I just don't know if I REMBER this' or something different? Goethe was not in doubt about the things having happened. Is he then implying 'I do REMBER this, but I don't know whether the *cause* of my REMBERING this was its having happened in my presence (as, let us suppose, it did) or my having been told?' – If it meant 'I just don't know if I REMBER this', then 'REMBERING' is not the kind of verb we tried to make it – for we ought not to be able to say 'I just don't know if I REMBER this', any more than we can say 'I don't know if I have a headache.' But if it means 'I do REMBER it but I don't know if that is from my having been there or from my having been told', then the above account of remembering as REMBERING + truth + having been there, and conscious, etc., is inadequate. For it appears that one can still say 'I don't know if I remember' though granting that I REMBER, the thing happened, and I was there, etc. What has to be added is the *causal connexion*. And how can that get established?

Of course it is possible for us to establish a causal connexion between someone's having an experience and a past event. But in order to do so we need to know how to tell that he has the experience and we must know when something is the expression (or manifestation) of the experience. Now for 'REMBERING' I have given no such criteria. For I coined the name as the name of a supposed 'simple idea of reflection' (in the terminology of the British empiricists) which is meant to be so to speak the core of 'experience' in remembering. I coined the word as a substitute for a circumlocution; and because it *ought* to be coinable if the philosophical implications of that circumlocution are correct. But I explained its sense only by way of the circumlocution. I do not know how we could tell that some simple expression in a natural language had this postulated sense.

The assumption that memory is an experience did make some people think that it consists in the special experience called 'having a memory image'. This is seldom believed now, because it has often enough been remarked that one *need* not have a memory image when one remembers. But even if somebody has one, and the memory image is just what he finds when he introspects to see what goes on 'when we remember', it *also* needs to be made clear that the memory image is not itself the remembering even on that occasion. One way of seeing this is to suppose the memory image replaced by an actual picture that one sees or draws. Referring an image to the past involves some belief; and it must be done by the person who has the picture before him, if to him it is even a false picture of the past. But in dismissing any image, as *the* experience of memory, we are by no means dismissing the 'experience of memory' itself. If this is a chimerical notion, that still has to be shown.

You may say: a person will at any rate have the experience in question, his expression *will* be the expression of it, if his expression *does* have the sense of 'I remember' as this relates, not to 'habitual' memory of information but to 'personal' memory. For in order that one's expression should have this sense of 'I remember . . .' there is not any absolute requirement that his memory should actually be true nor that he should actually have witnessed (that is, if he is not lying) what he relates. George IV was not using 'I remember' in a wrong sense, just because he said he remembered leading a cavalry charge at Waterloo and he wasn't even there.

That is what has led some thinkers to say that he *was* remembering. Thus Broad:

'In common speech we should be inclined to say that he "did not really remember" the event in question; just as we are inclined to say the drunkard doesn't "really see" pink rats. But in both cases this is to mix up psychological, epistemological and ontological considerations in a way which is most detrimental to philosophical discussion. Assuming that the First Gentleman of Europe was correctly describing his state of mind, he was the subject of a situation which has just as good a right to be called a memory situation as a veridical memory of the Duke of Wellington on the same subject-matter.'[1]

This passage exhibits the very assumption, complete with the assimilation of memory to sensation, which I am engaged in questioning. It is true that George IV will not have been misusing 'I remember', or using it in some sense other than the one normal in a purported account 'from memory' of a past action of the speaker. 'Remember' in his mouth here *was* the same as 'remember' in the supposed statement on Wellington's part. And if the assimilation of memory to sensation were right, that would mean that if he was sincere there was a sense in which what he said was true: he did remember, but what he remembered never happened.

The assimilation is shown false by the following fact: though what George IV thought he remembered need not have happened (in order for him to be using 'remember' correctly), nevertheless he himself could not *leave it open* whether the thing happened or not, whereas in contrast a man can leave it open whether what he sees is purely subjective or is really there. I mean 'subjective' in the sense that another could not check his seeing by looking himself. For example, if two people have taken a drug that makes them see white surfaces as coloured, a dispute between them about what colours the surfaces look would be farcical. A man may say what he sees without deciding whether the situation is one of that sort. Rarely, of course. But so is George IV's case rare. The difference between them remains.

Imagine the following dialogues:

1. 'Do you remember whether Jones was here last week?' – 'Yes, I remember his being here quite distinctly.' – 'Ah, well, so *Jones* was here, anyway. Now . . .' – 'Wait! I didn't say *that*! I only said I remembered that he was.'
2. 'Was Jones here last week?' – 'Yes, I remember that he was.' – 'Oh, someone told you, then? For you were far away yourself.' – 'No, no one told me, I just remember that he was.' – 'How do you mean – did you telephone him here, or something?' – 'No! Why do you keep asking such silly questions? I only said that I *remembered* that Jones was here. I wasn't here myself, and I

[1] C. D. Broad, *The Mind and its Place in Nature* (Routledge, 1925) p. 231.

didn't learn of it from anything; you know what remembering is like, don't you? *That* is what happened within me when by your question you brought the idea of his having been here before my mind.'

Neither of these dialogues makes sense, as they would have to if 'I remember' expressed an experience or, as Broad would put it, a 'state of mind' that one is saying one is in.

Let us go back to the remark: 'I don't know if I remember this, or if I was told it.' If I say this, is there any determining the question? We may certainly be able to determine it negatively. If you were not present on the occasion referred to, then you do not 'personally' remember it, i.e. you do not remember it except in the way you remember any familiar information.

One might wonder how we know this. Is it because we find it never happens? No; the second of the two dialogues above shows the absurdity of even speaking as if it did.

The past tense is heard by the learner of language, and then used by him to make spontaneous reports. By a report's being 'spontaneous' I shall here mean that the person making it did not receive any indications after the event, whether statements or evidence, that the thing happened. Now people do not usually produce spontaneous reports of past events (other than their own past acts, thoughts, sensations, observings, etc.) of which they neither were nor claim to have been *witnesses*. However, they sometimes do. Suppose that we are satisfied that a report is in the defined sense spontaneous, but the person makes no claim to have witnessed the happening – then, if the report is true, we are apt to say he must after all have been there; he 'must be remembering'. This fact alone should tell us that remembering is not (even, so to speak, in its core) quite generally an experience.

If a statement that something happened is spontaneous and true, but we know that the person was not there – what do we say then? According to circumstances, especially what else *he* says, we may say it was a guess (perhaps 'an inspired guess'), or a sudden irrational conviction that happened to be right; or even perhaps that he was a 'seer'. Or we might feel we did not know what to say, and leave the facts at that. But there is one thing we would *not* say. We would not both say that the person was in no way a witness of the previous event, *and* that he was personally remembering that it had happened. That is, 'remembering' does not stand for an occurrence which is what it is no matter what else has or has not already been the case, and which therefore we might introduce as an hypothesis in the situation I have sketched. This point serves to characterise the use of any *word* that *means* memory, and can thus justly be called a grammatical point.

But the point seems trivial *if* we can speak of REMBERING. The pure expression for this *would* stand for an occurrence which is what it is no matter what else has been the case. Now if there is such a thing, ought there not to be a 'simple' and primary expression for it? That cannot be 'I remember that . . .'; and such an expression as 'I remember . . . *as*' is not simple and primary but derivative, secondary. It inherits from 'I remember that . . .' the requirement of past presence. Furthermore, we *cannot* just disregard the facts about 'I remember that', for remembering is our starting point, REMBERING has to be something that is supposed always to occur in *remembering*. But now, why should there be any such thing? Remembering is presumably expressed by 'I remember'. This has to be an expression in a language in which people who have witnessed something make reports of this afterwards. The expression 'I remember' may precede such reports. In that case, the hearers are headed off by this precedent expression from bothering about the reporter's present evidence or his other sources of information. *That* will not be in question, but only his reliability first in judging, and later in reporting, things he has been present at. Or if an interrogator, say, does wish to probe into the man's subsequent sources of information, this will be perhaps through suspicion that the witness is not giving a pure memory report of the past. But the question simply does not arise here whether a present memory *experience* took place in someone who said 'I remember', or who simply spoke in witness of what had happened. *That* is not of the slightest concern. It is not what people are concerned with when they ask 'Does he *really* remember that?', nor would the absence of such a thing prove one had been wrong to say 'I remember'. This last consideration shows that it does not save for example Broad's view to say : 'Remember' is used in a variety of ways : admittedly we sometimes say 'That must have been a case of remembering, though he didn't know it', but 'remembering' then does not mean what it means when one says – and *means* – 'I remember.' The reply to this is : Say, if you like, that 'remember' is used differently in 'He must have been remembering' ('That must have been a memory, though he didn't know it') and in 'I remember'. So it is; and we have already given the difference. One man cannot, and the other one can, spontaneously say 'I remember'. So say if you like: 'We should really concentrate on the cases where one can spontaneously say 'I remember'. But even if one does give a privileged position to those cases, *still* it is false to think that 'there must be an experience *of* remembering, which is expressed there'. For in probing the question 'whether he is really *remembering* that, rather than influenced by the talk he has heard or the conclusion he has drawn' we are *not at all* concerned with the presence or absence of such an experience.

As I defined 'spontaneous', a report would not be 'spontaneous' if the one who makes it has also heard tell or received other indications of what he himself tells. This is an artificial restriction on the normal sense of 'spontaneous'. In the normal sense, a report would be 'spontaneous' – relevantly to our present interests – if the person *could* have made it quite apart from any subsequent indication that may have come his way. This comes close to the interest of Goethe's remark. The 'spontaneous' is what the man produces, so to speak, out of the home-baked goods in his store: that is why it seemed natural to introduce causality into the explanation of what Goethe said. It is a metaphor.

For if our account of 'I remember' and the past tense is right, this shows that the idea of the causal connexion was somehow wrongly introduced. I do not mean that we cannot speak of a causal connexion between memory and what is remembered. Quite the contrary. But we introduced it for the wrong purpose and in the wrong place, between the wrong terms. We introduced it in an attempted analysis and to resolve the perplexity aroused by Goethe's remark. On the supposition that the core of memory is an experience – which we are calling 'REMBERING' – Goethe would not be in doubt whether he had *that* or not. So, we suggested, he might have meant that, though he did have the experiences, he did not know whether they were caused by having witnessed the events he was going to recount.

There is a difficulty here, because there is such a thing as being reminded. A reminder elicits a memory. If the core of the memory is an experience, then the reminder will also be a cause of the experience. This seems to throw the whole subject into confusion. One wants to say something like: *that* is not the sort of 'causing' we had in mind. We want to know the true *parent*, the originating source, of the knowledge; it does not matter what foster parents it may have had.

Noting this difficulty, but boldly disregarding it, let us recapitulate our proposed theory of the meaning of Goethe's remark. First, there is a core in personally remembering an event or situation, which core is an experience. This experience may occur without being a core of remembering. We have called it 'REMBERING' and have disconcertingly failed to find any simple primitive term for it in our natural language. Second, REMBERING will be a core of remembering only if REMBERING is caused by having witnessed the events. The theory was: Goethe did have the experience in question but did not know whether it was caused in that way.

Now Goethe also *believed* – indeed he was confident that he knew – that the events had happened. We shall have to add a new component to the situation. We shall have to add that he did not know whether the *belief* was caused by the REMBERING or by something else.

We now find ourselves unclear about what, in this theory, we are identifying as the remembering. Is it the REMBERING, given that this has the right causal antecedents? Or is it the belief, given that *it* has the right causal antecedents, namely REMBERING with the right causal antecedents?

Now there seems to be no doubt of the following: in such a situation as Goethe describes, a man thinks that such and such occurred. And when he wonders if he knows these things from memory or from being told, he is wondering whether his thinking those things, or his knowledge of those things, *is* memory, not whether it is produced by something else which is a memory. If the supposed intervening experience (given the right provenance) were itself one of remembering that such-and-such occurred, then it would itself already be the judgement that such-and-such occurred: if it were not that judgement, then it would not just have to cause a judgement, but must itself be judged, or judged about: as, if one had an image that struck one as being, or 'felt like', a memory image, one could still not be said to be remembering (even falsely) unless one actually thought, believed, that 'things *were*, for example, as the image represents them'. (Or, again, 'as it does *not* represent them'.) But if one *can* judge 'things *were* as this represents them', why cannot one simply judge 'things were thus and so' – for example, 'Jones was there'? We have indeed seen that an image cannot play the part of our supposed experience of REMBERING because beliefs (i.e. memory beliefs) are involved in referring an image to the past. Presumably REMBERING must already contain such a reference, but without being or involving any judgement, any belief. If so, it still has itself to be judged, no less than an image would have to be; though here we can suppose the judgement to be merely *assent*, an inward 'Yes, *so*' in face of a present content which already (somehow) has a past reference. And the same consideration applies: if one can say 'Yes' to such a content of experience, why can one not equally say 'Yes' to the proposition 'This happened'? Why must there be an intermediary to have, as it were, the peculiar colour of memory? And if the intermediary is not a required element, neither is causality of it and by it.

Thus the *experience* drops out of the analysis, and the causality – if we are right in introducing it – is between the original witnessing of the event and the present thought, or again, that present state of a human being of which we speak when we say he knows that such-and-such occurred.

We should clear our minds of all prejudice on the subject of causality in considering what we know here. Here is someone, let us say, who knows that such-and-such occurred. Let us suppose that this is a surprising fact – we want an explanation. How *has it come about* that this person knows that? – we ask. And then we are convincingly told: 'Well, he was there, he witnessed it.' The mystery is removed: we are no longer puzzled about what brought about this state of affairs, which surprised us so much.

This is an original phenomenon of causality: one of its types – whether or not anyone has yet classified it as such.[2] No general theory about what causality is has to be introduced to justify acceptance of it. Nor does it have to be accommodated to any general theory, before it is accepted. It just is one of the things we mean by causality. Only in philosophy our minds tend to be

[2] Russell formulated a notion of 'mnemic causality' in the *Analysis of Mind* (Allen & Unwin 1921), pp. 85–6, which is close to the causality I am speaking of.

clogged by prejudices on the subject so that we are prevented from seeing the facts that are under our noses.

On the other hand, we do not analyse memory in terms of causality. It is rather that what we call (personal) memory of a past time we also call an effect of the original witnessing of its events. Something is not established as a memory by the discovery of a causal connexion, nor is ignorance whether something is a memory ignorance of whether it is the product of a known causal mechanism, first activated by an orginal event and remaining set to produce expressions of personal memory that such-and-such happened. (But also: that such-and-such did *not* happen.) We may form such a picture; we may also have a theory that there must be such a mechanism, and perhaps there *is*. But, whether there is such a thing or not, it is not what such a remark as Goethe's is referring to. He is not saying: my present knowledge, which of course (as anyone will agree) is a piece of habitual memory, may originally have been produced by either of two known mechanisms: the personal memory mechanism, or the belief mechanism activated by information; and I do not know which of these bits of machinery did produce it. He is saying only something like this: I am not decisively inclined to say, either that I remember these things happening, or that I do not remember these things happening. I have got this knowledge, and I do not know which sort of knowledge it is. Perhaps I do not know whether I witnessed certain events or not; and even if I did, I do not know whether I could have related them later even if no one had told me of them; nor do I know in every case whether anyone did tell me.

Overmastered by prejudice, someone may be unable to give up the idea of the experience of remembering, which occurs at a particular moment, as constituting the essence of what happens when someone personally remembers: it is a definite happening, which one is immediately conscious of; and everyone knows what it is like to have it happen within him. The cases of remembering without realising that one is doing so do not fit in with this, but no matter: 'remember' is, they may say, a 'family resemblance concept'; they are interested in the central concept, round which cluster some others. Using the central concept, one will say that a man who is not having the experience which, if he gave expression to it, he would express by saying 'I remember', *is* not remembering

(Thus Goethe *was* not remembering in this sense, just because he did not know he was.) This experience is necessary for one so much as to have the idea of the past. If such an experience is denied to be a memory on the ground that what it presents as having happened never did, that is like a man's having an hallucinatory sense impression. The hallucinatory sense impression is such because it is not caused by the object it makes one think is there; and similarly for the hallucinatory memory experience.

The dominant idea here is not just that of 'experience': it is that of a definite thing that happens, or a state of consciousness that occurs when (in the 'central' cases) a person *remembers* and which he speaks of when he says 'I remember'. This idea is common to the 'Cartesian', the British Empiricists, and to the materialist philosophers or proponents of the 'identity theory'. For the latter philosophers say that the mental events or states of mind in question are identical with some brain processes or brain states which neuro-physiology will be able to pick out. They would not say this if they did not unquestioningly accept the same basic assumptions as the 'Cartesian', i.e. if they were not hoodwinked by the suggestions of our verbal forms.

I will show that the role of the supposition of causal connexion, on such a view, is an unexpected one: that it serves only to rescue the theorist from a form of idealism.

It will of course be necessary that the peculiar experience of memory be quite generally identifiable without connecting it with the past as an actual memory of it. Rather as one could always identify a picture, and indeed as *this* picture, without connecting it with a sitter or an actual scene. The picture, we may say, is a portrait if it has a certain (complicated) causal relation to a sitter. Similarly the memory experience is supposed to be actually a memory, if it has a certain causal relation to a past event. But more must be demanded of the memory experience which is to be an actual memory, than of a picture if it is to be a portrait. For the picture does not after all have to resemble the sitter; but the 'content' of the memory experience, if having it is to be an actual case of remembering that . . ., has got to be *true*. The analogy reveals the incorrectness of that idea of the identifiable experience.

For if we explain the picture's being a portrait by its causal relation to a sitter, this will be because we give some causal account of the painter's *intending* this sitter, i.e. intending the picture to be a picture of *this* sitter. But in a memory experience, as we saw before, the 'past' reference, and indeed a quite particular 'past' reference, must already be contained *independently* of the causal relation which we may postulate. That reference would be as integral to the memory experience as the 'content' of the picture is to it; for how otherwise could it be a *memory* experience? It is that thing, which already makes a 'past' reference, about which we are now supposing a causal relation between it and the right past event, to ensure that it is an actual bit of remembering. But it now becomes difficult to see just why a causal relation *is* needed for this. The causal relation certainly does not effect the 'past' reference. I think it is obvious that its role is to secure that the 'past' reference is a real past reference. The 'past' reference that was necessarily involved in the experience is only 'past' in quotation marks. Experience, being present, cannot succeed in actual past reference; the 'past' which is in it is only something present, something to be seen in its own content.

The person believes, that is assents to, the content of this experience. This assent does not, as in our previous argument, involve judgement of what the memory experience presents. For no one has the idea of 'the past' except in the first place from memory, and hence if memory is an experience the idea of the past must simply be in the experience: one cannot bring any primary judgement about the past to bear on the presentation. It is indeed difficult to see what the belief or assent consists in, as it cannot involve assessment of the experience. This was a problem which Hume felt strongly, and could not solve. It seems that assent can only be : allowing the memory experience to feel 'solid'. Plainly we have fallen into idealism. If we are content to remain there, well and good; the causal connexion drops out, it is not needed. However we explain 'assent', the causal connexion is not needed to do so; and assent to a memory experience which is true is all that is needed for the person to be actually remembering. The distinction of true and false, veridical and non-veridical, will of course not be anything but a distinction between those memory ideas that belong to a coherent picture of the world, and the remaining 'wild' ones.

Thus, if we really adhere to that conception of memory as essentially and centrally a form of experience, the causal connexion drops out. This parallels the way in which we saw that the supposed 'experience' dropped out when we tried to give a proper account of Goethe's remark, and did not just dismiss what it describes as a peripheral matter. But the causal connexion with a past event outside the experience at once introduces a 'real' past, not yet involved in the memory experience.

I will now return to what I put forward before as the true view: for I consider the idea of the memory experience to have been refuted by my earlier arguments. I argued that there is no question but that there *is* a causal connexion between memory and remembered events, but that this is not something discovered: rather, here we are noting a particular type of causality: one of the kinds of things we *call* causation. The causality which is spoken of here comes in in two ways; one negative, one positive.

Negatively: a person's information about the past may be assigned to a source which excludes its arising from his own witnessing of the things in question. If it can be so assigned, then the beliefs he has in the matter will not be personal memories of his. This condition is for the most part satisfied only when his having witnessed something is actually excluded. (Though I imagine an exception to this below.) We must not lose sight of the fact that we sometimes take knowledge or belief as proof that the person is remembering and this in turn as proof of previous witnessing by him.

Positively, the original witnessing of a remembered event is a cause of any present memory (even a false memory) of that event.[3] And this may be seen as 'analytic'. Not so if, instead of speaking of memory we speak of present knowledge of, or belief about, a past event. An affirmative answer to the question whether the *source* of a man's present knowledge was his having witnessed the event is enough to determine that the knowledge is memory. This belongs in an account of how we use the word 'memory'. But also, of how we use the word 'source' in connexion with knowledge.

For being the source, and so a cause, of knowledge is not the same thing as occurring in some chain of causes or other that leads up temporally to the knowledge. Let us suppose that I witness something and tell others of it: then if I forget all about it and learn of it anew from others who got it directly or indirectly from

[3] See Norman Malcolm's first lecture on memory in *Knowledge and Certainty* for some useful observations on false memory, especially p. 190.

me, my original witnessing of it will be *a* cause of my present knowledge – but I shall not be remembering.

Perhaps a physiological causal mechanism might be discovered so that in its workings we had a 'right' causal chain: that is, a causal chain which was not detrimental to the present belief's being memory. But even if so, still the existence of a causal chain temporally leading from the original event to the later knowledge does not belong in an analysis of memory.

MAIN PUBLICATIONS

Intention (Blackwell, 1957)
An Introduction to Wittgenstein's Tractatus (Hutchinson, 1959)
Three Philosophers (with Peter Geach) (Blackwell, 1961)

THE SHAPE OF IGNORANCE

by

Renford Bambrough
Fellow of St John's College, Cambridge, and Editor of Philosophy

Ophelia Could beauty, my lord, have better commerce than with honesty?
Hamlet Ay, truly; for the power of beauty will sooner transform honesty from what it is to a bawd than the force of honesty can translate beauty into his likeness: this was sometime a paradox, but now the time gives it proof.
Hamlet, III, i, 112–17

Hamlet's paradox was true before the time gave it proof. The paradox was thought to be false, and is now seen to be true. Hamlet has discovered that things are not as they had seemed to be.

Macbeth also discovered something to be true that he and others had thought to be false:

> . . . the times have been
> That, when the brains were out, the man would die
> And there an end; but now they rise again,
> With twenty mortal murders on their crowns,
> And push us from our stools.
> *Macbeth*, III, iv, 78–82

But Macbeth's case is different. When Banquo's ghost shakes his gory locks at him he is showing that things are not as they were. A different account is given now because things are different, and not because how things always were has come to light.

Philosophers are traditionally concerned with timeless or eternal truths. If they give different answers at different times to the same question this should be because they have seen more of the truth than they had seen at first, and not because things have changed. Philosophers are Hamlets not Macbeths.

Or so I suggest. But I shall have to defend this suggestion, since many philosophers and many others think or seem to think that the truths that it is the philosopher's business to see and show and tell are different in different times and different climes. And it is not only about philosophical truths that they think this.

Collingwood tells us that he and I do not even ask the same questions as our philosophical predecessors. MacIntyre ties moral philosophy to the coat tails of morals and thinks that that makes moral philosophy fickle. Popper and his progeny see the philosopher's business changing as new questions and answers are posed and offered in science and in society. Feyerabend and Kuhn speak of scientific theories as mutually incommensurable; there cannot be permanent scientific *truths* to be *discovered* and *established* because a scientific conflict is between parties whose concepts are different, so that there is no single unambiguous question at issue between them, and hence no role for a crucial experiment or observation. In morals and aesthetics and criticism and religion it is easier still to find suggestions that truth is a shifting sand, that nothing counts as *how things are*, waiting to be discovered or unfolded.

I still think that philosophy is the pursuit of truth and understanding, and that there is a truth to be known and understood. I also think that this all applies to everything else that deserves the name of enquiry or investigation: the truths of mathematics, physics, history, psychology, theology, morals and criticism are all alike timeless. In so far as apprehension of any of them depends on the acquisition of particular concepts, then those concepts are in principle available to any enquirer at any time. The mastery of them is itself a species of understanding that one man or generation may have and another lack.

And all these truths and understandings are a unified truth and understanding to which it is not irrational to aspire, even though it may be unintelligible to suppose that it can be reached. My only reservation about this passage from Peirce is that it seems unduly to restrict the scope and subject matter of rational enquiry:

'There are Real things, whose characters are entirely independent of our opinions about them: these Reals affect our senses according to regular laws, and, though our sensations are as different as are our relations to the objects, yet, by taking advantage of the laws of perception, we can ascertain by reasoning how things really and truly are; and any man, if he have sufficient experience and he reason enough about it, will be led to the one true conclusion.'[1]

At this stage it will be useful to ask some of the questions to which these remarks are answers. The odd procedure of answering the questions before asking them is one that I have picked up from my opponents on these issues, who assume answers to questions that they have never clearly formulated and whose clear formulation is itself a useful argument against their answers:

Are there any logical or mathematical propositions which used to be true and are now false?

Are there any scientific propositions which used to be true and are now false?

Are there any historical/theological/aesthetic/moral propositions which used to be true and are now false?

It is not to be expected that the answer can be given in the same terms for all these fields of enquiry; and though I have already committed myself to giving the same answer in all cases, I must discuss them separately or at least in groups.

One of the clearest distinctions can soon be marked. There are some spheres in which it is obvious that Macbeth's experience is common: situations change and the changes are reported or recorded by historians, biologists, geologists, physicists. . . . To suggest the contrary would be to offer a paradoxical philosophical theory. There are other spheres in which to suggest that changes *do* occur is to be offering paradoxical philosophical theories: the truths of logic and mathematics do not change: if there are surprises in logic they are not unexpected turns of events. Attempts by tyrants to change the past or put the clock back are recognised as fraudulent representations of how the past was and is – except when they are recognised as insanities or at best as *façons de parler*.

In other cases there is room for controversy. Is it also madness or fraud or a mere manner of speaking when reformers attempt to change the future? Is there any change in morals where this does

[1] *Collected Papers*, vol. V, p. 384.

not mean a historical change in people's views or customs? Can a god be born or die or change in any respect? Can a statue lose its beauty without changing in any other respect?

But *discoveries* and *recognitions* are possible wherever there are questions: in mathematics, physics, history; and in theology, ethics and aesthetics, unless it can be shown, as it never has been shown, that these are 'without propositions'.

Neither Hamlet's way nor Macbeth's way of legitimately denying what was formerly legitimately affirmed gives any basis for the relativism that some of our contemporaries have sought to defend. If arguments for such a view are to be found they must be looked for elsewhere. I am predisposed to look on any such arguments with suspicion, not only because of what I have said above, but because of earlier and repeated commitment on my part to a reasoned faith in the scope and power of reason, and to a number of specific but wide-ranging theses of the same epistemological colour: that every question has an answer; that moral, aesthetic and religious disputes are as amenable to rational resolution as disputes in history or physics or logic; that a *total* disagreement between two people or two peoples is not coherently describable or in principle conceivable; that the necessary unity of the human species displays itself in the necessary unity of the human understanding.

To put all this in issue is to stretch near to breaking point the terms of an invitation to discuss 'some particular problem in a way which illustrates the way in which you think philosophy should be done now or what you consider particularly important'. But the particularity that is desired can be provided by concentrating on a number of objections that I have from time to time been called upon to answer. This will at the same time give this essay the character of 'personal statement' which the contributions to this series have traditionally borne, even if it also gives it a character, now less likely to commend itself to any but the traditionalist reader, of representing a summary statement of an outlook or even a system of doctrine.

The objections that have appeared in print are typical of many that have been put to me in public discussion and private conversation.

Professor Winch (in *Philosophy*, 1975) detects a hankering after transcendence, and Lady Oppenheimer (in *Theology*, 1974) suspects a hankering for a theology. The agreement in the diagnosis is interesting in view of the disagreement between them on another point: Lady Oppenheimer hopes for the hankering after a theology and Professor Winch fears the hankering for transcendence. This makes it more and not less likely that there is something in what they both say; but that in turn may make it puzzling that there is also something in what Dom Mark Pontifex says in his review of *Reason, Truth and God*:

'It is when we come to the discussion of God as transcendent that the disagreement with orthodox Christianity stands out most clearly. After all it can scarcely be denied that belief in a transcendent and also immanent God lies at the very heart of Christianity. The subject is obviously too vast to be discussed here, and indeed its treatment in this book is very summary. The question is asked: "Is it conceivable that God should exist, and yet that everything else should remain the same as if he did not exist?" (p. 52). Surely the theist would reply that, if God did not exist, nothing would exist, that when we reflect on the reality before us, we find we are aware, in and through the things around us, of the infinite "ground" of all. We are told on p. 92: "Transcendental ontology is made plausible only by an epistemological misunderstanding, by an unsure grasp of the nature of the ultimate grounds of our claims to knowledge". If this is so, of course there is nothing more to be said, but the question is, is it so?'[2]

The clue to untying this tangle is given in another remark by Professor Winch that I take as the compliment that it was not intended to be. Winch commits the *prima facie* inconsistency of comparing with *Spinoza* a writer whom he is at the same time accusing of hungering and thirsting after transcendence. I suppose it might be argued that Spinoza's insistence to the contrary was a symptom of the depth of his desire for what he said could not be attained, but the argument would not be plausible. There is a more plausible account of the situation, one that amounts to a defence both of Spinoza's posture and of mine, and which nevertheless makes it understandable that Winch and Pontifex and Oppenheimer should all say the things that they have said.

[2] Dom Mark Pontifex in *Downside Review* (July 1969), pp. 295–6.

Spinoza did not think that an aspiration after complete knowledge and understanding had to be given up by every thinker who denied the transcendence of the substance with which he identified both the object and the subject of all knowledge and apprehension. It is instructive to compare and contrast him with Schopenhauer, who writes in *Parerga and Paralipomena*, vol. I, p. 68:

'For it is with philosophy as with very many things; everything depends on whether it is tackled at the right end. Now the phenomenon of the world to be explained presents innumerable ends of which only one can be right. It is like a tangled mass of thread with many false ends hanging therefrom. Only the man who discovers the actual end is able to unravel the whole. But then one thing is easily developed from another, and from this we know that it was the right end. It can also be compared to a labyrinth that presents a hundred entrances opening into corridors all of which, after various long and intricate windings, finally lead out again with the exception of a single one, whose windings actually lead to the centre where the idol stands. If we have hit upon this entrance, we shall not miss the way; but by no other path can we ever reach the goal. I do not conceal the fact that I am of the opinion that only the will in us is the right end of the tangle, the true entrance to the labyrinth.'

The image of the tangled threads is as accurate as it is familiar, a natural representation of the plurality and complexity of the issues with which the philosopher has to do. There are other familiar metaphors that Schopenhauer rightly resists: 'My propositions do not rest on chains of reasoning.' What he offers is an intuitive perception of a truth that cannot conflict with itself from however many points of view it may be perceived. He contrasts the wide basis of his own philosophy with the concentrated 'foundations' on which other philosophers have thought it necessary or desirable to build their constructions:

'This is analogous to our sometimes not understanding the continuity and connection of a building's parts when we look at it for the first time and from only one direction; yet we are certain that such continuity is not wanting and that it will appear as soon as we have walked right round the building. . . . Accordingly, my philosophy has a wide basis whereon everything stands directly and thus securely; whereas other systems are like tall towers where, if one support breaks, the whole edifice collapses.' (pp. 130–1)

All this is excellent. But there is one element in the compound that compromises its claim to match the complexity of the structure that it is meant to represent, and it is just the one that Spinoza had tried most strenuously and effectively to remove from his picture. Schopenhauer clings closely at one point to the assumptions he is trying to question : he has not given up the idea that 'there is one right end to seize on in the tangled mass of thread that is the world'. This is a lapse into a thought that is at least parallel to the attachment to 'up and down methods' with which he taxes other thinkers, and it is to be accounted for in the light of his conviction that there is a truth to be discovered and displayed, combined with the conviction, which he shares with Winch, but which distinguishes him from Spinoza, that there cannot be a unified apprehension of a unified truth unless there is a single canonical point of entry to the maze.

You may start at Cape Town and I at Khartoum, but even if we never meet we are exploring the same continent. I may travel east while you are travelling west and we may meet only after we have both come full circle.

The innocent circularity of any exploitation that is comprehensive is one of the most fruitful sources of shame in those whose aspiration in philosophy is to abolish philosophy and its methods in favour of logic, science and their methods.

The suggestion is sometimes made that all this confidence in truth and reason is anthropocentric arrogance, or even that it is egocentric arrogance. Why should we or I think that I or we can know everything and understand everything? Why should there not be ultimate enigmas, irreducible mysteries, invincible ignorances?

To eat this humble pie is to forget the difference between saying that there is such a thing as knowledge and claiming myself to be in possession of such knowledge. My recognition that physics is a branch of knowledge does not involve a claim on my part to know much or any physics, and my ignorance of physics would be banished along with your knowledge if there were no such branch of knowledge as physics. And ignorance in general is yoked to knowledge in general: neither can lead where the other will not follow.

An expression of ignorance cannot intelligibly be an expression of *total* ignorance. What I do not know must have a shape, a specification: I must at least in sketchy outline know what it is that I do not know in order to know that I am ignorant. If you know that I am ignorant of something of which I do not know that I am ignorant, it must be possible for you to give such a specification.

Such specifications, whether given in expressions or in attributions of ignorance, are typically given in the form of questions: the very same indirect questions in which claims to or attributions of knowledge are typically cast. I may say that I do not know *how* the television set works, *why* it is dark at night, *whether* there will be a nuclear war, *when* the next Ice Age will happen, *what* makes Sammy run. You may say that I do not know *that* the game is up, or *who* has belled the cat, or *which* is the poisoned chalice, even if I have not framed or fathomed such a question. The shape of the question is what gives shape to my ignorance.

Ignorance, like knowledge, may be of a subject or subject matter. I do not know any or much geography. I have not studied set theory or Spanish. It is not hard to see that this way of expressing or attributing ignorance, if it cannot be reduced to the question form, is at least as clearly as that form itself one that depends on there being a shape to the knowledge that is said to be lacking and a direction in which it might be looked for.

We come nearer to the centre of the trouble when we take the cases where I don't know that I don't know, and where I have to be made to understand that there is a question before I can even see that I need an answer. Captain Schafer, in the American Airlines advertisement, teaches people things that they didn't even know they didn't know. I may take in hand the tribe, well known to philosophers even if never met by anthropologists, who count 'one, two, three, few, many' and teach them to see and count the seven stars in the sky, to aspire after an allotted span of three score years and ten, to forgive their brothers even until seventy times seven. Somebody may take me in hand and make me understand better than I do now what my ignorance of genetics amounts to.

In all these cases the deficiency of the individual or tribe is described by contrast and connection with a better understanding achieved by some other tribe or individual, or, in the case where the ignorance is universal, by reference to the part or parts of our knowledge, common or specialised, that gives rise and gives point and gives houseroom and gives what I have called *shape* to the question or quest that now taxes our talents. To be baffled is also to be in the picture. I cannot be puzzled if there is nothing that I understand.

The stress on relativity here is the answer to another complaint that I have learned to expect whenever I suggest (for example) that moral questions have answers. 'Where do you get these absolutes?' 'Who are you to say what is to count as a reason, an answer, a criterion . . . ?'

The most extreme and most interesting form in which I have met this response was one in which it was made into an accusation of ethnocentrism and/or of occidentocentrism. Once when I gave a lecture called 'A Proof of the Objectivity of Morals' a member of the audience suggested that I was misguided if I thought that I could refute a philosophical position by showing that it was self-contradictory. The law of non-contradiction was nothing but a local Western prejudice, as I could see by opening my mind to the wisdom of the East. The answer to this complaint is as old as Aristotle's *Metaphysics*, though it needs to be given again in new forms as the objection recurs in new guises and disguises. If we are to authorise contradictions the objector has no reason or right to think that I am misguided, since by his own method it can be allowed that he and I are both right, even though the point of his thesis was to contradict mine. And he was allowing that I had shown a certain thesis to be self-contradictory, even if not allowing that the demonstration was damaging to the thesis; how was this showing supposed to have been achieved if endless fluidity of terms and arguments and principles is to be tolerated?

More recently I have met the same objection in a less easily tractable form. This time the suggestion was that only racial bias and imperialism could prompt such an attachment to the unity and authority of reason as that to which I have given expression in some recent writings. The plausibility of the objection is again derived from the picture of reasoning as a journey up and down ladders that was rejected by Peirce and Wittgenstein and incompletely rejected by Schopenhauer. The same objection, deriving its plausibility from the same source, is made by Professor Gellner when he insists that no tradition must be a judge in its own cause. Surely, it seems reasonable to argue, it is not for me to be authorised to certify the canons of rationality by which my adherence to certain beliefs and opinions, and to certain canons of rationality, is to be examined. I must submit myself to external examination.

But if we take this tempting path we are heading for one or other of several familiar kinds of trouble. Just as the man who suspends the law of non-contradiction in his own favour must suspend it for others and so destroy the mutual understanding without which there cannot even be conflict, so the insistence on complete lack of overlap between what is criticised and the position from which it is criticised leads to the impossibility of communication between schools of thought or between individual thinkers. We are left only with rival solipsisms if I can never persuade you of anything without relying on something that you already accept and there is nothing that you and I both accept. It could not under these conditions be clear even that we were in mutual opposition. Conflict is a mode of contact.

Here then is what I 'consider particularly important' both theoretically and practically: that we should recognise that the traditional conflicts are resoluble and so give ourselves some hope of resolving them; but that we should also recognise the value of the conflicts themselves as contributions to the unified apprehension and understanding that we seek. The continuing conversation of mankind recurrently, and sometimes (at its best) concurrently, brings different parts of a single multifarious scene to light.

When I accused him of a momentary lapse into existentialism Professor R. W. Hepburn replied with a reference to John Stuart Mill:

'Again, it is one thing to acknowledge those aspects of the human predicament that evoke desolation or a sense of ultimate futility, and quite another thing to dwell upon these in a way that saps our vitality and moral stamina. As John Stuart Mill put it at the close of his *Three Essays on Religion*: "... in the regulation of the imagination literal truth of facts is not the only thing to be considered". For example: "it is not necessary for keeping up our conviction that we must die, that we should be always brooding over death"; and again: "the true rule of practical wisdom is not that of making all the aspects of things equally prominent in our habitual contemplations, but of giving the greatest prominence to those . . . which . . . can be modified by our own conduct". Here too, then, is a proper place for exercising choice.'[3]

My reply to his reply would be to allow that there is scope for choice about what deserves the emphasis in life or in a life, but to add that where there is scope for choice there is scope for conflict about the rightness of a choice, and hence a role for reason in the determination of the issue. Hepburn was facing some of the complexities but not enough: he was taking one step – one too many – on the journey that ends in facileness, in the choices of the existentialist or the posits of the positivist.

To offer such a strenuous method is to be able to give the answer in one movement even if not in one move to three further objections that I have more than once been called upon to meet. According to an anonymous critic in *The Times Higher Education Supplement* (31 May 1974) I am too optimistic in my faith in the power of the human understanding: 'He sometimes looks for reason beyond the point where it makes sense to do so. He keeps asking people what are their reasons for their values at the point that you recognise that their values *are* their reasons.'

This is the old story, the old structure of ultimate and ultimately arbitrary choice, *nomos* against *phusis*, the individual man as the measure for himself alone of what is and what is not true or false, good or bad, right or wrong, set up against the shared understanding of mankind.

The complaint is confused in another and revealing way, one that reveals the inescapability of the understanding that the complainant is trying to overthrow. To be too much attached to reason is presumably to be more attached to reason than it is reasonable to be; and this way of putting the charge does most of the work of counsel for the defence, as can be shown by setting some parallel cases beside it.

When a child is 'too good' there is something wrong with him – a lack of energy, spirit, enterprise or independence. A man who is 'too good to live' is perhaps a fragile creature, or a prig, or one

[3] R. W. Hepburn *et al.*, *Religion and Humanism* (BBC, 1964), pp. 88–9.

whose delicacy is said to be excessive only because it is not refined enough to see that some occasions do not call for delicacy. When the Hungarian expert in *Pygmalion* finds fault with Eliza Doolittle's speaking of English he condemns it as 'too good' to be genuine; it is too formally perfect to achieve perfection. A work of art that is too perfect is too rigid or too regular or too miniature to be perfect at all. In all these cases we have to do with oblique modes of expression of the attribution of defects. The nature of the defect is in each case expressed as an excess of a good quality, but the excess is a deficiency, and its diagnosis is far from being or involving a suggestion that the quality in question is not a merit.

This is put into relief by Professor D. D. Raphael's complaint, made in his comments on 'Appearance, Identity and Ontology'[4] that not *enough* scope had been allowed for rational argument.

We need to understand what are the opposing conceptions of reason that prompt these opposed complaints, and how the conflict between them contributes to the understanding of reason by helping to discriminate its modes. And we need to understand still and again that the modes are modes of reason; that the many are united in the one.

The same story of unity and diversity has a chapter on the notion of a *problem.* I caused some scandal when I claimed that Wittgenstein had solved the problem of universals. I could have made all the same points in an article beginning 'I believe that Wittgenstein altogether failed to understand the problem of universals' or 'Wittgenstein's denial that there are "problems of philosophy" has obscured from his readers, and from Wittgenstein himself, the nature of his own inadvertent contribution to the resolution of an ancient conflict'.

It was no doubt the recommendation and use of this slippery method that prompted the complaint or compliment from a graduate student that I was 'too literary to be a philosopher'. He was too philosophical, according to too narrow a conception of philosophy and its modes of expression, to recognise that the degree and kind of intricacy and complexity that has to be presented for the proper understanding and treatment of any interesting philosophical issue can be achieved or plausibly

[4] *Proc. Arist. Soc.,* vol. 75 (1974–5).

attempted only by the use of all the resources of expression available to us, including those that we forge and fashion for ourselves out of materials and sketch-designs bequeathed to us by our founders and benefactors.

Another graduate student, more sympathetic but still rather startled, said in the middle of a discussion, 'You say such *definite* things.' I tried to explain to him the advantages of a method in which what is complex and indefinite is presented by saying things which are simpler and more definite, but by saying enough of them and making sure that they have the relation of mutual support and complementarity that will cause some hearers to speak of contradiction and incoherence.

When Wittgenstein uses the method to which this method of mine is complementary, when he presents the detailed complexity directly, without any simplifying order or arrangement, he is accused by contrast of 'simply re-stating the problem'. For example: he says that the relation between a groan and a pain is not causal and is not analytic, but is logical. Professor Ayer will then ask how a connexion can be 'in some sense logical' without being inductive or deductive. But the idea that the connexion must be problematical if it is not of one or other of these two kinds is itself a philosophical idea that calls for argument and not just for assertion.

The determination to match the complexities of the themes and problems of philosophy with a complexity of exposition that is still not a bewildering maze is what Dr Ayers is thinking of when he speaks of the need for a *respect* for the difficulties of philosophy.[5] Such a respect is more commonly shown in strenuous conversation or discussion about the problems of philosophy than in books or lectures. The method of writing that I am preaching and practising is designed to preserve in print some of the merits of discussion, conversation, dialectic; to provide for the qualifications and complexities that can be entered by another speaker, or by the same speaker in another remark, in a conversation that can by this means supply both perspective and detailed apprehension. So it is not surprising that one common response to the practice of this method is to remember Hegel, who also and flagrantly ran

[5] M. R. Ayers, *The Refutation of Determinism* (Methuen, 1968), Preface, p. viii.

the risk of incoherence in the hope of achieving a comprehensive grasp without denying the complexity.

In returning to the form and manner of a 'personal statement' I am reacting against a reaction, and hence illustrating the dialectical pattern that I have described. Thirty years ago we thought that we were entering an age in which philosophy would and should be as impersonal as physics or logic. The omission of the autobiographical prefaces from the Third Series of *Contemporary British Philosophy* was one sign of the new times. In future the man would not matter but only the work, and we should all be technicians like . . . well, like whom ? Wittgenstein ? Moore ? Ryle ? Austin ? These are poor candidates for the role of bloodless clinicians.

I am not here withdrawing anything that I have said against subjectivism, irrationalism or existentialism; to recognise that a philosopher worth reading or hearing has an individual stamp and style and temperament is not to compromise the need for an impersonal and unselfish determination to seek a truth external to the mind; but the right analogy is not with the impersonality of the machine or the mechanic but with the integrity of the poet : 'The more perfect the artist, the more completely separate in him will be the man who suffers and the mind which creates; the more perfectly will the mind digest and transmute the passions which are its material.' (T. S. Eliot, 'Tradition and the Individual Talent'.)

The philosophical equivalent of this classic stance is described if not achieved by Collingwood when he speaks of the grand manner in philosophy :

'This grand manner is not the mark of a period; it is the mark of a mind which has its philosophical material properly controlled and digested. It is thus based on width and steadiness of outlook upon the subject matter; it is essentially objective, concerned not with the thoughts of others, whether to criticise or expound but with the features of the thing itself; it is marked by calmness of temper and candour of statement, no difficulties being concealed and nothing set down in malice or passion. All great philosophers have this calmness of mind, all passion spent by the time their vision is clear, and they write as if they saw things from a mountain top. That is the tone which distinguishes a great philosopher :

a writer who lacks it may or may not be worth reading, but he certainly falls short of greatness.'[6]

There is no suggestion here that there is no truth to be sought or found, and no hint that the individual thinker can seek or find it by solo flight, but there is the recognition, lacking even from much of the more intelligent philosophy that appears in books and articles today, that in philosophy as in literature the trappings of the sciences are out of place. Contributing to the progress of philosophy is not a matter of keeping up with the latest work, of joining a research team or a band or bandwagon, of building brick by brick.

Those who have tried hardest to stumble along in these heavy trappings have been prompted by shame at being mere philosophers, by a failure to see philosophy as the ancient and honourable profession that it still deserves to be.

[6] R G. Collingwood, *The Idea of Nature* (OUP, 1965), p. 158.

MAIN PUBLICATIONS

The Philosophy of Aristotle (New American Library, 1963)
New Essays on Plato and Aristotle (ed.) (Routledge and Kegan Paul, 1965)
Plato, Popper and Politics (ed.) (Heffer, 1967)
Reason, Truth and God (Methuen, 1969)
Conflict and the Scope of Reason (University of Hull Press, 1974)
Wisdom: Twelve Essays (ed.) (Blackwell, 1974)

IS LOGIC EMPIRICAL?

by

Michael Dummett

Fellow of All Souls College, Oxford

In 'Two Dogmas of Empiricism' Quine maintained that no statement, not even a truth of logic, was immune to revision as a response to experience. His example for the application of this thesis to the laws of logic was the suggestion that the law of excluded middle be abandoned in face of quantum mechanics. Two points need to be noted about Quine's claim. First, the claim was not merely that the laws of logic are not immune to revision. To support that claim, it would have been sufficient to refer, for example, to suggestions that we give up the law of excluded middle as applied to vague statements, or to statements about future contingents, or, as with the intuitionists, to mathematical statements. A claim of that kind would not, however, necessarily have been resisted by empiricists of the type Quine was attacking, since such empiricists are not to be thought of as holding ascriptions of analyticity or of logical truth as beyond the reach of philosophical criticism. In these three cases, we are concerned with a proposal, right or wrong, but not to be dismissed out of hand, that, under a proper analysis of the kind of meaning possessed by statements of some already familiar kind, certain classical laws will be seen not to apply to them : and an empiricist, however dogmatic, will hardly be prepared to deny in advance that any analysis could ever have that upshot. Quine's claim is that logical laws are not immune to revision *as a response to new empirical data* : and so he needed a case in which the proposed revision appeared to be such a response.

Secondly, it was essential to Quine's thesis that a proposal for such a revision have some merit. If the claim were merely that such proposals have been made, it would have little interest, although, indeed, it would be beyond dispute. But, to make out his case, Quine needed to produce an instance in which, even if the proposal were not ultimately acceptable, it had at least sufficient substance for us to be able to envisage the possibility that there should be some other proposal of that kind which we should accept. Within the limited scope of 'Two Dogmas', Quine had no room to argue for the merit of the proposed revision which he cited. There has, indeed, been very little attempt made to establish the thesis of the revisability, on empirical grounds, of logical laws by demonstrating, in any given case, that a revision of our logic on such grounds is both meritorious and properly described as occurring in response to experience. One such attempt is that of Hilary Putnam, in his paper 'Is Logic Empirical?' in the *Boston Studies for the Philosophy of Science* (vol. V, pp. 216–41). Putnam considers a different revision from that mentioned by Quine, one which leaves the law of excluded middle intact, but involves abandonment of the distributive law: the empirical theory to which this revision would be a response is again quantum mechanics.

In the meantime, Quine himself has totally reversed his position, as may be seen from the chapter on 'Variant Logics' in *Philosophy of Logic.* There, he begins by remarking that it is impossible for anyone to deny a law of classical logic: for, if he fails to accept some formula which a classical logician would take to be a formulation of such a law, this failure would establish a conclusive ground for saying that he was not attaching to the logical constants appearing in the formula the same meanings as those attached by the classical logician, and hence he had not denied anything held by the classical logician, but merely changed the subject. This is the celebrated 'change of meaning' argument frequently derided, in other contexts, by Quine and his followers as an ineffective bolthole used by meaning-theorists attempting to escape the rigour of Quine's arguments against traditional conceptions of meaning: it is therefore of some considerable general importance that Quine now believes that there is one type of context in which an appeal to this form of argument is legitimate. When he comes, in *Philosophy of Logic*, to consider the proposal that the law of excluded middle be abandoned in application to quantum-mechanical statements, Quine does not go into the arguments that have been adduced for doing so, but contents himself with remarking that a revision in physical theory, however extensive it may be, will always be less disruptive of our total theory than a revision in our logic ('our' logic being assumed to be classical), and hence always to be preferred to it. This argument, as thus baldly stated, is exceedingly weak: for, without examining what revision in physical theory would be required, or, indeed, whether any workable proposal for such a revision is to hand, one has no right to assume that an acknowledgement that classical logic does not hold within some restricted region of discourse really would involve a greater overall disruption. In any case, the conclusion of the argument is the very opposite of the thesis maintained in 'Two Dogmas': if it were correct, we could hold the laws of classical logic to be immune from any revision in response to experience, and perhaps in response to philosophical criticism also.

Putnam's initial explanation of quantum logic is that to each physical system S is co-ordinated a Hilbert space $H(S)$, and to each basic physical proposition $m(S) = r$ ('the magnitude m has the value r in the system S') is co-ordinated a subspace of $H(S)$. This co-ordination of propositions to subspaces is then extended to complex propositions by the following rules: where $S(A)$ is the subspace of $H(S)$ co-ordinated with the proposition A, $S(A \vee B)$ is to be the span of $S(A)$ and $S(B)$, $S(A \& B)$ is to be the intersection of $S(A)$ and $S(B)$, and $S(-A)$ is to be the orthocomplement of $S(A)$, while the quantifiers are to be treated like $\vee$ and &. Now, under these operations, the subspaces of $H(S)$ will form a complemented non-distributive lattice, and hence the propositions will form one also. In particular, it will not in general be the case that $A \& (B \vee C)$ implies $(A \& B) \vee (A \& C)$. We are then, Putnam says, faced with a choice: either the co-ordination is nonsense, or we must change our logic so as to give up the distributive law.

Putnam strongly recommends the alternative of 'changing our logic'. At this stage, however, this description of what we should be doing is highly tendentious. It is very dubious whether the most tenacious adherent of classical logic – for instance, Quine as he now views these matters – would want to deny that we may usefully, for one purpose or another, introduce logical constants which obey some but not all of the classical laws, and which were explained at the outset, not by the two-valued truth-tables, or by reference to any other Boolean algebra, but in some different way. What needs to be done, to make out the claim that accepting quantum logic would be rightly described as 'changing our logic', is to argue that the logical constants which appear in quantum logic are the same old constants we have always used. This Putnam later attempts to do: but, at this stage in the article, to speak of 'changing our logic' stands very much in need of justification.

If, Putnam says, we make this change in our logic, every anomaly vanishes from quantum mechanics. In particular, he claims that, once we have appreciated the structure of quantum logic, i.e. the failure of the distributive law but the validity of the law of excluded middle, we shall no longer be tempted to take a non-realist view of quantum-mechanical systems, for instance to say that the measurement of momentum 'brings into being' the value found by the measurement. Suppose, for example, that I have measured the position of a particle in a one-particle system, and that A records the position that I measured. And suppose that $B^1, B_2, \ldots, B_n$ are statements representing all the possible momenta that the particle can have. Then, for each particular i from 1 to n, the statement A & B_i is false. By 'smuggling in' classical logic, Putnam says, we pass from this fact and the fact that A is true to the conclusion that $B_1 \vee B_2 \vee \ldots \vee B_n$ is false, i.e. that the particle has no momentum. This is, however, a mistake: $B_1 \vee \ldots \vee B_n$ is *true*, in fact logically true, and it is therefore the case that the particle has some momentum. Furthermore, the statement A & $(B_1 \vee \ldots \vee B_n)$ is true; only, since the distributive law does not hold, we cannot pass from this to $(A \,\&\, B_1) \vee \ldots \vee (A \,\&\, B_n)$; this latter statement is in fact logically false, each one of the disjuncts being logically contradictory.

From this Putnam concludes that we can happily assert that, at any given time, a particle has a position and it has a momentum. What is more, if I measure the position, I shall find the position which the particle has, and, if I measure the momentum, I shall find that. Measurement does not bring either the position or the momentum into being: if a procedure were to distort the very thing it seeks to measure, it would be peculiar that it should be accepted as a good measurement (p. 225). If I have measured the position, then I cannot predict what the momentum is going to be after some fixed interval. Nevertheless, he says, there is some statement which is now true of the (one-particle) system which gives the momentum of the particle now, and from which it follows what the momentum will be after the given interval. The only trouble is that, having measured the position, I cannot know which statement this is. Thus inability to predict arises, in quantum mechanics as elsewhere, from ignorance: there is some statement which is true and which gives the momentum of the particle, but I do not know which it is. However, Putnam says consolingly, this ignorance is not *mere* ignorance, since it is not just that I do not know the statement, but that I *cannot* know it. I cannot do so because, knowing the truth of the statement giving the position of the particle, if I were also to know that of the statement giving the momentum, I should know a logical contradiction.

It is evident that Putnam is here appealing to some notion of truth distinct from that embodied in the quantum logic. It is a notion of truth which derives from his realist picture of the quantum-mechanical system. It looks rather as though it may be propped up by an appeal to counterfactuals: the momentum which the particle has now is that which I should discover if I were to measure it, which, unfortunately, I cannot do. If so, it may fairly be commented that an appeal to counterfactuals stands in serious enough need of justification when the antecedent is merely false; when it is actually impossible, the foundation for the notion of truth thus introduced is very flimsy indeed. However this may be, it seems inescapable that, if there is a statement which is true, even though I cannot know it, and if the reason that I cannot know it is that I already know another true proposition such that, if I knew them both, I should be knowing a logical contradiction, then there are two true propositions whose conjunction forms a logical contradiction. Well, one might say, they only form a contradiction in the quantum logic: they do not *really* form a contradiction. Exactly so: the notion of truth to which Putnam appeals when he defends a realist view of the quantum-mechanical system, and when he says that there is a true statement about the momentum which, knowing a true statement about the position, we do not know and cannot know, is a notion which obeys classical, two-valued principles. It is not Putnam's opponents, but Putnam himself, who cannot, for very long at a time, 'appreciate the logic employed in quantum mechanics'; it is Putnam, and not they, who 'smuggles in' distributivity. For Putnam's whole argument, at this point, depends upon distributing truth over disjunction; upon assuming that, because the disjunction $B_1 \vee \ldots \vee B_n$ is true, therefore some one of the disjuncts must be true. And, if we assume this, it becomes impossible to see how the law which distributes conjunction over disjunction can fail to hold, since, patently, truth distributes over conjunction on any view. But, for the notion of truth which is embodied in the quantum logic, truth simply cannot be distributed over disjunction. We are forced to say that, while the disjunction $B_1 \vee \ldots \vee B_n$ is true, there is no one B_i which is true; and hence that, while it is the case that the particle has some momentum, there is no one momentum which it has. And, in such a case, we cannot any longer maintain a realist picture of the quantum-mechanical system.

Perhaps, with slightly greater accuracy, the matter may be expressed as follows. Putnam's argument that, for some i from 1 to n, B_i is true depends upon taking truth to be distributive over disjunction. Hence, since A is true, if truth is distributive over conjunction, A & B_i must be true, although a logical contradiction. Putnam is thus faced with a choice between allowing that a logical contradiction may be true (and therefore that there exist true statements which it is impossible in principle to know to be true), and allowing that two statements may both be true, although their conjunction is false.

Putnam has, in fact, made the very mistake which he twice castigates in his paper: that of minimising a conceptual revolution. One possibility would be to give up the revolution. This would mean agreeing that A and B_i are not genuinely contradictory, i.e. that there is another type of conjunction (let us write it '.') over which truth distributes, and for which $A.B_i$ is not a contradiction (but is true); propositions formed by means of this connective are not co-ordinated with subspaces of $H(S)$. Truth need not then be required to distribute over the connective &. Such a view would be compatible with – in fact, it would be an expression of – realism with respect to quantum-mechanical systems; but it would entail relinquishing the claim that the operators of quantum logic were the only meaningful logical constants applicable to quantum-mechanical propositions. The awkwardness of this position would lie in the fact that, while the true proposition $A.B_i$ would not be a logical contradiction, it *would* still be in principle unknowable; and it is our reluctance to admit the existence of true propositions which cannot in principle be known to be true (at least where 'in principle' is interpreted in a very strong sense, to mean 'by beings however placed and whatever their observational and intellectual capacities') which in the first place motivates us to adopt a revised logic for quantum mechanics which will rule out such propositions. The other possibility is, then, to accept the conceptual revolution. This entails recognising that truth does *not* distribute over disjunction, and, therefore, that it may be that, while a particle has some momentum, there is no one particular momentum which it has. And this means abandoning realism for quantum-mechanical systems.

Putnam believes that the adoption of the von Neumann/Birkhoff logic which he advocates for quantum mechanics is consistent with a realistic interpretation of quantum mechanics. Indeed, he believes more than this: he believes that the adoption of quantum logic both compels and is required for a realistic interpretation. What is a realistic interpretation of statements of some given class? It is, essentially, the belief that we possess a notion of truth for statements of that class under which every statement is determinately either true or not true, independently of our knowledge or our capacity for knowledge. Putnam's realist doctrine plainly fits that characterisation. Now, it is by no means a requirement on realism that we deny that there is any use for, let alone that there is any intelligible interpretation of, non-classical logical constants as applied to statements of the class in question. But it *is* a requirement on realism that the classical two-valued constants can meaningfully be introduced. Since every statement is determinately either true or not, it must be *possible* to introduce a negation $\sim$ such that $\sim A$ is true just in case A is not true, even if this is not the negation which we ordinarily employ, or even the most useful one to employ. Likewise, it must be possible to introduce two-valued conjunction and disjunction.

Now consider the following argument against the claim that a realist interpretation of a given class of statements makes possible the introduction of the classical sentential operators. (The argument it not contained in 'Is Logic Empirical?', but was made by Putnam in the course of a private conversation.) A realist interpretation of a class of statements indeed allows the introduction of sentential operators which satisfy the two-valued truth-tables.

We cannot, however, assume from that that all the laws of classical logic will hold: for the use of the two-valued truth-tables to validate those laws presupposes, not merely that those truth-tables are *correct* for the connectives we are using, but also that the various lines of the truth-table together represent all the possibilities that there are. But the assumption that this is so presupposes the validity of the distributive law: without the distributive law, we cannot pass from saying that A is either true or false and that B is either true or false to saying that either A and B are both true, or A is true and B false, or A false and B true, or both are false. Hence we cannot without circularity deduce from the possibility of introducing connectives for which the truth-tables are correct that the distributive law will hold for them.

This is a very interesting and engaging argument. It bears a striking resemblance to the point much more frequently made, that the correctness of the classical truth-tables does not guarantee the validity of the law of excluded middle. The two-valued truth-tables are *correct* for the intuitionistic sentential operators: but one cannot use them to show that the law of excluded middle holds intuitionistically, because that would involve an appeal to the tacit assumption which governs their use in classical logic, that the lines of the truth-table exhaust all possibilities, i.e. in this case, that every statement is either true or false. The law of excluded middle can be validated by the use of the truth-tables only on the assumption of the law of bivalence; and, similarly, the distributive law can be validated from the truth-tables only on the assumption of a distributive law relating to truth and falsity.

This observation is certainly correct. But the analogy of intuitionism ought to raise a doubt whether it can be used to show that realism is consistent, not merely with the rejection of the distributive law, but with the denial that connectives can be introduced for which the distributive law holds. The anti-realist character of intuitionism is not shown by a denial that sentential operators can be introduced for which the classical truth-tables are correct, but by a rejection of the law of bivalence, which amounts to saying that no operators can be introduced for which the law of excluded middle is correct. The reply might be given that the law of bivalence was incorporated into the characterisation, given above, of what realism is, namely as involving that every statement is determinately either true or not true. But this characterisation used the connective 'or'; and it appears to me that, for the characterisation of realism so given to be adequate, the 'or' that was used must be taken as one for which the distributive law holds. To say that the distributive law fails is, in effect, to say that the rule of disjunction elimination fails: what follows from each of A and B, taken separately, need not follow from 'A or B'. An understanding of 'or' under which disjunction elimination fails is one which allows that it may be correct to say 'A or B', although there is no answer to the question 'Which of A and B holds?' – not just that we do not know it, but there is no answer to be known. To say that every statement was either true or not true, when 'or' was used in such a way, would not be an expression of realism: it was precisely this possibility that it was intended to rule out, in the characterisation of realism, by qualifying the phrase 'either true or not true' by the adverb 'determinately'.

For this reason, Putnam's entirely correct observation that the use of the two-valued truth-tables to validate the laws of classical logic makes a tacit appeal, not only to the law of bivalence but to the distributive law, fails to show that a belief that it is impossible to introduce connectives, applied to statements of a given class, for which the distributive law holds is consistent with a realistic interpretation of statements of that class.

The issue of realism concerning quantum mechanics, though an important one in itself, and one on which Putnam holds strong opinions, is nevertheless a side-issue in Putnam's paper, which is principally concerned to treat quantum logic as an illustrative case for the thesis that logical laws are revisable in the face of experience. Even if, as I have argued, Putnam is quite wrong in supposing that the replacement of classical logic by quantum logic is compatible with realism, this does not of itself affect his principal contention, that we have here an example of a revision in our logic which is forced on us by empirical considerations.

Putnam treats the distributive law as though it were something that we merely felt to be evident. He opens the paper by citing the Euclidean axiom of parallels, the proposition that nothing can be red and green all over, and the proposition that a bachelor cannot be married, as statements having an equal degree of intuitively evident necessity; and he later assigns the distributive law to the same category. The matter is presented as if the only reason anyone had ever had for thinking any one of these propositions to have a non-empirical status lay in an unanalysed *feeling* that they were necessary; as though no one had ever thought about them or attempted to investigate their relations with other statements or to uncover their internal structure. (And this even though Putnam himself once put forward a proof that nothing could be red and green all over.) In particular, the idea that the meanings of the sentential operators are given by truth-tables, and that, being so given, the distributive law cannot but hold for them, never gets a glance. Indeed, as we have seen, this idea needs supplementing by an appeal to the controlling assumption that the lines of the truth-table represent an exhaustive list of alternative possibilities; and, quite independently of whether or not this controlling assumption is integral to realism, as was claimed above, there is evidently a case to be made that, as a justification either of the law of excluded middle or of the distributive law, it involves a *petitio principii.* But, in 'Is Logic Empirical?' this case is not argued, because the conception that the sentential operators are to be explained in terms of the notions of truth and falsity is not so much as mentioned. Until very near the end of the paper, the only explanation of the sentential operators that is entertained at all is in terms of the co-ordination of propositions with subspaces of a Hilbert space; since the lattice formed by these subspaces is non-distributive, we have simply got to bite the bullet and dispense with the distributive law.

At the end of the paper, however, Putnam introduces 'operational' analyses of the sentential operators. He does so reluctantly, and with many apologies and cautions that operational definitions have only a heuristic value. Nevertheless, it is the first clear acknowledgement in the paper that there may be such a thing as an explanation of the meanings of the sentential operators, or that, in discussing the validity of logical laws governing those operators, we have any need to provide such an explanation and to justify our logical theory by reference to it.

Putnam's operational definitions are as follows. First, he says, we pretend that, to every physical property P there corresponds a test T such that something passes T if and only if it has P, where 'passes T' is interpreted to mean '*would* pass T, if T were to be performed'. Putnam remarks of this assumption that it is the usual operationalist idealisation. That is perfectly true: but the specifically operationalist part of the assumption is that to the effect that, for every property, there exists a test for its possession. The converse assumption, that, for every test (of some suitably restricted kind), there exists a property which is revealed by the test, and which, at any given time, each object either possesses or fails to possess, is not an operationalist assumption as such, but a *realist* one. (A parallel realist assumption is that, to each measurement procedure, there corresponds a physical quantity which possesses, at any given time, some determinate magnitude.) The possession or non-possession of the given property P is what gives substance to the truth of counterfactual statements about what the result of the test T, if it had been applied at a given time, would have been; the bivalence assumed for statements of the form 'The system S has the property P' guarantees that one out of every pair of opposite counterfactuals of this kind must be true. Conversely, the supposition that, of each such pair of opposite counterfactuals, there must always be one which is true, is tantamount to the realist assumption: the possession of the property can then be equated to the (hypothetical) satisfaction of the test, and will then, in virtue of the supposition about the counterfactuals, satisfy the law of bivalence. (The situation is similar in the parallel case of the measurement of quantities. It is essential, in this case, that it be assumed, not merely that each counterfactual whose antecedent relates to the performance of the measurement-procedure is determinately true or false, but that, of a range of such counterfactuals whose consequents together exhaust the possible outcomes of the procedure, some one should be true.)

Putnam goes on to say that tests are partly ordered by the relation $T_1 \leqslant T_2$ which holds whenever anything that would pass T_1 would also pass T_2. Then, if it exists, the test $T_1 \cup T_2$ is taken to be the least upper bound of T_1 and T_2 with respect to the partial ordering $\leqslant$: i.e. $T_1 \leqslant T_1 \cup T_2$, and $T_2 \leqslant T_1 \cup T_2$ and, for every T, if $T_1 \leqslant T$, and $T_2 \leqslant T$, then $T_1 \cup T_2 \leqslant T$. Dually, $T_1 \cap T_2$, if it exists, is taken to be the greatest lower bound of T_1 and T_2. We can take 0 as being the impossible test, which nothing is counted as passing, and 1 as the vacuous test, which everything is counted as passing; while, for any T, $-T$, if it exists, will be a complement of T, namely a test such that $T \cup -T = 1$ and $T \cap -T = 0$. Whenever $\cup$, $\cap$ and $-$ are defined, for any class of tests, these tests thus form a complemented lattice; for quantum mechanics, Putnam says, the operations are defined.

So far, of course, we have only a complemented lattice of tests, not a logic. Putnam's next step is to say that the proposition $A \vee B$ will have an operational meaning only if there is a test T which is passed by all and only the things which have the property expressed by A or the property expressed by B. Since he is here supposed to be giving an operational meaning to '∨', we must assume, to avoid circularity, that the 'or' occurring in the phrase 'the property . . . A or the property . . . B' is to be interpreted classically, i.e. by the two-valued truth-table; this must be legitimate, in view of the realistic character, already remarked, of the terminology of properties as revealed by tests. But, if so, Putnam's claim is unjustified. It is indeed true that, if there is a test T which is passed by just those things which either have the property P or have the property Q, where A expresses possession of P and B that of Q, then of course T will be the least upper bound of T_1 and T_2, where T_1 is the test for possession of P and T_2 that for possession of Q. But it may perfectly well be the case that every test which is passed by all the things having either the property P or the property Q is also passed by some other things, and yet that there is a minimal such test, i.e. one such that everything passing the minimal test also passes every test passed by everything having either the property P or the property Q. Thus Putnam expresses himself incorrectly when he says (p. 240): 'If there is *any* test at all . . . which corresponds to the disjunction $A \vee B$, it must [be] a *least upper bound* on T_1 and T_2.' This assertion is presented as following from the fact that a test passed by just those things which have the property P or the property Q will be a least upper bound of T_1 and T_2. He needs to say instead: 'We stipulate that the proposition $A \vee B$ is to be understood as corresponding to that test T (if there is one) which is the least upper bound of T_1 and T_2.' And then, while he can say that everything with either the property P or the property Q will pass such a T, he will have no right to assert the converse. He next goes on to say likewise: 'Similarly, if conjunction is to correspond to any test at all, it must be the test determined by the intersection of the subspaces S_A and S_B [that is, the subspaces co-ordinated to A and B respectively].' This remark, as stated, is ambiguous, according as we read it as the statement of a condition for the existence of a test corresponding to A & B, taken as already understood, or as a stipulation of what is to be the test corresponding to A & B, and hence as specifying the meaning of that proposition. Plainly, it ought to be understood as a stipulation, namely, in terms of tests, that A & B is to be taken to correspond to the test (if any) which is the greatest lower bound of the tests T_1 and T_2. Now suppose that P is a determinate position for the particle in a one-particle system, and Q a determinate momentum for such a particle. Putnam has precluded himself from denying that some system may have both properties; but, in this case, there is no test which anything passes, and such that everything that passes it has both the properties P and Q, i.e. would pass test T_1 and would pass test T_2: so the impossible test 0 may be taken to be the greatest lower bound for T_1 and T_2, so that A & B, interpreted operationally, becomes a contradictory proposition. B, however, neither is nor implies $-A$, since $A \vee B$ is not, under the operational definition, logically true, i.e. $T_1 \cup T_2$ is not the vacuous test 1. Thus, in all cases, and in the present case trivially, everything that passes $T_1 \cap T_2$ has both the property P and the property Q; but the converse, that everything having both the property P and the property Q passes $T_1 \cap T_2$ does not, in general hold (and, in particular, not in the present case).

Putnam is supposed to be giving operational definitions of $\vee$ and &. In doing so, he uses 'or' and 'and' in the metalanguage, to form disjunctions and conjunctions of properties; moreover, he tacitly assumes for them, in accordance with his realistic presuppositions, a classical two-valued meaning. It is then not in the least surprising that the 'or' and 'and' which he uses in the metalanguage do not agree, in the way that he claims they do, with the $\vee$ and & which are operationally defined. Actually, it is entirely unnecessary for him to use 'or' and 'and' in the metalanguage at all: the operational definitions of $\vee$ and & can be stated, as above, directly in terms of the lattice of tests. In drawing attention to the lack of justification for Putnam's claims, I am not just labouring again the point made earlier, that Putnam's realism is inconsistent with his acceptance of the quantum logic: the point involved here is critically relevant, as we shall see, to Putnam's claim that the adoption of the quantum logic constitutes a revision of our logic in response to experience.

Under the operational definitions in terms of the lattice of tests, we can see very easily that the distributive law fails. The question before us is: Can we, in this case, be said to have had to revise our logic; and, in particular, must we therefore acknowledge that logic, too, has an empirical character?

A change in the evaluation of the validity of a form of inference may represent a moderate or a radical revision of one's logic. By a moderate revision is meant here one by which a form of inference previously taken to be valid is recognised as invalid (or conversely) by appeal to more general principles for the evaluation of deductive arguments which were all along accepted as correct. For instance, someone who accepts a two-valued logic for the sentential operators may be disposed to allow a certain argument involving, say, five different constituent sentences, and then has it pointed out to him that there is a truth-value assignment under which the argument fails. A moderate revision of this kind is philosophically quite unproblematic. A radical revision is one which involves a replacement of some of even the most general criteria previously acknowledged for determining the validity of deductive arguments.

Now the idea of a radical revision of logic is an extremely puzzling one. By this I do not merely mean that it is perplexing for a philosopher to give an account of; I mean that the suggestion that we should make such a revision is one about which anyone is bound, at first encounter, to feel that he is unable to know what to make of it. Suppose that somebody with no philosophical training, but with a knowledge of classical physics, decides that he wants to find out something about quantum mechanics. What he reads at first puzzles him, because it appears to lead to antinomies. If, now, someone else says to him, 'You only think that because you are clinging to classical logic: if you just give up your adherence to the distributive law, the antinomies will disappear', he will not be at all consoled. On the contrary, the suggestion will strike him as mystifying in the same way as a child who has grasped that the square of a negative number is positive is mystified by the proposal to postulate the existence of a square root of -1. It is no help to tell the child that the employment of this number proves to be very useful in, say, the theory of electricity: he cannot see how it is possible to apply a proposition which, as he understands it, is simply contradictory. In order to remove the mystification, it is necessary first to explain to him that, in saying that there is a number whose square is -1, we are making use of an extended meaning for the word 'number'.

In just the same way, anyone will be quite right to resist the suggestion that we simply drop the distributive law, or any other previously recognised logical principle, without further explanation. He has, after all, learned to use deductive arguments as part of the procedure for testing any empirical hypothesis: a standard means of doing this is to derive, deductively, consequences of the hypothesis, and check them for consistency and against observation and already established facts. If, when this procedure leads a given theory into apparent antinomies, this is suddenly taken, not as a ground for revising the theory, but for adjusting the rules for deriving consequences, it is not merely a natural but a justifiable reaction to feel that we no longer know what is the content of calling a theory correct or incorrect.

The explanation that, in making a radical revision of our logic, we shall be giving altered meaning to the logical constants is a first step in providing a rationale for a proposal which, in the absence of any such rationale, remains merely absurd and unintelligible (just as the explanation that we are introducing a new meaning for the word 'number' is a necessary first step in getting the child to understand what is involved in speaking of $\sqrt{-1}$). Those like Harman who believe that Quine has eliminated the word 'meaning' from the philosophical lexicon usually claim that their opponents, who appeal to the notion of meaning, are indulging in mystification; we shall just speak about sentences – everybody knows what they are – and not about their meanings, which are quite obscure entities. But in fact the mystification proceeds from those who foreswear appeal to meaning; for such a person cannot explain what he is about when he proposes a radical revision of our logic, or, perhaps, of other well-embedded truths.

The idea that certain sentences could not be abandoned as no longer to be held as true, or certain principles of inference as no longer to be held as valid, unless some change in the meanings of some of the words involved had occurred is, of course, a fundamental principle of the conception of analyticity attacked by

Quine and by others, including Putnam himself. It ought to be unnecessary to remark that no one has ever maintained that there are sentences which could not be given up even under a change of meaning; but this trivial observation has, nevertheless, sometimes been overlooked by those arguing in favour of the 'Two Dogmas' view that there are no analytic, i.e. no unrevisable, sentences. In so arguing, they slip into supposing that all that they are required to show is that, for any allegedly analytic sentence, we can envisage circumstances in which we should not want to assert that sentence. Harman, for example, in his article on 'Quine on Meaning',[1] appeals to what he rightly calls the 'familiar point' that the use of certain words may be rejected by someone because he rejects 'the principles that give meaning' to those words (that is, in their customary use). The point is, indeed, a familiar one : what is unclear is whether it can be stated without an appeal, such as Harman twice makes in stating it, to the notion of meaning. Harman wishes (or wished, when he wrote that article) totally to reject the notion of meaning; it is therefore obscure what entitles him to invoke it when he himself needs it to state a thesis which he holds. It may be that the appeals he makes to the notion of meaning are intended as *argumenta ad hominem*; but the intention is unclear. However this may be, Harman goes on to appeal to this 'familiar point' to show how even the principle of self-identity might be rejected. Earlier (p. 128) he had claimed that this principle may reasonably be represented as recording a general feature of the way the world is, i.e. that the world happens to be such that everything in it is identical with itself. Now he backs up this claim by observing that someone who rejected the notion of identity itself, that is, who rejected certain uses of the verb 'is', would be bound to withhold assent from the principle of self-identity. (An example of a rejection of the notion of identity would be Geach's view that there is no absolute relation of identity, but only a number of relative notions; hence Geach must regard the remark that everything is what it is, and not another thing, not as banal, but as unintelligible.)

But, in fact, if there exist statements the rejection of which is intelligible only under the supposition of a rejection of one of the concepts involved in its expression, then such a statement would

[1] *Review of Metaphysics*, vol. XXI, pp. 124–51.

have a very high degree of analyticity indeed. Harman expressly conjectures that this is the case with the conjunction of the postulates of set theory: 'perhaps', he says (p. 134), 'it makes no sense to *deny*' this conjunction, 'since these postulates give meaning to "is a member of" '; but that does not impede someone from rejecting set theory, because he rejects the very notion of set-membership. The admission of such a possibility is the admission of the possibility of a very strong notion of analyticity, and not, as Harman seems to think, a refutation of it.

Analyticity has usually been claimed in a weaker sense than this, even for at least some of the laws of logic: they could be rejected only at the cost of changing the meanings of the logical constants, but not necessarily of rejecting those constants altogether.

Naturally, saying that a change of meaning is involved is only a *first* step towards explaining what one is after. The child will want to know what is the new sense of 'number' under which negative numbers can have square roots: and we are happily in a position to give him a clear answer. The fact that this answer seems so straightforward to us should not obscure the fact that it was attained long after complex numbers had first been introduced: in order to arrive at a clear understanding of the relation of the various number-systems to one another, and of what is needed in order to construct one from another, a great deal of work had to be done in the foundations of mathematics, by Dedekind, Cantor and many others, work which, when it was done, was a crucial necessity for the clarification of mathematical propositions. If mathematicians had rested content with saying 'Never mind what "number" *means* – whatever *that* may mean: just concentrate on the fact that we find these equations useful in dealing with empirical questions', then mathematics would have remained only one step away from magic. Frege rightly stigmatised it as a scandal that, while mathematics claimed the title of an exact science, no agreement existed on the fundamental questions what the objects of the various mathematical theories are or what justified acceptance of their axioms. The purpose of foundational work such as Frege undertook was not so much to establish the axiomatic bases of our theories with certainty, as to enable us to command a clear view of the structure of those theories and their interrelation. If, in Frege's day, the view which impatiently dismisses requests for explanations of meaning, and thinks the existence of empirical applications sufficient justification, had prevailed, then a great deal that is now taken for granted in mathematics would be unknown; and, in particular, we should be quite unable to give any account of what it is that gets applied and of what the application consists in.

In just the same way, it cannot be merely a matter of saying 'Let us give up the distributive law – of course, in doing so, we shall be altering the meanings of "and" and "or" ': we need to be told what these new meanings of 'and' and 'or' are to be, under which the distributive law will no longer come out valid. Such an explanation is provided by Putnam's 'operational' account of the logical constants.

Putnam's attitude to the issue about change of meaning is not easy to grasp. His most explicit remarks concern the choice of a geometry for the physical universe, which he expressly asserts (p. 234) to constitute a perfect analogy to the choice of a logic. He expresses himself as unwilling to pronounce on whether the replacement of Euclidean by Riemannian geometry does or does not involve a change of meaning in geometrical expressions like 'straight line'. He does, however, insist on two points: (*i*) that there is enough in common between the uses of 'straight line' in the two contexts for the use of the same expression not to be a mere equivocation; and (*ii*) we have not merely shifted the label 'straight line' from one set of paths to another. When a change of meaning is simply a case of relabelling, then we can still express the old meaning which a word used to have before its meaning was altered. Point (*ii*) is to the effect that this is *not* what happens in the geometrical case: even if 'straight line' has changed its meaning, we cannot, having adopted Riemannian geometry, use *any* expression with just that meaning which 'straight line' used to have when we adhered to Euclidean geometry.

This is a very important and completely valid distinction. Putnam does, indeed, grossly overestimate its novelty. Thus he claims (p. 219) that an appreciation of the distinction shows one 'that the usual "linguistic" moves only help to distort the nature of the discovery, not to clarify it'. But, even if the distinction had not previously been drawn in just those terms, it is a wild misrepresentation to suggest that philosophers who have tried to characterise a certain kind of necessity by the feature that a rejection of certain statements would involve a change of meaning have supposed that such a change of meaning would always be a case of relabelling.

However this may be, Putnam is clear about this: that, for his claim that the abandonment of the distributive law in the face of quantum mechanics shows logic to be empirical in the same sense that the replacement of Euclidean by Riemannian geometry shows the geometry of the physical universe to be empirical to stand, it must be possible to say that, if the logical constants undergo a change of meaning at all when the distributive law is abandoned, this is not a case of relabelling. If it were a case of relabelling, then we would have to be able still to express what we formerly meant by 'and' and 'or' when we accepted the distributive law: and then there would be no *proposition* that we had relinquished in response to experience, only a *sentence* to which we found it convenient to give a different meaning.

Let us assume that classical logic is at present in possession, so that a radical revision of logic will always be a revision from classical to some non-standard logic: let us call their advocates *C* and *N*. Then there are four possible cases, according to which of the following two pairs of alternatives hold. (1) *N* rejects the classical meanings of the logical constants and proposes modified ones; or (2) *N* admits the classical meanings as intelligible, but proposes modified ones as more, or at least equally, interesting. And (*a*) *C* rejects *N*'s modified meanings as illegitimate or unintelligible; or (*b*) he admits them as intelligible, alongside the unmodified classical meanings. If cases (2) and (*b*) both hold, then we are in effect in a position where only relabelling is involved: controversy, if any, centres round the degree of interest of the new constants.

Intuitionism, by contrast, clearly satisfies case (1): intuitionists reject the conception that the logical constants, at least as occurring in mathematical statements, can be explained by specifying truth-conditions for statements in which they are the principal operators, because they regard the notion of truth-conditions, as obtaining independently of proof or refutation, as unintelligible for mathematical statements.

How, then, does the matter stand with quantum logic? Putnam, considered as a revisionist, is much less radical than the intuitionists. For, as was argued earlier, the realistic terms in which he construes statements about quantum-mechanical systems cannot but allow as legitimate a purely classical interpretation of the logical constants as applied to such statements. If the atomic statements are considered to be ones assigning, with respect to a system S, a determinate magnitude to some one of various physical quantities at particular times, and the system is thought of as objectively possessing, for each such physical quantity and at each moment of time, a determinate magnitude, then there can be no possible objection to a classical use of 'and' and 'or' under which 'A and B' holds just in case both A and B hold, and 'A or B' holds just in case either A holds or B holds or both. (The circularity in these 'explanations' is inescapable for the classical connectives; the connectives used in the explanations are just those used by Putnam in speaking of disjunctive and conjunctive properties.) Hence Putnam cannot be thought to be *rejecting* the classical meanings of the constants in application to statements about quantum-mechanical systems. The situation is therefore *not* analogous to the geometrical one, where it is impossible to admit simultaneously, in application to the physical universe, both the Euclidean and the Riemannian meanings of 'straight line'. The classical and operational meanings of 'and' and 'or' will not, indeed, coincide, in the quantum-mechanical case, although, as has been seen, Putnam, with his penchant for committing the crime, which he so eloquently denounces, of minimising a conceptual revolution, does his best to obscure this fact. Not every system of which A and B are both true will pass the test $T_1 \cap T_2$, where T_1 and T_2 are the tests for the truth of A and of B respectively; not every system which passes $T_1 \cup T_2$ will be such that either A or B is true of it. Thus quantum logic, as presented by Putnam, involves the proposal to introduce new connectives '&' and 'v' explained operationally, alongside the classical connectives 'and' and 'or', explained truth-functionally; it is, therefore, alternative (2) which holds good in this case. Moreover, there seems no reason to doubt that alternative (*b*) also holds: provided that the relevant class of tests really does form a lattice, what objection could anybody have to the introduction of such variant meanings for '&' and 'v' provided that they were not confused with the classical meanings?

It thus seems that the situation is quite different from Putnam's summation of it. Putnam never once mentions the two-valued truth-functional explanations of the sentential operators; but he does suggest that his 'operational' explanations would be acceptable for them, as classically understood, and that this is therefore the only way they can be extended in the quantum-mechanical case. It is, however, simply untrue that the operational explanations would be acceptable to every adherent of classical logic. They would be accepted only by one who made the operationalist assumption that the class of testable statements is closed under all sentence-forming operations in the language (a statement being 'testable' if there exists a test for determining its truth or falsity). Such an assumption is, however, highly dubious for linguistic operations such as quantification and variation of time-reference (the use of past and future tenses), within a language understood classically. Furthermore, the operational explanation of the connectives would be admitted by an adherent of classical logic only on a further assumption that any test could always be carried out independently of what other tests are carried out; under this assumption, it will indeed be true that, if there is a test for possession of the property *P* and another for possession of the property *Q*, then there will be tests for possessing either the property *P* or the property *Q*, and for possessing both the properties *P* and *Q*, where 'and' and 'or' are classically understood. It is, however, just this assumption which breaks down in the quantum-mechanical case, leading to the result that '&' and 'v', explained operationally, diverge from the classical meanings and satisfy different laws.

The account of Putnam's position at which we have now arrived is different from that which was given earlier: it depends on which part of his article one is attending to. Earlier, I said that the failure of the distributive law made realism untenable: a particle has some position, but, since truth does not distribute over disjunction or existential quantification, there is not necessarily any one position which it has. For, in the earlier part of Putnam's article, the most prominent feature is the rejection of the distributive law, and so I was prompted to say that Putnam was not, as he claimed, entitled to take a realist view. But, in the later part of his article, the realism becomes highly explicit; and so it seems better to say instead that all that he is doing is to introduce new senses of '&' and 'v' *alongside* the old senses, without displacing the latter. Hence, in so far as this account is correct, Putnam is in no way rejecting the distributive law, as holding for 'and' and 'or' on their standard meanings; it remains as valid for him as for anyone else.

No pronouncement has been made, in the present paper, either for or against the adoption of quantum logic, nor yet for or against a realistic interpretation of quantum mechanics. All that I have been concerned to maintain is that it is inconsistent to combine, as Putnam wishes to do, a realistic interpretation with the thesis that the quantum logic should supplant classical logic. If the realism is upheld, then the two sets of logical constants must both be admitted as intelligible, when applied to statements about quantum-mechanical systems; and this entails that the situation is not parallel to the geometrical case, and does not involve the abandonment, in response to experience or otherwise, of any logical law formerly held.

But how would matters stand if the inconsistency in Putnam's position were resolved in the opposite way, namely by maintaining quantum logic, considered as supplanting classical logic, and abandoning the realistic interpretation of quantum mechanics? I suspect that Putnam himself would feel that such a modification of his view would blunt the cutting edge of his thesis that logic is empirical (as empirical as the geometry of the physical universe), since it would no longer be possible to claim that the discovery of the invalidity of the distributive law was a discovery *about the world.* But, if the world consists of all that we do not create, then the fact that certain statements cannot be interpreted realistically does not mean that they say nothing about the world.

Nevertheless, I should deny, in this case too, that logic had been shown to be empirical. The question is what kind of considerations they are, or should be, which would persuade us that, for quantum-mechanical statements, quantum logic ought to replace classical logic; and it appears to me that these considerations would be of exactly the same general kind as those which are invoked in favour of an intuitionistic logic, in place of the classical one, for mathematical statements. These considerations are not themselves mathematical ones: no mathematical discovery, no mathematical theory could justify or help to justify the rejection of classical logic and its replacement by intuitionistic logic within mathematics; to think otherwise would be to try to provide intuitionistic mathematics with a mathematical foundation, such as Frege and Hilbert each tried, in different ways, to provide for classical mathematics, but which the intuitionists repudiate as not required. The considerations which intuitionists invoke belong, not to mathematics, but to the theory of meaning: they relate to the question what is the correct model for the meanings which we confer upon our mathematical statements. A model of meaning, in this sense, is a model of understanding, that is, of what it is to know the meaning of a statement. It is really only since Frege that we have been able to construct anything which even approximates to being a plausible model of meaning; and it has been much easier to construct such models than to determine, let alone apply, the criteria by which any given model of meaning is to be judged correct or incorrect. But it is within the theory of meaning that the evaluation of the proposal to replace classical by intuitionistic logic within mathematics must take place, not within mathematics: the proposition that the correct logic for mathematics is the intuitionistic one neither is nor is dependent upon a mathematical proposition.

In just the same way, the issue whether, for quantum mechanics, classical logic should be displaced by quantum logic is an issue belonging to the theory of meaning; an affirmative answer would neither be nor be derivable from a proposition of quantum mechanics. There is an evident generic similarity between the two cases. Both employ a notion of meaning that relates to the means available to us for knowing the truth of statements of the relevant class: in the quantum case, in terms of measurements of physical quantities; in the intuitionist case, in terms of proofs of mathematical propositions. Since, if classical logic is admissible alongside the non-classical one, there can be no question of any *rejection* of a classical law, the crucial thesis, from the present point of view, is, in both cases, the negative one according to which, for statements of the relevant kind, meaning cannot be conceived as given in terms of conditions for the possession of truth-values which attach determinately to statements independently of our knowledge. This is an exceedingly deep, and extraordinarily difficult, question in the theory of meaning, one which we are unlikely to answer definitively until we have a far more penetrating insight into the way in which our language functions (in the present case, the mathematical and quantum-mechanical sectors of the language) than we now have. But it is a question which is irreducibly philosophical in character; one which we cannot hope can be answered, in the one case by any mathematical discovery, in the other by any discovery in quantum mechanics.

MAIN PUBLICATION

Frege: Philosophy of Language (Duckworth, 1973)

A THEORY OF SOCIAL JUSTICE

by

Antony Flew

Professor of Philosophy, University of Reading

'I have no respect for the passion for equality, which seems to me merely idealising envy.'

Oliver Wendell Holmes Jnr

For better or for worse *A Theory of Justice*[1] by John Rawls is now established as the reference point for contemporary discussions in this area. My remarks will, therefore, take the form of comments on his position. But I am not trying to write a Critical Notice.[2]

1. THE THEORY IN OUTLINE

Rawls opens with a trumpet blast:

'Justice is the first virtue of social institutions, as truth is of systems of thought. A theory however elegant and economical must be rejected if it is untrue; likewise laws and institutions no matter how efficient and well-arranged must be reformed or abolished if they are unjust. Each person possesses an inviolability founded on justice that even the welfare of society as a whole cannot override. For this reason justice denies that the loss of freedom for some is made right by a greater good shared by others. . . . Therefore in a just society the liberties of equal citizenship are taken as settled; the rights secured by justice are not subject to political bargaining or

[1] Cambridge, Mass, Harvard University Press, 1971, and Oxford, Clarendon, 1972.

[2] Some of the present material did however appear first as part of such a notice in *Encounter* for November 1973. I thank the Editor for allowing me to recycle this.

to the calculus of social interests. The only thing that permits us to acquiesce in an erroneous theory is the lack of a better one; analogously, an injustice is tolerable only when it is necessary to avoid an even greater injustice. Being first virtues of human activities, truth and justice are uncompromising.' (pp. 3–4)

The master concept which Rawls revives is that of a social contract. As in Rousseau[8] and Hobbes, but not in Locke, this contract is strictly hypothetical – a theoretical fiction:

'the guiding idea is that the principles of justice for the basic structure of society . . . are the principles that free and rational persons concerned to further their own interests would accept in an initial position of equality as defining the fundamental terms of their association. . . . This way of regarding the principles of justice I shall call justice as fairness.' (p. 11)

It is characteristic of these 'mere conditional and hypothetical reasonings' in Rawls that they take place behind 'The Veil of Ignorance' (p. 136). Wherever he sees a dimension of actual human differences which he fears might be improperly evaluated by interested persons, there Rawls rules that his hypothetical contracting parties must be ignorant of their particular personal parameters. These rulings together constitute a dramatisation of the procedural requirement of impartiality:

'First of all, no one knows his place in society, his class position or social status; nor does he know his fortune in the distribution of natural assets and abilities, his intelligence and strength, and the like. Nor again, does anyone know his conception of the good, the particulars of his rational plan of life, or even the special features of his psychology such as his aversion to risk or liability to optimism or pessimism. More than this, I assume that the parties do not know the particular circumstances of their own society. . . . The persons in the original position have no information as to which generation they belong [to]. . . . They must choose principles the

[8] In 'Rousseau and Equality' in *Encounter* for September 1974 Robert Nisbet sees Rawls as Rousseau redivivus. Nisbet's Critical Notice in *The Public Interest* (vol. XXXV, Spring, 1974) should not be missed.

consequences of which they are prepared to live with whatever generation they turn out to belong to.' (p. 137)

(It is curious, though not, I think, significant, that neither race nor sex is specifically included in this list of personal particulars not to be available to the contracting parties.)

'During much of modern moral philosophy', Rawls says, 'the predominant systematic theory has been some form of utilitarianism' (p. vii). One of his main aims is to develop 'the conception of justice as fairness as a viable alternative to the utilitarian tradition' (p. 150). So he makes a great deal of the theoretical, and often very practical, differences between, on the one hand, his own conception of a society governed by 'justice as fairness . . . a scheme of co-operation for reciprocal advantage regulated by principles which persons would choose in an initial situation that is fair', and, on the other hand, the classical utilitarian ideal of 'the efficient administration of social resources to maximise the satisfaction of the system of desire constructed by the impartial spectator from the many individual systems of desires accepted as given' (p. 33).

The two, or three, fundamental principles are: 'First: each person is to have an equal right to the most extensive basic liberty compatible with a similar liberty for others. Second: social and economic inequalities are to be arranged so that they are both (*a*) reasonably expected to be to everyone's advantage, and (*b*) attached to positions and offices open to all' (p. 60). These principles are arranged in what Rawls calls lexical order: the first, that is to say, has priority over the second; while 2(*a*), similarly, has priority over 2(*b*). (In an earlier discussion of the book I argued, as I now believe wrongly, that Rawls eventually gives 2(*b*) priority over 2(*a*).) It is these principles, he thinks, which 'persons' – if you can call such deprived and hypothetical contracting parties persons – 'would choose in an initial situation that is fair'. His candour about the measures necessary to ensure that it should be thus fair is exhilarating: 'We want to define the original position so that we get the desired solution' (p. 141).

2. JUSTICE AND SOCIAL JUSTICE

Rawls labels his massive work *A Theory of Justice*, without qualification. This is too broad a description of its actual scope. For, as he says himself, 'Our topic is that of social justice. For us the primary subject of justice is the basic structure of society, or more exactly, the way in which the major social institutions distribute fundamental rights and duties and determine the division of advantages from social co-operation' (p. 7).

That the actual title is misleadingly comprehensive matters little. What does is that Rawls has not recognised the need to relate the justice of social justice to that of other kinds. It is quite wrong to say that 'the primary subject of justice is the basic structure of society'. Such appraisal of the basic structures of societies is a pretty sophisticated activity. Our distant ancestors in closed societies must have spoken of other people getting or not getting their just deserts long before anyone brought the basic structure of any society into question. And today even those who later come to think of justice almost exclusively in terms of social justice first learn to apply words like 'just' and 'fair' in much less wide-ranging contexts. When one sister is given an orange it is only fair that the other sister should have an orange too; in a good old-fashioned Western both the goodies and the baddies get their just deserts; and so on.[4]

The question of primacy matters in two ways. It matters, first, because in the contexts which are in fact primary the claims of justice refer to antecedent deserts, obligations, and entitlements. These are not the same for all. They vary from person to person, according to what they have done or failed to do, and according to what their social position and social relations are. She has served well. But he has served badly, or not at all. I have an obligation to her because I am her son. And so on. To do justice requires that we take account of all these various deserts and obligations and entitlements. It is thus in at least one aspect an essentially backward-looking notion. Nor is what is available for distribution equally available for all. The history and social relations which give someone some claim on one store may give a different claim, or none at all, on another. That these are my daughters gives them claims on me quite different from any claims which the same two

[4] In a telltale passage of *The Liberal Theory of Justice* (Oxford, OUP, 1973) Brian Barry writes: 'For many working-class people in industrial societies "fairness" is virtually entirely comprised in the provisions of the welfare state' (p. 57). Illustrations in Ch. V of his earlier *Political Argument* (London, Routledge & Kegan Paul, 1960) suggest that he then knew better.

may have on anybody else. Everything is not up for grabs by all equally.

To recognise this should make us uneasy about the whole Rawls approach. For this starts from a fiction which is essentially forward-looking. The parties to his contract have no individuality, no past, and precious little present. Their whole existence and reason for existence lies in deciding how best to safeguard their future. It is also characteristic of their situation that in it there are no historically and socially determined antecedent claims on anyone or anything: 'You have nothing to lose but your ignorance, and all the world to win!'

This constitutes one reason why it is essential to try to relate the justice of social justice to that of other kinds. The second reason is that except in so far as there are connections, and close connections, social justice cannot genuinely be any kind of justice at all. Suppose that it is not. Then to commend a protagonist of social justice as by that token a champion of justice would be as misguided as to accept an apologist for Soviet or People's Democracy as an authentic democrat.[5] In both these cases it seems to be true that the unqualified element in the contrast possesses perhaps

[5] I am, of course, so using the word 'democracy' that the necessary condition of its proper application is not that they were voted in but that they may be voted out. Once we appreciate that this is indeed the crux, we see how wrong it is to take the sincerity of a commitment to achieving power only by getting voted in as the sincerity of a commitment to democracy. This is a common and dangerous mistake. It was made, for example, by the BBC's Political Correspondent, Hardiman Scott, while discussing the last national election in France. M. Marchais and his party may well now expect eventually to achieve power through the ballot box. But what is more relevant to Scott's question of the sincerity of their democratic professions is that they still offer the USSR and the other countries of the Socialist bloc as their paradigms of democracy.

If anyone does want nevertheless to construe these rival interpretations of the word 'democracy' as referring to different species of the same genus, then the genus will presumably have to be that of popular government; in a sense of 'popular' such that systems referring to the will of the people and systems referring to the needs and interests of the people are both properly popular. That the latter rather than the former is for a Muscovite Communist the heart of the matter comes out piquantly in a speech made by Janos Kadar shortly after the suppression of the Hungarian revolution of 1956, and his own inauguration by the friendly neighbourhood tanks of the USSR: 'The task of the leaders is not to put into effect the wishes and will of the masses . . . The task of the leaders is to realize and accomplish the interest of the masses.' (Reported in *East Europe* for July 1957, p. 56)

more than one sort of priority over the qualified, and that any prestige enjoyed by the latter is largely dependent upon its association with the former.

The actual phrase 'social justice', which has since become a cliché of the political platform, appears to have been introduced only in the 'sixties of the last century.[6] The first occurrence so far recorded by our dictionary-makers is in *Utilitarianism* itself: 'This', Mill writes, 'is the highest abstract standard of social and distributive justice'. Later, in *The Subjection of Women*, he denounced that subjection in marriage for 'laying the foundation of domestic existence upon a relation contradictory to the first principles of social justice'. However, although the phrase 'social justice' is comparatively new, the idea of social justice as 'the first virtue' of 'the way in which the major social institutions distribute fundamental rights and duties and determine the division of advantages from social co-operation' goes back at least as far as *The Republic*. And Plato, unlike Rawls, takes great pains to try to relate his very different account of social justice – justice, that is, writ large in the city state – to more primitive and commonplace manifestations of the same – justice writ small in the individual. It is no doubt by these labours that Plato hopes to earn for the proposed institutions of Kallipolis the respect which we all profess to think due to the just man or the just verdict.[7]

To cite Plato as a source on social justice may be, in the contemporary British climate, shocking. Among us today this particular expression is found almost exclusively on left-wing lips, while the arrangements in fact commended as socially just are more or less radically egalitarian. For Plato by contrast social justice demanded very drastic inequalities of both rights and duties between classes, inequalities based on big differences in hereditarily determined talents. I found a clear illustration of what is today taken for granted, and one agreeably distant from the rough and tumble of British party conflict, in a Central Office of Information pamphlet for visitors to Thailand: 'A further, important objective

[6] I thank Roland Hall for providing me with these dictionary facts, and for supplying a photocopy of the relevant page 247 of *Notes and Queries* for July 1965.

[7] I am not maintaining that his attempt was successful. See, for instance, David Sachs, 'A Fallacy in Plato's *Republic*', in Gregory Vlastos (ed.), *Plato* (New York and London, Doubleday, 1971, and Macmillan, 1972), vol. II.

. . . is to promote greater social justice by moving towards a more equitable income distribution and the expansion of social services for lower income groups. . . .'

The very width of the gulfs between such alternative systems of social justice is a further reason imposing upon their several spokesmen the obligation to try to vindicate the claims of their particular candidate to the diploma epithet 'just'. It will not, therefore, do for Rawls 'to leave questions of meaning and definition aside and to get on with the task of developing a substantive theory of justice' (p. 579). R. M. Hare is right in his despairing judgement on Rawls, a judgement made with many other moral words besides 'just' in mind: 'There is in fact a vast hole in his 600-page book which should be occupied by a thorough account of the meanings of these words. . . .'[8]

3. A LIBERAL THEORY OF JUSTICE

Brian Barry has described the Rawls account not as *A* but as *The Liberal Theory of Justice*. Barry's reason is that 'The essence of liberalism . . . is the vision of society as made up of independent autonomous units who co-operate only when the terms of co-operation are such as to make it further the end of each of the parties'; which vision Rawls presses 'to its logical limit by deriving the principles of justice themselves from a notional "social contract" '.[9] Another good or even better reason is that the first of these principles is that 'each person is to have an equal right to the most extensive basic liberty compatible with a similar liberty for others.'

Rawls is most emphatic in insisting that his principles are arranged in order of precedence: 'This ordering means that a departure from the institutions of equal liberty required by the first principle cannot be justified, or compensated for, by greater social and economic advantages' (p. 61). This grating insistence upon 'the institutions of equal liberty' has caused Rawls to be derided in some circles as a bourgeois liberal. Certainly his intentions are, as theirs are not, liberal; and no doubt he accepts

[8] p. 147 of his valuable two-part Critical Notice in *The Philosophical Quarterly* for 1974.

[9] pp. 166 and 167.

hostility from such a quarter with equanimity – even pleasure.[10] But the epithet 'bourgeois' is not appropriate. For Rawls maintains that his theory is in itself neutral as between private or public ownership of the means of production (p. 258); and to this Old Whig critic it seems that he is too little anxious about the difficulty perhaps amounting to impossibility of reconciling 'the institutions of equal liberty' with a wholly socialist economic order.[11]

There is room for a more belligerent and fruitful response to the contempt of authoritarian Radicals. Rawls' proposed priority can be made to serve as a touchstone of their egalitarian sincerity. For, even given the fullest meritocracy, and even given the narrowest spread of incomes, what kind of ideal of human equality has been achieved where uncriticisable rulers are installed irremovably in absolute power, whereas the ruled enjoy no 'freedom from arbitrary arrest and seizure as defined by the concept of the rule of law' (p. 61)? And so on. There may perhaps also be room, though this is none of our present business, for a similar argument about socialism and at least some measure of democracy. For can public ownership really be a kind of ownership save in so far as the putative collective owners exercise some collective control over whatever it is which they are said to own?

4. QUESTIONS ABOUT THE DIFFERENCE PRINCIPLE

Principle 2(*a*) as originally formulated requires that 'social and economic inequalities are to be arranged so that they are . . . reasonably expected to be to everyone's advantage'. This first formulation is said to be 'ambiguous' (p. 61). The official reading

[10] 'Le bon David', on the other hand, would have been distressed to find himself described as 'Hume, David (1711–1776) *English* bourgeois philosopher' (my italics). See V. I. Lenin, *Collected Works*, vol. 38, translated by Clemens Dutt and edited by Stewart Smith (London, Lawrence & Wishart, undated), p. 614.

[11] Compare, for instance, F. A. Hayek, *The Constitution of Liberty* (London, Routledge & Kegan Paul, 1960) and Samuel Brittan, *Capitalism and the Permissive Society* (London, Macmillan, 1973). Certainly the most hardworking contemporary enemies of any pluralist and open society are in no doubt on this issue. Thus the Institute of Marxism-Leninism in Moscow in a recent publication urging 'united front' tactics stated: 'Having once acquired political power, the working class implements the liquidation of the private ownership of the means of production. . . . As a result, under socialism, there remains no ground for the existence of any opposition parties counterbalancing the Communist Party' (see *The Economist*, 17 June 1972, p. 23).

is that 'inequalities . . . should satisfy the difference principle. Thus inheritance is permissible provided that the resulting inequalities are to the advantage of the least fortunate . . .' (p. 278). It remains altogether obscure to me why 'the advantage of the least fortunate' is thought to be an alternative interpretation of 'everyone's advantage'.

But there is a more important question : How is this Difference Principle supposed to be derived from the 'notional "social contract" '? Of any of its fictitious parties Rawls says : 'Since it is not reasonable for him to expect more than an equal share in the division of social goods, and since it is not rational for him to agree to less, the sensible thing . . . is to acknowledge as the first principle of justice one requiring an equal distribution' (p. 150). Rawls now asks : 'If there are inequalities in the basic structure that work to make everyone better off in comparison with the benchmark of initial equality, why not permit them?' Why not indeed? So he concludes : 'Inequalities are permissible when they maximise, or at least all contribute to, the long term expectations of the least fortunate group in society' (p. 151).

(*a*) Two gaps in the argument provoke questions. *First*, why do licit inequalities have to make everyone better off, as opposed to making at least some better off and none worse? The answer, I suggest, is that this is a consequence of a crucial basic assumption of the whole exercise. The very idea of social justice is taken to presuppose starting from Plato's 'clean canvas',[12] with all goods available for distribution at the absolute discretion of the distributing authority. Everything which one does not have is lacking only and precisely because it has been allotted to another. What to me looks like one getting more at no one else's expense, for the enthusiast of social justice becomes a matter of one being given something which perhaps ought instead to have been issued to another.

Consider a recent exchange on Radio Three. The Chairman, John Vaizey, was confronted with 'the idea that the state should determine everybody's rewards according to some system of fairness, and should determine prices accordingly . . . this is the acceptance of the view that there is a rational system of social justice which it is the business of the state to enforce . . .'. Vaizey

[12] *The Republic*, §501A.

agreed wholeheartedly: 'That's a view I should embrace very strongly. I believe that that is the way one ought to think about society.'[13]

If you do too, then you will be committed to a Hobbist view of property, in the widest possible sense of the word 'property'; the individual's enjoyment of any good is always and everywhere at the absolute discretion of the State. That impeccable Social Democrat Hugh Gaitskell once expressed this Hobbist commitment in a form which has since become in Britain an almost unchallenged commonplace: if any income is not taken away in taxes it is thereby given to the citizen. The 1959 Budget, he said, 'involved giving away 400 million pounds. Any Chancellor who could give this away could be described as lucky.'

Another usual though not perhaps essential element is the assumption that income ought to be received only as a reward. Barry dismisses any alternative in a peremptory parenthesis: '(and of course get rid of unearned income)'.[14] Gaitskell asserted categorically: 'The existence of unearned income is wrong in itself no matter how it is distributed'.[15] About this putative unacceptability of income from property I shall make one main point in my final section. Here I have to say that, both as a Treasury technicality and as an ordinary expression, 'unearned income' includes a great deal more than income from the property of plutocrats. It includes, for instance, interest on the already once taxed and saved earnings of the retired – interest at rates which in the present inflation are in real terms negative. It also includes many items which are not in any sense income from property – maintenance payments for abandoned wives with dependent young, for instance, and compensation for the thalidomide children. If social justice really requires the abolition of all such unearned income, or at least as now its heavier taxation from a low threshold, then social justice here displays a cruelly stern and to me unacceptable face. The immediate moral for us is: either that the notion that justice requires all income to be an earned reward must be abandoned; or that the claims of this first virtue ought from time to time to yield to others, such as those of humanity and compas-

[13] 'Whatever Happened to Equality?', *The Listener* (2 May 1974), p. 566.

[14] Barry, op. cit., p. 115.

[15] In *Socialism and Nationalization* (Fabian Tract No. 300, London, 1956), p. 6.

sion. Justice, even social justice, is not the whole of virtue; and the antithesis between justice and expediency is not the only antithesis in which justice has a place.

(*b*) *Second*, why does Rawls conclude that, in order to legitimate the advance of some group above 'the benchmark of equality', it is both necessary and sufficient to link this advance with an advance of the least advantaged? If Rawls wants to insist that everyone must be made better off, then it is not sufficient that the least advantaged benefit. Everyone must get more, or no one. If, alternatively, he were prepared to allow that it is all right for anyone to advance so long as no one is made worse off, then it would not be necessary that the least advantaged should also benefit.

In pondering this question we have to ask precisely what the hypothetical contracting parties are supposed to do. Are they in considering different social systems to decide which they would be prepared to enter, on the understanding that they might find themselves occupying any place in that system? Or are they in considering any social system to review every position in that system in turn, and to rule whether or not those in that position get a fair deal? The first is a matter of prudence, the second of morality.

In so far as it is the first, there is on the suppositions stipulated by Rawls little which can be said. The point made in the preamble to his statement of 'the first principle of justice' is met, since every potential contractor must take it that his chances of occupying any social position are the same as those of every other potential contractor. This makes it without question correct for them all to plump, all other things being equal, for any system in which some would be better and none worse off. It is not necessary, though it would of course be nice, to be offered an option in which everyone would be better off.

Suppose next that we try to derive a prudential analogue to the (moral) Difference Principle by urging that, as rational beings soberly dedicated to self-interest, the hypothetical contractors will always seek to improve the worst possibility. Not a hope. Rawls has stipulated that one of the things which they are not to know is their attitude towards risk; and a policy of maximising the minimum – maximin for short – is not essentially or uniquely rational. For instance: we surely cannot dismiss as irrational, or even perhaps as imprudent, all those millions who allocate a weekly investment to a football pool, and then with their eyes open choose to bet against the longest odds in order to maximise the maximum. Even if a maximin policy were demanded by reason, this would require only that we must choose a maximin option where there is one. It would not demand, as the Difference Principle apparently does, that we must never allow any advance above 'the benchmark of equality', save in so far as this advance is 'to the advantage of the least fortunate'. Maximin can tolerate, as the egalitarian Difference Principle cannot, that anyone may advance provided only that others are not thereby disadvantaged.

The alternative approach is for the hypothetical contractors to be asked to rule on every social position in turn. It now becomes important to distinguish two quite different interpretations of 'the first principle of justice', one formal and one substantial. Just as social equality may be taken, either as the ideal theoretical norm all departures from which provide purchase for sociological inquiry, or as the ideal moral norm all departures from which must be more or less scandalous,[16] so both the initial equality, and 'the first principle of justice' here equated with it, may be taken, either as involving only the formal point that there has to be a reason to justify anyone's having anything but an arithmetic mean share of any available goods, or as laying down the very substantial principle that such an equal share is what everyone is entitled to.

It is only in so far as Rawls is construing his first principle in this second and contentious way that it becomes endowed with the strength to require that, if any advances beyond 'the benchmark of initial equality' are to be just, then this can only be in so far as they are connected with advantages for others. Once granted this fundamental normative principle that everyone is entitled to an equal share of all goods, the hypothetical contractor must ask on behalf of any group of actual people who enjoy less than the average sum of all goods: Why not? The only answer compatible with the demands of justice according to Rawls will be that they have, in a vicarious and hypothetical social contract, agreed to waive this right to equality in return for a greater absolute sum

[16] Compare my 'Sociology and Equality' in *Question Eight* (London, Pemberton, 1975).

of goods than they would have enjoyed in a social system of complete equality. The reference to their agreement is essential to Rawls. Without it he will have to say that the richer alternative society, though no doubt justified on utilitarian principles, is still not just. And to accept such a justification would be a betrayal of the manifesto: 'Being first virtues of human activities, truth and justice are uncompromising.'

But now, if this is how the operation is to be conducted, the Difference Principle is inadequate. It is not only the least advantaged but every below average group which has to be bought off. Presumably too the just distance below that benchmark will in each case have to be such that any relative advance would be likely to involve that group itself in an absolute decline. Above the benchmark the same conception of social justice must, correspondingly, frown on any allocations greater than the minimum necessary to ensure the maximum absolute value of the average.

If this or anything like it is the correct explication of that putative 'rational system of social justice' in which Vaizey and so many other egalitarian intellectuals believe, then I suggest, rather diffidently, that everyone may be surprised to notice how impossibly difficult it would surely be to determine proper relative placings without the help of some refined and no doubt modified market mechanism. It is, therefore, very much to the point here to mention that the standard late scholastic account of a just price, or a just wage (a just price for labour), was in terms of what would be agreed in certain ideal conditions; which conditions specifically excluded all monopolies including – what are today by far and away the most powerful and least tractable – labour monopolies.[17]

5. THE CONFRONTATION WITH UTILITARIANISM

Rawls wants to develop an alternative to utilitarianism. He is, therefore, delighted to notice an incompatibility: 'Offhand it hardly seems likely that persons who view themselves as equals, entitled to press their claims on one another, would agree to a

[17] See J. Viner, 'The Intellectual History of Laissez Faire', *The Journal of Law and Economics* for 1960. I thank Brian Barry for this reference.

principle which may require lesser life prospects for some simply for a greater sum of advantages enjoyed by others' (p. 14). So it is worth noticing the ill-matching between the Rawls 'justice as fairness' and classical utilitarianism. For the latter, if we may take John Stuart Mill as its spokesman, offered a general standard of morality. The claims of justice appeared as presenting an awkward area of difficulty for any such account: notoriously Chapter V is the least happy in *Utilitarianism*. As a rule of legislation it has been and is often taken as equally comprehensive. Certainly it is in this comprehensive aspect that Rawls wanted to develop an alternative to utilitarianism. This was to be an alternative – the illustration is mine – to the political morality of the party in Arthur Koestler's *Darkness at Noon*; in which unlimited sacrifices must be imposed upon some people, and some generations, in order to achieve a more than equivalent sum of good for other people, and other generations.

Since justice is not the whole of morality, no account of justice, which confines itself to being an account of justice only, can stand forward as a well-matched opponent to any such comprehensive utilitarianism. Once you are, like Rawls, committed to this contest, there must be a temptation to stretch the notion of justice, to intrude other moral considerations into the idea of 'justice as fairness', and to insist that your principles of justice must be as uncompromisingly indefeasible as the utilitarian or any other criterion of morality has to be.

6. A CHALLENGE TO 'THE FIRST PRINCIPLE OF JUSTICE'

I have argued that the Difference Principle cannot be established on the Rawls foundations. I have suggested that it is in part because he confuses the two procedures distinguished in Section (4) (*b*), above, that he concludes that it can be. But I shall not propose any redefinition of 'the original position so that we get the desired solution'. For this is not a solution which I myself desire. I cannot recognise it as an imperative of justice that no group should do better than any other save in so far as 'the resulting inequalities are to the advantage of the least fortunate'. It also seems to me that any moral claims, not only of the least but also of the less advantaged, claims which are not necessarily claims of justice, must largely depend not on the relative but the absolute condition of the disadavantaged.[18]

The query I press here relates to something even more fundamental than the Difference Principle. Rawls limits himself to social justice within a single society: 'I shall be satisfied if it is possible to formulate a reasonable conception of justice for the basic structure of society conceived for the time being as a closed system isolated from other societies' (p. 8).

At first blush this restriction seems sensible. After all, if it is going to take 600 and more pages 'to formulate a reasonable conception of justice for the basic structure' of one isolated society, then what chance could there be of ever completing the corresponding job assignment for a whole United Nations? Such modesty is, nevertheless, not acceptable. Something, however brief and sketchy, has to be said about the international applications of this notion. For is not social justice supposed to be an, if not the, categorical imperative of morality? As such its principles must surely be of universal application. Certainly the strong normative egalitarian postulate which Rawls himself picks out as 'the first principle of justice' must explode beyond all national frontiers, even though its fallout is for him to be checked and offset by the Difference Principle.

To get the crux into sharp focus consider one reviewer's comment on A. B. Atkinson's *Unequal Shares: Wealth in Britain.* W. G. Runciman writes: 'there is no more reason to expect the lucky inheritors of fortunes to give them away than to expect left-wing intellectuals voluntarily to reduce their standard of living to that of the citizens of Upper Volta or Bangladesh . . .'[19]

Certainly this is true if the word 'expect' is read in a purely descriptive sense. Left-wing intellectuals are not conspicuously more willing than the rest of us to underwrite from their own pockets more than the merest token transfer payments to the citizens of poorer countries. But equally certainly, if the word 'expect' is read in the prescriptive sense, and if these left-wing intellectuals,

[18] I agree with Samuel Brittan that today's overriding concern for such relativities as parity or differentials, as opposed to absolute goods, is corrosive. See his disturbing address to the British Association in 1974 on 'The Economic Contradictions of Democracy', to appear in *The British Journal of Political Science.*

[19] *The Listener* (14 December 1972), p. 835.

or others, have proclaimed some form of egalitarianism as a moral imperative, then it is not true.

Runciman continues: 'Atkinson quotes from Isaiah Berlin to the effect that departure from the principle of equal division calls for special justification where adherence to it does not . . .' If, therefore, we are to be told that it is in deference to this principle that large and not so large fortunes must be taxed away, then we have to press the nasty question how it can consist with any such principle that only the compatriots of the rich thus soaked are to share in the resulting booty. What, in a word, is the 'special justification' which makes it moral for one lot of people to seize for their own enjoyment, or for the reward of their political supporters, the fortunes of those who are in their eyes offensively rich, while not requiring that all this loot – and a great deal more to be taken from, among others, those supporters – should be transferred forthwith to the too numerous foreigners in whose eyes almost all of us, both rich and poor, are even today rich?

To this Rawls would presumably have to respond that any international inequalities which can be justified at all have to be justified by reference to connected and compensating advantages to the least advantaged. Perhaps such a justification would start with the highly unpopular affirmation that almost all science, invention and cultural achievement has come and still is coming from a comparatively few richer countries; that that is one main reason why some of them became and remain rich. It would, I suspect, be an ungrateful task. Certainly I have no stomach for it. Instead I prefer to press a challenge to the whole Rawls approach, and in particular to his 'first principle of justice'.

For – without prejudice to the possibility of some universal and equal natural rights – if there are, as there surely are, any valid claims grounded in differences of past history and of present social relations, then it cannot be right thus to insist upon a total equality of entitlement as 'the first principle of justice'. I cannot, of course, prove that there are such valid claims. Suffice it here to point out that almost everyone in fact takes it for granted that there are; and that they may do it in a way which involves at the same time recognising legitimate differences in present income legitimately determined by the ownership of capital.

Consider, for instance, this universal deep assumption that any proceeds of soaking the British rich belong exclusively to the

British not-rich. Or consider the parallel assumption, which is in practice also taken absolutely for granted in all the countries of the Socialist bloc, that the stocks of artefacts and the natural resources currently available in each such country, and which are in fact very unequally distributed among these countries, are and must remain the collective property of citizens of those countries and their descendants. These assets at any rate are not to be redistributed internationally in accordance with 'the first principle of justice', for they are seen as already the property of the various peoples. Private property may be theft, yet still it is 'Scotland's oil'!

MAIN PUBLICATIONS

A New Approach to Psychical Research (C. A. Watts, 1953)
Hume's Philosophy of Belief (Routledge & Kegan Paul, 1961)
God and Philosophy (Hutchinson, 1966)
Evolutionary Ethics (Macmillan, 1967)
An Introduction to Western Philosophy (Thames & Hudson, 1971)
Crime or Disease? (Macmillan, 1973)
Thinking about Thinking (Collins Fontana, 1975)
New Essays in Philosophical Theology (edited, with Alasdair McIntyre) (SCM Press, 1955)

WHY LOGIC MATTERS

by

Peter Geach

Professor of Logic, University of Leeds

Before explaining why I think the study of logic matters, in regard to everyday reasoning and philosophical thought, I must say something about the inherent aim of logic itself. It would be generally agreed that logic is concerned with norms of sound or valid reasoning. However, it is also held that logic is concerned, even primarily concerned, with the discovery and orderly presentation of a special sort of truths, logical truths. The nature of logical truth is highly problematic; I shall come on to that problem in a moment. Let us just suppose that we have available some corpus of logical truths; how then do these relate to our appraisal of inferences as valid or invalid?

It clearly holds good that a pair of premises (abbreviated as) '*p*', '*q*', logically yield a conclusion (abbreviated as) 'r' iff (if and only if) the conditional 'If *p* and *q* then *r*' is a logical truth. But which depends on which? The validity of the inference on the logical truth of the conditional, or the other way round? We may look at this from another angle. Suppose that in order to show that from '*p*' and '*q*' there logically follows '*r*' we employ some logical truth (abbreviated as) '*s*'. How are we to put the logical truth of '*s*' to work? Let us suppose that we infer 'If *p* and *q*, then *r*' from '*s*' (I shall not discuss this part of the procedure), and then reason as follows:

1. We have *p*, and we have *q* : *ergo*, *p* and *q*.
2. *p* and *q*; if *p* and *q*, then *r*; *ergo*, *r*.
3. Since by (2) '*r*' follows from '*p* and *q*' with the addition of another premise that is a logical truth, '*r*' follows from '*p* and *q*' alone.

4. Thus we have *p*, and we have *q* : *p*,*q*, *ergo p* and *q*; *p* and *q*, *ergo r*; *ergo r*.

At every stage here we must appeal to a notion of logical validity, and to principles about valid inference, which cannot be explained in terms of logical truth. Step (1) might strike one as merely repetitious. But a conjunctive proposition is a single proposition, quite distinct from its two conjuncts; we see this by thinking of negation – a man may be justifiably certain that a conjunction is false, and accordingly assert 'Not both *p* and *q*', without asserting either the falsehood of '*p*' or the falsehood of '*q*'. So already step (1), *conjunction introduction* in the jargon, gives us a pattern of valid inference not reducible to some logically true proposition.

The same is even more glaringly true of step (2), *modus ponens*; Lewis Carroll long ago brought out the absurdity of making the validity of a *modus ponens* argument depend on an appeal to some logically true hypothetical. Frege's *Begriffsschrift*, the most thoroughgoing presentation of logic in terms of systematised logical truths rather than forms of inference, uses *modus ponens* as a form of inference that cannot be expressed by, or replaced by use of, a logically true proposition. Here as elsewhere, Russell and Whitehead are inferior to Frege; they had the extraordinary idea that the principle of *modus ponens* could be written down as an asserted logical axiom, so long as this was done in English rather than in logical shorthand!

In steps (1) and (2) we were concerned with patterns or schemata of valid reasoning. In steps (3) and (4) we are concerned with something quite different: with utilising already available valid arguments to generate other valid arguments. Stoic logicians gave the name *themata* to the procedures by which we may do this. Themata are radically different from schemata: a schema shows us how to get a proposition from one or more *propositions* as premises, and deriving an *argument* from other *arguments* is quite another matter. (Confusion on this point is by no means impossible; it is even likely, if someone is bemused by those presentments of 'natural deduction' in which schemata and themata are lumped together under the heading of 'introduction and elimination rules'.) In step (4) there is simply a plaiting together of two arguments into a chain, in which the ultimate conclusion is taken to follow from the original premises. That this can be done is ordinarily just taken for granted, not formulated as a distinct rule or principle; and we assume that this can be done arbitrarily often – a logical chain, unlike a physical one, can break only because there is a defective link, not because it is too long to bear its own weight. Clearly the use of this principle cannot be made to depend on the appeal to some logically true proposition.

In step (3) we have a more complicated thema: the principle that a logically true premise may be dropped and still leave us with a valid argument. This is not only more sophisticated, it is more problematic. Consider a proof *within* logic – a proof such as we were imagining used to get from '*s*' to 'If *p* and *q* then *r*'. The premises of such proof are of course logical truths: does this mean that any one of them could be dropped and the proof remain valid? Many logicians have said so, in writings on the theory of entailment; but if they act as examiners at universities, their practice belies their theory.

Imagine someone asked in an examination to prove some logical truth from certain axioms. He begins his answer with: 'This is a valid proof of the desired conclusion'; then he just writes down the premises and conclusion, as given in the question; then, he establishes that what he has written down *is* a valid proof, by the following metalogical comment. 'The conclusion follows from the set formed by the given premises *plus* itself; but it *is* a logical truth, or the examiners would not have asked us to prove it; therefore, it may be dropped from any set of premises in which it figures, without prejudice to the validity of the argument; therefore, the conclusion follows from the given premises.' Clearly this is not the sort of proof the examiners wanted – though they might give this candidate a good mark for ingenuity and cheek.

What the examiners wanted was a proof that was valid in virtue of its general pattern, without making any appeal to the logical truth of the conclusion: valid in virtue of a pattern recognisable also in other arguments, whose premises and conclusions are *not* logical truths. And if we allow, as the examiners would in practice allow, *only* proofs analysable into steps of this sort, then we can use the thema of step (3) only with certain restrictions. But even if this thema for *dropping* a premise that is logically true could lawfully be used unrestrictedly, it is clear that we could not replace an appeal to it by the use of one *more* logical truth in our body of premises.

Logical validity or logical following thus cannot be explained in terms of logical truth. I shall further maintain that logical truth itself is a notion not to be explained except in terms of validity. People have indeed tried to characterise logical truth in various other ways (it is hard to say which of these is more obscure than another): as necessary truth, or truth in all possible worlds; as truth in virtue of the meaning of the words used; as tautological truth, to know which is not really to know anything; and so on. I shall not try to follow these mirky tracks; the positive account of logical truth that I shall offer will, I hope, commend itself by its own light in contrast to these dark notions. I shall consider in detail just one account of logical truth that purports to be independent of validity: Quine's account, which unlike the others I have cited here, is not on the face of it obscure, but I think turns out unsatisfactory if we go into it.

Quine's key notion is the notion of a term's essential or inessential occurrence in a proposition: a term occurs inessentially iff uniform replacement of it by another term (of the appropriate category) can be effected *salva veritate* – otherwise it occurs essentially. For example, in the proposition:

(5) If every man is mortal and Socrates is a man, then Socrates is mortal

we cannot change the truth-value if we replace 'man' by another count noun or 'Socrates' by another proper name, or 'is mortal' by another predicable like 'lies sometimes'; these terms then occur inessentially. The only words that occur essentially are the logical words, 'if . . . then . . .', 'and', and 'every'. Quine characterises as logical truths those propositions in which *only* logical words occur essentially. Quine rejects the idea of a logical variety of truth: to say '*P* is true' is tantamount to saying the unadorned *P*, and if this does not contain 'true' or other allied semantical terms ('applies to', 'uniquely describes', etc.) then no problem arises about what ascribing truth to *P* amounts to; if *P* is 'Men are mortal', ascribing truth to *P* raises all and only the problems raised by ascribing mortality to men.

I applaud Quine's rejection of the idea that logical truths have a special way of being true. Indeed, if we rewrote (5) as follows:

(6) Either not every man is mortal, or Socrates is not a man, or Socrates is mortal

(6) would easily admit of empirical verification: if 'Socrates' is read as the name of a man, by verification of the last disjunct; if 'Socrates' is read not as the name of a man, but as the name of an owl or a mountain on the moon, then by verification of the middle disjunct. But that this counts as verification of (6) itself may well seem to rest on the validity of inferring a disjunction from any one disjunct. Let us waive this point, though. How can we pass from humdrumly verifying sentence after sentence, each one got from (6) by uniform replacement of the words occurring inessentially, to the confidence that *any* such sentence comes out true? And that indeed (6) itself could be known to be true regardless of any observation of the thing called 'Socrates'? Do we believe this on inductive grounds? A deservedly forgotten logical textbook, Alexander Bain's, did in fact maintain the like over the conversion of categoricals: most of us have learned by experience to distrust the schema 'If every *S* is *P* then every *P* is *S*'; but we still rely upon 'If no *S* is *P* then no *P* is *S*', since no counterexample has thus far turned up! Quine, I fear, writes at least sometimes in the spirit of Bain; it is thus that he can regard logical laws as if they were scientific laws, immensely well confirmed and of supreme generality – but by the same token, possibly fated to be overthrown in the next big scientific revolution.

Our confidence in the truth of (6) is in fact of quite a different kind; and people will often say that (6) is true by virtue of the meaning of the logical words. Of course the truth of (6) depends on the logical words having the meaning they have historically developed: for example, on the fact that 'either' has not at some stage in the history of English picked up a negative meaning (cf. German '*weder*', which is cognate with English 'whether' but means 'neither'). But this is not what is intended: the view is rather that truth can be determined *solely* by the meaning of words, regardless of 'the facts' or 'the world'. Logical truths would be just one particular case of meaning-determined truths: so this view is not going to show one what is distinctive about logic. And I agree with Quine in finding this explanation anyhow useless, because the supposed genus, of which logical truths are to be a species, really has not been characterised at all.

One example that would often be given of a meaning-determined truth is 'All fathers are male'. Another equally acceptable example would be 'Once a father, always a father'; or, more carefully put, 'If one animal is ever father of another, then the first is father of the second so long as they both shall live.' (Quine in a letter to me called this the thesis of sempaternity.) But from these two premises this follows: 'If one animal is ever father of another, then so long as they both shall live the first animal is male.' And this is certainly not true by virtue of the meaning of words; it is alleged (though I remain incredulous) that a human father can cease to be male and become female, and certainly this happens in other species. The truth about this is a matter of zoology, not of the meanings of words. A conclusion drawn from two premises 'true by virtue of the meanings of words' turns out to be not even true.

It looks, therefore, as though one of two premises supposedly endowed with meaning-determined truth were in fact false. There is indeed a way of salvaging the truth of both; we might say that the term 'father' did not mean quite the same in the two premises. But if the awkward conclusion had not been drawn, I think this suggestion would not be made. And if in such simple cases we feel driven to say that so familiar a word as 'father' can change its meaning unbeknownst to us, then once again our idea of meaning-determined truth begins to crumble. The reader should notice that the cases I have chosen are not marginal but such as would be used as paradigms; in oral discussion I have often heard one or other of my premises produced as a typical meaning-determined truth, and have then enjoyed giving the speaker the peculiar shock and outrage of realising that two such 'truths' together yield a false conclusion.

The mistake common to this view and Quine's is that of taking logical truth as the fundamental thing. What is fundamental in logic is not truth but validity; and we have already seen that the validity of an argument cannot be explained by throwing in some logical truths as extra premises. And the peculiarity of logical truths is that they can be logically proved from *no* premises – as people say, from the null class of premises.

This might well seem a contradiction in terms. And certainly one always needs to start with a premise or premises. But there are themata which enable us to derive from one valid argument another valid argument with *fewer* premises. Successive application of such themata gets rid of one premise after another, till finally we are left with a conclusion resting on no premises at all.

One thema with this property is conditionalisation. If we have a set of premises including 'p' and with conclusion 'q', then we may omit 'p' from the premises and derive 'If p then q' from the remaining premises. (It is worth while to observe how very confusing at this point is the jargon of 'introduction and elimination rules'. The rule whereby 'p or q' is derived from 'q' would be called an introduction rule for 'or', and the rule of conditionalisation, an introduction rule for 'if'. But the one rule gives a valid *schema*, for passing from one proposition to another; the other rule gives us a *thema*, by which if we start with a valid *argument* we can derive another valid *argument*. To assimilate the two sorts of rule is as gross a confusion as to confuse an argument with a proposition, or validity with truth.)

Let us take an example. The argument:

(7) Every volume on that shelf is blue
(8) There is a volume of Caesar's *Gallic War* on that shelf
Ergo (9) There is a blue volume of Caesar's *Gallic War* on that shelf

is patently valid. (There is indeed a silly and often repeated objection to this sort of argument: that it is 'begging the question', because (7) could be verified only by verifying of each volume on the shelf, including the Caesar, that it is blue. But a myopic man might well verify (7) directly when he could not see even how many volumes there were!) If now we take (7) alone as a premise, the thema of conditionalisation allows us to derive a conclusion with (8) as antecedent, (9) as consequent:

(10) If there is a volume of Caesar's *Gallic War* on that shelf, then there is a blue volume of Caesar's *Gallic War* on that shelf.

And now if we repeat the procedure, and construct a conclusion with (7) as antecedent, (10) as consequent:

(11) If every volume on that shelf is blue, then if there is a volume of Caesar's *Gallic War* on that shelf, there is a blue volume of Caesar's *Gallic War* on that shelf,

then we see that (11) no longer rests on the assumption of any premise at all. (11) can be proved – indirectly, by the use of a thema – to be derivable from *no* premise; that is what makes it a logical truth.

Not all logical truths have a conditional form: but our account is easily extended to other logical truths. Take the Law of Excluded Middle. Given the validity of the schemata '*p*, *ergo* (*p* or *q*)' and '*q*, *ergo* (*p* or *q*)', we see that '*p*, *ergo* (*p* or not-*p*)' and 'not-*p*, *ergo* (*p* or not-*p*)' are both valid argument forms. Now there is a thema: From two valid arguments sharing a conclusion, if one has '*p*' as a premise and the other 'not-*p*', we may frame a valid argument resting only on the premises of the two arguments other than '*p*' and 'not-*p*' and again reaching the same conclusion. For example: given that each of the premise-pairs:

{ (12) Herbert is not luckier than anyone who envies Herbert
  (13) Edith envies Herbert

and { (14) Edith envies anyone luckier than Edith
  (15) Edith does not envy Herbert

yields the conclusion:

(16) Herbert is not luckier than Edith

we can infer that (12) and (14) likewise yield (16). But if we similarly plait together the arguments '*p*, *ergo* (*p* or not-*p*)' and 'not-*p*, *ergo* (*p* or not-*p*)', we find that we can draw the conclusion '*p* or not-*p*' without relying on any premise at all.

Such proofs are plainly degenerate cases – in that use of the phrase in which '$0.x^2 - 4x + 8 = 0$' is called a degenerate case of a quadratic equation. The primary use of schemata is to derive non-logical propositions from non-logical propositions, and the primary use of themata is to derive valid arguments from valid arguments so that ultimately we have a conclusion still resting on premises.

Only if we see that logic is primarily concerned with the description of rules for valid inference, not with the building up of a corpus of logical truths, can we gain a just view of the relation between logic and other sciences. Logic is queen of the sciences, but a constitutional queen: she can put in a veto, but not initiate legislation. If logic claimed to supply a corpus of truths in her own right, then other sciences might claim to reach results damaging to this corpus. As it is, however, a logician may well be professionally competent to criticise what is done in other sciences in a way that admits of no comeback from practitioners of these.

A logician, let us suppose, says to a physicist, 'Your theory involves a contradiction' or 'Your argument is invalid'. There may yet be perfectly fair rebuttals of the charges. The alleged inconsistency may be a matter of the logician's misunderstanding technical terms. To imitate an example in Sextus Empiricus, not from physics but from physic: a logician might find this an inconsistent triad:

(17) When a disease abates, wine and a mixed diet are recommended

(18 Every disease abates before three days' sickness

(19) Wine and a mixed diet are not recommended in every disease before three days' sickness.

But the physician could correct him by explaining that 'abates' in (17) refers to the final convalescence and 'abates' in (18) to a temporary remission.[1]

Or again, the argument accused of fallacy may in fact rest on a number of premises too well known to physicists to be worth mentioning in a technical paper, but not known to the critical logician. With these premises filled in, the argument may be perfectly valid.

In either of these ways the criticism of a physicist's work by a logician may be shown to be misconceived. But what it does not lie in the physicist's mouth to reply is 'The latest work in physics shows the logical theories you are relying on to be very doubtful.' For logical criticism does not depend on any premises that the physicist can deny. Logic, like the House of Lords, is a court against which there is no appeal. Such a position obviously does not guarantee infallibility: logicians like other men err, and radically unsound doctrines, like the doctrine of distribution, have at times been part of the accepted norms of logic. But there is no remedy against bad logic but good logic. You can appeal, so to say, from the bad decision of an earlier House of Lords to the better mind of a later one, and the Lords are not bound to follow their own precedents; what you cannot do is to deny, or appeal against, the court's having jurisdiction.

[1] *Outlines of Pyrrhonism*, vol. II, §§ 237–8. I owe this reference to C. L. Hamblin's *Fallacies* (London, Methuen, 1970).

Accusations of fallacy and accusations of inconsistency are quite different; for what shows an argument to be invalid is not that it leads you into inconsistency, since a conclusion which does not follow from premises may perfectly well be consistent with them; moreover, the invalidity of an argument is established from the *consistency* of the contradictory of its conclusion with its premises. Let us then first consider how a charge of inconsistency can be rebutted. Certainly *not* by merely reiterating that our foursome (say) of propositions are known, or reliably established, and therefore cannot be inconsistent. What does constitute a successful rebuttal is to find *another* foursome, which the accuser must admit to be all true and moreover to be (as men say) 'on all fours with' the originally impugned foursome; any alleged derivation of contradiction from the old foursome could be matched by a parallel derivation from the new foursome; and since these four all come out true, derivation of a contradiction from them must be wrong. This would put the accused in the clear : the prosecutor is now in an awkward intellectual position, for he must hunt down the error in his original 'proof' of inconsistency.

The risk one takes in an accusation of fallacy is quite different. As Strawson pointed out long since, there is no one logical form that is *the* form of a given concrete argument; one and the same argument may correspond to more than one abstract schema; and accordingly an argument is not shown to be invalid by sharing *some* logical form with an invalid argument, for it may simultaneously have some form that makes it into a valid argument. (A schema, on the other hand, is shown irredeemably invalid if there is even one concrete instance that brings out true premises and a false conclusion; it is then no use pleading that in other instances of the schema the reasoning looks all right! This mistaken defence of invalid inferential forms is surprisingly frequent in philosophical articles.)

The charge of fallacy takes the following form. 'I do not see how your conclusion follows from your stated premises. Perhaps you are using unstated premises; if so, let us have them before us, however obvious they seem to you. I suspect, however, that you are deceived in this way : your argument is an instance of such-and-such an invalid schema, which looks valid; and I can show the invalidity of the schema by such-and-such a counter-example.' The accused now has more than one move open to him. He may alter the whole situation by claiming to have used unstated premises. He may deny that his argument is of the incriminated form, or even deny that the accuser's counter-example shows the form to be invalid at all. Finally, he may admit that his argument shares the form of some invalid arguments, but deny that it is itself invalid. But this last defence leaves an unsatisfactory situation: *A* saying 'It still seems to me to follow' and *B* saying 'It still doesn't seem so to me' – unless *A* can produce some *valid form* of which, as well as the invalid form, his incriminated argument is an instance.

The following illustration may help to make matters clear. The form 'Some *S* is *P*, *ergo* any *S* is *P*' is of course invalid – there are innumerable counter-examples. All the same, there are valid arguments of this form; the reader can easily check the validity of the following:

(20) As regards some dog: there is another dog such that one of the pair is white and the other is not white
Ergo (21) As regards any dog: there is another dog such that one of the pair is white and the other is not white.

Anyone misguided and confused enough to argue thus:

(22) Some argument from *some* to *any* is invalid
Ergo, by parity of reasoning:
(23) Any argument from *some* to *any* is invalid

produces an argument that must be invalid. For suppose the argument from (22) to (23) were valid; it is itself an argument from *some* to *any*, so if it is valid its own conclusion is *false*. But of course (22) is true; so if the above argument is valid its conclusion must be *true*. So if the argument is valid its conclusion is both true and false; so it is not valid. This just goes to show how mirky is the common idea of 'parity of reasoning' on which people, including philosophers, often rely. Parity of reasoning with a valid argument guarantees validity: parity of reasoning with a fallacious argument does not guarantee fallacy. After all, any two-premise argument, valid or invalid, is an instance of the invalid form '*p*,*q*, *ergo r*'.

Well then: why does logic matter? I use 'logic' here in the sense of a practical observance of good logical standards: *logica utens* rather than *logica docens*, to employ the old terms. Why should we aim at valid reasoning and consistent formulation of thought? The benefit of valid reasoning is that it never leads from truth to falsehood. Of course we do not always know that our starting-point is true: we may rather be concerned to test its truth. But as soon as we reach a false conclusion, we have acquired some further knowledge: namely, that falsehood lurks somewhere in our premises. Or again: we may be arguing with an opponent, and show by valid reasoning that premises he accepts lead to conclusions he rejects. This sort of thing is unpleasant for the victim; it seems victims have clubbed together to get the manoeuvre listed as a fallacy – the *ad hominem* fallacy. But *ad hominem* argument is not as such fallacious;[2] if it is formally valid, the argument is not even merely eristic – for, painful as the lesson may be, to learn that your present position is indefensible is a benefit. What would be a merely eristic victory would be for an opponent to use a form of argument against you which he knew to be fallacious, but could get away with because you were too inept a logician to discern the fallacy. An opponent who uses your own premises against you *ad hominem* is bringing you some light; one who uses your own bad logical principles against you leaves you in your original darkness.

The benefit of consistency is that you cannot be inconsistent without being wrong about something substantive; for truth cannot be inconsistent with truth. In so far as we will to think truly, as an end, we must will to think consistently, as a means; and to opt for self-deception is, in the words of the prophet, to hew out broken cisterns that will hold no water.

There is however perhaps something to be said on behalf of inconsistency: witness the so-called Paradox of the Preface. Authors very often admit in prefaces that despite revision some errors remain in the book. If there were no error in the book before, including such a preface ensures the presence of error; the whole corpus, text *plus* preface, is necessarily inconsistent. No paradox thus far; the odd thing is, however, that we judge the writing of such a preface to show greater wisdom than saying in the preface something like 'I thank all my kind friends who have

[2] In the *Euthyphro* Socrates argues from a premise of Euthyphro's (about feuds between the Gods) to conclusions Euthyphro wants to reject. I correctly described this argument as *ad hominem*, in an article I wrote on this dialogue; an indignant critic said I had 'accused' Plato of *ad hominem* reasoning!

suggested corrections, but I remain convinced that everything I have said in this book is true' – reading such words, as I have in fact done, makes one think the author a silly fellow, although unlike his more modest rival he has not run into any inconsistency. Is it then folly to be consistent, wisdom to be inconsistent? Our judgement of the matter is in fact easily explained. Given human frailty, both texts will in fact include error. The modest author recognises this, and incurs no further error by doing so; the conceited author compounds the errors of his text by denying their existence in his preface. The modest author must indeed admit that the totality, text plus preface, is inconsistent; but inconsistency matters, as I said before, just in so far as error matters; and he is not more in error for his preface than he was already – he does not fall into some peculiarly virulent form of error by being inconsistent.

We should notice that validity is not, as many authors suppose, to be *explained* in terms of avoiding inconsistency. On the contrary: any inconsistency except the flat inconsistency of contradictories has itself to be explained in terms of valid inferences from a set of premises, leading both to a conclusion and to its contradictory. Here as elsewhere, what comes first is that something logically follows from something else.

So much for *logica utens* and its benefits. *Logica docens*, the construction of formal logical calculi, never catches up with *logica utens*; logic is not and never will be what Kant called it, a finished science; for there will always be methods of reasoning that we rightly accept intuitively as valid but do not yet know how to codify. That is no reason for despising *logica docens.* To some fallacies the human mind appears particularly prone: notably to the fallacy of illicit operator-shifts. Only Frege's invention of quantification theory gave us a calculus in which this multiform fallacy could be systematically eliminated; the medieval rules against particular cases of the fallacy could not effect a radical cure. We may well suspect that there are other pervasive fallacies which we detect only by their grosser symptoms – which we cannot radically cure without further formal developments.

Nor do I think the avoidance of fallacy is the only use of *logica docens*. Progress in this gives us ever greater powers to draw out consequences of our knowledge and our hypotheses. It is of course quite idle to say that we 'implicitly' know these consequences already. And the continuing strength and progress of *logica docens* is of importance for the good health of all science and learning. As I have said before, only by being itself rigid can logic act as a lever to dislodge unsatisfactory theories; the way to defend such theories in face of contrary facts is to enervate the logic that shows the contrariety. Here, to change the metaphor, logic prunes away rotten limbs; but logic can also promote the growth of the tree in a positive way. To be sure, logic of herself cannot answer any substantial questions: as the goddess personifying logic said in C. S. Lewis's *Pilgrim's Regress*, she can tell us only what *we* know. But then, we often do not know *what* (in this sense) we know; not until logic tells us. And again, it is a matter for reflection that man is capable of logic, *logikon zōion*. But this is not a logical truth, and reflections on it do not belong in this paper.

MAIN PUBLICATIONS

Mental Acts (Routledge & Kegan Paul, 1957)
Reference and Generality (Cornell University Press, 1962)
Three Philosophers (with G. E. M. Anscombe), (Blackwell, 1967)
God and the Soul (Routledge & Kegan Paul, 1969)
Logic Matters (Blackwell, 1972)

THINKING

by

D. W. Hamlyn

Professor of Philosophy, Birkbeck College, University of London

To a certain sort of introspection the things that are most obvious about thinking are the things that, as John Wisdom once put it, float on the surface of the stream of consciousness – the images, the things that we say to ourselves, and in general the more easily identifiable manifestations to ourselves of the thought. I say 'a certain kind of introspection' since another kind of attention to what we are engaged in, at any rate in that kind of thinking which is intentional or even deliberate, is likely to reveal things about the direction of the thought, the strategies engaged in, etc.; and these features of the thinking are not plausibly to be thought of as part of the flotsam that floats on the surface of the stream of consciousness. Even where the thinking is not governed by intentions similar things may be true of it. It might be a point of some interest to speculate about the reasons why philosophers have so often tried to identify thinking with such things as a succession of images, inner speech and the like, but I shall not indulge in such speculation here. It is enough to say that it is part of a reductionist urge that may take many forms. Thus Ryle, for example, who has played a leading part in modern attempts to reject the identification of thinking with what have been called 'the bearers of the thought' – images and the like – has recently[1] given what is in effect an adverbial account of thinking. The concept of thinking, as he has said in several places, is a polymorphous concept, in that the activity of thinking may take many forms. In thinking there are many things that we may *do*. To characterise these doings as thinking is to put a kind of adverbial qualification

[1] Gilbert Ryle, 'Thinking and Reflecting', *The Human Agent, Royal Institute of Philosophy Lectures*, vol. 1 (1966/7), pp. 210–26.

on them, a fact which is reflected in the grammatical nature of the verbs that are used to describe the thinking; the class of verbs in question, Ryle says, might be termed the class of adverbial verbs. The implication of this thesis is that if one asks what takes place when one thinks, the answer is that nothing takes place but one or other of these things – saying things to oneself, humming, going through verbal constructions, or what have you. What makes these thinking is the context, the intentions and the like, something that is indicated by the qualifications expressed through the adverbial character of the verbs. This is a reductionist thesis in the sense that it reduces thinking to performing these activities in these circumstances – thinking is nothing but these things with the qualifications specified.

One might find a certain parallel to this point of view in some of the things that Wittgenstein has to say (although I believe that there are considerable differences too, since in Wittgenstein the reductionist impulse is missing). In the *Philosophical Investigations*, II, p. 211, Wittgenstein says that ' "Thinking" and "inner speech" are different concepts' (the words translated as 'inner speech' are 'in der Vorstellung sprechen'), and many of the remarks that follow *Zettel* 88 are directed to the same point. For Wittgenstein the idea that thinking might be characterised as inner speech had a special pertinence since in the *Tractatus* he had said that a significant thought, a thought with sense, *was* a proposition (*Tractatus* 4). But what had become clear to him about this matter is summed up in *Zettel* 110 – ' "Thinking", a widely ramified concept. A concept that comprises many manifestations of life. The *phenomena* of thinking are widely scattered.' Given the ramifications of the instances of thinking, to suppose that thinking could be identified with something like inner speech would be to embrace what he called 'the myth of the inner process'. One could understand the concept of thinking only by attempting to trace the various ways in which what we call thinking figures in our lives. To ape another of Wittgenstein's remarks, it would be foolish to suppose that one could get clear about the concept of thinking by studying the images, words, etc. that are now passing through one's mind.

It is, however, possible to accept this while recognising that there remains a problem about the exact role which is to be assigned to the images, words, etc. when they do pass through our mind in the course of thinking. For Ryle, provided they are 'intention parasitical, circumstance-independent', they are in effect the substance of the thought. That is to say that the activities of saying things to ourselves, going through things in our minds, is what thinking *is* provided that certain contextual conditions are satisfied; or at all events these are the only things we *do*, there is no further process called 'thinking'. Yet this account of the matter seems to me just false of some processes of thought, especially creative thought but also more trivial examples of thought such as trying to think of someone's name, or to recapture in memory some previous experience. The phenomenon of having something, as we say, at the tip of the tongue, or of knowing in a way what the experience was like without being able to give it any detail, is a peculiar one. It seems as if much lies under the surface, as it were, of the manifest thought, and may in some cases determine the direction that the manifest thought takes. Suggestions of this kind have been made much of, equally, by those who have tried to analyse creative thinking from a psychological or phenomenological point of view. What seems clear is that what comes into our mind in such circumstances may have a significance for us that is not always explicit to us. There lies at the back of the thought a mass of understanding which is being tapped without being explicit. Thus the thinking is in one way or another (and the ways in question may be manifold) an application of understanding and knowledge that one already has but need not have made explicit to oneself. It is significant that in trying to think of a name that one cannot quite remember one can be quite clear about what is *not* the name in question. I say that one 'can be' not that one necessarily *is* quite clear on this point; but even the fact that one *can* be clear is significant.

The significance lies in the fact that there seems to be a sense in which one knows already a great deal about the name without being able to make it, the name itself, explicit to oneself. The process of making it explicit may involve a course of thought that is not altogether under our control. That course may be determined in part by associations or factors that are entirely extrinsic to the problem at stake; but it cannot go in *any* direction and still be a case of trying to think of the name. For the course of thought is also delimited both by what constitutes the nature of the problem and by things that we know if only vaguely and indefinitely about the sort of thing that will constitute its solution. Something similar is true of creative thought. In composition, for example, of whatever kind, the course of thought may be largely determined by factors that are by any reasonable standard extrinsic, and if the course of thought leads to compositional success this may be in many ways a matter of luck. But once again, not anything will do as relevant to the compositional problem. One normally has some sense of what will do and will not do, even if it would be impossible to spell out in advance anything like a specification of it.

Ryle has said that 'it is not incidental to thoughts that they belong to trains of thought'.[2] There is a certain truth in this remark, but it is important to be clear about the basis of that truth, and I do not really believe that the basis is to be found where Ryle finds it – in the fact that the identity of the thought is to be found via its sequel. One can approach the matter by asking what it would be for a thought to stand by itself in isolation – an atomic thought, as it were. We may sometimes say 'out of nothing came the blinding realisation that . . ., the single thought that. . . .' Indeed the realisation that *p* may be to us like hearing the words that express *p*. It is of course important about this example that it is not like my previous cases an example of an intentionally guided thought; it just comes. It would be difficult to imagine a thought that was intentional standing by itself, since however we are to analyse intention the fact that it was intentional provides a context for the thought, and a context that must be in some sense a thought-context. The point about examples of sudden but, so to speak, involuntary thoughts is that that context is *ex hypothesi* not present. But the fact that there is no intentional thought-context does not entail that there is no context at all. For the thought to *be* a thought for us it must have a significance in terms of what already makes sense to us and means something to us. One might indeed ask by what criteria a thought counts as a single thought so that it could be atomic in the sense required. For a thought that *p* to be atomic it must be such that its description entails no further descriptions, such as that it involves thinking that *q* and *r*. But if the thought that *p* has significance for us then

[2] Gilbert Ryle, 'A Puzzling Element in the Notion of Thinking', *Proceedings of the British Academy* (1958), reprinted in P. F. Strawson (ed.) *Studies in the Philosophy of Thought and Action* (OUP, 1968), pp. 7–23.

what we think must be describable in terms other than p simply. One might put the point by saying that if it is to be a thought properly speaking it must come with a context ready supplied, so that the question whether one single thought took place or more is one that can be answered only relative to some more or less arbitrary criterion, and not in any absolute way.

Cannot one say that a certain thought occurred to one at a certain specific time, like Paul's conversion on the road to Damascus? Are not thoughts capable of being dated and timed? The answer is of course 'Yes'; there is nothing wrong with someone saying 'It was at half-past three exactly last Wednesday (I happened to be looking at my watch at the time) that the thought occurred to me that. . . .' The claim that it is not incidental to thoughts that they belong to trains of thought cannot be validly interpreted as a psychological or phenomenological claim; it must be interpreted as a claim about the identifying description of the thought. Even so it is not that for the thinker the identification of the thought is a matter of having to see what its context is, in what train it is a part; that would make no sense. It is rather that an account which specified the thought could involve reference to a single thought or to a train of thought equally, without there being any incompatibility. Moments of truth, blinding realisations that come suddenly and, as we might say, instantaneously, may still be extremely complex in their content, and it may be that it will seem to us that the only way to describe such a case might be in such terms as 'I had a great rush of thoughts all in an instant'. And this might be quite compatible with answering the question of just what actually passed through one's mind by saying that 'I heard clearly and distinctly, as if someone was saying them, the words "It's all over".' For the significance of those words for us might be immensely complex. It is in a sense impossible to give just one unequivocal description of what we thought.

So, to return to creative thought, if the solution of a problem comes to us, as we might put it, out of nothing, it still comes *as a solution*, in that context and with that significance. Or else it is a nothing and no *solution* at all. One might put the point paradoxically by saying that thoughts are possible only for those who already think; that is to say, only for those for whom things have significance. I have said that this would be paradoxical but it is really such only if one says that thoughts are possible only for those who have already thought. For in that case there immediately arises the genetic problem of how thinking ever gets started, if every thought presupposes prior thinking. But I did not say 'only for those who have already thought', but rather 'only for those who already think'; and this is simply another way of putting the denial of atomic thoughts. No sense is to be attached to the idea of a thought standing by itself in splendid logical isolation. But even if the slogan is innocent from that point of view, it cannot be said that it is very informative. For it does not say what interrelationship of thoughts is required for there to be thought at all. On the other hand it is not clear what can be said about that in general. That is to say that in certain particular cases if it is true of someone that he thought that *p* it may also be true of him that he thought *q* and *r*, simply because the applicability of the description 'thought that *p*' presupposes the applicability of the description 'thought that *q* and *r*'; whereas, it is important to note, if *p* entails *q* and *r* it does not follow that if someone thought that *p* he thought that *q* and *r*. The claim is that in all thoughts something of the former kind holds good, but that it is impossible to give any general rule for how it works out. The connexion between thoughts depends not only on what is presupposed in the objective description of a thought – something that philosophers may investigate – but also on what is presupposed for the individual thinker in thinking some thing under that description – something that might be a matter for psychology.

The general principle of the essential connectedness of thoughts remains valid and has certain implications. The main one for my present concern is that the content of the thought for the thinker can never be fully expressed in terms simply of what passes through his mind on the occasion in question. This explains why it so often seems to us that the expression of the thought in words provides a skeleton without the flesh. It explains why in creative thought the product, its expression in whatever form it is the aim of the creative process to achieve (a musical theme or structure, a series of words, or what have you), so often seems to fail to do justice to what has led up to it. The thought may seem to the thinker so much richer than its expression, or, what is perhaps a better term, its formulation. (Wittgenstein remarks at *Phil. Invest.*, I, 317 that it is a misleading parallel to say that just as the expression of a pain may be a cry so is the expression of a thought a proposition. So it is if 'expression' is used in *that* sense.) Vygotsky, the Russian genetic psychologist, has said that just as a word devoid of thought is a dead thing so 'a thought unembodied in words remains a shadow'.[3] How true is this and what significance has the truth that it has?

What I have been saying so far might be interpreted as claiming that a good deal of the substance of a thought lies in what is *not* embodied in the way that Vygotsky has in mind. Yet there is a certain plausibility in his assertion and an assessment of it will bring us face to face with the problem that has been my underlying concern all along: what role does the embodiment of the thought have in relation to the thought? That question is not answered simply by stressing that it is after all the *embodiment*, for it is the problem just what this is that is at stake. I have spoken earlier of the formulation of the thought and I suggested that 'formulation' might be a happier term than 'expression'. But 'formulation' should not be taken to mean the *ex post facto* summing up of the thought, when we have reviewed it and estimated its significance; it is not meant to be taken as a parallel in our own case to the description which we might offer of someone else's thought, when we have reached an estimate of its import. Yet it seems to me that when we think in words, so that words are in Vygotsky's sense the embodiment of the thought, there is an element of making our thought explicit to ourselves. It is not that we reflect on our thought and sum it up on a form of words; to that extent the form of consciousness used is, to use the term much beloved of the phenomenologists, pre-reflective – though to say that is merely to specify the problem, not to solve it. Someone might say that he has not really thought until the words are there, and it is presumably this that Vygotsky means when he speaks of the thought remaining a shadow if it is not embodied in words. But if what I have previously said is right, then if someone has thought that *p*, in the sense that the words that comprise *p* were the embodiment of his thought, it is a necessary truth that this cannot be all that he has thought. Hence while the words need not be his reflective summing up of the thought they must nevertheless constitute what is explicit to the thinker of his thought.

[3] See L. S. Vygotsky, 'Thought and Word', reprinted in Parveen Adams (ed.) *Language in Thinking* (Penguin, 1972), pp. 180–213, esp. p. 212.

Let me pose the problem in an acute form by asking whether thinking is possible which has no embodiment at all. It is clear that the embodiment need not take the form of words. In so far as other things that pass through our mind have a symbolic status, in so far as they have for us a significance in the way that words can, then we can certainly be said to think in them. This is true even if, for the thought to be described as the thought that *p*, there must be something about it that makes the description in propositional terms appropriate. The thought has, one might say, to be propositionally styled even if it is not embodied in words. The ramifications of that point are considerable; it implies among other things that the thought has a structure that might properly be termed 'grammatical' and that whatever embodiment it has must be capable of being construed in terms of a grammatical context. Thus if in having the thought that *p* all that passes through the mind as the embodiment of the thought is, say, the image of a table, the significance of that image does not simply lie in the fact that it represents or stands for something, whether an actual table or by some association of ideas something quite different. That would not be enough to make it the embodiment of a propositionally styled thought. Nor is it the case that the image must have a structure capable in some way of reflecting the grammatical structure of the thought. *That* does not seem to be the relation between the image and the thought. The image of some sunny spot might be the embodiment of the thoughts 'It was a good holiday' or 'How hot it was that year'; and we might know this in the sense that we might go on to formulate the thought to ourselves in some such words. Yet there was nothing in the image from which one could, as it were, read off that fact. If that leaves the relation between the thought and the image mysterious it promotes the question whether the thought could occur without anything of the kind occurring.

The subject of imageless thought has received at times discussion which has reached the level of heated controversy. However, as I pointed out some years ago,[4] I doubt whether the presuppositions of the classical debate on the subject bear examination, and it would be better to approach the subject from a different point of view. It is clear, as I have said, that there must of necessity be

[4] D. W. Hamlyn, 'The Stream of Thought', *Proc. Arist. Soc.* (1955–6), pp. 63–82.

more to the thought than what floats on the surface of the mind, than what comes explicitly into mind, than what we say to ourselves or conjure up in the way of images. If that is all that there is to the problem of imageless thought the matter may be taken as settled. But there are also cases in which over some period nothing has gone on in the mind that the thinker has been aware of, or at any rate nothing that was clearly to the point, and yet there are grounds for the claim that there has been thought. The most obvious cases are those on which Hadamard and others interested in the psychology of mathematical thought and discovery have concentrated – cases in which after a line of thought that has seemed abortive the thinker has reached in thought a solution to a problem, without anything apparently taking place during the interval. What is crucial to such cases is that they are not to be construed as ones in which a thought occurs to the thinker which, *as it happens*, is relevant to the previous problem. Rather it seems as if steps have been gone through in the interval and the process has produced the solution. It is easy enough, and no doubt true, to say that the brain has gone on working in the interval, but that does not help us to decide how to construe the thought itself. Should we, for example, say bluntly that no thought has gone on in the interval, but that the thinker, for reasons that we do not fully understand, has arrived at the final thought of the solution in a way that brings with it a consciousness of its connection with the previous thought? If so – and I am inclined to think that we should – these cases are not relevant to my problem.

For that problem is essentially one about intentionality and its relation to mental occurrences and doings. The thought, when it occurs, must be *of* something, *about* something; it must be directed towards an object in the way that Brentano had in mind in invoking the notion of intentionality. Is the occurrence of a mental item, an image, a saying, etc. essential to this? Or is it merely a convenient aide? For if it is the latter then its occurrence must be contingent only, and could in principle be dispensed with. In that case a period of thought with nothing occurring before the mind seems unobjectionable. But if the occurrence of the mental item is not just a convenient but contingent fact, what role does it play that makes it essential in some form to the intentionality of the thought? It is these problems that we are really concerned with in asking whether there could be a period in which thinking has gone on without there being any embodiment to the thought, and no amount of empirical investigation or inquiry will deal with those problems. They are essentially problems for the understanding.

One might get a clearer view of the situation by going to the other extreme and considering cases where mental occurrences of some form certainly seem necessary and not merely contingent. I have in mind here cases of imagining something or visualising something. To be asked to imagine some situation is in one sense to be asked to perform just as much of an intellectual feat as to be asked to think of it. Imagining, we might say, is a form of thinking; it can well involve a form of intellectual construction, the working out of the consequences or implications of the problem posed. But it also in a sense involves more. One can think out what is involved in a certain situation without doing that something extra which would be entailed if we were asked to *imagine* what is involved in the situation – displaying to ourselves in terms appropriate to one of the senses what there would be to perceive in the situation. For example, if the situation were such that construing it in visual terms would be the most appropriate way of approaching it in the imagination, then the appropriate way to imagine it would be to display it to ourselves in visual terms. Thinking of the same situation would be possible without this, by working out intellectually on the basis of a knowledge about visual properties of things what it would be for the things involved to have those properties in the situation. If, however, someone were to do just this he might well be accused of being unimaginative. In what way in this would he be falling short? The answer seems to me to be that he would lack a kind of insight into the visual nuances of the situation in something of the same way that the blind man may lack insight into the visual nuances of colour. A blind man may know a great deal about colours and their relationships, as long as the knowledge remains, as we might put it, on the formal level; but strictly speaking he cannot know just what it is like to see something as red. Similarly we can think out the implications of a given situation without presenting to ourselves anything of what the things involved look like. Visual images play in this respect something of the same role that sensations play with regard to perception; they provide the sensuous content in terms of which objects are to be imagined/seen.[5]

It would follow from this that for the imagination of a situation images or the construction of the situation visually in the imagination may well be essential. We could not conceive how imagining the scene could be carried out otherwise. Yet the object of the thought that is involved in the imagining is still the situation. We are thinking of the situation through the images, displaying it to ourselves visually (or in means appropriate to some other of the senses) by their means. Could we say that in thinking of a situation generally we display it to ourselves, without this display being necessarily sensuous or quasi-sensuous, in whatever mental item that is brought into our mind for the purpose? Analogously, when the thought just occurs to us is it displayed for us in whatever comes before our mind? And does it have to be displayed in anything? In this case the crucial words in 'display it to ourselves' are not 'display it' (for to use these words in this case is to rely on an analogy with the straightforward imagining case) but 'to ourselves'. They imply a certain reflexivity in the consciousness, which would be lacking if nothing were displayed. In other words the images, or whatever they are, bring to a focus for us whatever we bring to the object in thinking of or about it. Without this we could think of the object only, if this were possible, without thinking of it *as* anything. And it might well be said that this would scarcely deserve the name of 'thinking'. It might be asked in return why it is necessary for human beings that there should, when they think of an object or situation, be something which acts for them as a focus of the knowledge and understanding that they bring to the situation in thinking of it. What I have said suggests that while during a given period we might rightly be said to be thinking of *X* although nothing passed through the mind in the way of images, etc., we could not be thinking anything about *X* or of *X* as anything unless at some time in this context, even if outside the interval of time in question, something of the kind did pass through our mind. Why is this?

[5] I have said more about the role of sensations in this respect in a paper entitled 'Unconscious Inference and Judgment in Perception', given to the University of Western Ontario workshop on 'Images, Perception and Knowledge', May 1974, to appear in its proceedings. I am aware that my view of the role of sensations in perception is not entirely orthodox.

This question seems to me of fundamental importance for the philosophy of mind. If, in the case of perception, one believes, as I do, that the perception of something (the perception of it as such and such) involves among other things the occurrence of some sensory occurrence or set of sensations, it is easy enough to provide a blocking answer to the question why this is necessary, by saying 'It would not be perception otherwise'. A similar move is possible in the case of imagining something, and I made it myself earlier. But it is difficult to find such a move attractive in the case of thinking, and this invites a more significant construal of the situation overall. One thing is clear in all these cases, and that is that when the sensuous or quasi-sensuous occurrence takes place it is not to this that our attention is directed as such. Rather we attend to whatever the perception, visualisation or thought is *of*, and we are conscious of it as whatever it is through or by means of the sensuous occurrence. Thus if there is in it, as I suggested earlier, a certain reflexivity, it is not a full-blown reflexivity as there is in those cases in which when we do *X* mentally we *ipso facto* attend to the doing of X. Nevertheless it is that 'through or by means of' that is the crux of the problem. In the case of perception one might say that the sensuous occurrence or sensation provides the occasion and ground for application to what produces it of the conceptual understanding that is involved in seeing that thing as such and such. But just as any ground acts as a partial determinant of what can be built upon it, so the sensation acts as a partial determinant of the nature of the consciousness of the object. In the paper referred to in note 5, I have spoken of the sensation as 'colouring' the awareness of the object. It is through the sensation that the object is displayed for us, although other things are necessary too, for example the conceptual understanding of which I have spoken. In the case of imagination, since the image is not caused by the object of the imagining in the way in which the sensation is caused by the object of perception, one cannot speak of the image being displayed for us; rather we display it to ourselves, as I said earlier. In the case of thinking the connexion between the object of thought and the symbol, which the occurrence functions as, is even more remote. Hence it would not generally be right to say that in thinking of *X*, the mental occurrence is necessary for the object to be displayed to ourselves; for no *display* as such need occur. Yet the application to the object of thought of the concepts involved in the thought still requires a ground – something that can act as the focus for that conceptual understanding, in that it has something of that significance for us. That significance may well be idiosyncratic, but it must exist, and it is what philosophers have been getting at when they have spoken of images, etc. functioning as symbols.

In sum, any kind of consciousness of objects which involves the application of conceptual understanding and knowledge to those objects requires something which functions for us as the occasion and ground for that application. The way in which that something functions as such a ground determines in part the nature of the consciousness of objects which is in question. Thinking is no exception to this rule. The difficulty, which I am conscious of having surmounted only very partially, is to find a way to specify in words how this works in its case. The general principle, however, seems valid.

MAIN PUBLICATIONS

The Psychology of Perception (Routledge & Kegan Paul, 1957; reprinted with additional material, 1969)
Sensation and Perception (Routledge & Kegan Paul, 1961)
Aristotle's De Anima, Books II and III (Clarendon Press, 1968)
The Theory of Knowledge (Doubleday, 1970; Macmillan, 1971)

ETHICAL THEORY AND UTILITARIANISM

by

R. M. Hare

White's Professor of Moral Philosophy and Fellow of Corpus Christi College, Oxford

Contemporary moral philosophy (and the British is no exception) is in a phase which must seem curious to anybody who has observed its course since, say, the 1940s. During all that time moral philosophers of the analytic tradition have devoted most of their work to fundamental questions about the analysis or the meaning of the moral words and the types of reasoning that are valid on moral questions. It may be that some of them were attracted by the intrinsic theoretical interest of this branch of philosophical logic; and indeed it is interesting. But it may surely be said that the greater part, like myself, studied these questions with an ulterior motive: they saw this study as the philosopher's main contribution to the solution of practical moral problems such as trouble most of us. For if we do not understand the very terms in which the problems are posed, how shall we ever get to the root of them? I, at least, gave evidence of this motive in my writings and am publishing many papers on practical questions.[1] But, now that philosophers in greater numbers have woken up to the need for such a contribution, and whole new journals are devoted to the practical applications of philosophy, what do we find the philosophers doing? In the main they proceed as if nothing had been

[1] See, for example, my *Freedom and Reason* (*FR*) (Oxford, 1963), ch. 11; *Applications of Moral Philosophy* (London, 1972); 'Rules of War and Moral Reasoning', *Ph. and Public Affairs,* 1 (1972); 'Language and Moral Education', *New Essays in the Philosophy of Education,* G. Langford and D. J. O'Connor (eds) (London, 1973); 'Abortion and the Golden Rule', *Ph. and Public Affairs,* 4 (1975); 'Political Obligation', *Social Ends and Political Means,* T. Honderich (ed.) (forthcoming); and 'Contrasting Methods of Environmental Planning', *Nature and Conduct,* R. S. Peters (ed.) (London, 1975).

learnt in the course of all that analytical enquiry – as if we had become no clearer now than in, say, 1936, or even 1903, how good moral arguments are to be distinguished from bad.

I cannot believe that we need be so pessimistic; nor that I am alone in thinking that logic can help with moral argument. But surprisingly many philosophers, as soon as they turn their hands to a practical question, forget all about their peculiar art, and think that the questions of the market place can be solved only by the methods of the market place – i.e. by a combination of prejudice (called intuition) and rhetoric. The philosopher's special contribution to such discussions lies in the ability that he ought to possess to clarify the concepts that are being employed (above all the moral concepts themselves) and thus, by revealing their logical properties, to expose fallacies and put valid arguments in their stead. This he cannot do unless he has an understanding (dare I say a theory?) of the moral concepts; and that is what we have been looking for all these years. And yet we find philosophers writing in such a way that it is entirely unclear what understanding they have of the moral concepts or of the rules of moral reasoning.[2] It is often hard to tell whether they are naturalists, relying on supposed equivalences between moral and non-moral concepts, or intuitionists, whose only appeal is to whatever moral sentiments they can get their readers to share with them. Most of them seem to be some sort of descriptivists; but as they retreat through an ever vaguer naturalism into a hardly avowed intuitionism, it becomes more and more obscure what, in their view, moral statements say, and therefore how we could decide whether to accept them or not. Philosophy, as a rational discipline, has been left behind.

It is the object of this paper to show how a theory about the meanings of the moral words can be the foundation for a theory of normative moral reasoning. The conceptual theory is of a non-descriptivist but nevertheless rationalist sort.[3] That this sort of theory could claim to provide the basis of an account of moral reasoning will seem paradoxical only to the prejudiced and to

[2] See the beginning of my paper 'Abortion and the Golden Rule', cited in note 1.

[3] It is substantially that set out in *FR*. For the distinction between non-descriptivism and subjectivism, see my 'Some Confusions about Subjectivity', Lindley Lecture, 1974, University of Kansas.

those who have not read Kant. It is precisely that sort of prejudice which has led to the troubles I have been complaining of: the belief that only a descriptivist theory can provide a rational basis for morality, and that therefore it is better to explore any blind alley than expose oneself to the imputation of irrationalism and subjectivism by becoming a non-descriptivist.

The normative theory that I shall advocate has close analogies with utilitarianism, and I should not hesitate to call it utilitarian, were it not that this name covers a wide variety of views, all of which have been the victims of prejudices rightly excited by the cruder among them. In calling my own normative theory utilitarian, I beg the reader to look at the theory itself, and ask whether it cannot avoid the objections that have been made against other kinds of utilitarianism. I hope to show in this paper that it can avoid at least some of them. But if I escape calumny while remaining both a non-descriptivist and a utilitarian, it will be a marvel.

In my review of Professor Rawls's book[4] I said that there were close formal similarities between rational contractor theories such as Rawls's, ideal observer theories such as have been advocated by many writers[5] and my own universal prescriptivist theory. I also said that theories of this form can be made to lead very naturally to a kind of utilitarianism, and that Rawls avoided this outcome only by a very liberal use of intuitions to make his rational contractors come to a non-utilitarian contract. Rawls advocates his theory as an alternative to utilitarianism. Whether the system which I shall sketch is to be regarded as utilitarian or not is largely a matter of terminology. The form of argument which it employs is, as I have already said, formally extremely similar to Rawls's; the substantive conclusions are, however, markedly different. I should like to think of my view as, in Professor Brandt's expression, 'a credible form of utilitarianism';[6] no doubt Rawls

[4] *Ph.Q.*, 23 (1973); cf. my paper 'Rules of War and Moral Reasoning', cited in note 1, and B. Barry, *The Liberal Theory of Justice* (Oxford, 1973), pp. 12–13.

[5] See, for example, the discussion between R. Firth and R. B. Brandt in *Ph. and Phen. Res.*, 12 (1952) and 15 (1955); also D. Haslett, *Moral Rightness* (The Hague, 1974).

[6] R. B. Brandt, 'Towards a Credible Form of Utilitarianism', *Morality and the Language of Conduct*, H.-N. Castaneda and G. Nakhnikian (eds) (Detroit, 1963).

would classify it as an incredible form of utilitarianism; others might say that it is a compromise between his views and more ordinary kinds of utilitarianism. This does not much matter.

I try to base myself, unlike Rawls, entirely on the formal properties of the moral concepts as revealed by the logical study of moral language; and in particular on the features of prescriptivity and universalisability which I think moral judgements, in the central uses which we shall be considering, all have. These two features provide a framework for moral reasoning which is formally similar to Rawls's own more dramatic machinery. But, rather than put the argument in his way, I will do overtly what he does covertly – that is to say, I do not speculate about what some fictitious rational contractors *would* judge if they were put in a certain position subject to certain restrictions; rather, I subject myself to certain (formally analogous) restrictions and put myself (imaginatively) in this position, as Rawls in effect does,[7] and *do* some judging. Since the position and the restrictions are formally analogous, this ought to make no difference.

In this position, I am prescribing universally for all situations just like the one I am considering; and thus for all such situations, *whatever* role, among those in the situations, I might myself occupy. I shall therefore give equal weight to the equal interests of the occupants of all the roles in the situation; and, since any of these occupants might be myself, this weight will be positive. Thus the impartiality which is the purpose of Rawls's 'veil of ignorance' is achieved by purely formal means; and so is the purpose of his insistence that his contractors be rational, i.e. prudent. We have therefore, by consideration of the logic of the moral concepts alone, put ourselves in as strong a position as Rawls hopes to put himself by his more elaborate, but at the same time, as I have claimed, less firmly based apparatus.

Let us now use these tools. Rawls himself says that an ideal observer theory leads to utilitarianism; and the same ought to be true of the formal apparatus which I have just sketched. How does giving equal weight to the equal interests of all the parties lead to utilitarianism? And to what kind of utilitarianism does it lead? If I am trying to give equal weight to the equal interests of all the parties in a situation, I must, it seems, regard a bene-

[7] See my review of Rawls, *Ph.Q.*, 23 (1973), p. 249.

fit or harm done to one party as of equal value or disvalue to an equal benefit or harm done to any other party. This seems to mean that I shall promote the interests of the parties most, while giving equal weight to them all, if I maximise the total benefits over the entire population; and this is the classical principle of utility. For fixed populations it is practically equivalent to the average utility principle which bids us maximise not total but average utility; when the size of the population is itself affected by a decision, the two principles diverge, and I have given reasons in my review of Rawls's book for preferring the classical or total utility principle. In these calculations, benefits are to be taken to include the reduction of harms.

I am not, however, going to put my theory in terms of benefits and the reduction of harms, because this leads to difficulties that I wish to avoid. Let us say, rather, that what the principle of utility requires of me is to do for each man affected by my actions what I wish were done for me in the hypothetical circumstances that I were in precisely his situation; and, if my actions affect more than one man (as they nearly always will) to do what I wish, all in all, to be done for me in the hypothetical circumstances that I occupied all their situations (not of course at the same time but, shall we say?, in random order). This way of putting the matter, which is due to C. I. Lewis,[8] emphasises that I have to give the same weight to everybody's equal interests; and we must remember that, in so far as I am one of the people affected (as in nearly all cases I am) my own interests have to be given the same, and no more, weight – that is to say, my own actual situation is one of those that I have to suppose myself occupying in this random order.

Some further notes on this suggestion will be in place here. First, it is sometimes alleged that justice has to be at odds with utility. But if we ask how we are to be just between the competing interests of different people, it seems hard to give any other answer than that it is by giving equal weight, impartially, to the equal interests of everybody. And this is precisely what yields the utility principle. It does not necessarily yield equality in the resulting distribution. There are, certainly, very good utilitarian reasons for seeking equality in distribution too; but justice is something

[8] *An Analysis of Knowledge and Valuation* (La Salle, 1946), p. 547; see also Haslett, op. cit., ch. 3.

distinct. The utilitarian is sometimes said to be indifferent between equal and unequal distributions, provided that total utility is equal. This is so; but it conceals two important utilitarian grounds for a fairly high degree of equality of actual goods (tempered, of course, as in most systems including Rawls's, by various advantages that are secured by moderate inequalities). The first is the diminishing marginal utility of all commodities and of money, which means that approaches towards equality will tend to increase total utility. The second is that inequalities tend to produce, at any rate in educated societies, envy, hatred and malice, whose disutility needs no emphasising. I am convinced that when these two factors are taken into account, utilitarians have no need to fear the accusation that they could favour extreme inequalities of distribution in actual modern societies. Fantastic hypothetical cases can no doubt be invented in which they would have to favour them; but, as we shall see, this is an illegitimate form of argument.

Secondly, the transition from a formulation in terms of interests to one in terms of desires or prescriptions, or vice versa, is far from plain sailing. Both formulations raise problems which are beyond the scope of this paper. If we formulate utilitarianism in terms of interests, we have the problem of determining what are someone's true interests. Even if we do not confuse the issue, as some do, by introducing moral considerations into this prudential question (i.e. by alleging that becoming morally better, or worse, in itself affects a man's interests),[9] we still have to find a way of cashing statements about interests in terms of such states of mind as likings, desires, etc., both actual and hypothetical. For this reason a formulation directly in terms of these states of mind ought to be more perspicuous. But two difficult problems remain: the first is that of how present desires and likings are to be balanced against future, and actual desires and likings against those which would be experienced if certain alternative actions were taken; the second is whether desires need to be mentioned at all in a formulation of utilitarianism, or whether likings by themselves will do. It would seem that if we arrive at utilitarianism via universal prescriptivism, as I am trying to do, we shall favour the former of the last pair of alternatives; for desires, in the required sense, are assents to prescriptions. All these are questions within the theory

[9] Cf. Plato, *Republic*, 335.

of prudence, with which, although it is an essential adjunct to normative moral theory, I do not hope to deal in this paper.[10]

I must mention, however, that when I said above that I have to do for each man affected by my actions what I wish were done for me, etc., I was speaking inaccurately. When I do the judging referred to on page 116, I have to do it as rationally as possible. This, if I am making a moral judgement, involves prescribing universally; but in prescribing (albeit universally) I cannot, if rational, ignore prudence altogether, but have to universalise this prudence. Put more clearly, this means that, whether I am prescribing in my own interest or in someone else's (see the next paragraph), I must ask, not what I or he does actually at present wish, but what, prudentially speaking, we should wish. It is from this rational point of view (in the prudential sense of 'rational') that I have to give my universal prescriptions. In other words, it is *qua* rational that I have to judge; and this involves at least judging with a clear and unconfused idea of what I am saying and what the actual consequences of the prescription that I am issuing would be, for myself and others. It also involves, when I am considering the desires of others, considering what they would be if those others were perfectly prudent – i.e. desired what they would desire if they were fully informed and unconfused. Thus morality, at least for the utilitarian, can only be founded on prudence, which has then to be universalised. All this we shall have to leave undiscussed, remembering, however, that when, in what follows, I say 'desire', 'prescribe', etc., I mean 'desire, prescribe, etc., from the point of view of one who is prudent so far as his own interest goes'. It is important always to supply this qualification whether I am speaking of our own desires or those of others; but I shall omit it from now on because it would make my sentences intolerably cumbrous, and signalise the omission, in the next paragraph only, by adding the subscript '$_p$' to the words 'desire', etc., as required, omitting even this subscript thereafter. I hope that one paragraph will suffice to familiarise the reader with this point.

Thirdly, when we speak of the 'situations' of the various parties, we have to include in the situations all the desires$_p$, likings$_p$, etc.,

[10] The theory of prudence is ably handled in D. A. J. Richards, *A Theory of Reasons for Action* (Oxford, 1971); Haslett, op. cit.; and R. B. Brandt, John Locke Lectures (Oxford, forthcoming).

that the people have in them – that is to say, I am to do for the others what I $wish_p$ to be done for me were I to have their $likings_p$, etc., and not those which I now have. And, similarly, I am not to take into account (when I ask what I $wish_p$ should be done to me in a certain situation) my own present $desires_p$, $likings_p$, etc. There is one exception to this: I have said that one of the situations that I have to consider is my own present situation; I have to $love_p$ my neighbour *as*, but *no more than* and *no less than*, myself, and likewise to do to others *as* I $wish_p$ them to do to me. Therefore just as, when I am considering what I $wish_p$ to be done to me were I in *X*'s situation, where *X* is somebody else, I have to think of the situation as including *his* $desires_p$, $likings_p$, etc., and discount my own, so, in the single case where *X* is myself, I have to take into account *my* $desires_p$, $likings_p$, etc. In other words, *qua* author of the moral decision I have to discount my own $desires_p$, etc., and consider only the $desires_p$, etc., of the affected party; but where (as normally) I am one of the affected parties, I have to consider my own $desires_p$, etc., *qua* affected party, on equal terms with those of all the other affected parties.[11]

It will be asked: if we strip me, *qua* author of the moral decision, of all desires and likings, how is it determined what decision I shall come to? The answer is that it is determined by the desires and likings of those whom I take into account as affected parties (including, as I said, myself, but only *qua* affected party and not *qua* author). I am to ask, indeed, what I do wish should be done for me, were I in their situations; but were I in their situations, I should have their desires, etc., so I must forget about my own present desires (with the exception just made) and consider only the desires which *they* have; and if I do this, what I *do* wish for will be the satisfaction of *those* desires; that, therefore, is what I shall prescribe, so far as is possible.

[11] Professor Bernard Williams says, 'It is absurd to demand of such a man, when the sums come in from the utility network which the projects of others have in part determined, that he should just step aside from his own project and decision and acknowledge the decision which utilitarian calculation requires.' (J. J. C. Smart and B. A. O. Williams, *Utilitarianism: For and Against* (Cambridge, 1973), p. 116, and cf. p. 117n.) Christian humility and *agape* and their humanist counterparts are, then, according to Williams's standards, an absurd demand (which is hardly remarkable). What is more remarkable is the boldness of the persuasive definition by which he labels the self-centred pursuit of one's own projects 'integrity' and accounts it a fault in utilitarianism that it could conflict with this.

I wish to point out that my present formulation enables me to deal in an agreeably clear way with the problem of the fanatic, who has given me so much trouble in the past.[12] In so far as, in order to prescribe universally, I have to strip away (*qua* author of the moral decision) all my present desires, etc., I shall have to strip away, among them, all the ideals that I have; for an ideal is a kind of desire or liking (in the generic sense in which I am using those terms); it is, to use Aristotle's word, an *orexis.*[13] This does not mean that I have to give up having ideals, nor even that I must stop giving any consideration to my ideals when I make my moral decisions; it means only that I am not allowed to take them into account *qua* author of the moral decision. I am, however, allowed to take them into account, along with the ideals of all the other parties affected, when I consider my own position, among others, as an affected party. This means that for the purposes of the moral decision it makes no difference *who has* the ideal. It means that we have to give impartial consideration to the ideals of ourselves and others. In cases, however, where the pursuit of our own ideals does not affect the ideals or the interests of others, we are allowed and indeed encouraged to pursue them.

All this being so, the only sort of fanatic that is going to bother us is the person whose ideals are so intensely pursued that the weight that has to be given to them, considered impartially, outbalances the combined weights of all the ideals, desires, likings, etc., that have to be frustrated in order to achieve them. For example, if the Nazi's desire not to have Jews around is intense enough to outweigh all the sufferings caused to Jews by arranging not to have them around, then, on this version of utilitarianism, as on any theory with the same formal structure, it ought to be satisfied. The problem is to be overcome by, first, pointing out that fanatics of this heroic stature are never likely to be encountered (that no *actual* Nazis had such intense desires is, I think, obvious); secondly, by remembering that, as I shall be showing in a moment, cases that are never likely to be actually encountered do not have to be squared with the thinking of the ordinary man, whose principles are not designed to cope with such cases. It is therefore illegitimate to attack such a theory as I

[12] *FR*, ch. 9; 'Wrongness and Harm', in my *Essays on the Moral Concepts* (London, 1972).

[13] *De Anima*, 433a 9ff.

have sketched by saying 'You can't ask us to believe that it would be right to give this fantastic fanatical Nazi what he wanted'; this argument depends on appealing to the ordinary man's judgement about a case with which, as we shall see, his intuitions were not designed to deal.

A similar move enables us to deal with another alleged difficulty (even if we do not, as we legitimately might, make use of the fact that all desires that come into our reasoning are desires$_p$, i.e. desires that a man will have after he has become perfectly prudent). It is sometimes said to be a fault in utilitarianism that it makes us give weight to bad desires (such as the desire of a sadist to torture his victim) solely in proportion to their intensity; received opinion, it is claimed, gives no weight at all, or even a negative weight, to such desires. But received opinion has grown up to deal with cases likely to be encountered; and we are most *un*likely, even if we give sadistic desires weight in accordance with their intensity, to encounter a case in which utility will be maximised by letting the sadist have his way. For first, the suffering of the victim will normally be more intense than the pleasure of the sadist. And, secondly, sadists can often be given substitute pleasures or even actually cured. And, thirdly, the side-effects of allowing the sadist to have what he wants are enormous. So it will be clear, when I have explained in more detail why fantastic cases in which these disutilities do not occur cannot legitimately be used in this kind of argument, why it is perfectly all right to allow weight to bad desires.

We have now, therefore, to make an important distinction between two kinds or 'levels' of moral thinking. It has some affinities with a distinction made by Rawls in his article 'Two Concepts of Rules'[14] (in which he was by way of defending utilitarianism), though it is not the same; it also owes something to Sir David Ross,[15] and indeed to others. I call it the difference between level-1 and level-2 thinking, or between the principles employed at these two levels.[16] Level-1 principles are for use in practical moral thinking, especially under conditions of stress. They have to be general enough to be impartable by education (includ-

[14] *Ph. Rev.*, 64 (1955).

[15] *The Right and the Good* (Oxford, 1930), pp. 19ff.

[16] See my review of Rawls, cited in note 4, p. 153; 'Principles', *Proc. Arist. Soc.*, 72 (1972–3); 'Rules of War and Moral Reasoning', cited in note 1; *FR*, pp. 43–5.

ing self-education), and to be 'of ready application in the emergency',[17] but are not to be confused with rules of thumb (whose breach excites no compunction). Level-2 principles are what would be arrived at by leisured moral thought in completely adequate knowledge of the facts, as the right answer in a specific case. They are universal but can be as specific (the opposite of 'general', not of 'universal'[18]) as needs be. Level-1 principles are inculcated in moral education; but the selection of the level-1 principles for this purpose should be guided by leisured thought, resulting in level-2 principles for specific considered situations, the object being to have those level-1 principles whose general acceptance will lead to actions in accord with the best level-2 principles in most situations that are actually encountered. Fantastic and highly unusual situations, therefore, need not be considered for this purpose.

I have set out this distinction in detail elsewhere;[19] here we only need to go into some particular points which are relevant. The thinking that I have been talking about so far in this paper, until the preceding paragraph, and indeed in most of my philosophical writings until recently, is level-2. It results in a kind of act-utilitarianism which, because of the universalisability of moral judgements, is practically equivalent to a rule-utilitarianism whose rules are allowed to be of any required degree of specificity. Such thinking is appropriate only to 'a cool hour', in which there is time for unlimited investigation of the facts, and there is no temptation to special pleading. It can use hypothetical cases, even fantastic ones. In principle it can, given superhuman knowledge of the facts, yield answers as to what should be done in any cases one cares to describe.

The commonest trick of the opponents of utilitarianism is to take examples of such thinking, usually addressed to fantastic cases, and confront them with what the ordinary man would think. It makes the utilitarian look like a moral monster. The anti-utilitarians have usually confined their own thought about moral reasoning (with fairly infrequent lapses which often go unnoticed) to what I am calling level 1, the level of everyday moral thinking on ordinary, often stressful, occasions in which information is sparse. So they find it natural to take the side of the ordinary man

[17] Burke; see *FR*, p. 45.
[18] See 'Principles', cited in note 16.
[19] See note 16.

in a supposed fight with the utilitarian whose views lead him to say, if put at the disconcertingly unfamiliar standpoint of the archangel Gabriel, such extraordinary things about these carefully contrived examples.

To argue in this way is entirely to neglect the importance for moral philosophy of a study of moral education. Let us suppose that a fully-informed archangelic act-utilitarian is thinking about how to bring up his children. He will obviously not bring them up to practise on every occasion on which they are confronted with a moral question the kind of archangelic thinking that he himself is capable of; if they are ordinary children, he knows that they will get it wrong. They will not have the time, or the information, or the self-mastery to avoid self-deception prompted by self-interest; this is the real, as opposed to the imagined, veil of ignorance which determines our moral principles.

So he will do two things. First, he will try to implant in them a set of good general principles. I advisedly use the word 'implant'; these are not rules of thumb, but principles which they will not be able to break without the greatest repugnance, and whose breach by others will arouse in them the highest indignation. These will be the principles they will use in their ordinary level-1 moral thinking, especially in situations of stress. Secondly, since he is not always going to be with them, and since they will have to educate *their* children, and indeed continue to educate themselves, he will teach them, as far as they are able, to do the kind of thinking that he has been doing himself. This thinking will have three functions. First of all, it will be used when the good general principles conflict in particular cases. If the principles have been well chosen, this will happen rarely; but it will happen. Secondly, there will be cases (even rarer) in which, though there is no conflict between general principles, there is something highly unusual about the case which prompts the question whether the general principles are really fitted to deal with it. But thirdly, and much the most important, this level-2 thinking will be used to *select* the general principles to be taught both to this and to succeeding generations. The general principles may change, and should change (because the environment changes). And note that, if the educator were not (as we have supposed him to be) archangelic, we could not even assume that the best level-1 principles were imparted in the first place; perhaps they might be improved.

How will the selection be done? By using level-2 thinking to consider cases, both actual and hypothetical, which crucially illustrate, and help to adjudicate, disputes between rival general principles. But, because the general principles are being selected for use in actual situations, there will have to be a careful proportioning of the weight to be put upon a particular case to the probability of its actually occurring in the lives of the people who are to use the principles. So the fantastic cases that are so beloved of anti-utilitarians will have very little employment in this kind of thinking (except as a diversion for philosophers or to illustrate purely logical points, which is sometimes necessary). Fantastic unlikely cases will never be used to turn the scales as between rival general principles for practical use. The result will be a set of general principles, constantly evolving, but on the whole stable, such that their use in moral education, including self-education, and their consequent acceptance by the society at large, will lead to the nearest possible approximation to the prescriptions of archangelic thinking. They will be the set of principles with the highest acceptance-utility. They are likely to include principles of justice.

It is now necessary to introduce some further distinctions, all of which, fortunately, have already been made elsewhere, and can therefore be merely summarised. The first, alluded to already, is that between specific rule-utilitarianism (which is practically equivalent to universalistic act-utilitarianism) and general rule-utilitarianism.[20] Both are compatible with act-utilitarianism if their roles are carefully distinguished. Specific rule-utilitarianism is appropriate to level-2 thinking, general rule-utilitarianism to level-1 thinking; and therefore the rules of specific rule-utilitarianism can be of unlimited specificity, but those of general rule-utilitarianism have to be general enough for their role. The thinking of our archangel will thus be of a specific rule-utilitarian sort; and the thinking of the ordinary people whom he has educated will be for the most part of a general rule-utilitarian sort, though they will supplement this, when they have to and when they dare, with such archangelic thinking as they are capable of.

The second distinction is that between what Professor Smart[21] calls (morally) 'right' actions and (morally) 'rational' actions.

[20] See 'Principles', cited in note 16.

[21] Smart and Williams, op. cit., pp. 46f.

Although Smart's way of putting the distinction is not quite adequate, as he himself recognises, I shall, as he does, adopt it for the sake of brevity. Both here, and in connexion with the 'acceptance-utility' mentioned above, somewhat more sophisticated calculations of probability are required than might at first be thought. But for simplicity let us say that an action is rational if it is the action most likely to be right, even if, when all the facts are known, as they were not when it was done, it turns out not to have been right. In such a society as we have described, the (morally) rational action will nearly always be that in accordance with the good general principles of level 1, because they have been selected precisely in order to make this the case. Such actions may not always turn out to have been (morally) right in Smart's sense when the cards are turned face upwards; but the agent is not to be blamed for this.

It is a difficult question, just how simple and general these level-1 principles ought to be. If we are speaking of the principles to be inculcated throughout the society, the answer will obviously vary with the extent to which the members of it are sophisticated and morally self-disciplined enough to grasp and apply relatively complex principles without running into the dangers we have mentioned. We might distinguish sub-groups within the society, and individuals within these sub-groups, and even the same individual at different stages, according to their ability to handle complex principles. Most people's level-1 principles become somewhat more complex as they gain experience of handling different situations, and they may well become so complex as to defy verbal formulation; but the value of the old simple maxims may also come to be appreciated. In any case, level-1 principles can never, because of the exigencies of their role, become as complex as level-2 principles are allowed to be.

A third distinction is that between good actions and the right action.[22] The latter is the action in accordance with level-2 principles arrived at by exhaustive, fully-informed and clear thinking about specific cases. A good action is what a good man would do, even if not right. In general this is the same as the morally rational action, but there may be complications, in that the motivation of the man has to be taken into account. The good (i.e. the morally

[22] See my *The Language of Morals*, p. 186.

well-educated) man, while he is sometimes able and willing to question and even to amend the principles he has been taught, will have acquired in his upbringing a set of motives and dispositions such that breaking these principles goes very much against the grain for him. The very goodness of his character will make him sometimes do actions which do not conform to archangelic prescriptions. This may be for one of at least two reasons. The first is that when he did them he was not fully informed and perhaps knew it, and knew also his own moral and intellectual weaknesses, and therefore (humbly and correctly) thought it morally rational to abide by his level-1 principles, and thus did something which turned out in the event not to be morally right. The second is that, although he could have known that the morally rational action was on this unusual occasion one in breach of his ingrained principles (it required him, say, to let down his closest friend), he found it so much against the grain that he just could not bring himself to do it. In the first case what he did was both rational and a morally good action. In the second case it was morally good but misguided – a wrong and indeed irrational act done from the best of motives. And no doubt there are other possibilities.

The situation I have been describing is a somewhat stylised model of our own, except that we had no archangel to educate us, but rely on the deliverances, not even of philosopher kings, but of Aristotelian *phronimoi* of very varying degrees of excellence. What will happen if a lot of moral philosophers are let loose on this situation? Level-1 thinking forms the greater part of the moral thinking of good men, and perhaps the whole of the moral thinking of good men who have nothing of the philosopher in them, including some of our philosophical colleagues. Such are the intuitionists, to whom their good ingrained principles seem to be sources of unquestionable knowledge. Others of a more enquiring bent will ask why they should accept these intuitions, and, getting no satisfactory answer, will come to the conclusion that the received principles have no ground at all and that the only way to decide what you ought to do is to reason it out on each occasion. Such people will at best become a crude kind of act-utilitarians. Between these two sets of philosophers there will be the sort of ludicrous battles that we have been witnessing so much of. The philosopher who understands the situation better will see that both are right about a great deal and that they really ought to make up their quarrel. They are talking about different levels of thought, both of which are necessary on appropriate occasions.

What kind of philosopher will this understanding person be? Will he be any kind of utilitarian? I see no reason why he should not be. For, first of all, level-2 thinking, which is necessary, is not only utilitarian but act-utilitarian (for, as we have seen, the specific rule-utilitarian thinking of this level and universalistic act-utilitarianism are practically equivalent). And there are excellent act-utilitarian reasons for an educator to bring up his charges to follow, on most occasions, level-1 thinking on the basis of a set of principles selected by high-quality level-2 thinking. This applies equally to self-education. So at any rate all acts that could be called educative or self-educative can have a solid act-utilitarian foundation. To educate oneself and other men in level-1 principles *is* for the best, and only the crudest of act-utilitarians fails to see this. There will also be good act-utilitarian reasons for *following* the good general principles in nearly all cases; for to do so will be rational, or most likely to be right; and even an act-utilitarian, when he comes to tell us how we should proceed when choosing what to do, can only tell us to do what is *most probably* right, because we do not know, when choosing, what *is* right.

There will be occasions, as I have said, when a man brought up (on good general principles) by a consistent act-utilitarian will do a rational act which turns out not to be right; and there will even be occasions on which he will do a good action which is neither rational nor right, because, although he could have known that it would be right on this unusual occasion to do an act contrary to the good general principles, he could not bring himself to contemplate it, because it went so much against the grain. And since one cannot pre-tune human nature all that finely, it may well be that the act-utilitarian educator will have to put up with the possibility of such cases, in the assurance that, if his principles are well chosen, they will be rare. For if he attempted to educate people so that they would do the rational thing in these cases, it could only be by incorporating into their principles clauses which might lead them, in other more numerous cases, to do acts most likely to be wrong. Moral upbringing is a compromise imposed by the coarseness of the pupil's discrimination and the inability of his human educators to predict with any accuracy the scrapes he will get into.

The exclusion from the argument of highly unusual cases, which I hope I have now achieved, is the main move in my defence of this sort of utilitarianism. There are also some subsidiary moves, some of which I have already mentioned, and all of which will be familiar. It is no argument against act-utilitarianism that in some unusual cases it would take a bad man to do what according to the utilitarian is the morally right or even the morally rational thing; good men are those who are firmly wedded to the principles which *on nearly all actual occasions* will lead them to do the right thing, and it is inescapable that on unusual occasions moderately good men will do the wrong thing. The nearer they approach archangelic status, the more, on unusual occasions, they will be able to chance their arm and do what they think will be the right act in defiance of their principles; but most of us ordinary mortals will be wise to be fairly cautious. As Aristotle said, we have to incline towards the vice which is the lesser danger for *us*, and away from that extreme which is to *us* the greater temptation.[23] For some, in the present context, the greater danger may be too much rigidity in the application of level-1 principles; but perhaps for more (and I think that I am one of them) it is a too great readiness to let them slip. It is a matter of temperament; we have to know ourselves (empirically); the philosopher cannot tell each of us which is the greater danger for him.

The moves that I have already made will, I think, deal with some other cases which are well known from the literature. Such are the case of the man who is tempted, on utilitarian grounds, to use electricity during a power crisis, contrary to the government's instructions; and the case of the voter who abstains in the belief that enough others will vote. In both these cases it is alleged that some utility would be gained, and none lost, by these dastardly actions. These are not, on the face of it, fantastic or unusual cases, although the degree of knowledge stipulated as to what others will do is perhaps unusual. Yet it would be impolitic, in moral education, to bring up people to behave like this, if we were seeking level-1 principles with the highest acceptance-utility; if we tried, the result would be that nearly everyone would consume

[23] *Nicomachean Ethics*, 1109 b 1.

electricity under those conditions, and hardly anybody would vote. However, the chief answer to these cases is that which I have used elsewhere[24] to deal with the car-pushing and death-bed promise cases which are also well canvassed. It is best approached by going back to the logical beginning and asking whether I am prepared to prescribe, or even permit, that others should (*a*) use electricity, thus taking advantage of my law-abidingness, when I am going without it; (*b*) abstain from voting when I do so at inconvenience to myself, thereby taking advantage of my public spirit; (*c*) only pretend to push the car when I am rupturing myself in the effort to get it started; (*d*) make death-bed promises to me (for example to look after my children) and then treat them as of no weight. I unhesitatingly answer 'No' to all these questions; and I think that I should give the same answer even if I were perfectly prudent and were universalising my prescriptions to cover other perfectly prudent affected parties (see above, page 119). For it is not imprudent, but prudent rather, to seek the satisfaction of desires which are important to me, even if I am not going to know whether they have been satisfied or not. There is nothing in principle to prevent a fully informed and clear-headed person wanting above all that his children should not starve after his death; and if that is what he wants above all, it is prudent for him to seek what will achieve it, and therefore prescribe this.

Since the logical machinery on which my brand of utilitarianism is based yields these answers, so should the utilitarianism that is based on it; and it is worth while to ask, How? The clue lies in the observation that to frustrate a desire of mine is against my interest even if I do not know that it is being frustrated, or if I am dead. If anybody does not agree, I ask him to apply the logical apparatus direct and forget about interests. Here is a point at which, perhaps, some people will want to say that my Kantian or Christian variety of utilitarianism, based on giving equal weight to the prudent prescriptions or desires of all, diverges from the usual varieties so much that it does not deserve to be called a kind of utilitarianism at all. I am not much interested in that terminological question; but for what it is worth I will record my opinion that the dying man's interests *are* harmed if promises are made to him and then broken, and even more that mine are

[24] See my paper 'The Argument from Received Opinion' in my *Essays on Philosophical Method* (London, 1971), pp. 128ff.; *FR*, pp. 132ff.

harmed if people are cheating me without my knowing it. In the latter case, they are harmed because I very much want this not to happen; and my desire that it should not happen is boosted by my level-1 sense of justice, which the utilitarian educators who brought me up wisely inculcated in me.

Whichever way we put it, whether in terms of what I am prepared to prescribe or permit universally (and therefore also for when I am the victim) or in terms of how to be fair as between the interests of all the affected parties, I conclude that the acts I have listed will come out wrong on the act-utilitarian calculation, because of the harms done to the interests of those who are cheated, or the non-fulfilment of prescriptions to which, we may assume, they attach high importance. If we add to this move the preceding one which rules out fantastic cases, and are clear about the distinction between judgements about the character of the agent, judgements about the moral rationality of the action, and judgements about its moral rightness as shown by the outcome, I think that this form of utilitarianism can answer the objections I have mentioned. Much more needs to be said; the present paper is only a beginning, and is not very original.[25] I publish it only to give some indication of the way in which ethical theory can help with normative moral questions, and to try to get the discussion of utilitarianism centred round credible forms of it, rather than forms which we all know will not do.

[25] Among many others from whose ideas I have learnt, I should like in particular to mention Dr Lynda Sharp (Mrs Lynda Paine), in whose thesis *Forms and Criticisms of Utilitarianism* (deposited in the Bodleian Library at Oxford) some of the above topics are discussed in greater detail.

MAIN PUBLICATIONS

The Language of Morals (OUP, 1952)
Freedom and Reason (OUP, 1963)
Essays on Philosophical Method (Macmillan, 1972)
Practical Inferences (Macmillan, 1971)
Essays on the Moral Concepts (Macmillan, 1972)

DIRECT PERCEPTION AND THE SENSE-DATUM THEORY

by

Jonathan Harrison
Professor of Philosophy, University of Nottingham

My object in this paper is to attack, and, I hope, to dispose of, a view which has been predominant among the great majority of Anglo-Saxon philosophers for the last thirty years or so. This view is that the sense-datum theory is wrong, and that the problems to which it gave rise are pseudo-problems. To the extent that any one doctrine has been put in its place, that one is, I suppose, the doctrine that we do not see material objects through the mediation of sense-data, but 'directly'. In style I propose to be slightly polemical, if for no better reason than that a view so firmly embedded in the minds of most of my contemporaries will need a pinch of dynamite if it is to be disposed of. Erroneous philosophical theories should be treated to some extent like people. Those which are weak and sickly, as well as erroneous, should be treated gently, and with consideration. It is to be hoped that they will die anyway. Theories which are as vigorous as they are wrong-headed, however, may be, and perhaps must be, treated with less respect. Indeed, they must be treated somewhat roughly, if the person attacking them is to gain a hearing. Philosophers are only a little less prone to the sheep-like vice of being over-impressed by what is the prevailing fashion than more common mortals, and they will need to be shaken just a little, if they are to be aroused from their dogmatic slumbers over this particular question. For a similar reason, I shall be fairly crude in my methods of expounding the sense-datum theory itself, the reasons why it has been held, the reasons for rejecting it, and the doctrine that has been put in its place.

According to the sense-datum theory, whenever we perceive

such things as chairs, tables, hills, rivers, valleys, the sun, the moon, the stars and the bodies of ourselves or other people, we do not see these things 'immediately'. What we are aware of immediately, when we look at the top of our table, is a trapezoidal patch of colour; when we look at the moon what we are aware of immediately is a yellow disc or silver crescent; what we are aware of immediately when we look at our house from a distance is a small white dot. Similarly, with perception which is not visual, what we are aware of immediately is not the Flying Scotsman, but the noise the Flying Scotsman makes; what we are aware of immediately is not the rose, but the smell which emanates from the rose, what we are aware of immediately, when we touch our friend on the arm, is not his arm, but sensations of pressure. It should be said that though the term 'sense-datum' is a comparatively modern one, the doctrine itself is old, and has been held by philosophers of the very greatest eminence. Locke and Berkeley called them ideas. Hume called them impressions. Kant called them *Anschauungen*, or 'intuitions'. Sometimes, more recently, they have been called sensations, sometimes sensa, sometimes sensibilia, sometimes perceptions. As might be expected, there are small differences between the views of the people who used the different words, but I am not at the moment concerned with minute details, and these differences may, for my present purposes, be neglected. Incidentally, the fact that the sense-datum theory has so long a history makes one suspect that those who so unequivocally reject it are guilty of an arrogance that is based on temporal parochialism.

Once you make the distinction between perceiving an object like the moon, and being immediately aware of a sense-datum of the moon which, allegedly, interposes itself between us and the moon, and *via* the mediation of which the moon is seen, a number of problems arise. The first of these, of course, is the question of how we can know that there is a moon, for there might be nothing at all hiding behind that small silver crescent. It looks as if, if we are not immediately aware of the moon, its existence must be some kind of inference, hypothesis or postulation, evolved, perhaps, by our primitive ancestors in order to explain why we have the appearances or sense-data of it that we do. The nature of the moon itself, as opposed to that of its appearances, was also a problem. The silver crescent itself could hardly be supposed to exist apart from the perceptual apparatus of a sentient being, for that we saw a crescent of this size and colour at all must be due to the pattern of stimulation of the rods and cones, which itself was determined by the nature of the light coming from the moon, and it was difficult to believe that it could exist independently of them. The official scientific theory on the matter is that the moon itself consists of a simply enormous collection of minute particles, which possess primary qualities (shape, size, position, and velocity) but not secondary qualities (colour, smell, taste, etc.). The only two respectable alternatives to this theory known to me are the view (held by Hume and by, at one time, Russell and, in a way, by Berkeley and Leibniz) that material objects consist of vast collections of things just like sense-data, except that, since no one is aware of them, they are not the sense-data of any person or animal; and phenomenalism. Phenomenalism is the theory that since statements about material objects can be translated into statements about sense-data – mostly hypothetical statements about the sense-data observers would have if they were differently situated in space and time from the way in which they in fact are – material objects are no more something over and above sense-data than nations or rowing clubs or limited liability companies are something over and above people.

The motives for rejecting the sense-datum theory are, I think, as follows. One motive is materialistic, the reluctance to admit that the world contains anything over and above the entities studied by physics. These entities have mass, three-dimensional shape and size, occupy a volume of space, are publicly observable, and leave traces which can be detected by ordinary measuring instruments. Another motive is anti-sceptical, and arises from the feeling that the sense-datum theory interposes a veil between ourselves and the outside world which makes our knowledge of this world problematic, and its existence doubtful. A third motive arises from a tendency, deriving from Moore (though this philosopher accepted the sense-datum-theory), to be very reluctant to allow any view which appears to conflict with common sense. The fourth, allied, motive is a tendency to dislike any philosophical theory which cannot be expressed in ordinary language, coupled with the view that 'sense-datum' is a philosophers' invention, for which there is no equivalent in ordinary language. This word, consequently, is supposed to give rise to unreal problems because, as it has no properly defined use, the questions asked in sentences containing it do not, in the last resort, make sense. The fifth motive is a dislike of 'privacy', of what cannot be publicly observed and checked, coupled with the belief that, if we admit the existence of sense-data, then these private entities impose not only a barrier between oneself and the external world, but a barrier between the contents of one person's mind and his experiences and those of another.

Hence, I suppose, it is not surprising that I should be opposed to such philosophers. I believe that materialism is a gross over-simplification; and that though common sense is likely to be right for the most part, failure to set it aside, when there seems good reason to do so, is likely to lead to a second-rate and unimaginative conservatism. I have an innate scepticism, which I would not be without. I believe that ordinary language should be treated with only as much respect as is deserved by a partially evolved instrument designed by an organism of limited intelligence, which instrument is likely to be as much capable of improvement as man is of discovering new information to record and convey, and of new uses to which to put it. I think, however, that to use it whenever possible is both courteous to one's readers, and a prophylactic against pretentious and confused verbosity. And, as I value my solitude, I think, and welcome the fact, that the mind of man is essentially private; that he does not have to disclose its contents unless he wants to; and detest the compulsory social fraternisation that the opposite view would entail.

The number of objections which have been levelled in the last few decades against the sense-datum theory is simply enormous, and I neither can nor wish to give a detailed consideration to any of them; most of them I shall simply have to ignore. The most convincing line of attack, I think, is as follows. In introducing the noun 'sense-datum', philosophers have, in departing from ordinary language, misrepresented a number of facts which, if expressed in the proper way, give rise to no problems, and then built upon these flimsy foundations a superstructure which they are totally unable to bear. It is perfectly good ordinary English – or ordinary any language, so far as I know – to contrast the way things are with the way they look, taste, feel, smell and sound, and, of course, a perfectly ordinary common-sense view that these may be different. One and the same thing may look small when it is large, look khaki when it is red (my car used to do this under certain kinds of street lighting), feel hotter than it is, taste like sawdust when it is not sawdust, smell putrid when it is perfectly wholesome. Again, one and the same thing may look, taste, feel, smell and sound in different ways to different people, from different places, under different conditions, and at different times. If one sticks to ordinary language to state these platitudes, no trouble arises, but, once we start talking the sense-datum language, or attempt to derive from these facts a theory that interposes between ourselves and the objects we perceive visual, tactile, auditory, olfactory or gustatory sense-data, which actually have the properties that the things we perceive seem to have, we get into difficulties at once. For one thing, we clutter the universe with a jungle of quasi-Meinongian objects, existing either in space, or in the private spaces of different percipients or different senses, which extravagant proliferation of entities could have been avoided by the discipline of a more rigorous and economical philosophical analysis. For if I persist in saying, when I see a penny which, because it is tilted towards my eye, looks (roughly) elliptical, that I am aware of something which is elliptical, it immediately follows that what I am aware of cannot be the penny, which is not elliptical. If the penny looks brown to me under some conditions, but pink under others, and I persist in saying that, in the first case, I am aware of something which is brown, and in the second case of something which is pink, it immediately follows, or seems to follow, that what I am aware of the first time I saw the penny cannot be the same as what I was aware of the second time I saw the penny. And if, instead of saying, when two people look at the same thing from different distances, that it looks bigger to one than it does to the other, they persist in saying that one of these people is aware of an entity which is large, and the other is aware of an entity which is small, they naturally derive the conclusion that these people are aware of different entities, neither of which is the thing they are looking at. If we talked in ordinary English, which we know how to handle, we would not draw these strange and paradoxical conclusions.

To the extent that the motive for this manœuvre is materialistic, it can be replied to as follows. One can, perhaps, get rid of the suggestion that the world, besides material objects, contains strange things like sense-data, but only at the cost of conceding that things have characteristics which, though not exactly strange – we are, indeed, all perfectly familiar with them – are at least characteristics which objects possess in addition to those which are investigated by scientists in general, and physicists in particular. For physics tells us how things are, and it is only a matter of incidental concern to the physicist how they look. Hence, in rejecting the sense-datum theory, these philosophers have got rid of 'queer' entities only at the cost of introducing queer characteristics. If you accept the sense-datum theory, you have ordinary characteristics like being coloured, having a certain size, shape and position, but two different kinds of thing to have these characteristics. If you reject the sense-datum theory, you may have only one kind of thing, but these things must possess two kinds of characteristics, the characteristic of being such-and-such and the characteristics of looking, tasting, smelling, feeling such-and-such to a sentient being, from a certain place, at a certain time.

The anti-sense-datum philosopher is not without a reply to this. Sometimes people are ill, at other times they seem to be ill. (There is no reason, of course, why they should not both look and be ill.) It would be absurd to suppose that men and women possess two quite different kinds of characteristic, exemplified by being ill on the one hand, and seeming to be ill on the other. When we say that a man seems to be ill, we are not (confidently) attributing to him a peculiar characteristic, the characteristic of seeming to be ill, we are rather judging tentatively that he has the quite normal characteristic of being ill, or saying that we are inclined to suppose, or that there is something about him which makes it probable, or not impossible, that he is ill. Similarly, it has been argued, if we judge that something looks red, we are not attributing to it the peculiar quality of looking red, so much as suggesting that there is some reason to think that it is red. There are not, then, two different kinds of characteristic, the characteristics of looking so-and-so and being so-and-so, so much as the one set of characteristic, some of which we know or firmly believe things have, and others of which we suspect, tentatively opine, or are inclined to think that they have.

This attempt to explain away the characteristics which things appear to have simply will not do. If we look at doric pillars in the distance, we may confidently judge that they are bulgy, because they look straight; hence, when we judge that they look straight, we cannot be tentatively judging that they are straight. It is true that we do have some inclination to believe that they are straight, which is inhibited by our knowledge that they are bulgy, but why do we have this inclination to believe that they are straight unless it is that, from that distance, they present a straight appearance, or, in common parlance, look straight. Again, to the extent that we have any inclination at all to believe that a tilted plate is elliptical, this must be because of the prior fact such plates look elliptical. Nor can you get rid of the basic and irreducible fact that a tilted plate looks elliptical by saying that it looks as an elliptical but untilted plate would look, for this, though true, is true simply because of the equally basic and irreducible fact that untilted elliptical plates also look elliptical. If we see the moon, and it looks crescent shaped, it seems incredible that anyone should have more than the very slightest inclination to judge that it is crescent shaped, and to the extent that the idea of a crescent shape enters our heads at all, it must be because, from that distance and in those circumstances, it looks crescent shaped.

There are, then, a class of characteristics, those which things look to have, which are distinct from and cannot be reduced to the ones they actually do have. Describing such characteristics is a matter of phenomenology, but it must not be supposed that they are of concern only to the artist or poet or descriptive writer or psychologist or oculist or those interested in curious facts for their own sake. They have a logical importance, which is, or should be, of concern to the professional philosopher. He, to the extent that he is an epistemologist, is interested in the basis of our ascription of properties to things, and there is a close logical connection between the way things look and the way things are. This has been carefully investigated by some very eminent philosophers whose work does not nowadays receive the attention it deserves, partly because it is supposed that, because their writings presupposed the sense-datum theory, and the sense-datum theory is wrong, they are not worth reading. An example of one of these problems is this. Sometimes, when things change their looks, we say that this is because they are moving; at other times we say it is because we are moving, or because both we and they are. The eliciting of the principle which guides us in distinguishing between what have been called objective and subjective successions is an interesting philosophical task, and one which cannot be accomplished simply by reflecting on the meanings of words. We need to go to the appearances, and carefully consider what it is about them that makes us sometimes say that we are moving, or sometimes say that the thing we are looking at is moving. In general, knowledge of the shape, size, position, colour, mass, etc., of objects must to a large extent be based upon knowledge of how they look, and to investigate the relationship between the two is a proper task for the philosopher.

Once it is recognised that things have these two sets of properties, many of the characteristic problems of the sense-datum theory come creeping back again. It seems fairly obvious that, when we say how something looks to us, from this place, at this time, we are not saying something which we have to infer from anything else. We do not infer that the moon looks crescent shaped (though we may infer that it is a moon or satellite which looks crescent shaped) to us, now, from where we are – though we may infer that it looks crescent shaped to someone else, or that it will look crescent shaped to us on some future occasion, or would look crescent shaped from some other place. That the moon looks crescent shaped, and yellow, is a basic proposition, as is that the penny we see looks elliptical, that our house in the distance looks small, and that our jacket and trousers look the same colour in this light. And when we consider colours, at any rate, it seems obvious that what colour something is is a matter for inference. Things which both are and look green do not look any different from things which look green, but are not. The colours things are hide themselves, so to speak, behind the colours they look. If something looks one colour we can only infer that it also is or that it is not that colour, from such things as our knowledge of the nature of the material and the conditions under which it is illuminated. If it looks green, we may infer that it is blue, if we know that things like that look green in artificial light or, alternatively, we may infer that it is green if it is seen in daylight, and we know that our eyesight is normal. The situation is not so clear, however, with the spatial characteristics of things. One can make out a case for saying that, if we see a penny which is round, but looks elliptical, both its round shape and its elliptical look are equally present to us, and neither is inferred. This case, however, would be a mistaken one. A small object which looks small does not necessarily look any different from a large object which looks small, and, if it does, it is not so much that it looks a different kind of smallness, as that we infer that it is large (and so distant) from various visual clues, such as the fact that it looks as if it were the kind of object which we know is large. The characteristics objects have, then, are inferences from the characteristics they seem to have, just as the sense-datum theorists supposed them to be inferences from non-inferential knowledge of the properties of sense-data. Talking about how things appear, then, does not bring us any closer to non-inferential contact with the external world than does talking of sense-data.

Is it possible to go farther than this, and say that the external world is hidden behind its appearances, as it was supposed that it was hidden behind a veil of sense-data, and that, perhaps, behind the veil of appearances or the veil of sense-data there might be nothing at all? I think that this is possible – logically possible – though this does not mean that it might be true. That this is possible is something which is difficult to express in the language of appearances. It is difficult because, in the language of appearances, it is always necessary to use some noun which is a noun for some material thing, and to say that it is this thing which appears to have whatever perceptual characteristic it is that is in question. It is the penny which looks elliptical, the moon which looks crescent shaped, my house which looks small and white. If this is so, the penny, the moon and my house must all exist in order to bear the properties of looking so-and-so, just as they have to exist to be the bearers of the properties of being so-and-so. But it would be absurd to infer from this fact, which is a fact about our terminological habits, anything about the world, or about whether an external world might or might not exist at all. To say that there must be chairs and tables because otherwise we couldn't describe the phenomena of experience by saying that chairs look so-and-so and tables such-and-such would be to make much the same mistake as those philosophers are alleged to have made in arguing that the swans in Australia must be white, because swans are by definition white. Of course we do have expressions such as 'seem to see a dagger, the handle of which seems to be turned towards me' and to some extent it is possible to express the possibility that all our experience is a consistent hallucination in the language of appearances just as much as in the sense-datum language. It should scarcely be necessary, had it not been denied, to point out that, if we seem to see a dagger, this must be because, whether you care to use the sense-datum language to describe it or not, our visual field is modified in just the way in which it is modified when we see a real dagger. The former modification of course is not produced by light waves, but is 'proceeding from the heat-oppressed brain'.

To a large extent, then, the problems to which the sense-datum theory gives rise are genuine and unavoidable, and arise naturally out of the distinction between statements describing how things appear and statements describing how things are. Considering the difference between these two kinds of statement ought also to make us reject the theory, if anything so obscure and ill considered is worth the name, that we perceive material objects directly. What exactly those philosophers maintain who have held that we do perceive material objects directly is far from clear. 'Perceive directly', unlike 'hear directly' (which means to be told by someone who has been told by someone else), is not an expression in ordinary English. It is to be presumed that since those philosophers who held it, however unclear they were about their positive view, were unequivocal enough about their negative contention that the sense-datum theory was false, they must think that the existence of the things we perceive neither is nor presupposes an inference. But in thinking this they are quite, and quite obviously, mistaken. If I claim that what I see is a pig, however good the light, and however normal its environment, I am making claims about how it will look to other people, how it will look to me and others at later times, and how it would look to me or others from other points of view. If it looks as a pig looks to me, but to everyone else it looks just as a cow looks, or if it looks like a pig now, but immediately and for ever after looks like a goat, or if it looks like a pig from here, but looks like a sheep when I get closer to it, or if it looks like a pig to me from where I am now, but all the hypothetical propositions to the effect that it would look like a pig to observers at different places, if there were observers at these places, are false, then it simply is not a pig. We have already seen that we infer how things look to other people, or to ourselves at other times or from other places, and it is even more obvious, if this is possible, that how it would look to observers situated at different places is something which has to be inferred. It does not follow from this that what we see might not be a pig (though it does follow that it is logically possible that it is not a pig), nor that we ought not to be certain that it is a pig, nor that we do not know that it is a pig. To suppose the contrary is to make the common philosophical mistake of thinking that there can always be error where there is inference, and so inferring from the fact, which I am inclined to concede, that there cannot be error, that there cannot be inference. But there is inference, at least in the sense that the statement 'That is a pig' entails an enormous number of statements which can be known only by inference, and which are such that the statement that it is a pig would have to be false if they were false.

Consequently, a great deal of what can be said in the sense-datum terminology can be said in the ordinary language of looks and is. Not all of it can be so said, however. There are well-established rules for deciding whether one and the same thing looks the same or different to different observers, and the question whether they are aware of the same or different entities (sense-data) does not seem to arise in the language of looks as it does in the sense-datum language – though it must not be forgotten, however, that the fact that something looks brown to Tom is not the same fact about it as that it looks brown to Dick, and that Tom knows that it looks brown to Tom in a different (and non-inferential) way from the way in which he knows that it looks brown to Dick. And there are occasions when we get on ill if we have not a word which is a word for an entity. One of the most striking of these is when we want to say – as some philosophers do – that the view we get of the front of, say, a cabinet fits together with the views we get of its sides, back, top and bottom to enclose a region of space, which region we normally think is inhabited by those microscopic objects which, scientists tell us, is what the cabinet is composed of.

Once we start talking about a different class of entities from chairs and tables, rivers, mountains and seas, we are likely to get into trouble from those philosophers who want to hold that the world contains nothing but the objects which are of concern to the physicist. We do not, however, get into as much trouble as we would have when those philosophers who rejected the sense-datum theory were in their hey-day. Professor J. L. Austin, in *Sense and Sensibilia*, has quite rightly pointed out (with the intention of criticising the sense-datum theory, though such facts were also pointed out by sense-datum philosophers such as C. D. Broad and H. H. Price many years before Austin wrote) that the world contains many more things than material objects. And perhaps we will get into less trouble still if we insist that not everything which we wish to talk about belongs to the category of substance, in that sense of 'substance' in which substances are things capable of existing by themselves. If you look through a dictionary, you will find that the vast majority of nouns do not refer to things which belong to the category of substance, but that does not stop anyone from talking about them, or describing them, or making statements about them. If something does not belong to the category of substance, of course, it is tempting to suppose that all statements about it can be translated into other, equivalent, statements about something which does. Statements about accidents, which are not substances, can perhaps be translated into statements about cars, which are substances, bumping into one another. Statements about tunes, which are not substances, can perhaps be translated into statements about composers and players and audiences and musical instruments, which are substances. Philosophers, however, have attempted, and then with doubtful success, to carry out this attractive programme with only a very few of those classes of things which may or may not be substances. They have tried to do it for space, time, points, classes, properties, propositions, minds, matter, but there are an enormous number of things reductions of which have never even been attempted. Hence, to my mind, it is quite harmless to talk about sense-data, and leave open the question – which was answered by only a minority of philosophers (for example, Hume) explicitly in the affirmative – whether they are substances, and, if they are not substances, to what statements about substances statements about them must be reduced. (If you take the view that statements about sense-data are statements about how material objects look, you may regard statements about them as having to be reduced to statements about material things, or both material things and the sentient being who perceives them, a manœuvre which will not work very well in the case when we have hallucinations, see reflections, liver spots and the phenomena we perceive when at the oculist. Alternatively, you may wish to attempt to reduce, in a Berkelian manner, statements about sense-data to talk about the way in which sentient beings experience, a manœuvre which works quite well for tactile and kinaesthetic experience or with the sensations of our own body, but badly for visual sense-data, or, at least, the clearly delineated ones).

But at this point it will be objected that I am going too quickly. I have not yet established that there is anything to be gained by talking about sense-data, or explained how this noun is to be anchored to experience. I think that this is not nearly as difficult to do as has commonly been supposed, because, contrary to common opinion both among sense-datum theorists and their opponents, the sense-datum language is a part of ordinary language. Ordinary language, of course, does not have the generic term 'sense-datum', which is a philosopher's invention, but it does have many words which can sensibly be regarded only as words for particular sense-data, or classes of sense-data. The really hard-line anti-sense-datum view is that verbs of perception must always take things like chairs and tables as their objects; this view may, and has, been weakened to allow us to perceive less solid entities like reflections, shadows, rainbows, and the aurora borealis. In fact, however, it is perfectly good English to go farther than this, and talk of seeing coloured patches, yellow discs, silver crescents, bright specks, and so on. Austin, for example, himself talks in this way. Once you allow yourself to do this, however, a great number of the most characteristic contentions of the sense-datum theory have implicitly, through inadvertently, been conceded. It seems obvious, really, that, when we look at the moon, it can be true to say that we see a yellow disc or silver crescent. That one does see a yellow disc, too, is a basic proposition, and one which does not need to be inferred from anything else. It would not turn out to be false if further investigation showed that there is no round or even spherical object above the earth. It is also, one hopes, true to say that we see the moon. But that we see the moon is not a basic proposition; indeed, a great deal of astronomic theorising is presupposed by our making this assertion. It is logically possible that what we see when we look at the sky and see a silver crescent is not the moon, but a very large cheese, or something painted on the concave surface of a great sphere. If it is objected that the moon was called the moon by people ignorant of astronomical theory, the reply is that it is then a matter of inference that the moon is a material object at all, and not a purely visual phenomenon which entirely disappears from a few miles above the surface of the earth. That we see a silver crescent, then, is something not inferred; that we see the moon is, and two very fundamental contentions of the sense-datum theory must be conceded straight away. But not only this, seeing the moon entails seeing a silver crescent, or something similar, whereas seeing a yellow disc or silver crescent does not entail seeing the moon. If one were to look at the sky, and not see anything but a uniform expanse of black, then it could not be true that we saw the moon. On the other hand, it logically could be the case that, though we saw a silver crescent, we did not see the moon, or, at any rate, some material object which is a satellite of the earth. As we have seen it could be the case that the moon is a purely visual phenomenon. It could be the case that the silver crescent was a visual phenomenon that only one person saw. It could be the case, even, that it was a short-lived visual phenomenon, and that when we look at the sky on subsequent occasions we do not see it.

Two more central contentions of the sense-datum theory must, therefore, also be conceded, namely, that seeing material objects entails seeing (though sense-datum theorists would not have liked the word 'seeing') sense-data, and that seeing sense-data does not entail seeing material objects. It does not, of course, follow from this that the silver crescent is private, as the majority of sense-datum philosophers supposed sense-data to be, but at least there is a sense in which material objects like the moon are public and objects like silver crescents are not public. Material objects like the moon have to be public; if only one normal observer can see them, then they are not material objects like the moon. On the other hand, the statement that one person sees a silver crescent does not entail anything at all about what anyone else sees. If I look at the sky, and see a silver crescent, it is logically possible, however improbable, that no other observer should see a silver crescent when he looks at the sky, if for no other reason than that it is logically possible that the rods and cones on my retina should be activated in the way which causes me to see a silver crescent, although no one else's rods and cones are activated. It was once fashionable to deny this possibility, for example by trying to reduce hallucinations to a kind of false belief that one was seeing anything at all, but few people try to do this nowadays, and the view is so unplausible as not to deserve serious attention. And not only does seeing the moon entail seeing some such things as silver crescents, but not conversely; all our knowledge of the latter is derived from our knowledge of the former.

Why then, if Austin admits the existence of nouns in ordinary

English which function much as words for sense-data are supposed to function, does he wish to deny that there are sense-data? I think there are two reasons for this, one which he acknowledges, the other which he does not. The one he does not acknowledge is this. Simply saying that I am aware of a silver crescent, or a bright speck, or a white dot, or a blue expanse, or an elliptical brown patch suggests, though it does not assert, that I am unable to identify the object which I am looking at. It seems to be a convention of language that, if I do not give maximum information when I very easily could have done, it must be because I am not in a position to give it. Hence it is misleading, though not false, to say that I am to meet a relative when I am to meet my mother (although my mother is a relative) for, since I could just as easily have said I was to meet my mother, my not saying this suggests that I am not in a position to say it, although I am in this position. Hence, usually, when I say I see a white dot, I am suggesting that I am unable to identify this as my house, which is misleading, though not false, if I am able to identify it. So a 'colour patch' language is much more natural in the case of distant objects than it is in the case of near ones, for they are often not so readily identified, and the associations by which an appearance of visible solidity is almost overwhelmingly conveyed (so overwhelmingly that I suspect that many anti-sense-datum philosophers simply do not notice that it is not visibly present) are not so compulsive.

The second reason why Austin failed to notice that he had opened the door to readmit sense-data was that he thought that yellow crescents, bright specks, white dots, and so on, just were material objects (or, at any rate, presumably, just were things like shadows, reflections, apparitions, etc.) and because he thought that, if they were material objects, then it followed that they were not sense-data. On the latter point, he was quite mistaken. The word 'sense-datum' was introduced by the best sense-datum philosophers in such a way as to leave open as many questions as possible about them; hence it was left possible for it to turn out that sense-data just were material objects, though none of them were so wrong-headed as to suppose that they would do so in fact. The nearest they got to this rather implausible view was to hold that some sense-data were identical with the front surfaces of material objects. And, of course, it is really quite ridiculous to suppose that the silver crescent is the moon, that

that bright speck just is Sirius, that that white dot just is my house. That Austin did suppose it is, I think, because there is a quite common and perfectly legitimate use for 'That white dot is my house', but where the 'is' is not the 'is' of identity. We can say 'That cloud of dust in the distance is Tom on his motor-bike' and 'That cloud of spray in the distance is Dick in his speed-boat' without in the least intending to imply that Tom is numerically identical with a cloud of dust, or that Dick is numerically identical with a cloud of spray. And, without going into the rather needless intricacies which have evolved over discussion of the point, it is surely obvious enough that my house is not numerically identical with a white dot; that the moon is not numerically identical with a silver crescent; that Sirius is not numerically identical with a bright speck, and so on for everything else one cares to think of. And even if they were identical, none of the epistemological contentions I have made about the relations between them would have to be abandoned.

A great deal of prejudice against the sense-datum theory, enshrined in the belief that the sense-datum theory imposes an iron curtain, or better, a painted veil of sense-data between us and the external world, arises from a misconception about the logical interrelations between propositions about sense-data and propositions about material objects. It is not that we would see the external world so much better, were it not for sense-data getting in our way; without the sense-data we would not see it at all. We logically could not see the moon from this distance without seeing some such thing as a yellow crescent; logically could not see stars if we did not see such things as silvery specks; logically could not see our house if we did not, from a distance, see a white dot (or, from closer to, a white expanse); and logically could not see a penny if we did not see a round or elliptical patch. Indeed, if the yellow crescent is an appearance of the moon, and not an hallucination, it is both true to say that we see a yellow crescent and true to say that we see the moon. This is not for the reason that Austin supposed that it was, viz. that 'yellow crescent' and 'the moon' were different descriptions of one and the same thing. It is more for the reason that to kick a panel of a wardrobe and to kick a wardrobe (when the panel is part of a wardrobe, and not detached from it) is one and the same thing. One (logically) cannot kick a wardrobe without kicking some part or other of the wardrobe, and it would be absurd to complain that one could not kick wardrobes because the parts of the wardrobe were for ever getting in the way. And from this, of course, it neither follows that the parts of wardrobes and wardrobes are one and the same thing, nor that we kick a wardrobe in one sense of 'kick', but kick the panels of wardrobes in a different sense of 'kick'. Why should it follow, from similar facts, that 'yellow crescent' and 'the moon' are different descriptions of one and the same thing, or that we see the yellow crescent in one sense of 'see', and the moon in a different sense of 'see'? What does follow, of course, is that more is necessary to establish that it is a wardrobe I am kicking than to establish that it is a panel that I am kicking and, similarly, that more is necessary to establish that what I am seeing is a moon than that it is a yellow crescent. This is so obvious that it could only be disingenuous openly to deny it, and sheer obscurantism to seem to make resounding claims, such as that we perceive things directly, if one is not going to deny it.

Sense-data, then, are not an iron curtain between us and the real world, and there is simply no such thing as coming face to face with a material object as opposed to seeing it in seeing them. To suppose that there is, is rather like to suggest that, because our eyes, which may be astigmatic, short-sighted, colour blind and in any case are sensitive to light waves of only a limited range of frequency, can give us only a distorted picture of reality, we would see much better if we had them removed. Only God, the idea might be, who does have eyeless vision, sees things as they really are. It is obviously silly to suggest that we might see without eyes, or some artificial substitute for eyes, and less obviously silly to suggest that we might have, or even have some idea of, a seeing which did not involve seeing sense-data. Nevertheless, the fact remains that man's eyes, upon which the existence of visual sense-data causally depend, are all different from one another, and different from the eyes of non-human animals, and that they are sensitive to only a limited range of the radiation which emanates from objects, which radiation takes a finite length of time to reach them, and the nature of which depends upon the intervening media and conditions in the observer's environment. Consequently, it is very unlikely that everyone sees things the same way, that different animals do not see things very differently, and that the world does not contain beings whose perceptual apparatus gives them a view of the universe which is almost completely different from ours.

In other words, perceiving the world is a process of sampling it. The sample is, relatively, almost infinitesimally small. We only see the side of things which is turned towards us, their backs are seldom and their insides hardly ever explored. They are only viewed intermittently, seldom from close to, and enormously the great part of the universe is never seen at all. Furthermore, there is every reason to suppose that the sample on which all our knowledge of the universe is based is not a fair sample, for there is every reason to suppose that the presence of sense organs in a region of space, which is how the sample is taken, makes a difference to what is going on there. Worse than this, that process of sampling in which perceiving consists is unlike the process of sampling the opinions of housewives, for though in both cases there are different ways of obtaining one's sample – with and without spectacles, for example – in the case of housewives, sampling is made necessary only by shortage of time; it would be possible, if the worst came to the worst, to ask them all. But in the case of perception there can be no such thing as checking on the sample by viewing everything all at once from every possible point of view, or viewing things without eyes to avoid being responsive to only a selection of the radiation which emanates from objects.

A corollary of the view that we perceive material objects directly, without any intermediary, is the view that the only cognitive faculty in the human mind necessary to enable us to know that what we see is, say, a chair, is having seen chairs before and remembering having been told that they are chairs – that is, the faculty of recognition. This simplistic view, however, ignores an important distinction. There are two different experiments a psychologist might make on some rather unintelligent subjects. First of all, he might wish to test their powers of recognising things they had seen before; so he flashes on a screen before them pictures of chairs, pictures of tables, pictures of lions, pictures of people and then when, as they probably will, they say of the picture of a lion, 'That is a lion', he gives them a good mark for getting the answer right. In this experiment, all the subjects need to be able to do in order to give correct answers is to recognise things that they have already seen. The word 'lion' is being used in a somewhat emasculated way, for, as both experimenter and subject well know, the things on the screen are not really lions, but pictures of lions. The second experiment is a little more complicated. Sometimes the psychologist flashes pictures of lions on a screen; at other times he makes the screen instantaneously transparent, and shows his subjects real lions behind the screen. The object of the game is for the subjects to guess correctly when they are being shown lions and when pictures of lions, etc. In this case, if they say of a picture of a lion that it is a lion, they will not, as in the former experiment, be getting the answer right, but getting it wrong. And, in order for them to get the answer right, more will be necessary than for them to have a capacity for recognising things that they have seen before. They must, in addition, have at least a capacity for making predictions on the basis of past experience, for, a subject of the second experiment, in saying that what he sees is a lion, is making predictions which he is deliberately not making when he says of this lion-looking thing that it is a lion. This does not mean that a capacity for recognising things seen before, together with a capacity for making inductive inferences (both of which capacities presuppose memory) are the only cognitive capacities involved in perception. In addition we must, at the very least, have a capacity for fitting together successively perceived bits of a vast mosaic to form a simultaneous unitary and coherent picture of the world in a single space and time. But to go into this question in any detail would be a task for at least one other paper.

The final reason why I deplore the disrepute into which the sense-datum theory has fallen is that it removes from philosophers an opportunity of exercising their imaginations, a faculty which is at least as important to a philosopher as analytical skill. Perception throws a pin-point of light on the vastness of the universe, and what is in the darkness beyond is a matter for speculation. Such speculation is, of course, a proper activity of natural scientists. There is, however, a great deal to be said for the view once expressed by Bertrand Russell, that natural scientists put forward theories about the form of the universe, not about its matter. They put forward theories about the laws governing the universe, but not about the inner nature of the things which obey those laws. But these things must have some inner nature or other, and perhaps speculating about what it is is one function proper to philosophy. It might even be possible to find interpretations for physical laws which make these laws apply to things quite unlike what physicists suppose their laws apply to, if, indeed, they suppose anything at all about this. In particular, it does not seem to me that Russell's once-held view that things are just vast systems of mostly unsensed sensibilia or, if modified, the Leibnizian view that they are about the interconnected perceptions of rudimentary minds, are so absurd as they have been supposed to be by some. Since it is logically impossible that we should ever be able to settle this question by observation, we are allowed to be weighted by considerations of coherence and aesthetic elegance. Indeed, we have no alternative. Aesthetically, a Leibniz–Russell view has much to recommend it. But if we reject the sense-datum theory, we are unlikely even to ask the questions to which such theories are an answer, and, to this extent, we shall be intellectually the poorer. It is in an attempt to reopen options such as these that I have written this paper.

MAIN PUBLICATIONS

Our Knowledge of Right and Wrong (George Allen & Unwin, Muirhead Library of Philosophy, 1971)
Hume's Moral Epistemology (OUP, forthcoming)

TIME-TRANSCENDENCE AND SOME RELATED PHENOMENA IN THE ARTS

by

R. W. Hepburn

Professor of Moral Philosophy, University of Edinburgh

The words 'transcend', 'transcendence' and their cognates make occasional appearances in descriptions of experience of the Arts. Some of these appearances are entirely trivial and philosophically insignificant, for in them 'transcend' could be replaced by various other 'going-beyond' words without metaphysical or religious implications. Other appearances, however, are certainly intended to carry such implications, and sometimes even to resonate with ideas of divine transcendence and of a divine mode of awareness. I begin by noting three specimen contexts in which this may occur.

1. From the side of metaphysics and theology: if a writer is trying to give some content to the notion of a transcendent and perfect deity, and in particular to the mode of awareness such a deity might be thought to have, he may well reflect that since he cannot avoid extrapolating from human experience, he ought to draw on that experience where it is least deficient and can point towards still less deficient forms. Now, among human experiences aesthetic experiences are peculiarly valued not least because of their abnormal intensity, their facilitating of expansions of consciousness, synoptic grasping of complexes, and other features I shall mention shortly. It is not surprising that analogies from aesthetic experience have been found tempting by theistic writers in characterising some aspects of the conjectural divine awareness.

2. Working the other way: a writer on aesthetics may wish to put some aspects of art-experience in a new light, to show up

certain connections, perhaps continuities, which he discerns between the aesthetic and the religious. Again the vocabulary of 'transcendence 'may be judged relevant.

3. My third sort of case is very different. On occasion, a writer may want to relate the domains of art and religion much more closely and boldly, seeing art as able to intimate a divine transcendence, presenting the world in a way that carries what H. D. Lewis has called clear 'traces of a sphere beyond that of finite experience'. With this third sort of claim (deeply interesting though it is) I shall not be centrally concerned in this paper.

There is no stable, unified aesthetic use of transcendence-language, and I am not trying to pretend that there is. I am aware also that there is marvellous scope for vague and inflated uses, for dressing up the commonplace in pretentious and solemn clothes. Nevertheless I believe that the language can, in some contexts, play a useful, illuminating role, can bring out certain important connections among the different arts and between the values of art and of religion: provided it is used cautiously and with full awareness of its perils.

One recurrent use of the language relates to the overcoming of successiveness, the transcending of *time*. Poetry and music both, as arts of time, consist necessarily of temporally successive parts. Yet sheer successiveness does not exhaust their natures as we experience them. We do not let each element, word or note fall from awareness as soon as it is uttered or sounded. We build them into meanings, melodies and even larger unities if the work assists us, approaching a grasp of a complex work as a totality. It is natural and not uncommon to speak of this ideal grasp of the whole as a 'transcending' of the temporal flux. (This is transcendence, clearly, in an epistemological, not an ontological context.) Gabriel Marcel wrote, of music, for instance: 'Gradually, as I pass from tone to tone, a certain *ensemble* emerges, a form is built up, which very surely cannot be reduced to an organised succession of states. It is of the very essence of this form to reveal itself as duration, and yet to transcend, in its own way, the purely temporal order in which it is manifested.'[1]

It is clear from this, that though, like Marcel here, I am going to draw my material from the Arts, the subject-matter could

[1] 'Bergsonism et musique', *La Revue Musicale*, VII, 3 pp. 223f.; quoted S. K. Langer, *Feeling and Form* (Routledge, 1953), pp. 116f.

readily be extended beyond them. Collingwood, in *The Principles of Art*, considers the experience of hearing a thrush singing. 'By mere sensation', he writes, 'I hear at any given moment only one note or one fragment of a note. By imagination what I have been hearing continues to vibrate in my thought as an idea, so that the whole sung phrase is present to me as an idea at a single moment' (p. 253). I am, in fact, simply breaking off a small part of the agenda for a study of time-consciousness in general, and of temporal synthesis more particularly.

On poetry and time-transcendence there is an interesting study by P. A. Hutchings (University of Western Australia) in *The Journal of Aesthetics and Art-Criticism* (1970–1), 'Imagination: "as the Sun Paints in the Camera Obscura" '; also a companion paper, in *Philosophical Studies*,* ' "Words After Speech". . .' (I shall comment here chiefly on the first of these.) By way of a discussion of Lessing, Herder and particularly Coleridge, Hutchings describes the ideal of so integrating a poem, making the internal relations of its elements so tight, that the reader is enabled to grasp its meaning as nearly as possible instantaneously or non-successively. 'The mind follows the words in time; and takes the meaning a-temporally' (p. 66); although an utterance 'takes time to say', it may not take time 'to mean' (p. 65). In a poem like Keats's ode *To Autumn*, where we have a record of revisions to the text, we can observe the poet tightening the unity of the poem, enabling 'the mind to surround the core of meaning, and to take it panoramically, rather than . . . serially and temporally' (p. 74). Hutchings sums up: 'Poetry would transcend the essence of its own medium, escaping from the serial into the instantaneous; and this transcendence is of the essence of poetry' (p. 74).

For a further example, consider George Poulet's account of Maurice Scève's poetry, in vol. IV of *Études sur le temps humain* (*Mesure de l'instant*, 1968). This is a poetry in which a dense, compact complexity of thought and feeling is presented in a minimum of duration. All the elements are so closely intertwined that the effect can register only as *one*. It is all there, gathered up, not as yet unfolded ('ramassé . . . non encore déroulé'). If complex, then at the same time *simple*, because unified. (See pp. 9, 15.)

To state the obvious: these accounts imply very clearly that to

* Vol. XXII, pp. 17–37.

transcend time, to experience a non-temporal unity, is *better*, is a more valuable state of affairs, than to remain merely a recipient of successive events. The temporality of a temporal art is something to be at least partially overcome. Such a view of time and the non-temporal has, of course, a long and distinguished ancestry; discussion of it continues today. Something needs to be said about the view in general, before we consider further its appearances in aesthetic theory, and I begin by quoting a few sentences from Plotinus's Tractate, 'On Eternity and Time' (*Enneads*, III, 7), which played a vital part in giving philosophical articulation and imaginative force to that view:

'we must think of eternity not only in terms of rest, but of unity . . . as without extension or interval One sees eternity in seeing a life that . . . always has the all present to it, not now this and then again that, but all things at once, . . . a partless completion, as if they were all together in a point . . . 'always in the present, because nothing of it has passed away . . . That, then, which was not, and will not be, but *is* only, [that] which is static . . . is eternity. The life all together and full . . . is eternity.'[2]

The soul has, in a sense, 'fallen' from eternity into time, due to its 'restlessly active nature'. Because of this 'unquiet power', it 'did not want the whole to be present to it all together'. In this context, Plotinus uses an important simile: soul is like a seed, initially compressed, condensed and concentrated, timelessly holding all its being in unity. It advances itself, or so it imagines, towards self-enhancement in growth; but in fact this amounts instead only to a squandering and dissipating of its unity outside itself, and it 'goes forward to a weaker extension'. This is the outcome of soul's 'putting itself into time'.[3] (Note, in passing, how close Poulet, in 1968, comes to Plotinus's simile, in the aesthetic context I quoted. 'Tout est là, ramassé, non encore déroulé.')

We cannot here follow through the development of these ideas and the modifications they underwent in passing into Christian thought. Boethius is, of course, the key (and much quoted) author in the initiating of this development.

[2] Plotinus, op. cit., III, 7; Sections 2, 3 (trans. Armstrong).
[3] ibid., III, 7, Section 11.

It is not at all difficult to understand how the life of temporal successiveness could be seen as a second-best life. Deficiency does seem involved where past states are inaccessible or 'lost', and future states are inaccessibly 'not yet'. Not even an infinite succession of temporal states – a 'sempiternal' existence – would overcome these particular deficiences: only a possession of experience *totum simul*, as a simultaneous whole.[4]

To show the religious impressiveness and *prima facie* inevitability of this idea of time-transcendence is not, however, to demonstrate its ultimate *coherence*. There may well be insurmountable difficulty in trying to hold on to the notion of mental activity and awareness together with a complete annulling of all successiveness. Various philosophers have argued that if we seriously think away all successiveness, we thereby whittle away to nothing any idea of mental activity. Even if we do have moments of experience that are particularly rich, compressed or 'meaningful', they are moments preceded and followed by other moments in the flux of time; and we can attach no meaning to a claim that all our experience (or that God's experience) might be wholly devoid of temporal flow.

Other recent criticisms include the argument that eternity as a timeless *totum simul* is a contradictory or self-defeating idea, because '*simul* is itself a temporal notion'. 'Things in time happen either successively or together (*simul*) and to say that the parts of time, past, present and future happen together is to deny the necessary condition of simultaneity.'[5] Or again, there is contradiction in the claim that an eternal, non-temporal being (God, in the first instance) could have *knowledge*; for knowledge is essentially 'datable', that is to say, *in time*.[6] N. Pike argues, in his *God and Timelessness* (1970), that a timeless being could scarcely be counted as a person: 'a timeless being could not deliberate, anticipate, or remember'. It 'could not be affected or prompted by another . . . could not respond' (p. 128).

[4] For a recent argument on these lines, see A. C. Ewing, *Value and Reality* (George Allen & Unwin, 1973), pp. 279ff. God's perfection requires that the whole time-series should be present to him. Ewing discusses the matter, interestingly, in the terminology of McTaggart's *A* and *B* series.

[5] M. Kneale, *Proc. Arist. Soc.* (1968–9), p. 227.

[6] E. J. Khamara, 'Eternity and Omniscience', *Philosophical Quarterly* (1974); see also W. Kneale, 'Time and Eternity in Theology', *Proc. Arist. Soc.* (1960–1).

Supposing these criticisms are justified, they would not prevent us from still attaching high value to various approaches to the experience of a 'timeless whole': but it would now be misleading to think of the temporal mode of experience as second best to a mode of experience from which all successiveness has in fact been removed. For the latter cannot be coherently described. Our situation, then, would be one in which temporal successiveness is basic and necessary, but in which partial transcendings of time are possible, and can be highly prized for their intensity and richness of content presented with unusual immediacy. We should be capable, in some limited measure, of 'living more fully' – to recall Boethius (*amplius*) – than we live in the 'fleeting and transitory moment'.[7]

In the case of works of art – to return to aesthetics – the peculiar unity-to-perception of some temporal works furthers that synoptic grasping which occurs in the appreciation of poetry and music both. But, it has to be stressed, it is from *time*, the temporally spread-out, that the non-temporal structure emerges: and, further, it is because we remain aware of the temporally serial nature of the medium – never completely transcended – that we experience delight and astonishment at the partial transcendence. The approach I am suggesting (to repeat) does not see aesthetic time-transcendence as an 'earnest' of a wholly non-successive eternal life hereafter, nor is it a salvaging and secularising of a religious conception which just happens not to be actualised in a deity. But let us develop the aesthetic implications in more detail.

I am saying, to put it somewhat crudely, that we should not have a more aesthetically interesting situation if the 'meaning' or 'structure' of a work could be somehow presented by a wholly non-temporal medium. The noteworthy thing is the co-presence of successiveness, vividly registering on the senses, and the non-

[7] *Consol.* V § VI, lines 16ff. We can distinguish two kinds of case in which an endless approach is made to an ideal of experience or of behaviour or of theoretical understanding. (1) In the first of these, the goal, even if unattainable, is at least coherently conceptualisable. For instance, the unifying of moral principles or virtues, or the unifying of fundamental laws of nature. (2) In the second, a 'direction of approach' is still discernible, but the goal itself is not at all surely conceivable, and may even in fact be finally incoherent. Nevertheless, the pursuit of this goal may still bring about real, not illusory, value. A possible instance may be the idea of an approach to 'direct' or 'certain' knowledge of another's mind.

successive structure that emerges. The transcendence is *necessarily incomplete*. One of Hutchings' example-poems – Keats's 'To Autumn' – undoubtedly lends itself to his purpose of showing the actual tightening of organisational unity by a poet in his corrections and revisions. But no less could the same poem remind us of the importance for poetry also of the sound of the words, their sensual values, the varying tempi required by them as they are read aloud. The poem is what I shall call 'temporal adventure' as well as non-temporal structure or meaning. The same is true of the tiny poem by Aldous Huxley to which Hutchings also appeals:

A MELODY BY SCARLATTI

How clear under the trees,
How swiftly the music flows,
Rippling from one still pool to another,
Into the lake of silence.

This certainly does exemplify, and speak *about*, simultaneity of comprehension and 'stillness' after serial presentation of elements; but in addition it displays the importance of temporal adventure. The movement, the flow, of the verse, follows the flow of the water, and both image the flow, the individual movement, of the Scarlatti music.

In *musical* aesthetics also there is a danger that if a writer is impressed by phenomena of temporal synthesis, simultaneous, synoptic grasp (and these are indeed remarkable), he may tend to dwell on them too exclusively, in a way that may in the end impoverish his overall account. In his *Introduction à J-S Bach* (1947), B. de Schloezer shows this onesideness:

'Si l'acte intellectuel qui permet à l'auditeur de comprendre l'oeuvre musicale, si la synthèse effectuée au cours de l'exécution exige un certain laps de temps de telle sorte que l'exécution achevée cet auditeur peut constater qu'elle a duré tant de minutes, ce qu'il a écouté et compris, l'oeuvre est intemporelle comme sont intemporels un poème, une dissertation philosophique, et pour la même raison : comme eux elle a un sens. Elle est hors du temps, bien que son audition se fasse dans le temps. . . . Elle m'est présente en la totalité de ses parties comme l'est un tableau'. (p. 30)

'Organiser musicalement le temps, c'est le transcender'. (p. 31)

De Schloezer is criticised by Mikel Dufrenne on the score that his approach 'over-intellectualises' music.[8] 'Music', writes Dufrenne, 'is not an object of the *intellect*, but a *perceived* object.' My own complaint is rather that in this passage de Schloezer risks seriously downplaying the musical values that belong essentially to 'temporal adventure'. For an excellent and clear corrective, we could turn to Charles Rosen, in *The Classical Style* (1971):

'In too much writing on music, a work appears like a large system of inter-relationships in which the order, the intensity, and, above all, the direction of the relations are of secondary, and even negligible, consideration. Too often, the music could be played backward without affecting the analysis in any significant way. This is to treat music as a spatial art. Yet the movement from past to future is more significant in music than the movement from left to right in a picture . . . There must be a constant interaction between the individual motif and the direction of the piece – the intensity and proportions of its gradual unfolding'. (pp. 40f.)[9]

Hutchings, in ' "Words after Speech". . .', quotes an apposite passage by Gabriel Marcel on *reading*. Consider the series of acts of consciousness by which I attend to the constituent parts of the discourse I am reading. 'These acts,' Marcel writes, 'however, appear on reflection to be completely exterior, indifferent to' the 'intelligible total, the *totum simul*'. I want rather to say: in prose, normally, this is so; but in poetry and in music the relation between serially presented components and final 'meaning' or pattern is by no means 'exterior', but very intimate. Marcel himself, however, stressed the two aspects together impeccably, when he wrote the words already quoted earlier: 'It is of the very essence of [musical form] to reveal itself as duration, and yet to transcend, in its own way, the purely temporal order in which it is manifested.'

[8] *Phénoménologie de l'expérience esthétique* (1953), p. 276.

[9] Contrast de Schloezer's comparison between a piece of music and a picture.

Music as we know it is not a falling short of an ideal of *totally* non-temporal presentations. That is an unimaginable ideal – indeed an incoherent notion. We can apprehend a musical structure only if note follows note in temporal succession. The transcending of time depends on the continuing flow of the music in time, the flow that keeps bringing nearer the final cadence. The time-transcendence is real enough, but once more it is a necessarily incomplete transcendence. We are not on the way to (or catching a glimpse of or experiencing an earnest of) a thorough eliminating of successiveness. We are experiencing how from the temporal, or with the temporal as a necessary and continuing base, there can emerge what *prima facie* is incompatible with the temporal. A sense of the *Distance* between these can be, or can become, a lively element in our aesthetic experience itself. And I shall use the word 'Distance' in this way in the remainder of this study. From this perspective we are not seeing the intermittent and fugitive nature of the time-transcending experiences as a lamentable 'fall' from an eternal mode of being, a dragging down of the soul by the sensuous and material, with their *partes extra partes*. On the contrary, we can see the time-transcending as a product of the interaction of mind precisely with the sensuous and the material. In this context, these latter are experienced not as its enemies, nor to be superseded, but as the necessary conditions of its activity.

Before going further, I ought to acknowledge one oversimplification. I have been contrasting temporal adventure with timeless meaning or structure. This contrast is rough and provisional only. For temporal adventure cannot be analysed in terms of sheer successiveness. A sense of climax, anticipation, tension, release from tension, of gaining or losing momentum – these are essentials of temporal adventure, and they all involve minor syntheses, or minor synopses, the grasping of successive drifts and directions of change; and they are thus themselves impositions of order upon the flux, even if of a subordinate kind. It is only at the limit – with an unstructured succession of sounds, or when sounds are heard in a state of extreme passivity, as in semi-consciousness – that synthesising is attenuated towards vanishing-point.

Have I not come very near to precisely that thesis which I have supposedly rejected – namely that it is the synthesised, timeless 'meaning' that is alone the aesthetically significant thing? Not altogether; for the sense of temporal adventure needs to be analysed in terms of a multiplicity of successive and overlapping minor syntheses, their very temporal successiveness being itself crucially present to awareness. What is certainly and profoundly right about the thesis of timeless meaning is that in a closely organised work of art all the minor syntheses have a plainly partial, provisional, incomplete character. We have to acknowledge hierarchies of synopses or syntheses, at the highest level of which we seek the meaning or sense or overall structure of a work of art as a whole, in a single intuition.

Another study in musical aesthetics which has relevant and arresting things to say on these topics is Victor Zuckerkandl's *Sound and Symbol* (English edition 1956): 'The force that gives meaning is in the tone as life is in a face; . . . non-physical, it is yet one with the physical appearance and cannot appear save through a material medium, which it nevertheless infinitely transcends' (p. 68f). Music is essentially motion and direction; but it is motion neither of psychical contents nor of bodily things. This pure or 'primal' motion involves a transcending of spatiotemporal bearers. It can be called an 'internal transcendence'; for it is one that 'does not lead away from the phenomenon but into it, to its core' (p. 147). Zuckerkandl is not at all tempted to over-stress the simultaneous-whole, time-transcending aspects of music. Rather, for him, the phenomenon of music calls in question any claims that a perfect mode of consciousness would be exclusively a-temporal. In fanciful vein he writes: A God 'beyond time in timeless eternity would have to renounce music'. And this 'argues against God's timelessness. Are we to suppose that we mortals, in possessing such a wonder as music, are more privileged than God'? (p. 151). Fanciful, yes: but serious as well, and it agrees with the claim that time-transcendence, if it *ousted* temporal successiveness, would make for an attenuating-to-vanishing-point, not an enriching, of experience.

Zuckerkandl is both interesting and unsatisfactory on the question of how to analyse in more detail our synthesis of musical elements, as we do in hearing a rhythm or a pulse or in grasping a melody. He takes an example of the simplest sort. If we are to hear the second beat of a bar *as* the second beat, the first beat must not be 'lost in non-existence'; for then ' "two" [beat two] would be simply a second "one" and nothing more' (p. 225). But Zuckerkandl denies that this is a matter of remembering 'one' while 'two' is sounding. To recall the previous tone, to be vividly aware of 'one' in memory, would cause the cessation of 'all perception of meter' (p. 227), and cause us to lose the thread of any melody. Conversely, any *anticipating* of beat or continuation of the music is again incompatible with the concentration on the present that is necessary to experiencing musical metre. Ruling out memory, Zuckerkandl is forced to say that 'the present of "one" is a present directed toward the future, pregnant with future' (p. 226). 'The present of musical metre, then, contains within it a past that is not remembered and a future that is not foreknown . . . as a thing directly given in experience itself' (p. 227). 'Time itself stores' the past, and 'the future is not an impenetrable wall . . . because the being of time is an anticipating itself' (p. 228).

It seems to me that Zuckerkandl is forced into these paradoxes about time through working with over-simplified notions of memory and anticipation. Certainly an episodic and fully-heeded *recalling* of beat 'one' would block rather than facilitate the perception of a metrical pattern, when beat 'two' is sounding; and a lively auditory image of an anticipated following tone would destroy one's hearing of a melody. But memory is much more than recall-episodes and images, and expectation is more than episodes of imagining future events. I need not *recall* episodes of a person's past behaviour to be aware, through memory, of his present behaviour as characteristic or unusual for him. If I come to hear a beat or a phrase as 'pregnant with' a particular future, this can happen only if the past has given me some perceptual ground for that continuation. It cannot be *simply* the present beat or phrase that has its future contained within it, in monad-fashion. For that beat or phrase would be in itself no different, were it to have *no* future – whether due to the performer breaking off his performance, or the composer having changed his time-signature or interrupted his melody.

Summing up the main argument so far. The language of 'transcendence' makes appearances in aesthetics. When referring to the arts of time, transcendence language often connects, directly or remotely, with the pair of metaphysical correlates, 'time'/'eternity'. On the one hand, I have argued that an important source of the interest and value of temporal works of art is indeed their ability to elicit 'time-transcending' structures and meanings. On the other hand, I am doubtful whether the notion of eternity in its thoroughgoing metaphysical development is a fully coherent notion. More bluntly, it may be that all we can have of eternity, indeed all there is of eternity to have, are such time-dependent deliverances from time; and they are none the less remarkable for that, perhaps the more to be valued. Even in the aesthetic context, however, we can prize them too exclusively. There are aesthetic values proper to flow as well as to stasis; and it is only if we are keenly aware of *both* in one aesthetic experience, that the gulf between them, the Distance as I am calling it, and the emergence nevertheless of the one from the other, can be wonderingly appreciated.

In the same volume of *The Journal of Aesthetics and Art-Criticism* as Patrick Hutchings' article, there appeared also a long article by W. V. Spanos, called 'Modern Literary Criticism and the Spatialization of Time: an Existential Critique'. The juxtaposition of the two articles is interestingly relevant to the present study; for Spanos, instead of seeing the time-transcending moment of literature as a high fulfilment, sees the aspiration for simultaneity as misguided and harmful. Since human life is fundamentally life in time and contingency, if literature is to engage seriously with the problems of human existence, it must resist the 'impulse to disengage' from that temporality and contingency: must not see these as 'defilement'. Yet, Spanos argues, such disengagement has recurrently been sought, over recent decades.

Wilhelm Worringer (1908) wrote of the urge to abstraction, the geometrical and dehumanised, and of a quest for 'tranquillity' in a universe perceived as an alien, arbitrary 'flux of happening'. Art, in this aspect, seeks to 'eternalise' objects 'by approximation to abstract forms', wresting them out of the flux. Imagist aesthetics (e.g. T. E. Hulme) caught up this theme; and a poem was characteristically described as a static, timeless artefact, very often in metaphors drawn from the static *visual* arts. The implied metaphysical depreciation of the temporal world was expressed no less clearly. Furthermore, the erstwhile New Critics repeat the same emphases, even the visual metaphors, such as Urns and Icons, seeing a literary work 'as if it were a static visual object, an unmoving whole without sequence, and thus, unlike life, devoid of those qualitative distinctions . . . between one moment in time and the next . . . that give motion to or better, that dramatize experience'. To the New Critics and like-minded readers, 'the critical act begins . . . only after the reading . . . terminates; at the vantage-point, that is, from which, like an omniscient god, which . . . man cannot be, no matter how good his memory – one sees all its temporal parts *at once* as a whole . . . thus radically minimizing the sequential dimension and reducing the existential experience'. Spanos comes down on the side of Lessing, against Herder (and Hutchings). That is to say, despite Imagists and New Critics, a literary work 'is not *in fact* a piece of sculpture or a painting'. He regrets and opposes 'the obsessive effort of the modern literary imagination to escape the destructive impact of time and change' in favour of the 'timeless eternity of the aesthetic moment' (p. 91) – a 'futile solipsistic pursuit' (p. 98). In place of an urge to the abstract, he commends an 'urge to engagement, or dialogic encounter with the dreadful world of crisis generated by temporal flux', one that does not 'reject or subdue the temporal' (p. 95). As examples of writers who have been impelled by this urge to engagement, Spanos cites, among others, the author(s) of the Book of Job, Shakespeare, Tolstoy and Dostoevsky. Finally, Spanos sees continuations of those tendencies which he deplores, in the cult of the psychedelic, in the Happening, in Anti-art generally and the currently fashionable down-playing of subject-matter in literature.

My contact with this article is indirect, in that I am concerned rather less with the recent-historical succession of artistic styles, movements and fashions (with their manifestos) and more with locating fundamental features of art and aesthetic experience, features common to many movements, though I do not dare to say all. Art may have no non-historical essence. But if my contact with Spanos is not head-on, I do contact him obliquely.

His article is probably correct that an out-and-out, exclusive pursuit of the values of timelessness and simultaneity has often been linked with a metaphysic unsympathetic to the world of temporal change, and failing to take time-involved life seriously enough. I can see no reason, however, why this pursuit need be exclusive; it may coexist with other pursuits, and the implied metaphysic may be neither onesidedly world-denying nor world-affirming. Analogously, the responsible Christian mystic is not permanently disengaged from the world of time and action. In both cases there can be movement back and forth between temporal and eternal concerns. Indeed, the condensed, gathered-up realisation of a complex meaning simultaneously may effect just such revision of life-commitments as Spanos takes with particular seriousness. That is, there is no sharp or necessary opposition between the instantaneously grasped vision or meaning-complex, and the moral or political–existential relevance of a work of literature. The point can be illustrated by a Blake Song of Innocence or Experience, or, in prose, by a tightly organised story like Solzhenitsyn's 'For the Good of the Cause'. In the case of art, to 'take out of time' is not necessarily to deflect the arrows of relevance between art-works and human temporal existence.

In a word : there are temptations of very different and understandable kinds to overemphasise onesidedly the aspect of timelessness and the aspect of temporal flow. But why be onesided? A concern with both aspects is legitimate : and the interplay between the two levels, flow and instantaneous-grasp-of-meaning, itself enters – as I have argued – as a constituent in the enjoyment of poetry and music. So too does the actual experienced *emergence* of the latter from the former – transcending, without discarding or annulling, the experience of temporal movement, direction and change.[10]

If we make too much of the alleged continuities between Imagist-apologetics, Anti-art and psychedelic experience . . . we are likely to blur a vital distinction. This distinction can, I think, best be made in terms of two kinds of 'immediacy'. The first is an empty, contentless immediacy, sought after by those who radically distrust or repudiate all available forms of articulation. In the pursuit of it no new forms are created. So there is resort to psychedelic euphoria, or to mystical experience of a quite unfocused kind. The second sort of immediacy is very different. It has a rich

[10] Among literary critics Murray Krieger is particularly alert to the dangers of onesided emphasis on the timeless emergent structure. See his study, 'The Ekphrastic Principle and the Still Movement of Poetry; or *Laokoö* Revisited' (*The Play and Place of Criticism* (J. Hopkins Press, 1967)), to which Patrick Hutchings' second paper drew my attention. 'Through pattern, through context, [literature] has the unique power to celebrate time's movement as well as to arrest it, to arrest it in the very act of celebrating it' (p. 125). '. . . the aesthetic desire for pure and eternal form must not be allowed merely to freeze the entity-denying chronological flow of experience in its unrepeatable variety' (p. 126). If the flow of time is neglected, 'poetry is hardened into static, Platonic discourse that has lost touch with . . . our existential motions' (p. 127).

Krieger does justice both to the 'empirically progressive and [the] transcendent conversion of the empirical into the archetypal, even as it remains empirical' (p. 127).

content and is the instantaneous grasp by the mind of a complex meaning, pattern or way of seeing or articulating. It is clearly this second type of immediacy which is facilitated by the temporal works of art chiefly referred to in this study. It involves a rich content that can, if we wish, be made explicit in subsequent analysis, although in actual appreciation the whole is experienced as a single, vivid and convincing vision – whether it be of autumn, or love or death or the human predicament as such.

The pursuit in art of 'empty immediacy' amounts to a capitulating before the problems of how to fashion adequate and fresh articulations of experience, free from cliché. 'Full' or 'dense immediacy', in literature for instance, adds creatively to the resources of language. A new context is fashioned, a field of force set up by means of which words are made to say what they had not said before. In more general terms, dense immediacy retains and celebrates the sensuous base of experience, though it transforms it very far from the qualities of the sheerly and serially 'given': the result is both sensuous and the synthesis of new unities. *Because* it retains that sensuous base, it is happily free from the moral ambiguities of certain radically world-denying and world-transcending forms of mysticism.[11]

We now need to ask – though very briefly – whether there are other effects, in any of the arts, at all significantly analogous to the time-transcendence effects we have been considering. I take the main features to be these: (1) 'transcendence' in the sense of the emergence from some medium of an aesthetic effect seemingly incongruous in some fundamental way with that medium (as non-temporal structure is with temporal flow); (2) the necessarily incomplete character of the transcendence, retaining the sensuously given while transforming it; and (3) the sense of Distance between medium and emergent effects. At this point I need to give myself a renewed reminder of the dangers of a purely verbal and unilluminating extension of terminology.

I think it is possible to single out a roughly analogous set of cases in the non-temporal visual arts. But I am not going to claim either that the vocabulary of 'transcendence' is as a matter of

[11] On the latter, see John Passmore, *The Perfectibility of Man* (Duckworth, 1972), especially chs 14 and 15, his article in *Encounter*, April 1974, and his book, *Man's Responsibility for Nature* (Duckworth, 1974). Also relevant is J. E. Smith, 'Being, Immediacy and Articulation', *Review of Metaphysics* (1971).

fact used in writing about these cases, or that one cannot sensitively describe them without that vocabulary. All I am claiming is that bringing the vocabulary into play here may make connections that are worth making.

Consider, for example, a pen or brush drawing, of trees and buildings in brilliant sunshine. (For an actual example, Rembrandt's 'Cottages Beneath High Trees in Bright Sunlight', pen, ink and wash. It is reproduced in Philip Rawson's *Drawing* (1969), p. 312.) Let it be executed with few lines, and yet those few lines capture the dazzle, the essence of a sun-drenched scene. The drawing is very far from being a mere *reminder* of a piece of countryside in sun, nor is it a substitute for that. We cannot fail to be aware as we look at it that no more than some exiguous black marks on white are before us – *prima facie* quite inadequate to evoke sun, dazzle and shimmer.[12] But they do evoke it; and a sense of that Distance between the *prima facie* capacity of the medium and the actual aesthetic effect remains a primary ingredient in the enjoyment of the drawing: a sense which, of course, we cannot have when we confront a sun-drenched vista in nature. The analogy with the temporal cases is not too remote: out of the temporally successive (and transcending it) comes the non-temporal meaning; out of the meagre, seemingly insufficient scribbles and blobs comes a most vivid impression of an extensive, variously-lit world. Analogously too, we do not wish the transcending could be 'complete': that is to say, we do not want the medium to obliterate itself, to become transparent and disappear, the drawing or painting to become a *trompe l'oeil*, like a window on nature. For if it did, there would vanish also the sense of Distance and hence of aesthetic transcendence, for these require the medium to remain clearly perceptible, in its inkiness or paintiness. The aesthetic experience would be less highly valued, not more highly, were these obliterated.[13]

A contrasting example may make this clearer. A stereoscopic viewer produces a strong sense of three-dimensionality from a pair

[12] Compare E. Gilson, *Painting and Reality* (Routledge, 1957), p. 120: 'Some pen drawings by Corot are enough to give existence to charming landscapes that seem to be made from nothing, and almost with nothing'. See also Gilson's plate 40: Corot, 'The Broken Bridge'.

[13] Cf. Stuart Hampshire, *Feeling and Expression* (H. K. Lewis, 1961), pp. 14f.: quoted Wollheim, *On Drawing an Object*, § 21. A revealing representation needs an alien or resisting medium through which it is filtered.

of two-dimensional pictures, pictures of the same scene from view-points some two or three inches apart. But, when we view, the two-dimensional picture-surface wholly disappears. The perception of depth may well give pleasure; but the relevant contrast here is between our knowledge that the pictures are flat and our perception of depth, not between the simultaneous perception of picture-plane and represented depth. So Distance, in the metaphorical sense I have introduced, cannot be savoured as it can in a painting or drawing, where the medium remains a focus of perception.

Distance is threatened in another way when an artist's drawing conventions are stereotyped formulae, coded allusions to objects. The graphic means used may in such cases again be exiguous, but to the extent that it approaches a lazy symbolic script, it loses visual immediacy. That is to say, transcendence and sense of Distance certainly have a place among the criteria of aesthetic achievement, here again as in poetry and music; and they are not mechanically attainable by means of economical but stale representational formulae, like the formulae of a typical strip-cartoon. Further, there is no automatic guarantee that the choice of a medium or representational mode very distant from the overt subject-matter of a work of art will *necessarily* evoke an experience of Distance, of the kind we are discussing. Minute carvings in ivory, yes, but hardly in granite: the song of the lark ascending – in the violin, but not in a consort of trombones.

The topic of apparent inadequacy of means appears interestingly if briefly in Reynolds' *Discourses.* In *Discourse Eleven* (1782) he argues that the close resemblance between a waxwork and its original object may be actually disagreeable to the spectator; and that, thus, our pleasure in imitation is 'not increased merely in proportion as it approaches to minute and detailed reality; we are pleased, on the contrary, by seeing ends accomplished by seemingly inadequate means' (ed. Collier–Macmillan, p. 171). 'To express distances on a plain surface, softness by hard bodies, and particular colouring by materials which are not singly of that colour, produces that magick which is the prize and triumph of art.' Moreover, on occasion, the 'effect of imitation' is 'fully compassed by means still more inadequate': when 'the power of a few well-chosen strokes, which supersede labour by judgment and direction, produce a complete impression of all that the mind demands in an object'. The pleasure, once again, is clearly in the revealing of unlikely potentiality, in actually experiencing, contemplating, the emergence of the effect from the unpromising materials – soft from hard, three-dimensions from a two-dimensional surface, and we can add, in the art of time, the timeless from temporal flow. Oriental aesthetics as well as Western has seen this as an important theme to reckon with in any account of the arts. In China and Japan artists, under Zen and Taoist influence, have sought to obtain the maximum effect with the most exiguous means.[14]

A Platonist aesthetic can celebrate the compression and pregnance, the effects of *multum in parvo*, the capturing in few lines of what nature achieves only with great complexes of material bodies. But where my account diverges, once again, from a typically platonic one is in not in any way regretting or disparaging the bodily and sensuous media through which the aesthetic transcendence is attained; rather, enjoying these, together with a sense of the gap, the Distance, between them and the emergent effect. We experience a this-worldly transcendence that may not even intimate an other-worldly continuation or completion. To speak of compression and pregnance is in a sense to speak of an *attenuation* of the material, but one in which the material remaining is proportionately indispensable and necessary – every line and blob of it – to the resultant effect. The effect (in the drawing example and much representational art) is the capturing of the perceptual 'gist', the seizing of perceptual *character*, masses, light, dazzle, gloom, but without at all duplicating nature's own means – means that are *prima facie* indispensable.

We can make a further and, for this paper final, extension of topic to cover certain aesthetic effects which Susanne Langer brackets together as 'secondary illusions'. 'In the emergence of a secondary illusion', she writes,[15] '. . . an element is created which seems to belong to a different symbolic projection altogether from the substance of the work'; and she cites as examples a 'sudden impression of color in music', 'harmonic space', the expression of movement in a painting, a cathedral experienced as *drama* (p. 237, quoting Le Corbusier). Although she withholds

[14] Cf. P. Rawson, *Drawing* (OUP, 1969), p. 284.

[15] *Mind: An Essay on Human Feeling* (Johns Hopkins Press, 1967), vol. I, p. 230.

the honorific label 'transcendence' from all but a very small class of phenomena, she certainly sees these 'secondary illusions' as of peculiar interest and importance, and her reasons are relevant to our present themes:

'The art symbol . . . reflects the nature of mind as a culmination of life, and . . . exhibits first of all . . . the mysterious quality of intangible elements which arise from the growth and activity of the organism, yet do not seem entirely of its substance. The most powerful means to this is . . . the creation of secondary illusions.' (pp. 229f.)

'. . . All secondary illusions . . . have the same character of suddenly coming into existence from nowhere, . . . and fading again into nothing . . . Like fantasies, secondary illusions seem to have no somatic being; they are disembodied, yet they come out of the created form and heighten its livingness . . .' (p. 240)

Now let us connect these cases with my own last example of the drawing, and the comments made on that. In Mrs Langer's cases once more we have the emergence of an effect seemingly incommensurate with its means, whether visual or auditory: also a sense of 'strangeness' (p. 239) at the transition from one mode or level of consciousness to another. The impressiveness of some of these examples derives, I am sure, from the fact that what is caused to emerge, in the interplay between artefact and our invigorated imagination, are basic categorial features of experience – 'space' where there is literally no space but only sounding musical harmonies, 'movement' where nothing in fact shifts from one place to another. In other words, here are features of our experience under which we are normally quite passive become amenable to our initiative, responsive to our fiats. The more basically 'given' the feature, the more remarkable that we should acquire any dominance over it.

This helps us to understand some of the value attached to these aspects of art: but not all of it. The emerging of the timeless from time, of motion where no space is traversed, a sense of space in the wholly successive (and so on) can be experienced also as a mitigating or overcoming of the mutual exclusiveness of the ordinary modes of being and perceiving. And to exhibit meaning, intelligible structure and expressiveness in a peculiarly intense and concentrated form in the sensuous and the material, at least temporally reduces the sense of the foreignness of the material and spread-out to the mental and intentional. The outcome is a partial reconciliation to certain of the fundamental conditions of our existence, by way of a vivid and striking disclosure of their interconnections and mutual implication. Here again, the interpretative ways fork. The theist, Platonist and mystic will read all this as intimating a fuller and ultimate unity of being in God or the One; and will see its value in its reflecting of and witnessing to that ultimate unity. But it is also open to a person who has no confidence at all in any ultimate unification to set a high value upon that partial, and as far as he surmises incompletable, transcendence of the ordinary fragmentariness of experience. As I suggested in the case of 'eternity', so I suggest with respect to this much wider field at which we have latterly been glancing, that possibly the transcendence here may *consist* in the disclosure of those inter-communicatings and counter-intuitive emergings: and that we misinterpret these in taking them as pointing to a mysterious completion beyond our experience, since such completion cannot be coherently described.

From the viewpoint of a theistic apologist, the value of aesthetic transcendence phenomena is problematical. He could properly use them, along with other and more pervasive phenomena, to establish a foothold for the concept of transcendence as such. There is transcendence in passing from mere sense-experience to material objects, and from the behaviour of others to the minds of others; and in the field of the arts – time-transcendence and medium-transcendence. Analogously, he may argue, the world as a whole mediates our awareness of a being who altogether transcends that world. One has to concede that materials are provided, plentifully, for such an analogy, but the main apologetic weight would of course fall on the *additional* argument necessary to show that the world is in fact so transcended.

Again, the more stress is laid, in the aesthetic cases, on the idea of *emergence*, the less apologetic help these cases will offer. For God certainly cannot in any traditionally acceptable sense be said to 'emerge' from the world as a landscape emerges from an artist's brush-strokes.

Lastly, from a range of experiences, taken as 'necessarily

incomplete transcendence', there can be no direct argument to a total divine transcendence of the material, spatial and temporal world.

It may be thought that these reflections belong to a level of generality and abstraction very remote from the particularities with which one deals when confronting an individual work of art. It does not follow, however, that they are irrelevant to the activity of appreciating a work of art. In appreciation, the attention is of course directed to particular elements of a work, but it may operate simultaneously on several levels. Enjoying a painting, we look both at the two-dimensional picture-plane and at the represented depth; and we relate the two. In watching a drama we are often – even typically – aware both of a character in his particularity *and* of the general insights he yields about humanity-at-large (Hamlet the man, for instance, and the Hamlet in men). In reading a poem, as we have noted, appreciation attends to both the sensuous-temporal and the non-temporal emergent meaning. It attends also to the Distance between them. So, in general, a realisation of 'aesthetic transcendence' in some of the forms discussed – necessarily incomplete transcendence – can certainly be an ingredient in aesthetic appreciation itself. We would be held back from acknowledging this very obvious fact only by some dogma that 'aesthetic surface' or the given particular alone, is the proper object of appreciation. The particulars are indeed vital: for it is through them that works of art are discriminated from one another and their individual character established. Attention to the particulars is compatible, fortunately, with simultaneous awareness of more general features of aesthetic achievement. It is a legitimate task for philosophy to call attention to such features, and thereby in the end perhaps to enhance aesthetic experience itself.[16]

[16] Versions of this study were given as lectures in Edinburgh and Stirling Universities, and in Dundee as part of my Margaret Harris Lectures on Religion.

MAIN PUBLICATIONS

Christianity and Paradox (Watts, 1958; Pegasus, 1968)
Metaphysical Beliefs (in collaboration): SCM, 1957)

Contributor to:
Collected Papers on Aesthetics (ed. Barrett: Blackwell, 1966)
British Analytical Philosophy (ed. Williams and Montefiore: Routledge & Kegan Paul, 1966)
Hobbes and Rousseau (ed. Cranston and Peters: Doubleday, 1972)
Education and the Development of Reason (ed. Dearden, Hirst and Peters: Routledge & Kegan Paul, 1972)
Philosophy and the Arts (ed. Vesey: Macmillan, 1973)

ON THE SUBJECT MATTER OF PHILOSOPHY

by

Stephan Körner
Professor of Philosophy, University of Bristol

The apparently innocuous assumption that philosophical thinking has a subject matter and may issue in genuine theses about it, is itself a controversial philosophical thesis. It has, for example, been rejected by the logical positivists and is incompatible with many *dicta* of Wittgenstein.[1] The aim of this essay is to defend the thesis by characterising the subject matter of philosophy (or at least part of it) and by propounding some subsidiary theses based on its characterisation. The essay is divided into two parts. The first demarcates the subject matter of philosophy as comprising certain aspects of specific cognitive and practical systems (1), supreme cognitive and practical principles (2) and the relations of these principles to each other and to reality (3). The second indicates the bearing of these demarcations on two philosophical problems, namely the structure of philosophical arguments (4) and the limits of cognitive and practical relativism (5). It concludes with some relevant autobiographical remarks (6).

1. ON SPECIFIC COGNITIVE AND PRACTICAL SYSTEMS AS BELONGING TO THE SUBJECT MATTER OF PHILOSOPHY

In being aware of the world we find ourselves in a cognitive and a practical position. The former is determined by our beliefs, including the beliefs about the practical options which are open to us; the latter by our practical attitudes towards these options.

[1] See, for example, *Tractatus*, 4, 112, and *Philos. Untersuchungen*, I, 128.

Both within our beliefs and within our practical attitudes we discern some comparatively stable systems. Examples of systems of beliefs or cognitive systems are on the one hand interconnected common-sense assumptions about various fields of experience, about mathematical and about logical relations; on the other the refinements of these common-sense systems in scientific, mathematical and logical theories. Examples of systems of practical attitudes or practical systems are on the one hand interconnected common-sense prudential attitudes towards different ways of adjusting a person's conflicting interests, towards different ways of adjusting conflicting interpersonal interests and towards the adoption of codes of conduct; on the other the refinements of these common-sense systems in some branches of decision-theory, welfare-economics and jurisprudence.

All these cognitive and practical systems clearly have a subject matter. In the case of cognitive systems it consists of propositions – a proposition being anything that can be the object of a belief. In the case of practical systems it consists of real or apparent options – an option being anything whose realisation or non-realisation can be chosen in accordance with the chooser's preference for one over the other or his indifference between either. That a belief or practical attitude has an object neither implies, nor excludes, that the possession of the belief or attitude is itself the object of a belief; or that the option, if any, of accepting rather than rejecting the belief or attitude is itself the object of a practical attitude. And what applies to the objects of separate beliefs or attitudes applies equally to the collection of these objects which form the subject matter of cognitive and practical systems.

In order to indicate some of the ways in which a specific cognitive system, say, $C = \{f_1 \ldots f_n\}$ each of whose propositions is believed by a person S or a specific practical system, say, $P = \{a_1 \ldots a_m\}$ each of whose practical attitudes is held by S, can become the subject matter of philosophical thinking and of philosophical theses, it will be useful to consider four kinds of statement which can be made about these systems. They are (*i*) factual statements to the effect that S believes f, or that he holds a; (*ii*) logical statements to the effect that f stands in a certain logical relation (logical inconsistency, consistency, implication) to some other proposition g or that a stands in a certain formal, practical relation (practical inconsistency, consistency, implication), to some other practical attitude *b*; (*iii*) factual statements to the effect that *f* stands in a certain substantive, i.e. non-logical, relation to a proposition *g*; or that *a* stands in a substantive, i.e. non-formal, practical relation to a proposition *b* (e.g. that *g* is a simplification of *f* or *b* a simplification of *a*); (*iv*) evaluative statements to the effect that *f* falls short of certain desiderata which make its replacement by another proposition desirable or that *a* falls short of certain desiderata which make its replacement by another practical attitude desirable.

Whether within each of these kinds there can be found characteristically philosophical propositions and, if so, how they can be identified are questions which cannot be answered with equal assurance for each of these kinds. As regards the first kind one might for example argue that some statements to the effect that *S* believes *f* belong to the history of philosophy and are philosophical in so far as the history of philosophy is philosophy. However, the view that the history of philosophy is philosophy follows from certain rather special metaphysical positions and is by no means generally accepted. As to the second kind of statements one might similarly argue that some statements about logical relations between propositions belong to logic and hence, in so far as logic is a branch of philosophy, to philosophy. But there are good reasons for holding that logic, though it once was philosophy, is now a separate discipline. A stronger case might be made for regarding the study of the formal relations between practical attitudes as a branch of philosophy with a well defined subject matter on the grounds that the so-called 'logic of preference' and 'deontic logic', which on some views is closely related to the logic of preference, are still far from having reached the independent status of a logical theory as usually understood. (For some very brief remarks on practical consistency and other notions belonging to the logic of preference, see sections 2 and 4.)

It is easier and less controversial to identify characteristically philosophical statements about specific cognitive or practical systems among the statements of the third and fourth kind. Examples are found in the philosophy of mathematics, of science and, more generally, of any at least partly cognitive system; as well as in the philosophy of economics, of law and, more generally, of any at least partly practical system. Thus, to choose examples from the third kind of statements, it is a philosophical and not a mathematical thesis that the application of mathematics to the physical world involves the identification of non-empirical with empirical propositions in certain contexts and for certain purposes; and it is a philosophical and not an economic thesis that a certain code of strict regulations for the distribution of income does not satisfy one's conception of economic justice. To choose examples from the fourth kind of statements, it is a philosophical and not a mathematical thesis that in so far as classical mathematics assumes the existence of infinite totalities, it stands in this respect in need of improvement; and it is a philosophical and not an economic thesis that in so far as any principle of arriving at economic decisions by maximising a purely economic quantity ignores the possibility that the result of the maximisation may be immoral, it too stands in this respect in need of improvement.

Exclusive concentration on the philosophy of specific cognitive or practical systems may help to create the impression that philosophy is mere clarification or analysis of meaning. Admittedly a statement to the effect that a proposition *f* is believed or a practical attitude *a* held by *S* and a statement to the effect that a proposition *f* logically implies a proposition *g* or an attitude *a* practically implies an attitude *b*, might be metaphorically described as clarifying a thought without adding to it anything that has not been implied in it. But the metaphor does not fit statements to the effect that a proposition or practical attitude stands in a certain non-formal relation to another or that it stands in need of modifying improvement. For such statements about a specific cognitive or practical system depend not only on what is implicit in it, but on its place in a wider context. And this relationship is in its turn a subject matter of philosophical thinking.

2. ON SUPREME COGNITIVE AND SUPREME PRACTICAL PRINCIPLES AS BELONGING TO THE SUBJECT MATTER OF PHILOSOPHY

A person's specific cognitive or practical systems may contain beliefs or practical attitudes which serve as standards of cognitive or practical adequacy in these systems. Cognitive adequacy does not imply truth so that, for example, a scientist may claim that a theory is cognitively adequate without claiming it to be true. In order to explain the notions of cognitive adequacy and its supreme principles and to compare it with the analogous notions of practical adequacy and its supreme principles, it is convenient to start by examining the relation of cognitive domination between beliefs.

A person's belief, say, that p_0 cognitively dominates a system of beliefs C if, and only if, he believes that no proposition is cognitively adequate to C unless it is logically consistent with p_0. The beliefs C if, and only if, he believes that no proposition is cognitively dominated in a wider system which includes p_0. But it may be cognitively supreme in the sense that the person believing that p_0 also believes that no proposition whatever is cognitively adequate unless it is logically consistent with p_0. A person's cognitively supreme beliefs, as here defined, are universal in the sense that if in their light he judges some proposition to be cognitively inadequate, he judges it to be cognitively inadequate *for everybody including himself* – not just for himself. They include his logical beliefs, i.e. those beliefs whose objects are his logical principles. But they usually include also some non-logical beliefs. Both kinds of cognitively supreme beliefs may vary from person to person, but the variation among the non-logical ones appears to be much greater. The objects of a person's non-logical supreme beliefs may be principles of great generality, such as the Kantian analogies of experience, or singular propositions such as G. E. Moore's common-sense truism that the earth has existed for many years before his body was born.[2]

To the role of logical consistency and cognitive domination in welding beliefs into cognitive systems there corresponds the role of practical consistency and practical domination in welding practical attitudes into practical systems. In order to explain these notions attention must be drawn to the familiar fact that, at least, some people's practical attitudes are stratified into levels. Thus a person may prefer smoking to not smoking (a practical preference which he manifests by never refusing a cigarette) and at the same time (*a*) have a second level preference for a first level preference for not smoking over smoking over his actual first level preference for smoking over not smoking (a practical preference of second level which he manifests by undergoing an aversion therapy against smoking); (*b*) have a second level preference for the

[2] See 'A defence of common-sense', *Contemporary British Philosophy*, 2nd series, J. H. Muirhead (ed.) (London, George Allen & Unwin, 1925).

presence of his first level preference over its absence; or (*c*) have a second level attitude of indifference towards the presence or absence of his first level attitude. It is natural to say in all these cases that his first level preference is practically dominated by his second level preference, more particularly that in the first case it is positively dominated, in the second case negatively dominated and in the third case indifferently dominated. The third case in which a practical preference is indifferently dominated must be distinguished from the case in which it is not dominated, that is to say in which the practical attitude is not the object of *any* higher level attitude.

Because of a possible stratification of a person's practical attitudes we must distinguish between two kinds of practical inconsistency of which one applies to practical attitudes of the same level and the other to practical attitudes of different levels. Two practical attitudes of the same level are practically inconsistent if, and only if, they are not jointly realisable. Two practical attitudes of different levels are inconsistent if, and only if, one of them is negatively dominated by the other. Calling the first kind of inconsistency 'joint unrealisability' and the second 'discordance', it must – without further elaboration – be noted that there are different species of joint unrealisability (for example, logical and empirical) and that the notion of discordance can be generalised to cover not only two successive levels, but also levels which do not immediately succeed each other. Just as the notion of logical inconsistency can be used in defining a notion of logical implication, so can each of the two kinds of practical inconsistency, as well as their disjunction, be used to define corresponding notions of practical implication.[8]

The definitions of an attitude's practically dominating a system of attitudes, of a supreme practical attitude and of a supreme practical principle are straightforward and similar to the corresponding notions in the cognitive sphere: A person's practical attitude, say, a_0 dominates a system of his practical attitudes say P if, and only if, he regards no attitude as practically adequate to P unless it is practically consistent with a_0. A person's practical attitude is practically supreme if, and only if, it practically dominates some

[8] In the present context we may ignore a third kind of practical inconsistency which is definable in terms of the other two. For details see 'Rational Choice', *Proc. Arist. Soc. Suppl.*, vol. XLVII (1973), pp. 1–17.

attitudes of lower level, is not practically dominated by any attitude of higher level and is practically consistent with any practical attitude of the same level as itself. It is a supreme practical principle if, and only if, in addition it is directed towards lower level attitudes which one possesses not only as an individual, but as a member of the class of all human beings and if the lower level attitudes towards which it is directed are themselves directed not only to particular situations, but to situations of some general kind. An example of a practical attitude dominating a specific system of practical attitudes is a practical preference towards maximising one's pleasure over not doing so in all situations which are morally neutral. An example of a supreme practical attitude, which is also a supreme practical principle, is Bentham's principle of utility.

Awareness of cognitive and practical domination within specific cognitive and practical systems and of supreme cognitive and practical principles suggests a systematic inquiry into these systems and principles which would aim at making them explicit, examining their interrelations and conjecturing their relation to a reality beyond man's cognitive and practical position. This inquiry has always been philosophical – partly philosophical when as philosophy of a special subject shared with its practitioners, exclusively philosophical when as epistemology, ethics and ontology concerned with the structure and function of supreme cognitive and practical principles.

3. ON THE RELATIONS OF A PERSON'S COGNITIVE AND SUPREME PRINCIPLES TO EACH OTHER AND TO REALITY AS BELONGING TO THE SUBJECT MATTER OF PHILOSOPHY

The philosophical inquiry into the structure and function of supreme cognitive and practical principles makes it necessary to devise a suitable terminology and taxonomy for describing and classifying systems of such principles and for asking and answering questions about them. Examples of technical notions which seem to prove useful for this purpose are the concepts of a categorial framework and the notion of a practical framework. Both are based on traditional philosophical distinctions, drawn in reflecting on one's own supreme principles while yet not prejudging the question of the extent to which an epistemological, ethical and ontological pluralism is not only an historical fact but a defensible philosophical position.

A person's categorial framework embraces, among other supreme cognitive principles, a categorisation of all particulars into maximal kinds (*summa genera*) with each of which is associated a set of constitutive principles expressing logically necessary and sufficient conditions for a particular's belonging to it; a set of individuating principles expressing logically necessary and sufficient conditions for the distinctness of any of its members from any other; and a set of logical principles presupposed, for example, in formulating logically necessary and sufficient conditions.[4] A person's practical framework embraces his supreme practical principles, which though part of his morality do not necessarily exhaust it, at least if one admits the possibility that a person's moral attitudes may be supreme practical attitudes but not also supreme practical principles. The notions of a categorial and a practical framework – themselves descendants of older conceptual tools – are in the course of being used expected to suggest improved versions of themselves.

With this proviso one may regard categorial and practical frameworks as belonging to the subject matter of philosophy about which questions of varying degrees of generality can be, and have been, asked and answered by philosophers. One very general question concerns the extent to which a person, group of persons or everybody explicitly or implicitly adheres to a certain categorial or practical framework as opposed to vacillating between two or more of them or of being incapable of any definite adherence. This question is similiar to the grammarian's question about people's adherence to a grammar or an anthropologist's question about their adherence to rules of conduct covering a sphere in which correct and incorrect actions are distinguished. It was, for example, asked and answered by Kant in his so-called metaphysical exposition of the synthetic *a priori* propositions presupposed in the common sense and science of his day and in his analysis of the common-sense concept of duty as implying the categorical imperative.

The question of the relation between theoretical and practical

[4] For details see *Categorial Frameworks* (Oxford, Blackwell, 1970 and 1974).

thinking, reasons or Reason is a second philosophical question of high generality which can be naturally and usefully construed as the question or, at least, as implying the question of the relation between categorial and practical frameworks. *Prima facie* all practical thinking, that is to say all practical preferences between possibilities which are believed to be realisable, presupposes distinctions between these possibilities and thus theoretical thinking. It is consequently subject to the principles of theoretical thinking and thus ultimately dominated by the chooser's supreme cognitive principles which define his categorial framework. Common sense hardly contains obvious examples of situations in which theoretical thinking presupposes practical thinking. Science, on the other hand, may involve deliberate choices between theories – and thus beliefs – which for some reason or other are preferred to others. And in so far as the acceptance or rejection of a theory is a matter of choice, it is subject to the chooser's supreme practical principles.

While this description of the interrelation between theoretical thinking within some categorial framework and practical thinking within some practical framework will on the whole be accepted by most philosophers as *prima facie* correct and as a useful starting point for a deeper analysis, various deeper analyses will not necessarily yield the same result. Thus a person whose categorial framework comprises – as does the Leibnizian – an unrestricted principle of sufficient reason and the principles of classical logic might argue on ontological and logical grounds that any practical preference and any choice which implements it can only be apparent. On ontological grounds since every event is uniquely determined by the principle of sufficient reason; on logical grounds since every proposition, even if it refers to the future, is eternally or non-temporally either true or false. Again, a person whose categorial framework comprises – as do some recent neo-Kantian ones – a maximal kind of facts conceived as human constructions and also the principles of intuitionist logic, might argue on ontological and logical grounds that factual thinking which simply ascertains facts can only be apparent. On ontological grounds since every construction implements a practical preference between genuine alternatives; on logical grounds since according to the intuitionists existence is constructibility. Lastly, there are philosophical positions which allow for a defence of the *prima facie* view of the relation between theoretical and practical thinking as also ultimately correct.

The dependence of the answers to some philosophical questions on the questioner's categorial framework, his practical framework or both leads to a third, very general question about them, which is recognisably a version of the traditional question of the relation between thinking and being. It concerns, not the sense and criteria of the adequacy of a belief to a categorial framework or of the adequacy of a practical attitude to a practical framework, but the sense and criteria, if any, of the adequacy of a categorial or practical framework to reality. However, the inquiry into the structure of categorial and practical frameworks and of their relations to each other, as well as to specific cognitive and practical systems, can be separated from the speculation about the relation of categorial and practical frameworks to a transcendent reality. Their separability manifests itself in the logical independence of theses resulting from the inquiry on the one hand and the conjectures resulting from the speculation on the other. It will be confirmed by the following examples which apart from illustrating the nature of these two philosophical pursuits are also attempts at answering some specific philosophical questions.

4. ON THE STRUCTURE OF DEDUCTIVE, PHILOSOPHICAL ARGUMENTS

In any specific discipline such as mathematics, physics or jurisprudence, deductive reasoning proceeds from premises which are characteristic of the discipline by inferences based on logical implications, that is to say deducibility-relations based on the formal logic underlying the discipline. Deductive reasoning in philosophy is sometimes claimed to be inferior by lacking premises which are of characteristic philosophical content; and it is sometimes claimed to be superior by providing apart from the implications of formal logic also informal implications which, though not logically or formally valid, are no less apodictic than logical implication. The former claim is made by those who hold that philosophy has no subject matter, the latter by Cartesians, Hegelians and others who hold that besides formal logic there also exists a non-formal logic, as well as by some modern philosophers who contrast the 'formal' notions of consistency, inconsistency and necessity with the informal notions of coherence, incoherence and 'conceptual', 'informal' or 'material' necessity.

In the light of the preceding account of the subject matter of philosophy both claims must be rejected. The first for the simple reason that supreme cognitive and practical principles are both characteristically philosophical and perfectly suitable to function as premises in ordinary deductive arguments. The second because in so far as the notions of informal implication, material necessity, coherence and similar notions employed in the cognitive and the practical sphere are not irremediably obscure they can be analysed in terms of supreme cognitive or practical principles and of logical or practical inconsistency (which latter notion is in turn definable in terms of logical and empirical concepts together with the notion of practical preference).[5]

Such an analysis is suggested by the following observations: When a philosopher asserts that a certain factual proposition – for example that a miracle happened or that miracles never happen – is incoherent, conceptually or materially impossible, odd, etc., he implies that the proposition in question, though not violating the principles of logic, is nevertheless violating some standards of all factual thinking. He usually acknowledges that these non-logical standards of factual thinking are less widely shared than the principles of logic. These observations, to which others based on the history of philosophy and on the writings of contemporary philosophers could be added, suggest that a person's non-logical standards of all factual thinking (for example, Kant's second analogy, Leibniz's principle of sufficient reason, Bohr's principle of complementarity) should be identified with the supreme cognitive principles demarcating his categorial framework and that the notion of incoherence or material impossibility be defined relative to a categorial framework.

More particularly, if F is the set of supreme cognitive principles demarcating a categorial framework, then a proposition, say, g can be defined as materially impossible (incoherent, etc.) with respect to this framework if, and only if, g is not only false but logically inconsistent with F. In terms of material impossibility one can define some other relative concepts such as material necessity,

[5] For details see, for example, 'On Some Relations between Logic and Metaphysics', *The Logical Enterprise,* Essays in honour of F. B. Fitch (forthcoming in Yale University Press).

possibility and the notion of a materially necessary implication which, though sometimes considered characteristic of philosophical reasoning, is left undefined by those who employ it. Instead of a systematic exposition of these notions it is sufficient to indicate the definitions of material necessity (conceptual necessity, etc.) and of materially necessary (conceptually necessary, etc.) implication. A proposition *g* is materially necessary *with respect to* F if, and only if, *g* is true and, in addition, logically implied by *F*. A proposition *g* implies a proposition *h* with material necessity if, and only if, the conjunction of *g* and not-*h* is materially impossible *with respect to* F.[6]

The role played by a person's supreme practical principles in his philosophical reasoning about practical options is analogous to the role played by his supreme cognitive principles in his philosophical reasoning about matters of fact. Once the notion of practical inconsistency between practical attitudes, including supreme practical principles, is understood, the notions of practical possibility, impossibility, necessity and implication can be defined, as well as the notions of practical possibility (coherence), impossibility, necessity and implication *with respect to* a set of supreme practical attitudes, say, *P*. The following two definitions will be sufficient to illustrate the spirit of a more systematic treatment.

A practical attitude, say *a*, practically implies another practical attitude, say *b*, if, and only if, *a* and $\neg b$ (where $\neg b$ is the disjunction of the attitudes practically inconsistent with *b*) is practically inconsistent. A practical attitude, say *a*, is practically incoherent with respect to a set of supreme practical attitudes, say *P*, if, and only if, *a* is not only morally unacceptable but also practically inconsistent with *P*. (The reason for distinguishing between moral unacceptability and practical incoherence is that, at least, in some moralities the morality or otherwise of an action is independent of supreme practical principles even though it is dependent on supreme practical attitudes.)

The deduction by means of logical or practical implications of cognitive or practical conclusions from supreme cognitive or practical principles is no more peculiar to philosophy than the deduction by means of logical implications of mathematical conclusions from mathematical axioms is peculiar to mathematics. What

[6] For details, see 'Material Necessity', *Kant Studien* (1973), no. 4.

distinguishes the two disciplines is not the nature of the logical deduction in them, but the content of their first principles and, hence, of the conclusions deduced from them. In each case the first principles may appear to be indubitable – a feature which requires explanation.

Traditionally, their indubitability has been explained either by their material necessity or by their self-evidence. Yet neither explanation will do. If one applies the notion of material necessity to a person's cognitive principles then their material necessity for a person means that they are true and logically implied by themselves, i.e. that they satisfy two conditions which do not guarantee their indubitability. Similar remarks are in order if one applies the notion of practical necessity to a person's practical principles. Again, to explain the indubitability of first principles, be they mathematical or philosophical, by their *self*-evidence will not do, if it is not acknowledged by everybody. The two explanations were intended – for example by Descartes and Kant – to demonstrate not only the indubitability of philosophical and mathematical principles for their acceptors, but also for everybody who thinks correctly.

Fortunately, most of mathematics and much of philosophy do not depend on proving this claim or even on making it. And if one forgoes it, one can understand the indubitability of a supreme cognitive or practical principle for a person or group of persons as a simple empirical fact, namely as an inability to think or act without adopting this principle or as an inability to think or act more effectively by adopting an alternative to it. To show to others that – possibly only for the time being – they too suffer from a similar inability as their philosophical interlocutor, is the true core of many Kantian, Cartesian and other philosophical arguments which ostensibly rely on some universally acknowledged material necessity or self-evidence. But there is no reason falsely to plead eternal necessity or self-evidence when one can truly show that as yet no other or better alternative is available.

5. ON THE LIMITS OF COGNITIVE AND PRACTICAL RELATIVISM AS A PHILOSOPHICAL PROBLEM

The apparent plurality of systems of supreme cognitive and of systems of supreme practical principles or, more briefly, of categorial and practical frameworks implies an apparent relativity of people's cognitive and practical standards and raises problems about its limits. Of these problems some are clearly empirical, for example the problem of determining the categorial and practical frameworks which have so far been adopted by common-sense thinking and formulated by philosophers and of making empirical hypotheses about what is common to all such systems. Yet even tackling these problems requires some knowledge of the structure of the general frameworks and their relation to more specific beliefs and practical attitudes, that is to say some philosophical knowledge. Among the characteristically philosophical problems about the limitations of cognitive and practical relativism are the problem of the nature of philosophical understanding and of the extent to which it can bridge the gap between alien categorial and practical frameworks; and the speculative problem of the extent to which they all depend on a reality of which they and their users are transient aspects. In considering these two problems here, it is again more important to exhibit their philosophical character than to propose detailed answers.

Understanding another's cognitive or practical position ranges from the unattainable ideal of putting oneself completely into his position to being able to co-operate with him in simple tasks which are separable from understanding his cognitive or practical principles. Between these extremes lies the characteristically philosophical understanding of an alien categorial or practical framework by interpreting it in one's own. It will be sufficient to explain and to exemplify two methods of interpretation. The first of these, which is applicable only in the cognitive sphere and in it only under special conditions, might be called the method of ontological subordination. It consists in replacing statements about entities which are ultimate in the interpreted – but not the interpreter's – categorial framework, by logically equivalent statements which are ultimate in the interpreter's categorial framework. In this way Leibniz interprets Democritean atoms by the monads of his ontology and Whitehead material objects by events, so that Leibniz's interpretation of physical atoms as well-founded *phenomena* and Whitehead's interpretation of material objects as abstractions can each be regarded as a version of interpretation by ontological subordination.

The second method of interpretation, which is applicable both in the cognitive and in the practical sphere, might be called the method of fictitious identification. It consists in treating non-identical features of the interpreted and the interpreter's categorial frameworks or practical systems *as if* they were identical – in contexts and for purposes in which such identification is justifiable. Thus a Platonist might, in order to understand G. E. Moore's common-sense ontology, identify Moore's classes of common-sense material objects with Platonic forms in all contexts in which the difference between an object's being an element of a class and its participating in a Platonic Form can be neglected. Again, a person who employs moral rules as mere simplifications of non-deontic moral principles might, in order to understand another's genuinely deontic morality, identify that person's genuine deontic principles with his own merely simplifying rules – in any context in which he would regard himself as justified in substituting a simplifying rule for one of his non-deontic principles. Among the reasons why the notions of ontological subordination and of fictitious identification are well suited to the interpretation of another's cognitive and practical principles is their familiar use in one and the same person's cognitive and practical sphere. For example, the method of ontological subordination is used whenever a reductionist thesis is adopted, while the method of fictitious identification is used whenever pure mathematics is applied to sense-experience, or a legal fiction to social relations.

So far we have distinguished two kinds of limitation to cognitive and practical relativism : one which is based on common features which as a matter of empirical fact or hypothesis are shared by all categorial or practical frameworks; another which is based on the possibility of interpreting some of these frameworks within others. There is a third kind of limitation which is based on speculative conjectures about the relation between categorial and practical frameworks on the one hand and a transcendent reality on the other. Any such conjecture must satisfy certain negative and certain positive conditions. As to the former, it must be logically consistent and coherent with respect to the speculative thinker's supreme cognitive and practical principles. The positive conditions which it must satisfy are that it must give him not only some intellectual and emotional satisfaction, but greater intellectual and emotional satisfaction than alternative speculative conjectures. Remembering a famous phrase of Kant's, one might say that by conforming to the negative conditions of any speculative conjecture one makes room for one that conforms to the positive conditions of its adequacy.

Instead of attempting a classification of speculative conjectures which bear on the problem of cognitive and practical relativism and of comparing their virtues and shortcomings, two rather crude illustrations must here suffice. Although one of them, namely ontological perspectivism, seems in the main to limit cognitive relativism, and the other, namely the metaphysics of self-transcendence, seems primarily to impose limits on practical relativism, the two conjectures supplement and, it could be argued, reinforce each other. Versions of either speculative conjecture are deeply rooted in Western and Eastern culture.

A starting point for a quick – though not perhaps the most persuasive – approach to ontological perspectivism is the observation that the principles of an alien categorial framework may be incoherent with respect to one's own and yet cognitively useful, for example, as heuristic fictions. Calling such alien principles and the categorial framework defined by them 'categorial distortions' of one's own categorial framework, one may further note that the categorial distortion of one categorial framework by another is often reciprocal. From here it is not far to ontological perspectivism, i.e. the speculative conjecture that categorial frameworks do not only distort other categorial frameworks, but a reality which transcends them all and that even if one's own categorial framework is less of a distortion than the others, each of them is an aspect of reality which it is preferable to grasp than to miss. This preference can be partly explained by the intellectual enrichment felt as the result of understanding a hitherto unknown neglected mode of apprehending the world – an enriching experience familiar to natural scientists, anthropologists, historians and anybody acquiring a new language.

A starting point for a quick – though not perhaps the most persuasive – approach to a metaphysics of moral self-transcendence is the observation that although the supreme principles of one morality may be practically incoherent with respect to another, all moral attitudes are directed towards attitudes not of a particular person as such but to this person *qua* human being. From here it is not far to a metaphysics of moral transcendence, i.e. the conjecture that every morality is a more or less, but never wholly, successful attempt at transcending the limitations of one's separate selfhood and particularity. The metaphysics of self-transcendence supports ontological perspectivism since, in conceiving every morality as an attempt at overcoming selfhood and particularity, it suggests that the distinction between particulars and characteristics which is presupposed by every categorial framework is not ultimate.

In concluding this overcursory sketch of ontological perspectivism and the metaphysics of self-transcendence, it cannot be emphasised too strongly that they are at best speculative conjectures which give intellectual and emotional satisfaction to some people. They will no doubt appear too soft and mystical to those who like their speculations to *seem* as tough and down to earth as mathematical deductions from indubitable premises or uncontroversial reports of transparent experiments. Yet the speculative position of, say, a cognitive and a moral correspondence theory, according to which there exists one and only one categorial framework and one and only one moral system which is fully adequate to reality, gains its aura of toughness from the tacit assumption that one can compare reality as apprehended through a categorial framework and a morality with reality as apprehended independently of them. And this assumption implies an even more direct access to a transcendent reality than do the two speculative conjectures which served as an illustration of a subject matter of philosophy beyond specific cognitive and practical systems and systems of supreme cognitive and practical principles.

6. SOME AUTOBIOGRAPHICAL REMARKS SUPPORTING THE PRECEDING ACCOUNT OF THE SUBJECT MATTER OF PHILOSOPHY

A person's intellectual development may provide a context in which his philosophical views are more clearly understood. For this reason and because of the nature of this essay a few remarks on its author's philosophical development may not be out of place. It began with an overriding interest in the metaphysical systems of Spinoza and Leibniz – an interest which was, however, soon discouraged by the (spurious) arguments of the Austrian and German logical positivists. The resulting philosophical doubts led, together with uncertainties of a very different kind, to four long years of studying law. During this period it became clear that legal systems are specific practical systems which stand in explicitly acknowledged and implicit relations to other specific practical and cognitive systems and that the internal and external relations of all these systems require 'philosophical analysis'. At first – but not for very long – this activity seemed more rewarding in the cognitive than in the practical sphere. Engaging in it led to the recognition that the philosophical analysts' notion of philosophical analysis was itself obscure. Trying to clarify it gave rise to a distinction between an analysis which merely exhibits implicitly adopted concepts, statements or rules and an analysis which replaces those of them which fall short of certain standards by others which conform to these standards.

The standards themselves were first conceived as regulative principles which govern and constrain the construction of theories. Further inquiry into the internal structure and external relations of mathematical and philosophical theories, as well as an attempt at understanding the Kantian account of them, yielded two general conclusions relevant to the topic of this essay. One was that some regulative principles may put constraints on all cognitive systems of a person, including his common sense. The other that different sets of such principles may be – and have been – adopted by different persons or groups of them. Making these comprehensive regulative principles the object of examination revealed some of them as backed by indicative principles demarcating categorial frameworks. The assumption of the possibility of alternative categorial frameworks and the – admittedly rare – occurrence of deliberate choices between two such frameworks made it necessary to inquire afresh into the complex structure of practical systems and the relation between man's practical and cognitive position. Even though this inquiry is still proceeding, it is unlikely that it will compel a change in the conception of the subject matter of philosophy as expounded in this essay.

MAIN PUBLICATIONS

Kant (Penguin, 1955)
Conceptual Thinking (Dover Publications, 1955)

The Philosophy of Mathematics (Hutchinson, 1960)
Experience and Theory (Routledge & Kegan Paul, 1966 and 1969)
Categorial Frameworks (Blackwell, 1970 and 1974)
Fundamental Questions of Philosophy (Penguin, 1971 and 1973)

ENTITY AND IDENTITY

by

P. F. Strawson

Waynflete Professor of Metaphysical Philosophy, University of Oxford

A slogan – 'no entity without identity' – and a phrase – 'criterion of identity' – have achieved great popularity in recent philosophy and have been used with more freedom than caution. I shall first discuss the slogan and shall argue that it expresses no very powerful principle. In doing so I shall make an uncritical use of the phrase. Then I shall turn my attention to the phrase and shall argue that, as at present employed, it expresses no single clear idea and should either be dropped from the philosophical vocabulary or be employed only under quite severe restrictions.

I

1. 'No entity without identity.' The slogan sounds well, but how are we to understand it? Does it mean: (*i*) 'There is nothing which is not itself'? This seems to say too little. Does it mean: (*ii*) 'There is nothing which does not belong to some sort such that there is a common, general criterion of identity for all things of that sort'? This says, I think, too much. Does it mean: (*iii*) 'Some things belong to sorts such that for each such sort there is a general criterion of identity for all things of that sort, while other things do not: only things of the first kind are *entities* (objects), things of the second kind are not'? This sounds like nonsense or, at best, a stipulation of which one would wish to know the point.

Another possible interpretation of the slogan, less vacuous than the first, more cautious than the second, less mysterious than the third – though vaguer than any of them – might run something like this: 'There is nothing you can sensibly talk about without knowing, at least in principle, how it might be identified.' I have nothing to say against *this* admirable maxim; I shall return to it at the end of the paper.

How has the slogan been used? It has been used, for one thing, to discredit attributes or properties in comparison with classes. For the latter we have a general criterion of identity: the class of α-things is identical with the class of β-things if and only if all α-things are β-things and conversely. No such general recipe can be supplied for determining property-identity. Given the intention to discredit attributes, the comparison is unimpressive, even on its own terms. For it leaves open the possibility that properties or attributes, like, say, saleable things or things with spatial position, fall into sub-categories for which, or for some of which, general criteria of identity can be given. But my immediate interest in this application of the slogan is not in its adequacy or inadequacy on its own terms but in its revelation of what those terms are. The terms are those of either the second or the third interpretation (of either (*ii*) or (*iii*) above); and presumably the third. For, as I have already suggested and shall now show, 'There is nothing (or nothing identifiable) which does not belong to a sort such that a generally applicable criterion of identity can be given for things of that sort' is fairly obviously false.

I remarked just now that the fact that there were no generally statable criteria of identity for attributes, properties or qualities did not exclude the possibility of attributes, etc., falling into sub-categories for which such criteria could be given. But in fact such criteria cannot in general be given for the sub-categories either. There are no general criteria of identity for colours,[1] intellectual qualities, qualities of character or affective attitudes. Nor are there – to extend our range – for smells, feels, timbres, ways of walking, manners of speech, literary styles, architectural styles or hair-styles. But under all these heads there fall things we can identify or learn to identify, can recognise or learn to recognise, as the same again in different situations.

The cases differ. Suppose someone has mastered the use of the expressions 'blue', 'witty', 'cheerful', 'loves'. He knows how to apply them to visibilia, persons and pairs. Then, and so far, he knows how to identify the corresponding colour, intellectual

[1] There might be said to be for 'minimally discriminable shades' of colour: but even here there would be difficulties.

quality, quality of character and affective attitude. The criterion of application of the predicate *is* the individual criterion of identity of the *individual* quality or relation. The sense of the general term gives the individual essence of the general thing. So there is no need for *general* criteria of identity for things of the kind to which the general thing belongs.

Consider next smells or musical *timbres*. There are no general criteria of identity for them. Nor are they directly named, as blue, wit, cheerfulness and love are directly named. Yet they are often as distinctive, as easily recognisable, as anything in our experience. We borrow names for them, of course, from the kinds of things they are causally associated with: but it is only adventitiously true, if true at all, that the smell of α-kind things is the same as the smell of β-kind things if and only if α is the same kind as β. So in smells we have general things which can be ostended and recognised as the same again even though there is neither a general criterion of identity for them nor any set of names or general terms which gives for each its essence.

Consider now ways of walking, manners of speaking, characteristic styles of gesture. They can be *demonstrated* by any skilful mimic: '*This* is the way he walks.' They too are among the most readily recognisable, most readily identifiable features of our experience: how often we identify a distant friend or acquaintance by recognising such a feature. These features again, if they have names, have in general only derived names: X's manner of speaking, Y's way of walking. But we cannot draw criteria of identity from the possibility of derived names. Not only can the mimic reproduce, but someone else (another member of the family perhaps) might untheatrically exhibit, the very manner of speaking which we first encountered in X.

I will not linger on literary styles, architectural styles or hair-styles. There are no general criteria of identity for them either. But they are things that any trained eye or ear can recognise and any competent specialist can reproduce. Often they too have derived names, but the names indicate no exclusiveness of possession. Strawberry Hill Gothic is not found only at Strawberry Hill, and not all buildings in the Palladian style were designed by Palladio.

It will be said that the identities I have been speaking of lack sharpness of definition. And so they do – in more than one way.

The extensions of the corresponding predicates have no sharp cut-off points. It is not quite clear where wit ends and (mere) sarcasm begins, where cheerfulness turns into boisterousness, when we no longer have the Transitional style, but the true Gothic. But nor is it quite clear when we have left the town or are out of the wood, where the mountain ends and the foothills begin or when the estuary becomes the sea. There is another aspect of indeterminacy, turning, not on the indefinite limits of application of a name or general term, but on variation in the fineness of discrimination required. I suppose heights, weights and temperatures are things for which general criteria may be said at least to be stipulatable, in so far as we have balances, and measures, and in so far as we can give these quantities numerical values. But then there are variations in the sensitivity of balances and measures, variations in the degrees of deviation from indiscriminability of level which we are interested in, variations in the number of decimal places to which we are concerned to take our numerical values. And upon these variations will depend the answers we give to questions of the form: Is the weight/height/temperature of this the same as the weight/height/temperature of that? We find similar variation in the case of colours, which we learned to identify long before we associated *them* with numerical quantities. Is the colour of her eyes the same as the colour of the material of her dress? Yes, because they are both blue. No, because her eyes are a lighter blue. Is the blue of the sky in Oxford on this cloudless day in July the same blue as the blue of the sky in Florence on that cloudless day in June? Is your hairstyle the same as mine? Do he and she have the same way of walking? It depends. It depends on how fine we want our discriminations to be.

2. I shall take it as agreed that the identifiability of something does not require that it be of a sort such that there exist general criteria of identity for things of that sort.[2] That is, I shall take it that (*ii*) is false; which leaves us to consider (*iii*). It may now be said that many of the identifiable things I have been discussing are really

[2] Anyone unconvinced by the examples may be invited to reflect that it would be very odd to hold that *criteria* of *identity* were not themselves identifiable. It will hardly be appealing to hold that they form a single sort with one (self-applicable?) criterion of identity for all members of the sort; and the difficulty will simply be postponed by the suggestion that they fall into subsets with a different criterion of identity associated with each subset.

nothing but principles of discriminating among, or grouping together, independently identifiable things which do belong to sorts such that, for each such sort, there exists a criterion of identity for things of that sort. This may not be so for all the things I have been discussing – perhaps not, or not always, for colours and certainly not, in general, for smells. But though not all the things I have been discussing are merely general characters or features of independently identifiable things, many of them are: qualities of character and intellect belong to, or are manifested by, people; so are affective attitudes; manners of walking and talking are exhibited by things which walk and talk; architectural styles are exemplified by buildings, literary styles by literary works, hairstyles by heads of hair. And people, buildings, books and heads do belong to sorts such that there exist general criteria of identity for things belonging to those sorts. Does this not begin to show a point in the third interpretation of our original dictum, the interpretation which I said was at best a stipulation, at worst nonsense?

I will return later to this thought or half-thought. First I want to ask a question which is not, I think, normally asked. It is agreed that some identifiabilia belong to sorts such that there exist general criteria of identity for things of those sorts, while other identifiabilia do not. Now what accounts for this difference? Why do some identifiabilia belong to the first class (the class favoured by our slogan on its third interpretation) while others do not? There is no reason to think that the explanation will take the same form for all identifiabilia of the first or slogan-favoured class.

It has been said* that animal species belong to a sort such that there exist general criteria of identity for things of that sort. The same has been said of chemical substances. If we imagine a primitive tribe who encounter, say, wolves, sheep and bison, they may reasonably be supposed to distinguish and identify these animal-kinds. They have, of course and thereby, general criteria of identity for animals belonging to these kinds. But there seems no reason for saying that they have general criteria of identity for animal-kinds. They discriminate and group as they find it natural and useful to do so. That is all. We, or the experts among us, are in a different position. We have a systematic taxonomy of orders, families, genera and species: principles for deciding whether or

* By Michael Dummett in *Frege: Philosophy of Language*.

not to count a given plant or animal as belonging to a hitherto unknown species or as a member of an already recognised species. It is the *system* which gives sense to the idea of criteria of identity for species. It is the development of a science which underlies the possibility of such general criteria.

As in the organic, so in the inorganic realm. Our savages, no doubt, distinguish and identify various sorts of stuff. But they have no general criteria of identity for *kinds* of stuff. In the chemical notions of element, compound and mixture, however, and the analysis of these, we find what may reasonably be regarded as such criteria. The science of chemistry supplies such criteria because it supplies systematic principles of classification.

Perhaps something similar now holds good of diseases and of medically interesting conditions in general. I do not know. The general point is clear enough. It is when unsystematic classification gives place to systematic classification that we can begin to make sense of talking of general criteria of identity not just for things that belong to kinds, but for the kinds themselves.

As far as *kinds* found in nature are concerned, this answers the question: what underlies the possibility of general criteria of identity? Natural history gives birth to natural science and in so doing gives birth to this possibility. But art history and literary history are not likely to have any comparable progeny; and unless they do, there will never be general criteria of identity for literary or architectural styles. The sensitive and learned discriminate and name; and the rest of us learn from them.

3. As far as universal or general things are concerned, we have, then, a partial answer to our question. General things divide roughly – only roughly – into those which belong to sorts such that there exist general criteria of identity for things of those sorts and those which do not. Styles, smells, colours, traits of intellect and character and pre-scientifically distinguished kinds of organism or stuff are identifiable without benefit of general criteria of identity for smells, styles, traits, etc. Because biology, botany, chemistry, supply principles of systematic classification, we may say that biological, botanical and chemical kinds *are* subject to general criteria of identity. But in spite of this difference, the cases are not really so very far apart. We might say that where the general thing is directly named, a full grasp of the sense of the

name carries in every case a grasp of the *individual* criterion of identity for the general thing named; the difference is that when we have a principled system of classification, a science, a full grasp of the name carries also a grasp of the principles of classification, and hence a grasp of what we have agreed to call general criteria of identity associated with the sort to which the general thing belongs.

How different is the case of particular things, the case of spatio-temporal particulars! That particular things should belong to sorts such that there exist general criteria of identity for things of those sorts seems, on the face of it, no refinement of science but an absolute requirement of the identifiability of such things. If such a thing has a name, the fact that command of its name puts us in the way of a capacity to identify that thing (if it does) seems to depend essentially on the fact that our grasp of the name includes our knowledge of a sort to which the thing belongs and which is such that there exist general criteria of identity for things of that sort. Now what is the general principle underlying the identifiability of particular things belonging to sorts? The standard and essentially correct answer adverts to the special relationship which obtains, in the case of such things, between space and time on the one hand and some recognisable general form on the other. In the case of relatively enduring particulars – horses, men, beds, billiard balls, mountains – it is, with some familiar qualifications, some characteristic continuous manifestation of some recognisable general form through some space-time tract that yields the particular individual. So you can identify the individual because you can identify the form and, in principle, track the space-time path of a particular characteristic continuous manifestation of it. Of course there are qualifications to be made here – some beds, for example, can be dismantled and reassembled, though horses cannot; and there are many subordinate types of particular which should be distinguished and discussed in any full treatment. But if the account is *substantially* correct, there is one consequence which we should note at once – not a new consequence, rather a truth almost as old as our subject: viz., that the identifiability of a particular individual of a certain substantial sort depends upon and presupposes the identifiability of a certain general form.

This should cause us to review that half-thought I mentioned earlier. The suggestion was that, setting aside the awkward case of sense-qualia (colours and smells), those identifiabilia which did not belong to sorts such that there existed general criteria of identity for things of those sorts were all, as it were, dependent identifiabilia. They were, it was suggested, essentially general features or characters or modes of being or behaving exemplified by other independently identifiable things – people or buildings for example – which did belong to sorts such that there existed general criteria of identity for things of those sorts. Here, it was suggested or half suggested, lay a ground of preference for things of the latter kind, for awarding them the status of entities and denying it to things of the former kind. Let us distinguish these kinds by speaking of 'g-sorted' identifiabilia (i.e. those belonging to sorts such that there exist general criteria of identity for things belonging to those sorts) and 'g-unsorted' identifiabilia. Qualities of character or intellect (like cheerfulness, generosity or wit) are g-unsorted identifiabilia, people (like Tom, Dick and Harry) are g-sorted identifiabilia; and it is true that you can only distinguish and identify qualities of character or intellect because you can distinguish and identify people. But this and comparable facts supply no general or conclusive reason for the preference in question. For, as we have just seen, you can distinguish and identify those individuals which are pre-eminently g-sorted identifiabilia only because you can distinguish and identify the form of the sort. And the forms of the sorts are not, or not originally, g-sorted identifiabilia. So if we are to find any ground for the stipulation about entities – for interpretation (*iii*) of our slogan – it must be another ground.

A general argument to the same conclusion is this. Some sorts of g-sorted identifiabilia must themselves be identifiable as a condition of applying the criterion of identity for the sort. But on pain of infinite regress not all sorts can themselves be g-sorted. So the ultimate identifiabilia – those upon the identifiability of which the identifiability of all else depends – must be themselves g-unsorted.

I lay little weight on this general argument. It has altogether too abstract a character to be entirely convincing or trustworthy.

4. Before returning to the main line of the discussion, I should like to pursue a little further the question, why spatio-temporal particulars must be g-sorted. As I have remarked, it may seem

obvious, even trivial, that they must be. For if we inquire in the most general terms into the basic nature of the particular – the nature of the primary particulars we distinguish – we must come to an answer somewhat like this: the being of the particular consists in a certain unique disposition in space and time of some general and in principle repeatable pattern or form (where we allow this notion – of a pattern or form – to include that of development over time). For any (primary) particular there must be such a pattern or form which is sufficient to yield a principle of identification for all particulars that exemplify it: it would be possible, in principle, in the case of any such particular, to give its identification, to say which or what it was, by specifying the general pattern and specifying the appropriate disposition of the pattern in space and time. Now this thought is wholly theoretical and, it might seem, *practically* empty. Yet it may have the merit of leading us to enquire what kinds of concepts of forms must be evolved if there is ever to be the practical possibility of identifying particulars as we do. It is clear, for example, that some forms must be such as to be themselves reasonably readily identifiable – and also such as to yield the possibility of relating our particulars in space and time, i.e. of supplying a space-time framework for the general determination of particular spatio-temporal dispositions of forms. Thus there emerge the sortals under which we primitively identify those particulars which supply the organising framework of all our historical and geographical knowledge – concepts of space-occupying things, characteristically featured, some static, some mobile, with some endurance through time, concepts which allow for change in individual members of the sort and for variation of character from one member to another of the same sort. Once the framework exists, particulars of subordinate categories – notably sorts of event or process – become generally identifiable in relation to it.

This is familiar ground. I traverse it again, partly to emphasise the gap that exists between (*a*) the bare theoretical thought that the general notion of a particular already implies that of a g-sort to which it belongs, and (*b*) the make-up of the actual conceptual apparatus of sorts which we evolve to meet our needs. But, further, the question might be raised whether the bare theoretical thought is even correct. Could we not devise techniques for identifying particular space-occupying things which had histories but were not covered by any plausible sortal? Is it not clear that, even as things stand, we acknowledge particulars of which we might well hesitate to say that their being consists in a certain particular disposition in time and space of a certain general *pattern* or *form*. Particular *loads*, *cargoes*, *consignments* trace paths through space, have histories, suffer accidents. Yet we could scarcely identify a common *form* in their case. Again, for political or proprietorial reasons, we make certain divisions of the physical world which, those reasons apart, would seem quite arbitrary: the resulting *domains*, as we may generally call them, are surely particulars too. Such examples, however, do not by themselves constitute a serious objection. It is clear that these are particulars of derivative types, defined in relation to more 'natural' sorts; and there is really no reason why we should hesitate to count 'load', 'cargo', 'consignment' and various domain-terms as sortals, though derivative sortals. The examples simply show that we can frame more sophisticated concepts of particulars on the basis of more primitive ones.

Now consider what seems a more radical objection. Suppose we made a camera pan more or less at random for half an hour through the streets and countryside, and then declared that there was an individual object, lasting half an hour, composed, at any moment, of all and only what, at that moment, was being photographed, taken to a certain specified depth below the visible surface. Given suitable care in the manipulation of the camera, this object would be a spatio-temporally continuous individual with a striking enough history of development; for it would keep on gaining and losing parts. There could perhaps be other techniques for defining similarly arbitrary individuals, the common aim of all such techniques being that of detaching the idea of a spatio-temporally continuous individual (hence, *a fortiori*, a particular) from that of a covering sortal of any kind. Such individual particulars would resemble waves, or short-lived shifting sandbanks, in their successive occupation of different and overlapping parts of space and in their steady loss and compensating gain of parts; but would be covered by no such familiar sortal as waves or shifting sandbanks.

The objection fails. For we could define a sort of such particulars by reference to the technique employed in delimiting them; and this would yield a general principle of identity applicable to all the particulars delimited by a specified general technique. The case is not altogether dissimilar to that of a load or that of a domain. The major difference is that whereas there is a practical human point in distinguishing and identifying particular loads and particular domains, no point has so far been supplied for distinguishing and identifying the particulars delimited by the camera-panning technique.

Yet surely, it may be said, there are exceptions to the principle of the necessary sortedness of particulars. What of those items which some philosophers have spoken of as 'parcels' or 'quantities' of stuff, for example the gold which, as it happens, at this moment, is the gold in this room? Or the water which happens, at this moment, to be the water in this glass? Would it not be too illiberal a handling of the concept *particular* to deny such items the status of particulars? And would it not be too liberal a handling of the concept *sortal* to allow 'quantity of water' and 'quantity of gold' as sortals, either primary or derivative? For these phrases incorporate no notion of a distinctive form and none, either, of any such delimiting principle as we can find in 'load' or 'domain' or the artificial example just considered; for it is quite adventitious that the particular quantity of water in question happens just now to be all the water in this glass, and the past and future history of this particular allows for any mode and degree of scatter.

Suppose these items, then, admitted as particulars; and let us admit, too, that the relevant concepts, 'quantity of gold', 'quantity of water', are neither primary nor derivative sortals. Yet if it is insisted that these concepts are concepts of particulars which are all in principle capable of being identified as the same again, then it must be admitted that they are concepts of g-sorted particulars. Lacking sortal forms or delimiting principles, these particulars must, from the point of view of reidentifiability, be viewed simply as aggregates of the smallest portions of the relevant stuff, gold or water, of which they are constituted. So we see the identity of each as reducible to the identity of its constituent stuff-particles; and thus find a general criterion of identity, in the case of each kind of such particulars, for all the particulars of that kind. Of course, except in artificially favourable circumstances, it would be impossible to *apply* the 'criterion' with any strictness. So what is the value of the claim that it is a criterion? To this we reply: it has exactly the same value as the claim that these are genuinely reidentifiable particulars.

These last reflections gain a certain poignancy from the considerations of Part II of this essay.

5. But now I return to the main question of Part I: what justification, if any, is there for the third interpretation of our original dictum, i.e. for the doctrine that identifiabilia qualify as entities only if they are g-sorted identifiabilia? We have considered the suggestion that the identifiability of the g-unsorted always presupposes that of the g-sorted and not conversely; and found it false. I shall suggest instead that the appeal of the doctrine arises from two very different sources, the mingling of two very different kinds of consideration, which nevertheless, and not accidentally, reinforce each other in a certain way and up to a certain point. The first is the simple thought that it is the readily distinguishable material individuals of the world, the solid perceptible things, that are the real entities, the original, pre-eminent, undeniable objects: not form alone, or formless matter, but form and matter both – even though the form may simply be that of a *lump*. I have nothing to say against this ancient, earthy and respectable prejudice. I merely wish to examine how it marries with another thought. For the moment we are to note simply that these preferred and concrete objects are, of course, g-sorted identifiabilia, and sorted, for the most part, under the primary sortals which sort our particulars.

The second and more sophisticated thought construes the notion of 'object' or 'entity' in a different style, a logical style. Objects are, briefly, those identifiabilia which are the subjects of indispensable first-order predication: the greater the range of such predications and the more evident their indispensability, the more securely entrenched as objects those identifiabilia are. This thought yields us what we might call the 'predicate-worthiness' test for the status of entity.

It is evident that substantial objects – objects in our first and earthy sense – pass this test with flying colours. We tell the day-to-day story of our world, describe the changing postures of its states-of-affairs, essentially by means of predications of which such objects are the subjects; and we cannot seriously envisage any alternative way of doing so. What makes the story so rich in contingency, so essentially news, is just the fact that these objects, which supply, as I said, the organising framework of all our historical or geographical knowledge, though they are essentially of this or that sort, have no *individual* essences. Each such object can be caught hold of, as it were, or identified, by this or that speaker or thinker, by this or that or the other of its unique characters or relations, but for no such object is there any unique character or relation by which it *must* be identified if it is to be identified at all. This is why it makes no sense to ask, impersonally and in general, of some individual object or person, what makes him or it *the* individual object or person it or he is; and this is why proper names for such objects or persons have no individual 'sense', though they may be said to have a general 'sense' (i.e. a sense they share with names of other objects of the same sort). And here we can see again the supreme importance of the covering sortal which links together all the uniquely exemplified characters or relations by which the particular object may be, at different times and by different thinkers, identified.

So, then, g-sortedness, predicate-worthiness and the status of earthy or substantial object hang splendidly together. Now nobody wants (or nobody would admit to wanting) to defend the thesis that all entities are g-sorted simply on the ground that all substantial objects are g-sorted and only substantial objects are entities. And nobody, surely, wants to defend the thesis by reducing it to the truism that only g-sorted identifiabilia are g-sorted. A more interesting and attractive form of the thesis would be this: all entities (objects) are predicate-worthy and only g-sorted identifiabilia are predicate-worthy; therefore only g-sorted identifiabilia are entities (objects). But in this form the thesis seems to be untrue. What is true, as I have just remarked, and what in part, as I have suggested, accounts for the attractiveness of the thesis, is that g-sortedness and predicate-worthiness go splendidly together in the case of our model, earthy objects. But it is not true that predicate-worthiness always implies g-sortedness. I earlier mentioned styles, architectural, literary and other, as identifiabilia which are not g-sorted. And surely styles are predicate-worthy. At any rate they are so treated in criticism, an activity which would be crippled, or at least severely handicapped, if critics were not allowed the freedom to predicate of styles. Of course it might be said that criticism is anyway a dispensable activity; for it forms no part of natural science. From such philistinism as this we can only avert our eyes.

Among other g-unsorted identifiabilia I mentioned certain sense-qualia, viz. smells and colours, and also ways of talking, walking, laughing, etc. It will hardly be denied that the former are predicate-worthy. It may be questioned whether the latter are. We say such things as: 'He has the same laugh as his father – a loud, coarse, guttural laugh.' I suppose we could say instead: 'When either of them laughs, you cannot tell (or are very hard put to it to tell), just by listening, which it is; and whenever either laughs, he always, or almost always, laughs loudly, coarsely and gutturally.' I suppose, at a pinch, this would do. (It will be noticed that, anticipating the needs of a certain style of structural semantic analysis, I have made the *adverbial* qualifications amenable to replacement by predicates attaching to particular episodes of laughing rather than to a kind of laughter.) But it would be a pinch. And this is a particularly simple case. One should try giving the sense of 'He speaks with a Bronx accent' without reference to *ways* of talking.

The important points are these. *First*, we need only one case of an identifiable which is both predicate-worthy and g-unsorted in order to destroy the thesis in its present form; and in the face of so many challenges (I have not by any means exhausted the list) the task of defending the thesis seems hopeless. Moreover – and this is the *second* point – the effort to do so is not really worth while. For the concept of predicate-worthiness is not an absolute one. Richness of range of predications is clearly a matter of degree; and so, in those cases in which it is sensible to raise the question, is the matter of their dispensability. But do we want the status of being an object or an entity to be a matter of degree or of more or less arbitrary line-drawing? This is not, I take it, how philosophers have thought of the status.

Not only does the concept of predicate-worthiness fail to be an absolute concept. It seems plausible to hold – and this is the *third* point – that the concept of g-sortedness does so too. Games and sports, for example, I take to be predicate-worthy. Certainly we have plenty to say about them and we should find it difficult, at least, to say what we have to say without using their names. I know of no theory of games which sorts them as biology sorts species and chemistry chemical substances; and it might seem that only a mad authoritarianism would try to do so. On the other hand someone might hold that there was something like an incipient theory in our current practice of classification and naming. I do not wish to be dogmatic on the point. There is, simply, a dilemma. Either games are clearly g-unsorted, in which case we have yet another kind of example of predicate-worthy g-unsorted identifiabilia. Or they are neither clearly g-sorted nor clearly g-unsorted, in which case g-sortedness is not an absolute concept and we have an independent reason for querying the association between g-sortedness and entity-status.

We have seen, by now, a fairly complete collapse of the thesis that only g-sorted things are entities. It cannot be successfully argued for along the lines: *entity* implies *identifiability* implies *g-sortedness*; for, as we saw long ago, the last implication does not hold. It cannot be successfully argued for along the lines: *entity* implies *predicate-worthiness* implies *g-sortedness*; for again, as we have just seen, the last implication does not hold. We have also seen the interest of the thesis dwindle in the light of the fact that neither predicate-worthiness nor g-sortedness marks any generally clear or sharp division among identifiabilia. I think the moral to draw is that we should give up any attempt along any such lines as these to distinguish, among identifiabilia, between those which enjoy the privileged status of object or entity and those which do not. Belonging to all the kinds of identifiabilia I have mentioned and to many more – for example, customs, religions, social conditions (like war and peace), techniques of many sorts (for example, acupuncture, wireless telegraphy), dishes (for example, Boeuf-en-Daube, Crême Brûlée) – there will be items which we shall sometimes find it convenient or pointful to make subjects of first-order predications. We should revise our notion of predicate-worthiness and regard the capacity of an identifiable item to support a pointful predication as a sufficient attestation of worthiness to do so. Then indeed we might regard predicate-worthiness as the mark of an object. It will be a notably unexclusive mark.

Of course – the point should not need making, but perhaps it had better be made – this does not mean that we forfeit the power, or forgo the right, to distinguish between true and false existence-claims. We are no more committed, by a categorial catholicism of entities, to admitting Pegasus among the horses or the golden mountain among the mountains or the rational square root of two among the numbers or witches among the women than is the adherent of more restrictive doctrines. Exclusionists and catholics alike know how to distinguish between the names which really do name identifiabilia of a certain kind and the names which only purport, or are mistakenly supposed, to do so.

Anyone disposed to worry about inflated ontologies, proliferation of entities and so forth will not, evidently, be pacified by this point. In so far as such a one thinks that ontological catholics are deluded into supposing that properties are like people or that objects need have anything more in common than being identifiable subjects, he does not deserve to be pacified. In so far as he simply deplores the untidy richness of the vernacular in this respect and yearns for a sparser style, he manifests a quasi-aesthetic preference which can be respected, if not shared. In so far as his point is that category-catholicism is no substitute for philosophical elucidation and that the latter enterprise may sometimes be forwarded by even partially successful efforts at analytic paraphrase, he can be agreed with; but should also be reminded that if ontological generosity is no substitute for elucidation, it is no bar to it either.[3]

II

6. So far I have taken largely for granted the connexion between the idea of a (primary) substance-sort and that of a general criterion of identity for things of the sort. What is the nature of the connexion? Is there one criterion of identity for dogs and another for cats? Any disposition to answer this question affirmatively receives at least an initial check in a further question: Is there one criterion of identity for wolfhounds and another for terriers? One for Scotch terriers and another for smooth-haired

[3] This is not to deny that there is quite a good case for a conservative reform of our terminology here, as regards both the word 'object' and the word 'ontological'. Thus we might distinguish between a 'logical' sense and an 'ontological' sense of the word 'object'. Objects in the first sense would be all predicate-worthy identifiabilia whatever. Objects in the second sense—our earthy, substantial objects—would form one ontological category among others, such as events, processes, qualities, numbers, species, states, types, etc., etc.; though, doubtless, the *first* among them.

terriers? So one may be inclined to ask whether there is not, rather, one criterion of identity for all animals, a criterion which they share with nothing else. This time the check comes from the opposite side. Why not shared with, say, plants? And if with plants, why not with some non-organic substantial things? Why not with all? Why not a common criterion of identity for all substantial things?

Wherever we set the limits for a common criterion of identity, we must be able to say what that criterion is. And a criterion is something that is *applied.* So saying what it is should reveal how it is that we are able to apply it.

We might say: if a is a substantial individual and b is a substantial individual, then $a = b$ if and only if there is a substantial kind which a is of and which b is of and there is no time at which there is a volume of space occupied by a which is not occupied at that time by b.

Could we delete the reference to kinds? One reason against doing so is this. Suppose John dies in his bed and William dies by being blown to smithereens. Then if we delete the reference to kinds, we should have to say that William is identical with his body while John is not.

The reference to kinds has another and more general importance. How could we begin to apply such a criterion as is here proposed unless we thought of any item to which it applied as occupying some more or less determinate volume of space at any time? And doing so, at least in principle, *observably* or *surveyably*? Perceiving, or thinking of, an object as falling under some substantial kind concept, we meet this requirement.

But there remains something profoundly unsatisfactory about the alleged criterion. It seems that in order to apply it we must already be operating a principle of identity: for how else could we be sure that we had the identical individual, a, in all those positions in which we are then to ask whether we had, at the same times, the individual, b? As what it is supposed to be, viz. a criterion of identity, what we are offered is otiose. All it really says is that the occupation of a given volume of space by an individual substance of a certain sort at a certain time excludes the simultaneous occupation of that volume of space by a different individual of the same sort. An important principle, certainly; but not, it seems, exactly what we were seeking.

But were we seeking the right thing? Such classical examples of clearly statable criteria of identity as those for directions of straight lines or numbers of members of sets have two features which seem quite inappropriate in the present connexion. First, reference to the items for which criteria of identity are given is eliminated in the statement of the criteria: reference to lines or sets is retained, but not to directions or numbers. In fact the statements could be viewed simply as reductive analyses of the predicates 'has the same direction as' or 'has the same number of members as', two-place predicates of lines and sets. This feature seems quite alien to our present object. Second, and more vaguely, these criteria of identity have a rigidity and clear-cutness which seem equally out of place where individual substances are concerned.

Does this mean that the whole notion of a criterion of identity is here inappropriate? That might seem a desperate thing to say. At least it presents us with a quandary – or two quandaries. For in the first place we have assumed throughout that substantial individuals are prime examples of g-sorted identifiabilia, i.e. of identifiabilia belonging to sorts such that there exist common general criteria of identity for things belonging to those sorts. And in the second place we are familiar enough with perfectly intelligible discussions of questions which are at least presented as questions about the criteria of identity for men, say, or ships or buildings.

To clear a little space for manoeuvre, let me revert to the point that concepts of substance-kinds range from the highly general (animal, plant) to the highly specific – of which any botanist or biologist will be forward with examples. Between the extremes lies an extensive middle ground, and in it, we may plausibly suppose, fall substance-kind concepts which are both ontogenetically and phylogenetically primitive. Such concepts as these I have already roughly characterised in a general way: they are concepts of space-occupying things, characteristically featured, some static, some mobile, with some endurance through time, capable of change in characteristic ways and exhibiting some variation of character from one member to another of the same kind. Associated with each such middle-ground substance-concept is a whole cluster of readinesses for variation *between* individual members of the kind and of expectations of typical continuities and typical modifications *in* individual members of the kind.

It is impossible to specify fully and precisely these expectations and readinesses. If we made the attempt, we should find ourselves launching into a disquisition on typical histories and varieties of organism, non-organic natural object and artefact. A consequence is that when we attempt a reasonably brief, yet full and precise, statement of a criterion of identity for some substance-kind, we either overshoot the mark or fall short of it. We overshoot the mark when – as in the case of the general criterion for substance-identity lately considered – it would not be clear how we might apply the criterion unless the ability to keep track of the identical individual were presupposed. If we try to avoid such presupposition, we do so at the price of inadequacy. We might seek to avoid the presupposition, for example, by saying something like: we have one identical dog at all points on a spatio-temporally continuous path of manifestation of caninity (or the dog-form). But it is not clear that this excludes, as surely we want it to, some phantasmagoric sequence of transformations of dachshund into wolfhound into Pekinese, etc. Indeed it is not clear that it excludes the result that the dog at one end of a regimented line of shoulder-to-shoulder dogs is identical with the dog at the other end. Indeed, and more shortly, it is not clear at all. The difficulty is only aggravated by the substitution of a more general substance-form concept; and it is not significantly alleviated by substituting one more specific. We are not prepared for individual dogs, even of the same sub-kind, to exhibit successively the variety of characteristics which we accept with equanimity as between different individuals of the sub-kind.

What, then, of my earlier remarks about the necessary g-sortedness of particulars – g-sortedness being explained in terms of the existence of general criteria of identity? Some revision, or reinterpretation, of those earlier remarks is certainly called for. But this does not mean that we lack an explanation of our ability to identify and reidentify substantial particulars. We have only to reflect on the general character of substance-kind concepts to see that possession of any such concept necessarily carries with it the ability to distinguish one individual of the kind from another; to count such individuals (if one can count at all); and to apply the notion of 'the same one' of the kind. For they essentially are concepts of things which occupy space and endure in existence in characteristic ways. It would be harmless enough to say that each such kind-concept *is* a principle of identity for all individuals of the kind. What is mistaken is the supposition that we can analyse such kind-concepts as conceptual compounds of an identity-preserving element and something else. An example of such an attempt is the suggestion just now cited that substantial identity is to be analysed in terms of the spatio-temporally continuous manifestation of something general, say, a form. Here spatio-temporal continuity of manifestation is thought of as the common identity-preserving element in a vast range of substance-kind concepts, while the form is what varies from kind to kind. But we have no concepts of forms which will fill this analytical bill.[4] Rather, in the case of a given substance-kind, the concept of the form inextricably involves expectations of characteristic modes of continuance in existence of the individuals belonging to the kind – which is not, of course, to say that we can learn nothing from experience about their typical histories.

Now we are in a position to deal formally with the first of my quandaries. We can adopt either a stricter or a looser interpretation of the notion of a criterion of identity. Here is one possible strict interpretation. The notion of a criterion of identity pertains,

[4] One source of the belief that we have may perhaps be found in the concepts of our infancy or the infancy of our concepts. It is natural to describe the responses of very young children to certain experimental tests by saying that the subjects possess powers of recognition of patterns or forms exhibited by certain sorts of objects, or even by individual objects of a sort, before they master any appropriate sortal concept; and it is natural to find in these primitive powers of recognition the germ of the power to form sortal concepts. (Cf. the discussion of the distinction between the concept of the cat-feature and the sortal concept, *cat,* in *Individuals* (Methuen, 1964), pp. 207–8.) But to fill the analytical bill we require not only that the concept of a certain sort-form should be distinct from and theoretically independent of the concept of the sort. We require also that the latter should be analysable in terms of the former. The mental life of adults supplies no sort-form concepts which satisfy even the first of these requirements. If we waive these requirements, we can indeed maintain *a* distinction between, say, a horse-form concept and the concept of a horse. For older children, and we ourselves, find *intelligible* those myths or fantasies in which something assumes, perhaps in rapid succession, a variety of forms. What, in such a fantasy, takes the form of, or appears as, a horse is not, whatever it is, a horse; even if the hero saddles and rides it. It is, perhaps, a horse-phantasm. But *this* concept of a horse-form or horse-phantasm is clearly *derivative* from that of a horse, and no more available for the analysis of the latter than that of a toy horse is.

firstly, to those things to which a certain form of analysis is appropriate. The form of analysis in question is this: the α of x is identical with the α of y (*or* x has (or is an instance or a token of) the same α as y) if x and y are R-related; where no expression in the analysans includes a reference to αs and where the R-relation is not itself that of identity. The notion applies, secondly, to those things of which the identity is essentially and simply reducible, in some clearly statable way, to the identity of other, *constitutent* things. Thus it applies also to sets. (These are intended as two sufficient tests, not necessarily mutually exclusive.)

If we adopt some such strict interpretation of the notion of a criterion of identity, we shall loosen the connexion between this notion and that of g-sortedness. We shall count individuals as g-sorted so long as they fall under essentially individuative concepts, whether or not we can associate general criteria of identity, *sensu stricto,* with those concepts. Thus we shall count substantial individuals as g-sorted because they fall under essentially individuative concepts of space-occupying and enduring things; each such concept *is* a principle of counting, and hence identifying, the individuals which fall under it. But we shall not count intellectual qualities or literary styles or colours or smells or ways of walking or talking as g-sorted; because the concepts 'intellectual quality', 'literary style', etc. are not counting principles, though we can identify intellectual qualities, literary styles, etc.

The alternative is to be content with a loose notion of criterion of identity which allows us to associate the notion with any individuative concept whatever, as well as with anything which satisfies either of the two tests I have just mentioned. On this alternative we can allow the original explanation of g-sortedness and the entire terminology of Part I to stand unrevised. But I favour the first alternative. It would limit the application of a phrase which is apt to come too easily to one's lips. It would not, of course, affect the substance of the thesis maintained in Part I; only its mode of expression.

What of the second quandary? What of those discussions of problem-cases which are presented under the head of investigations into the criteria of identity of substantial individuals of certain interesting kinds? I have remarked that a substance-kind concept involves a whole cluster of expectations of typical continuities and discontinuities and, one might add, of typical terminations, to which individuals of the kind are subject. History sometimes, and mildly, and ingenious philosophers more frequently, and starkly, present us with cases in which these expectations receive a certain sort of shock. The recipe for administering the shock is to contrive some striking dislocation of normal continuities, perhaps in such a way that we may seem to be presented with rival claimants to a single identity. It is the essence of such cases that they should be quite outside the range of normal experience. Indeed, obviously, they could not have the shock-effect I have mentioned if they were not. Whatever is commonplace, or merely unusual, is taken in the stride of our normal conceptual apparatus; and the same would hold of the philosophers' imaginings if they *became* commonplace. They would be absorbed by conceptual adjustments: additions, refinements, decisions. We can amuse, and instruct, ourselves by imaginative anticipation of such adjustments; but we should recognise *this* exercise for what it is.

7. So much, for the moment, then, for substantial particulars. What of non-substantial particulars? I shall consider some examples from the large and heterogeneous class of substance-dependent non-substantial particulars: particular deaths, smiles, battles, falls, walks, etc.[5] I call these substance-dependent because they are essentially happenings to, or processes involving, or modifications of, substantial individuals, space-occupying continuants. The concepts they fall under are often directly, though sometimes rather loosely, individuative; or if, as in the case of the noun 'fall', they apply to happenings which a wide range of substance-kinds can suffer, they can be made to yield individuative concepts by appropriate substance-specification, for example 'fall of a horse'. Are we to say that the notion of a criterion of identity is in place in connexion with these concepts? Not, certainly, if we take that notion in the strict sense I have mentioned. Do they present, then,

[5] By a *particular walk,* I do not of course mean such things as the walk from the house across the fields, along the towpath and back past the Rectory – the walk we recommend to visitors and take ourselves every Sunday. The walks I mean are unrepeatable tokens rather than types. Type-walks, such as the one just described, are yet a further example of g-unsorted identifiabilia. Madder by far than any individuative principle for games would be the authoritarianism of a principle which determined how many *walks* there were in a certain district.

a stronger case for widening the notion to embrace them than concepts of substantial individuals do?

I think this much can be said. The nature of these concepts is such that there is often a relatively standard way of giving or fixing or specifying the identity of the particular individuals which fall under them. This is particularly obvious in the case of certain kinds of event which are such that no substantial individual is liable to endure more than one event of that kind – for example a death, a destruction, a final going-hence. We often enough say what death is in question by saying who it is who suffered it. But the principle holds for many substance-dependent event- or process-kinds which do not have this once-for-all character; only in these cases an important part is often played by an appropriately precise specification of the time at which the event occurred or over which the process extended. Such time-specifications supplement specification of agents or sufferers or locations of the events or processes in question to yield relatively standard ways of giving their identities.

It is difficult, however, to find in these facts a sufficient reason for discriminating in the way suggested between substantial particulars and non-substantial substance-dependent particulars. It might be said of some substantial particulars too that there exist relatively standard ways of specifying their identities. An obviously standard way of specifying identities in the case of relatively static substantial particulars such as geographical features, cities or individual buildings is to give, with sufficient precision, their spatial location.

The issue here may be crossed by, and perhaps confused with, another issue. Suppose we could say, of some kind of particular individual, that for each such individual there was a uniquely possessed complex relational property of a certain general sort, distinguished from other uniquely possessed properties of other sorts which typically characterise individuals of that kind by being, in the case of each such individual, the property the possession of which constituted the *individual essence* of that individual or 'made it just the particular individual it was'. Then we might be inclined to think that we indeed had hold of something which deserved to be called a general criterion of identity for individual particulars of that kind. For example, suppose we thought that the individual essence of a smile smiled by a certain person at a certain moment consisted in its being smiled by *that* person at *that* moment; and that each smile had a uniquely possessed essential property of this sort. Then we might think that in the general idea of being smiled by some person at some moment we had a general criterion of identity for smiles. (I will not set it out in form : it is obvious how it would go.)

This suggestion owes such attractiveness as it has to distinguishing each such relational property, as an essence-constituting property of the smile which uniquely possesses it, from every other uniquely possessed property which the smile might exhibit (for example, being smiled at a certain time by lips occupying a certain spatial position at that time). For it is a trivial general truth that if a property is uniquely possessed by an individual, then any individual which possesses that property is identical with the given individual; and unless we make a special claim for the property in question, it is no more than one application among others of this trivial truth to say that if a certain smile is smiled by a certain person at a certain moment, then any smile smiled by that person at that moment is identical with that smile.

Of course, it is true of any smile that it must be smiled by someone at some time, and that no other smile can possess just that particular combination of these properties that a given smile possesses. But neither this nor any other unique combination of properties constitutes the individual essence of a particular smile; for there is no such thing. The notion of an individual essence belongs not to particular things but to general things; just as the notion of an individual sense belongs not to the names of particular things, but to the names of general things. If it were the case, for some particular thing, that there was just one of its uniquely possessed properties which it *had* to be identified by if it was to be identified at all,[6] then it would be reasonable to extend the notion of individual essence to such a particular thing. I remarked earlier that this was not the case for any substantial particular. Neither is it the case for any non-substantial, substance-dependent particular. Competitions can be organised on the basis of the principle that it is *not* required that one know *who* smiled a certain smile in

[6] Let no one say that, for any particular, there is such a property, namely the disjunction of all its uniquely possessed properties !. To identify an item by means of some uniquely possessed property, you have at least to know what that property is.

order to know what smile it was. The schoolmaster need be in no doubt at all as to what utterance he has in mind when he asks 'Who said that?'

There remains the point which I began this section by making. The sorts of non-substantial substance-dependent particulars are such that there often exist relatively standard ways of specifying the identities of particulars belonging to these sorts, of saying which or what individual member of the sort is in question. This is less frequently true of the sorts of substantial particulars. But this difference of degree is hardly one on which we can found a case for saying that the precise-sounding notion of a criterion of identity is appropriate to the former class of individuative concepts but not to the latter.

8. I turn now to some individuating concepts of another kind, concepts of things which fall within a general classification sometimes indicated by the use of the word 'type'. The examples I shall consider are those of musical or literary compositions of certain forms: for example, sonnet, ode or, more generally, poem; story or novel; song, sonata, symphony. About these I should like to make two very different points. The first is not a very serious point and perhaps could hardly be sustained. I make it by way of exaggerated anticipation of a possible objection to the second. It is that the practice of the activities of poetising, story-telling, music-making, does not have as an immediate necessary consequence the existence of any *individuative* concepts of these kinds. I do not mean simply that certain forms might not have been devised. On the contrary the point is that the existence and practice of, for example, the sonnet-form does not strictly necessitate the existence of sonnets. We are familiar with, and can easily accommodate, the notion of different versions or variants of the *same* composition. But we can perhaps imagine this notion pushed to self-destructive lengths; to the point at which the ideas of identity of composition and hence of versions and variants of the same one are altogether lost. We can perhaps imagine a general practice of poetising or story-telling or even sonneteering accompanied by such a habit of slight continuous variation as had the consequence that what, as things are, we should unhesitatingly describe as the tellings of two different stories or as copies of two different sonnets had a place on a continuous story- or sonnet-

spectrum on which no lines of demarcation could be drawn to separate one from another.

The point, even if it could be sustained, is not to be pressed. As things are, we do have individuative concepts of these kinds. At most it has been shown that their existence and utility, as individuative concepts, rest on certain general facts about our practice in these areas.

Now for the second point. These individuating concepts, sonnet, novel, symphony, etc., strikingly emerge as far better candidates than those lately considered for the status of concepts of things for which there exist general criteria of identity in a strict sense. They pass without difficulty the first of my sufficient tests. Neglecting for the moment the matter of versions and variants, we may say, for example: *a* is an inscription of the same sonnet as *b* if *a* is an inscription of words in the sonnet-form and so is *b* and the words and their arrangement in the form are identical in both cases. We can take account of versions or variants by qualifying 'identical' with some expression like 'approximately' or 'nearly enough' – a useful reminder of the point already made. Clearly this pattern of statement of a criterion of identity can be generalised for all such types.

What of the second of my sufficient tests, the one designed for sets. Evidently, a sonnet or a sonata is not simply a set of words or a set of notes. But each is, *and is essentially*, a particular set of words or notes ordered in a particular clearly specifiable arrangement. *This* reduction is quite in order; though again minor qualifications are required to allow for versions and variants. If we interpret this second test, then, with reasonable liberality, sonnets and sonatas pass it as well as the first. We could say: the criterion of identity for compositions is their composition.

Now this might, for an unreflective moment, encourage the resurgence of a general error. It might, for example, be said: then haven't we, after all, a general criterion of identity for all material substances or bodies? For a body *a* is identical with a body *b* if *a* at any time is composed of the same material particles as *b* is composed of at that time. There are many objections to this, implicit in what has gone before. It is enough to say that a criterion is something that is *applied*. But I will add this general comment. It is futile to suppose that you can devise anything which deserves to be called a criterion of identity for things falling under some concept of high generality simply by applying the general *logical* characters of identity to any feature you happen to think of which universally characterises things which fall under that concept. A specimen of this futility is the recent suggestion that a criterion of identity for events is to be found in the identity of their causal relations.

9. It would be instructive to consider how the notion of a criterion of identity fares in the case of yet other general sorts of individuals than those I have selected. But this paper is already long enough. I have, I think, assembled enough evidence to support the proposal that the phrase should either be dropped altogether from our professional vocabulary or be employed only under some such restrictions as I have suggested. As things are, the phrase has a spurious and thought-stopping authority. Criteria should be both clearly statable and actually applicable, actually applied. Criteria of identity are at their best in the case of certain sorts of abstract, general thing. It is pointless to extend the notion to individuative concepts in general, to all concepts of the g-sorted; it is even more futile to try to extend it to concepts – like that of an event – which are so general that they are not themselves individuative at all, although they cover a range of concepts which are.

Nevertheless useful results may sometimes be achieved with inappropriate tools or weapons; and the waving of this weapon may sometimes have forced us to a conceptual clarification, or a recognition of conceptual unclarity, which we had previously missed. These beneficial results, however, could equally well have been secured by a steady attention to that sober maxim which I suggested as an unexceptionable gloss on our original slogan, 'No entity without identity' : viz., you cannot talk sense about a thing unless you know, at least in principle, how it might be identified. This principle of conceptual clarity applies equally to the g-sorted and the g-unsorted : to souls, for example, on the one hand, and to telepathy on the other. You do not know what you mean by 'telepathy' unless you know how to identify it, i.e. how you would tell that you have a case of it. You do not know what souls are unless you know how to tell one from another and to say when you have the same one again. And if someone should say that this is just old verificationism writ small, or loose, then I am quite content with that.

MAIN PUBLICATIONS

Introduction to Logical Theory (Methuen, 1952)
Individuals (Methuen, 1959)
The Bounds of Sense (Methuen, 1966)
Logico-Linguistic Papers (Methuen, 1971)
Freedom and Resentment (Methuen, 1974)
Subject and Predicate in Logic and Grammar (Methuen, 1974)

PERSONS AND PERSONAL IDENTITY

by

Richard Swinburne

Professor of Philosophy, University of Keele

This paper is concerned with important differences between our standards for identifying, counting, and re-identifying inanimate material objects of a specified kind, such as tables and chairs, and our standards for identifying, counting, and re-identifying persons, including human beings.[1]

When we ask what are the grounds for applying some concept ϕ to some object (for calling some object 'ϕ'), we may be asking one of two questions. First, we may be asking what are logically necessary and sufficient conditions, such that if those conditions hold, then – of logical necessity – the object in question is ϕ, and if they do not hold, then it is not ϕ. We may say that a philosopher asking for such a set of conditions is asking for an analysis of ϕ. Secondly, we may be asking what are the public phenomena, the occurrence of which makes it probable that the object in question is ϕ. By a phenomenon being public, I mean that observers can find out whether it occurs and no one observer is of logical necessity in a better position than any other to find out whether it occurs. A philosopher asking this question is asking for the public evidence for ϕ. Two kinds of answer may be given to the evidence question. The question may be answered by producing public phenomena which constitute criteria of the object being ϕ. I understand by x, y, and z being the criteria of q, that q is made probable to the extent to which x, y, and z are satisfied – and that this is so as a matter of logical necessity. If x, y, and z are well satisfied then it is probable that q; if they are not well

[1] I understand by a human being, a member of the same biological species as ourselves, and allow for the possibility that there may be persons other than human beings – e.g. inhabitants of some distant planet.

satisfied, then it is not probable that q. (I count it being certain that q as an extreme case of its being probable that q.) This suggested use for the term 'criterion' is, I think, a more precise version of that which has become familiar as a result of Wittgenstein's discussion of criteria and of other minds. As Albritton and others have pointed out, Wittgenstein did not himself use 'criterion' in a very precise sense – sometimes he seems to think of it as above, at other times he seems to think of a criterion as something akin to a necessary or sufficient condition.[2] Alternatively the evidence question may be answered by producing public phenomena which constitute inductive evidence (or 'symptoms' as Wittgenstein calls them in *The Blue Book*) for the object being ϕ. I understand by x, y, and z being inductive evidence of q that x, y, and z make q probable and that this is so in virtue of some other known non-logical fact w. In that case it will be a necessary truth that w makes x, y, and z evidence of q; and so w will be among the criteria for x, y, and z being evidence of q. Philosophers interested in persons and personal identity have not always made it clear when asking for the grounds for applying some concept, which question they have been asking; nor, in so far as they have been asking the second question, which kind of answer they have been providing.

Full investigation of some concept ϕ which applies to objects involves the philosopher in asking three questions, each of which can be subdivided along the lines of the distinctions made in the last paragraph. The first question is the question with which the last paragraph was explicitly concerned, the grounds for identifying an object as ϕ; which we will call the identification question. Here our concern may be with analysis or with public evidence, either criterial or inductive. In the study of persons one concern of the philosopher is with analysing the concept of a person, giving logically necessary and sufficient conditions for something being a person; and another concern is with the public evidence that something is a person, both with any evidence which is criterially related to a thing's being a person and with any evidence which is related only inductively.

[2] He distinguishes too between 'a criterion' and 'the defining criterion', but does not make the distinction very clear. See Rogers Albritton, 'On Wittgenstein's use of the term "Criterion"', *Journal of Philosophy*, vol. 61 (1959), pp. 845–57.

The second question with which the philosopher investigating a concept ϕ will be concerned is the question of the grounds for saying that a certain ϕ is the same ϕ as another ϕ at the same time, which we will call the counting question. Two objects may evidently satisfy the criterion for being ϕs, while being picked out by different names or descriptions which leave it open whether or not the objects are the same ϕ. (In referring to a ϕ as 'another ϕ' I mean only a ϕ picked out by a different name or description, not a ϕ which is necessarily a different ϕ from the first ϕ; and likewise in talking of 'two ϕs' I mean only ϕs picked out by two different names or descriptions, not necessarily two distinct ϕs.) Thus a car may be described as 'my car', and a car may be described as 'the car at the bottom of the hill', and it be an open question whether these cars are the same car. In his concern with this matter the philosopher needs to distinguish – along the lines drawn in connection with the identification question – the question of what it is for two ϕs to be the same ϕ from the question of what is the public evidence that ϕs are or are not the same ϕ, and he needs to distinguish criterial from inductive evidence on this matter. In our field the philosopher must analyse what it is for two persons to be the same person, and what is the public evidence, criterial or inductive, that we have one person or two at a certain location.

The third question with which a philosopher investigating a concept ϕ will be concerned is the question of the grounds for saying that a certain ϕ is the same ϕ as a certain ϕ at an earlier time, which we will call the reidentification question. Here again there is a question of analysis and a question about public evidence. The philosopher concerned with persons is interested in the question of analysis – what are the logically necessary and sufficient conditions for a person P_2 at a time t_2 to be the same person as a person P_1 at an earlier time t_1. He is also interested in the different question of what is the public evidence that P_2 is the same person as P_1, and with whether any such evidence is criterial or inductive.

In stating that philosophers concern themselves with questions of identification, counting, and re-identification, I do not in any way commit myself to the form which answers to these questions must take. We may be able to answer the question of what are the logically necessary and sufficient conditions for something being a lorry, or a car, a chair or a mountain by providing an analysis which does not mention any particular objects – for example, a lorry is any motor vehicle suitable for transporting heavy and bulky loads. Or, in order to answer this question we may need to mention particular examples – for example, a mountain is anything which resembles Mount Snowdon, Mont Blanc, Mount Everest, etc., etc., in the ways in which these resemble each other. That is, an answer may be in terms of genus and differentia or in family resemblance terms. Adequate answers of either kind may need to be quite long answers, much longer than some of the brief summaries which I give by way of illustration. In the application of many concepts there are bound to be borderline cases, objects which are borderline cases for satisfying the analysis of those concepts. An object which is a borderline case for being ϕ is an object of which it is as near to the truth to say that it is ϕ as to say that it is not; for such an object there is no one right answer to whether or not it is ϕ.

We made a distinction between questions of analysis and questions of evidence; but the fact that there are different questions here in no way guarantees that their answers are different. And, indeed, for inanimate material objects of a specified kind an answer to a question of analysis will cite public criterial evidence, and an answer to a question about evidence can be given in terms of criteria which will provide an analysis. Take identification questions first. To be a lorry is (roughly) to be a motor vehicle suitable for transporting heavy and bulky loads. This analysis is, I suggest, on the right lines, although it needs more elaboration and precision. And what is the public criterial evidence that something is a lorry? Roughly, that it is a motor vehicle and that it is suitable for transporting heavy and bulky loads. The criteria would need to be made more precise in just the same way as the analysis. The same point applies in respect of answers to the counting and re-identification questions. Where a ϕ is a kind of inanimate material object, to be the same ϕ as another ϕ at the same time is to consist of the same matter. My car and the car at the bottom of the hill are the same car, if and only if they consist of the same matter. And what is the public criterial evidence which – of logical necessity – makes it probable that two ϕs are the same (where a ϕ is a kind of material object)? That they consist of the same matter. Again, where a ϕ is a kind of inanimate material object, what is it to be the same ϕ as a ϕ at an earlier time? Roughly, it is to consist of matter which is the same as that of the ϕ at the earlier time or has been obtained from it by gradual replacement of that matter. This too constitutes the criterial evidence that ϕs at different times are the same ϕ. In all these cases the criterial evidence makes it certain that the object is ϕ or the same ϕ as another object.

However, a main thesis of this paper is that there is a contrast between persons and inanimate material objects of specified kinds in that, for persons, unlike for inanimate material objects, the answers to analysis questions will always differ from the answers to evidence questions – and that this holds for identification, counting, and re-identification questions. I shall argue for this as a claim about the identification question fairly briefly; but I shall argue for it at greater length as a claim about the other two questions – for the reason that in the latter form the claim has received far less attention from philosophers than it has received in the former form. Let us however begin with the identification question. Clearly something is a person if and only if it has mental events, that is thoughts, sensations, and perceptions of a certain degree of complexity; and if also it can perform actions of a certain degree of complexity. (I understand by an action something which an agent does intentionally, that is, does meaning to do it.) The degree of complexity required can be illustrated by examples. Further conditions would have to be satisfied for something to be a person of a particular kind, for example a human being. This account leaves open the disputed question of whether persons have to have bodies. Some philosophers have claimed that something could not be a person unless it had a body, and others have denied this. I shall however in subsequent discussion consider only embodied persons, i.e. persons which are – whether accidentally or essentially – material objects. To do so will simplify the discussion in a way, superficially, most favourable to opponents of the case which I wish to make.

Now a person's having certain specific thoughts, feelings, and sensations is not generally analysable in terms of public phenomena, nor is his performing certain specific actions; although the public phenomena provide very strong, normally overwhelming, evidence of a man's thoughts and actions. I appeal briefly to the intuitive obviousness of this point, which is nowadays, I would think, fairly generally accepted by philosophers. Those who have in the past sought to analyse mental events or actions in terms of public phenomena have been either behaviourists or what I may term brain-analysts. The behaviourist analyses a person having a mental event in terms of his exhibiting certain public behaviour. But such analyses have been recognised to fail. To have a pain clearly is not simply to scream out and say that you have a pain,[8] or anything similar. For it is logically possible that the public behaviour occur and yet the person not have a pain, and conversely. The same applies to actions. For me to perform the action of moving my hand is for me to move my hand intentionally, i.e. meaning to do so. But this is not simply for my hand to move and for me to say that I meant to move it, or anything similar. My intentions are not public phenomena. The brain-analyst tries to analyse mental events and actions in terms of brain events (and sometimes also of public behaviour as well). But such an analysis is even less plausible. My having a pain is not analysable in terms of there being certain disturbances in my brain. This point has been admitted even by mind-brain identity theorists who, while wishing to affirm the identity of mental events with brain-events, have claimed that the identity is a contingent, not a logical one. Yet while having mental events is not analysable in terms of public phenomena, the latter constitute strong, often overwhelming, evidence of the existence of the former. A similar point holds for the relation between actions and public phenomena.

The public phenomena which constitute the best public evidence of a person's mental events (and the intentions in his actions) will be what he says about them, his non-verbal behaviour and the things which happen to him. The best possible public evidence of a person having toothache are his saying that he has toothache, his face being contorted and his crying out, and the existence of damage to his tooth. Such phenomena make it probable that he has toothache, so probable that others can rightly claim to know that he has toothache, but they do not constitute his having toothache. I shall not discuss whether such phenomena constitute criterial or only inductive evidence of the person having toothache. If they were inductive evidence, they would be so in virtue of some other known non-logical fact – for example, correlations between

[8] I assume that someone's saying something is a public event, although someone's saying something intentionally is not. Such an assumption makes the behaviourist position as plausible as possible.

toothache and crying out, the existence of damage, etc., in the experience of others. There are well-known objections to the view that the phenomena are inductive evidence,[4] but these may be superable.

To claim that the occurrence of mental events is not analysable in terms of public phenomena is not to deny a very important point due to Wittgenstein. This is that we could not have mental-event concepts, such as the concepts of pain, after-image, and thought, unless we had in our public language words to denote such events. We would not have such words unless there were characteristic public phenomena which were taken as evidence of the occurrence of mental events – for example, screaming, grimacing, and making statements about being in pain, which are taken as evidence of the presence of pain. This point in no way affects my main point. The fact that we could not have a concept of *x* unless we observed *y* and took *y* as evidence of *x* does not show that *x* can be analysed in terms of *y*.

Given that a person's having this or that mental event or performing this or that action cannot be analysed in terms of public evidence, and given that being a person is a matter of having mental events and performing actions, it would seem not implausible to generalise the former result and conclude that being a person cannot be analysed in terms of public evidence. The public evidence that some material object is a person is evidence that that object has mental events and performs actions. This will be a matter of its reactions to stimuli, observable goings-on within it, its public behaviour, and what it says – i.e., broadly, its history, physiology and public behaviour. But now consider some highly sophisticated robot developed in a laboratory, or some creature from another planet. They may scream when we stick pins into them, utter long meaningful sentences in English or some other language, show goal-directedness in their behaviour, and generally behave and react like humans. Are they persons? Yes, if they have sensations and consciously pursue their goals. No, if they are unconscious robots. Yet however much we know about their history, physiology, and public behaviour, it seems consistent to wonder whether or not they are persons. For it seems consistent with what we know about them to suppose either that they are

[4] See, for example, P. F. Strawson, *Individuals* (Methuen, 1964), ch. 4.

unconscious, like simpler robots, or conscious like the humans which their public behaviour imitates. So their being persons is not constituted by the public evidence that they are. But if an analysis cannot be given in terms of public evidence of what it is for such creatures to be persons, then, generally no analysis can be given in terms of public evidence of what it is for a material object to be a person. For, if it could, then we could set it out and see whether the sophisticated robot satisfied it or not. Yet public evidence could not, we have seen, entail an answer to the question whether the robot is a person. But that is not to deny that in normal cases we have strong, nay overwhelming, evidence whether or not some object is a person.

Note that the doubt whether some sophisticated robot is a person is not a doubt which arises from the object being known to be a borderline case for being a person, in the sense of 'borderline case' delineated earlier. For if it were, then we would know that it would be as true to say that that object was a person as that it was not. Yet our difficulty is that we do not know which claim is nearer to the truth; we are in doubt over a genuine factual matter. It is not like doubting whether some blue-green object is blue or green. Here, either answer is as near to the truth as the other, and this we know. We are not in this position when we doubt whether some sophisticated robot is a person.

If being a person cannot be analysed in terms of the public phenomena which are evidence for there being a person, it would not be surprising if being the same person at a given time or at a different time also could not be analysed in terms of the public phenomena which are evidence of two persons being the same. That that is so I shall argue both with respect to the counting question and with respect to the re-identification question. My arguments on these two questions will, I hope, reinforce my brief arguments on the identification question.

Let us start with the counting question. What are necessary and sufficient conditions for two persons at a given time to be the same person? Two persons are the same person if and only if they have (numerically) the same mental events and do (numerically) the same actions. And what is the public evidence that we have one person as opposed to two? We are assuming that persons are material objects, i.e. are embodied. So clearly the answer to the question is that the typical unity which we observe in the behaviour and reactions of an ordinary human body makes it very probable (well nigh certain) that it is the body of one person. And likewise the typical disunity between the behaviour and reactions of distinct human bodies makes it very probable (well nigh certain) that they are the bodies of distinct persons. But awkward cases are conceivable, cases where there is a doubt whether there is only one body, or whether one body is the body of two persons, or two bodies are both the bodies of one person. We can describe in these cases what is the public evidence which makes it probable that we have one person, or, as the case may be, two. But it is logically possible that what the public evidence shows is not the case. That could not be if there being one person was analysable in terms of the public evidence. It should be added that in these cases, as in the similar case discussed in connection with the identification question, the doubt concerns a factual matter; it is not a doubt arising from the cases being known to be borderline cases.

I put forward two imaginary cases. Suppose we have before us a thing *B* which is, physiologically, one living organism, but which consists of what is, anatomically, a normal human body with an additional head. Do we have two human bodies merged from the neck downwards, or one body with two heads? We should, I think, say that there are two bodies, if there are two persons here; one body, if there is only one person. There is one person and one body if disturbances in and to *B* are correlated with the mental events of only one person, and if only one person can perform basic actions,[5] by moving parts of *B*. There are two persons and two bodies if disturbances in and to certain parts of *B* are correlated with the mental events of one person, and if disturbances in and to other parts of *B* are correlated with the mental events of a different person; and if one person can perform basic actions by moving some parts of *B*, and a different person can perform basic actions by moving other parts of *B*. Or again consider the case where we have clearly two human bodies, but the person whose body is the first body seems to feel disturbances in and to the second body and seems able to perform basic actions by moving parts of

[5] A basic action is an action which one does, but not by doing any other action. Thus moving one's hand is a basic action, whereas opening the door is not, because one opens the door by moving one's hand. See Arthur C. Danto, 'Basic Actions', *American Philosophical Quarterly*, vol. 2 (1965), pp. 141–8.

the second body; and conversely. Do we have here one person with two bodies, or two persons? Clearly, we have one person if disturbances in and to both bodies are correlated with the mental events of only one person, and if only one person is able to perform basic actions by moving parts of both bodies. We have two persons if disturbances in and to one body are correlated with the mental events of one person who can move parts of that body but not of the other as a basic action; and disturbances in and to the other body are correlated with the mental events of a different person who can move parts of that body but not of the first body as a basic action.

The public evidence in these cases that we have one person or two will be provided by the unity or disunity of behaviour and reactions. In the case of *B* disunity would be illustrated by phenomena such as the following. If I stick pins into the right side of *B* only out of the right mouth will come screams and acknowledgement of suffering. If I block the right pair of ears and then make a request to *B* to make movements with his right and left legs, only the left leg is moved, and out of the left mouth comes a statement that the agent requested can only move the left leg and not the right. And, more generally, out of the two mouths come acknowledgements of different mental events and admissions of performing basic actions with different limbs. All this would be evidence that we have here two persons. Consider now the two-body case. The normal reactions and behaviour of two bodies indicate two persons. But suppose the following. We separate the bodies, and ask the person whose body is the first body to move the limbs of the second body, and those limbs move. Likewise a request to the person whose body is the second body to move the limbs of the first body is followed by the movement of those limbs. Damage to either the first body or the second body leads both the person whose body is the first body and the person whose body is the second body to show the symptoms of pain and to claim to feel pain. All this would be evidence that we have only one person.

It would however be a mistake to equate the existence of such public evidence for there being one person (or two, as the case may be) with the existence of logically necessary and sufficient conditions for there being one person (or two, as the case may be). For there are other logically possible hypotheses compatible with the public evidence. Thus suppose that the public evidence indicates in the way illustrated in the last paragraph, that B consists of two merged bodies of two different persons. It is nevertheless compatible with the evidence described there (and also with any further similar public evidence) that in fact there is only one person who is pretending to be two or who is psychologically conditioned so as to react with his left side and mouth to disturbances to his left side and remarks heard through his left ears, and to react with his right side and mouth to disturbances to his right side and remarks heard through his right ears. Likewise it is compatible with the two-body situation described in the last paragraph to suppose that there are two persons who are telepathically in contact, have deep sympathy with each other's feelings and are anxious to fulfil each other's requests. In each case the public evidence of unity or diversity, although it makes very probable the claim that we have one person, or, as the case may be, two persons, does not provide an analysis of the claim in question.

I leave open the issue as to whether the public evidence cited is criterially or only inductively related to the claim that two persons are (or are not) the same person. If the evidence was related only inductively, it would be so in virtue of some other non-logical known fact. This fact could not be that similar evidence in the past has been found to be correlated with the existence of only one person – for the latter could not be known on other occasions save via the former. But it might be some such fact as that in the past the various pieces of evidence which we now take as evidence that there is one person had been found to be correlated with each other on different occasions in the past and never to occur in isolation.

Finally, we come to the re-identification question. What is it for a person P_2 at t_2 to be the same person as a person P_1 at an earlier time t_1? Clearly P_2 is the same person as P_1 if and only if those mental events which P_2 has and those actions which P_2 does are (numerically) the same mental events as those which P_1 will have and (numerically) the same actions as P_1 will do.

And what is the best public evidence that P_2 is the same person as P_1? Clearly, there can be evidence of three kinds: (1) P_2 claims to remember things that P_1 did and experienced; and, in so far as this can be established independently, P_1 did and experienced those things; (2) P_2 behaves like P_1; (3) P_2 has the same body as P_1. (3) itself will not normally be known by direct observation –

appearance, fingerprints, and blood groups are indirect evidence that (3) holds. Obviously (1), (2), and (3) need spelling out a bit, and other philosophers have devoted some attention to this task. Some wish to replace 'body' in (3) by 'part of the body, the states of which are causally correlated with the memory-claims and character of the person whose body it is', which part is, scientific evidence shows, the brain. I shall not discuss the detailed exposition of (1), (2), and (3), nor how they are to be weighed against each other (an issue over which philosophers have differed greatly), but shall suppose that there is some agreed way of weighing them which tells us what to say in a particular case – for example if (1) and (2) are satisfied but (3) is not – viz. whether or not to say in these circumstances that P_2 is the same person as P_1. Then we can talk of (1), (2), and (3) being satisfied on balance or not being satisfied on balance. Once we have filled out the details of the extent to which (1), (2), and (3) respectively are evidence of personal identity, the question arises as to whether personal identity over time is constituted by the satisfaction on balance of (1), (2), and (3), or not.

I have argued at some length elsewhere[6] that personal identity is not so constituted, and I will repeat my arguments briefly here. Basically, they appeal to the conceivability of situations where P_1 and P_2 are the same person, even though (1), (2), and (3) are not on balance satisfied, and conversely.

Consider two cases. First, the resurrection of the dead (whose dead bodies have decayed). Most men uninfluenced by philosophical dogmas judge that their own resurrection from the dead is a coherent supposition (though, of course, some believe that they will rise again and some believe that they will not). If they are right about this, then P_1 can survive even if (3) is not satisfied. But in such a case P_1's survival will, on the view being criticised, consist in the existence of a person P_2 for whom (1) and (2) are on balance satisfied. But in hoping to survive I do not hope merely for the future existence of *a* person making the memory claims which I would be expected to make and behaving like me. I hope for the future existence of me, even if I am somewhat changed in memory and character. The survival for which P_1 may hope does not *consist in* the future existence of a person satisfying on balance

[6] 'Personal Identity', *Proc. Arist. Soc.*, vol. 74 (1973–4), pp. 231–47.

(1), (2), and (3). Secondly, more fashionably, consider a man P_1 undergoing a severe operation. If you suppose that satisfaction of (3) is a matter of brain-continuity, let it be a brain operation. According to the view being criticised, personal identity over time is a matter of the satisfaction of (1), (2), and (3) to a definite degree, which can be spelt out in a detailed analysis. But this can be seen to be implausible if we consider cases where the operation has the consequence that (1), (2), and (3) are only just satisfied or only just not satisfied, on whatever detailed analysis is offered. Thus suppose that the analysis requires that P_2 has to have half of P_1's brain-matter subsequent to an operation in order to be the same person, and that I am P_1 undergoing an operation in which I shall lose more than half my brain-matter. Yet despite the analysis if I hope to survive the operation I seem to have a coherent hope. Surely I am not refusing to look logical facts in the face if I hope to survive an operation in which I lose more than half my brain-matter. Any attempt to provide the detailed analysis in terms of the amount of continuity of the whole body, and/or of similarity of memory and character, runs into similar difficulties. Either the theory has rather demanding conditions for survival (for example, continuity of 90 per cent of body matter), or it has less demanding conditions (for example, continuity of 10 per cent of body matter). In the former case it seems a coherent hope to hope to survive even if the conditions are not fulfilled; and in the latter case it seems a coherent fear to fear that you will not survive even if the conditions are fulfilled. A detailed analysis of personal identity in terms of the extent of satisfaction of (1), (2), and (3) does not seem plausible. The alternative suggested by the cases which I have discussed is to suppose that (1), (2), and (3) are merely fallible evidence of personal identity. I put forward no view as to whether they are criterial evidence, or merely inductive evidence.

So generally I have argued that the existence, distinction, and continuation of persons are not analysable in terms of public evidence, although normally (i.e. except in awkward cases) public evidence gives very probable, nay well-nigh certain, verdicts. What arguments could an opponent bring against my conclusion? He might claim that my descriptions of the imaginary cases which I set out are not coherent descriptions. But they appear to be coherent descriptions, and it is hard to see how they could be shown not to be without recourse to some general principle of meaning. This might be a principle about the meaningfulness of statements – for example, that only a statement which can to some extent be verified or falsified by observational evidence has factual meaning, and it might be suggested that my examples fall foul of it. But the principle would need to be proved first, and in so far as the arguments for or against it appeal to examples of statements which apparently have or lack factual meaning, then necessarily the examples discussed in this paper would not favour its truth. More interestingly, my opponent might appeal to some principle about the meaningfulness of words or phrases. He might suggest that words purporting to denote properties or relations possessable by material objects can only have a meaning in a language if they can be analysed in terms of words denoting public phenomena. If that principle were true, then on my account 'person' and 'is the same person as' would be expressions empty of meaning. He might claim, further, that I could give no account of how a man could come to learn to use these expressions He might object, yet further, that I could not give a satisfactory account of how we are in a position to know that the public phenomena which we treat as evidence for identifying, counting, and re-identifying persons do constitute such evidence. I shall reply to these objections in the form of objections to my account of the grounds for re-identifying persons. It will be seen that if my counter-arguments succeed in defending my account of re-identification, similar counter-arguments would succeed in defending my accounts of identification and counting.

It is true that 'is the same person as' cannot be analysed in terms of words denoting public phenomena. But then, as we saw earlier in the paper, neither can such expressions as 'is in pain', 'has an after-image', 'feels a worse pain than', 'has a different colour sensation from'. Yet clearly such expressions denote properties and relations which can be possessed by material bodies, viz. embodied persons. Some of them denote properties the existence of which can be known incorrigibly by one person; whereas others denote properties and relations, the presence of which no person can know incorrigibly. Although a man may be in a good position to be reasonably confident that his present colour sensations differ from those of someone else or from his own earlier sensations, he may always be mistaken. Likewise whether P_1 feels a worse pain than P_2 is something which neither P_1 nor P_2 nor anyone else can know incorrigibly. So the further fact that the truth of statements about personal identity over time cannot be known incorrigibly, even by the individuals to whom they refer, also does not count against the meaningfulness of 'is the same person as'. Most words of our language are related to the publicly observable phenomena which give them meaning in a somewhat rough and loose way which nevertheless suffices to give them meaning. 'Is the same person as' has a meaning because standard examples can be provided of persons who are – very probably – the same and of persons who are – very probably – different; and because some of the entailments of statements made by the sentences in which it occurs can be set out. For example 'P_1 is the same person as P_2' entails 'if P_2 is not the same person as P_2*, then P_1 is not the same person as P_2*'. Again, it entails that P_2 is responsible for what P_1 did, to blame for his misdeeds, to praise for his good deeds. Again, it entails that if P_2 suffers, P_1 has something to fear – and so on.

The next objection claimed that I could not give an account of how a man could come to use the expression 'is the same person as'. Here, however, is a plausible account. The account assumes that (1), (2), and (3) above are criteria of personal identity. A somewhat different account would be needed if one held the view that they were inductive evidence. A child hears others say to him such things as 'Yesterday you went to Granny's', 'This morning you got up late'. They have made these statements by using criteria (2) and (3), to judge that the child before them is the child who went to Granny's yesterday, etc. The child learns that what they are saying is the same as what he would say if he uttered the same sentences using the word 'I' instead of the word 'you'. After hearing many such statements made, the child finds himself uttering similar sentences – for example, 'Last week I had my birthday', 'This afternoon I had my rest', straight off – without using criteria. Yet what he says is the same as others do and would say if they were to use criteria (2) and (3). They therefore judge him to have got hold of the concepts involved, and commend him for making true statements. Since they now judge him to have got hold of the concepts involved, they take similar sentences uttered by the child in future as statements about his past activities, as memory claims, and so, by criterion (1), as evidence that he is the same person as a person who did the things claimed, that is, as evidence of his past activities. In consequence the child gains confidence in his ability to make true statements about his own past activities – he feels certain to be true and certain to be false, straight off. Further, the child observes others making judgements about the activities of third persons and sees the criteria which they use for doing this – in effect criteria (1), (2), and (3). He then learns the use of the expression 'same person' by being told that if *P* who is so and so today (for example, in the same room as himself) did such-and-such yesterday, then the person who is so and so today 'is the same person as' the person who did such-and-such yesterday. He has thus learnt that (1), (2), and (3) are the criteria for personal identity. By hearing fairy stories about persons changing bodies, he learns that (1), (2), and (3), while being criteria of personal identity, do not constitute it. 'The same person', he learns, means the same in 'I am the same person as the person who went to Granny's yesterday' (a statement which is true if and only if he went to Granny's yesterday) as in 'The prince on Tuesday is the same person as the cobbler on Monday'. So what (1), and (2), and (3) are criteria of is a relation between persons, one example of which being something of which the child has immediate non-inferential knowledge – that he was (the same person as) a person who did so and so yesterday. He means by 'is the same person' in 'The prince on Tuesday is the same person as the cobbler on Monday' whatever he means by it in 'I am the same person as a person who did so and so yesterday'.

Who he was, what he did, are among the most basic things about which an individual has strong convictions not based on inference, convictions which normally amount to knowledge. What he knows cannot be fully defined in public terms. Within the framework of the public rules for the use of the terms, an individual denotes by such expressions as 'is the same person as' a specific relation, of instances of which he is aware in his own experience. Public use of such judgements as 'You did so and so' provide the words for a child to recognise and then describe a fact of which he becomes aware (though not incorrigibly aware) in his own experience.

The final objection claimed that I could not give a satisfactory account of how we are in a position to know that (1), (2), and (3) are evidence of personal identity. But clearly we are taught, as we first learn language, certain criterial knowledge. We must have such criterial knowledge – of what is evidence for what – if we are to have knowledge of anything beyond what we immediately experience. We acquire and come intuitively to see as correct certain standards of what is evidence for what. Either we are justified in adopting such standards as we see intuitively to be correct, or we are not. If we are, then it would appear that by adopting such standards we acquire criterial knowledge of what is evidence for what. Among such knowledge (either on its own or as a consequence of some other piece of criterial knowledge) is the knowledge that (1), (2), and (3) are evidence of personal identity. If we are not, then all claims to knowledge of anything beyond immediate experience are unjustified. If an opponent is unwilling to accept this latter conclusion (as most opponents will be), he will have to admit that the final objection fails.

I conclude that a number of objections which might be made against my account of the status of our grounds for re-identifying persons fail. Similar objections to my accounts of the status of our grounds for identifying and counting persons will fail for similar reasons. In default of more powerful objections,[7] I reaffirm the thesis of this paper that there are important differences between persons and inanimate material objects, in that the existence, distinction, and continuation of kinds of inanimate material objects is analysable in terms of public phenomena, whereas the existence, distinction and continuation of persons is not so analysable – although public phenomena provide evidence (normally well-nigh conclusive evidence) about the existence, distinction and continuation of persons. Human beings may have evolved from inanimate material objects, but what has evolved is qualitatively very different from that from which it has evolved.

[7] I do not have space to discuss all the objections which might be made against my thesis. One objection which I have not been able to discuss is the objection that although I might accurately have described our present conceptual scheme, the advance of science would suggest for the future a different scheme, in which the concept of person would have no place. But if we were to have rational justification for adopting the new scheme, it would need to be shown that it did no less justice to basic facts of our experience than did the old scheme. And, initially, it would seem that in failing to allow talk of persons and their conscious states and doings, it would do a great deal less justice to basic facts of experience than did the old scheme. How too, one wonders, could claims to knowledge be justified in the new scheme. For surely a man's claims to knowledge are justified ultimately by claims about what he has experienced. But what *he* has experienced is only something which can sensibly be talked about if he is a person who continues to exist over time.

MAIN PUBLICATIONS

Space and Time (Macmillan, 1968)
The Concept of Miracle (Macmillan, 1971)
An Introduction to Confirmation Theory (Methuen, 1973)
The Justification of Induction (ed.) (Oxford University Press, 1974)

THE PERFORMING ARTS

by

J. O. Urmson

Fellow of Corpus Christi College, Oxford

There is a distinction between works of art which is logically fundamental; some works of art include a series of events and thus take time, while others include no events and do not take time. Thus each of Beethoven's second and third symphonies includes a series of audible events; each has a duration; each takes time. It makes sense to say that the third is longer, takes more time than the second; this is in fact true, though it raises some minor philosophical difficulties, since an exaggeratedly slow performance of the second could be made to take longer than an absurdly fast performance of the third. This fact must be distinguished from two other facts, neither of any relevance to the questions raised in this paper, namely that the second symphony has existed longer than the third and that both took time, to be reckoned in months rather than in minutes, to create. Let us mark the fact that such works as these take time by calling them temporal works of art.

But some works of art do not take time. Thus Botticelli's 'Birth of Venus' and 'Primavera' do not take time, include no events, have no duration, though both have no doubt existed for some time and took some time to create. It does not make sense to ask which is longer, unless the word 'longer' is interpreted spatially. Let us mark the fact that such works as these do not take time by calling them atemporal works of art.

It is clear that all works of music and all dances are temporal works of art. In the original, narrower sense of 'drama' all dramas, including plays, operas, mimes, marionette shows and charades are inevitably temporal works; they are listened to, or watched, or listened to and watched. This seems to be a necessary truth. It is also clear that the conventional works of painting, sculpture, pottery, tapestry and landscape-gardening are atemporal works. There are, indeed, nowadays, temporal works of art such as mobiles, where the viewer witnesses changes in three-dimensional relationships and works where the viewer witnesses changes in two-dimensional patterns of colour. If these be classified as works of painting and sculpture, then it is not a necessary truth that works of painting and sculpture are atemporal. I have heard one ex-painter of traditional canvases who had changed to making mobiles say that he had done so because painting was a static art. Let us at present (for linguistic convenience and without implying any philosophical or aesthetic thesis) side with him verbally and use 'painting' and 'sculpture' as names for arts of which the products have the traditional atemporal character.

Rather surprisingly, there are works of art which are not *obviously* temporal or atemporal. I have especially in mind works of literature. Thus, if one asks whether *War and Peace* and Milton's sonnet on his blindness are temporal works, one may be inclined to say that they are atemporal since one witnesses no events in reading them; one may read about events, but that is not to witness them. One, indeed, takes longer to read than the other; but it also takes longer to look at a vast mural than at a miniature, and this fact does not make them temporal works. Since there are also arguments on the other side, I propose to leave literature entirely out of consideration for the present and to return to it at the end when certain general points have been clarified.

Obviously the distinction between temporal and atemporal works of art is in itself noteworthy. But it might be thought to be more significant than has yet emerged since it seems to carry a number of other very considerable differences with it. This I shall now attempt, provisionally, to show.

At least if we confine our attention to the essentially temporal works of music, dance and drama on the one hand and to conventional works of painting and sculpture on the other, which are atemporal, we shall find that the two groups are distinguishable in many ways beyond the temporality and atemporality already noted.

First, music, drama and the dance would seem to be performing arts, while painting and sculpture are not. In calling the former performing arts I have in mind such points as the following:

1. We distinguish the maker (creator, composer) of a work of music, dance or drama from the performer or performers. While the creator of a musical or balletic solo, or a monologue, may perform it himself and on his own, it is clear that the creator of a typical symphony, opera, ballet or play could not perform it unaided. Even if creation and first performance are simultaneous, as in the case of a musical improvisation, the distinction remains; a second performance can be given by the composer or by another, given sufficient musical memory and competence. It is a contingent question whether the composer joins in the performance of his creation. We can, on the other hand, attach no significance to the expression 'performance of "The Birth of Venus" ' in the case of painting, or 'performance of the "David" ' in the case of sculpture; *a fortiori* we can attach no meaning to the expression 'second performance' in either case, though the original artist or another can no doubt make a copy, which is something very different.

2. In music, drama and dance we recognise two distinct skills, that of the creator and that of the performer. The composer of a violin sonata may not have the technical skill to perform it, while the performer may lack the teachable (and regularly taught) skills of composition; there are many great performers who do not know how to write a fugue. Since there is no performance, this distinction cannot be made in the case of painting and sculpture. But this point does not depend on the special temporal meaning of 'performance', for we seem to have no use for a distinction between creator and executor in these arts. The questions 'Who painted it?' and 'Who carved it?' are questions also about creation. We have no use for such expressions as 'created by Michelangelo, executed by Raphael', and there are no creative but non-executive artists in this field. Though one artist may suggest a subject of a painting to another, the latter, not the former, is regarded as the creator.

Thus the temporal arts seem to be also performing arts, while at least such pre-eminent atemporal arts as painting and sculpture seem to be non-performing arts. But this is not all. There appear to be other interesting distinctions between the same two groups.

One further point to note is that while music and drama are essentially audible, the making of a work of music or drama does not necessarily involve the making of any sounds; some composers compose 'at the piano' and some do not. Similarly, while dancing essentially involves movement, the composing of a ballet does not, even if notation of the steps involves movement of the pen-hand. We may even distinguish the composition from the writing down on paper. Mozart habitually composed pieces of music completely before he undertook the (for him) pedestrian task of committing them to paper. 'I composed the fugue first and wrote it down while I was thinking out the prelude', he wrote to his sister on 20 April 1782. But the creation of a painting or of a sculpture essentially involves painting or sculpting; we should not allow that a painting or sculpture had been created before the painted canvas or carved stone was completed.

Thus we do not regard the conception and execution of a painting or sculpture as being even a partial parallel to the conception and performance of a drama, dance or musical work. The execution is part of the creation, and until the painting or sculpting has been undertaken the work is at most projected. But a piece of music, or a drama, or a ballet may exist before it has been performed, if it ever is.

A further difference between the two groups, a final difference for the purposes of this paper, may be noted. Setting aside the views of Croce, we may say that the identity of a work of painting, sculpture, architecture or tapestry is unproblematic; it is this or that configuration of pigment, this or that piece or carved stone, this or that building or this or that stitched cloth. In short, it is a physical object. But the identity of a play, a symphony or a ballet is a notorious aesthetic problem (it arises also with regard to novels, poems and other literature, but the reader will remember that the status of literature has been left for separate consideration). Certainly we cannot identify the work with a series of performances, finite or otherwise, since to do so would make all unperformed works identical with the null-class and hence with each other.

Thus it seems that we have two groups of arts between which a whole group of differences can be discerned. On the one hand we have a group of arts

(*a*) that are temporal,
(*b*) that require a distinction between performer and creator,

(*c*) where the creator does not as such produce those things (sounds, movements) of which the witnessable work consists,
(*d*) where the identity of the work of art is philosophically problematic.

On the other hand we have a group of arts

(*a*) that are atemporal,
(*b*) that permit no distinction of creator and performer,
(*c*) where the creator does produce just those things of which the witnessable work consists,
(*d*) where the work can be unproblematically identified with *some* particular physical thing.

I have no doubt that, if we consider the main tradition of Western art, these two groups, so strongly distinguished, do exist and that music, dance and drama belong to the first group and painting and sculpture to the second. Nor, I believe, is this a mere accident. But perhaps the tie between the various features that we have ascribed to the two groups is not so close as it may seem. This is the question for immediate investigation.

It might seem that the tie is very close indeed. It might be argued that since the work created by the painter or sculptor is a physical object and not a sequence of events the two arts are inevitably atemporal and the identity of the work will be clear and unproblematic; and since the work is an enduring physical object the creator of it can have no need of an ancillary artist with the status of a performer; it will also be inevitable that the creator produces the witnessable work himself. But, the argument continues, the creator of a theatrical or musical work, or a dance, inevitably produces a temporal work; since what is witnessed can only be a performance of the work, the work itself cannot be identical with what we witness; so there must be a separate act of creation and a separate act of performance. There we have one extreme view.

It might, perhaps, be argued on the other side that the distinctions set out above are really superficial. One might attempt to break down the distinction between, for example, painting and music (with easy application to the other arts mentioned) in the following way. We must remember, it might be said, that in music the performer, as well as the composer, is regarded not only as a technician, but as an artist. This is so because the performer is in fact a joint composer. Thus the musical score prepared by the composer is merely an approximate sketch of the musical work; it may be very approximate at the one extreme, as when in his 'Ode on St Cecilia's Day' Handel at one point writes 'Organ ad lib.', but it is still only approximate in the scores of, for example, Elgar and Stravinsky, laden as they are with performing directions. Two performances may be very different and yet have equal right to be counted as acceptable performances of the same work. So it may be claimed that the distinction between composer and performer is unimportant. What we hear is a joint composition by so-called composer and so-called performer. It is as if in painting one man laid down the general structure of the picture and another filled in the details.

Now it is importantly true that scores are approximate and that the performer has to make decisions continuous with those of the composer, which determine the precise character of the performance. The suggested argument based on this truth is, however, quite mistaken. To mention just one point, but a decisive one: in a joint painting, however the work is divided, each artist paints, while in the case of music the composer makes no sound – all the sound is produced by the performer.

So we must embark on a more careful examination of the matter than that on which either of the extreme views just outlined could rest. We cannot do better than to start with a consideration of the relation of composer and performer in a temporal art.

If we want a reasonably exact parallel (logically, not aesthetically) to the relation of composer to performer drawn from some atemporal art we shall find it not in a joint painting, as suggested above, but in the relation of recipe-maker to cook. As the creator of music, play or ballet makes no relevant sounds or movements, as such, so the creator of, say, the Dundee cake cooked and made nothing edible, as such. The recipe may well be the result of experiments in cooking, but so may the score be the result of experimental performance. So to invent a dish in cookery is to think out, and normally write down, a recipe, as to invent a musical work is to think out and, normally, write down a score. As in the case of the musical score, the recipe will be more or less approximate ('mix well', 'add seasoning to taste') and the cook has to interpret it. Thus chef A's Dundee cake may differ from that of chef B much as maestro C's 'Eroica' will differ from that of maestro D. In neither case need the difference be caused by differences in skill and facilities; it may be caused by interpretative choices. Cooking, as conducting, is an art.

So, I suggest, what the composer of music, plays or dances produces is a recipe or set of instructions; the performer follows the recipe with more or less skill and greater or less aesthetic judgement and imagination. When a composer of music writes a minim G on the second line of the treble clef, followed by a crotchet A in the space above, with a 'hair-pin', open-end to the right, below, and gives the value of the crotchet as M.M. = 60, he is saying to the performer something similar to what the recipe-maker says to the potential cook when he writes 'Take two eggs and beat briskly'. Logically the composer, instead of using musical notation, could have written: 'Hold the G above middle C for two seconds and then the A immediately above for one second, getting louder all the time'. This is exactly equivalent to the musical notation described above. Needless to say, there are the strongest practical objections to such a notation. But it remains that the composer is using a special notation for giving a recipe, and imperatives in ordinary words do occur from time to time (*non affrettarsi*, *muta in A*, *la cadenza sia corta*, etc.). Because of the special notation the score is perhaps more like knitting instructions than a cookery recipe.

The case of ballet seems so clearly similar that it requires no separate discussion. Also the playwright who puts in the script:

Lady Macbeth: Out damned spot.

can be regarded as giving an abbreviated version of performing instructions which might have cumbersomely read: 'Next, the performer of the part of Lady Macbeth is to say "Out damned spot".'

For ephemeral purposes and in simple cases the explicit recipe can be replaced by demonstration, which is itself a sort of recipe – 'Do it like this'. The explicit recipe is also frequently supplemented in this way by composers, playwrights, producers, conductors and others with suitable authority and talents. But an explicit recipe in writing is clearly a practical necessity for complex works which are to have any permanence.

Thus we may see things this way:

(*a*) what the composer writes down is logically comparable to the autograph of the cookery-recipe.
(*b*) the type-score is logically comparable to the type-recipe.
(*c*) a performance of, say, the 'Eroica' is logically comparable to a particular Dundee cake.
(*d*) the 'Eroica' symphony is logically comparable to *the* Dundee cake.

To say that the 'Eroica' symphony exists (that there is such a work) is to say that there is a recipe, or set of instructions, any performance in accordance with which will count as a performance of the 'Eroica'; to say that the Dundee cake exists (that there is such a cake) is to say that there is a recipe any piece of food made in accordance with which will be counted as a Dundee cake. We must construe 'performance in accordance with' in terms of intention rather than success; partial failure to follow the instructions correctly will make the performance a bad one, but it will still be a performance of the work.

Thus the Dundee cake has the same abstract character as a work of the temporal arts. But cookery is not a temporal art; the Dundee cake does not take time, even if it takes time to bake a Dundee cake and takes time to eat one. A Dundee cake, not a making or eating of a Dundee cake, is parallel to a performance of the 'Eroica' symphony. Thus we can see that it is not the fact that music, dance and drama are temporal arts that explains why works in these arts have their abstract character; for products of atemporal arts can have the same abstract character. The explanation is that in the temporal arts the creator is normally the producer of a recipe. In both temporal and atemporal arts, when creation consists in the production of a recipe the work will have an abstract character.

It is clearly no accident that the temporal arts have, with traditional resources, been performing arts, where the creator provides only a recipe. Only in this way could there be permanent works of any complexity in the temporal arts; in simple cases a demonstration by the creator, without notation, can serve as a recipe, but an enduring opera or five-act play can scarcely exist without a written recipe. It is also clear why in cookery and other applied temporal arts, such as dress-making, pottery, furniture-making and rug-making, the creator should be a recipe-maker, though the reasons are different; we commonly need an abundance of the things for practical reasons (twelve dinner plates, not one) beyond what a single artist would wish or be able to make, and they themselves are ephemeral and liable to be worn out. But when these arts aspire to the condition of the fine arts we revert to thinking of them as we think of painting and sculpture. Whatever may be the case with regard to commercially available dinner services bearing famous names, a Leach pot is one turned on the wheel by Leach himself; a Lurçat rug hung on a museum wall was worked by Lurçat, and you may copy but not multiply it; for varying purposes a Chippendale chair is one made to Chippendale's design by anybody, or one made under Chippendale's supervision, or one made with his own hands.

If the above is correct, it is easy to see both how such atemporal arts as painting and sculpture could become arts admitting both a creative recipe-maker and an executive artist and why they in fact are not. For them to become such, parallel to music, drama, dance and cookery, one person, or group of persons, who would be conceived of as the creator, would have to write down, in some notation, a recipe or set of instructions for painting or sculpting. Anyone who followed these instructions would be an executive artist and what he produced would not be *the* painting of which the recipe had been given, but *a* painting made to that recipe; it would be parallel to a Dundee cake, not to the Dundee cake. The work created by the maker of the painting-recipe would have the same abstract status as the 'Eroica' symphony and the Dundee cake.

That things should be as described in the last paragraph is not logically impossible. Something very like it does actually occur for the amusement of children. One may give an approximate recipe for a stylised cat-drawing made by tracing circles round coins of different sizes, for example. But in serious painting and sculpture it is too easy to see why this type of procedure is not followed for it to be worth detailed explanation. It is obvious that it would be very difficult to devise a notation determining even approximately the character of a painting in cases of any complexity; if such a notation were devised it would probably be too difficult to follow. So one could give instructions most easily by providing an exemplar oneself. But since the exemplar would be relatively permanent and very difficult to copy with the fidelity required in the fine arts, it is natural to think of it as the work of art itself (like the Leach pot and the Lurçat rug) and to regard other productions not as following the recipe but as copies.

But while it is natural to think of the work of the creative painter as the work of art of which only copies can be made rather than as a pattern which any number of executants could follow, it is not inevitable. The point I have in mind may be illustrated from music. While the musical score is approximate and could be made more accurate only at the cost of increasing difficulty in writing, reading and performance, this approximate character has by no means always been thought of as a limitation. Composers have often left their scores more approximate than they need in order to leave a choice to the performer; the variety in performance that resulted was considered an asset. If an auditor of, say, Handel's own embellished performance of one of his own scores had reproduced it exactly in a further performance, everyone, including Handel, would have thought him a very dull dog. Further, it is always recognised that the pace and other features of any musical work must be partly determined by the specific performing conditions, such as the resonance of the building. There is nothing impossible about treating painting in a similar fashion. A painting could be thought of as a pattern, similar to a Handel first performance, a modified version of which by another executant artist could be thought of as an agreeably varied version rather than as an imperfect copy. Or, thinking of it as a pattern, we could have small versions of it for small rooms and large versions for large rooms, brighter versions for dark rooms and darker versions for lighter rooms, and so on. Each could be thought of as an execution of the (type) painting. There would, I repeat, be nothing impossible about this way of regarding things, though we do not do so, and would not wish to. But we could imagine a situation in which all drawing was done on tide-washed beaches. Perhaps then we might regard successive outlines in the sand of approximately similar character rather as examples of one abstract drawing than as mere copies of the first, lost, work of art.

If we could, then, assimilate our way of regarding such arts as sculpture and painting to our way of regarding the temporal arts in many respects, is the reverse also possible? How far could we regard music, dance and drama as we regard painting and sculpture?

If we are willing to abandon the notion of a permanent work of art in temporal fields, it is easy to see how it *could* be done. We *could* think of what we now regard as the first performance as the work of art and what we now think of as further performances as copies. In these circumstances there would be no unperformed works; if a score were made prior to any performances, its making would have to be regarded not as the creation of a work but the planning of it. We should have no use for the notion of the work persisting beyond the period of its performance. We should also have abolished the distinction between composer and performer. The work will have lost its abstract character; what one hears on any occasion will be the unique work, not a performance. This is all possible; it might be practically possible in the case of solo works or even simple group-works. Perhaps we do approach such a conceptualisation in the case of a charade or a jam-session. But so long as our temporal arts include such highly organised structures as five-act plays, operas and ballets this type of revision of concepts seems unlikely, at least. A complex painting can be composed as it is painted, alterations being made as necessary, but in the temporal arts the very complex structure must be determined in advance; one can make corrections only in a further performance. We may discount the chances of evolving an opera by group improvisation.

But in certain ways new developments are permitting, or even demanding, some revisions in our conceptualisation of the temporal arts. Prior to the invention of recording techniques our concept of the performance of a work of art was such that every performance had a date as well as a duration. Perhaps we can speak of, for example, Beecham's 'Jupiter' as a type-performance, having no assignable date, but then there must be performances which are tokens of that type which have a date. But the invention of the gramophone record and sound- and video-tapes has changed our way of speaking. A recorded performance can be replayed many times, but it is regarded as a token, not as a type. If I hear Beecham's 'Jupiter' three times in the concert-hall I shall have heard one type-performance, but three token performances. But if I listen three times to Beecham's recording of the 'Jupiter' symphony I have in no sense of 'performance' listened to three performances; I have heard repetitions of a single performance. In this way recorded performances have become permanent: they have a duration but no date, since they are repeatable. Moreover, I hear the same performance if I listen to three different shellac discs, if they are all prepared from the same master tape or disc. So we can now speak of a performance being preserved for posterity and being as likely to survive as any painting.

We now, indeed, find composers who compose directly on to tape, synthesising many sounds electronically. No score is made, and no score of traditional character could be made. The traditional distinction of composition and performance has gone. There are also colour-tapes showing mobile abstracts on the television screen. In this way, then, there can be some assimilation of the temporal arts to the atemporal, since we can obliterate the distinction between composer and performer, without sacrificing the permanence of the work of art. We perhaps have longer-established examples of this in the case of films composed, so to speak, on the set.

My conclusion is that there are very clear and important differences between the traditional temporal and atemporal arts, so far as we have considered them. These differences have stemmed from their temporal or atemporal character, against the background of existing techniques, technology and aesthetic goals. But we have found that there is no inevitability in this, and that, with less traditional techniques and goals, and with new technology, the sharp boundaries may begin to blur.

Being limited in space, I have ignored many arts in this discussion, some of which can easily be fitted into the scheme of things as here represented, others less easily. What space remains must be devoted to the interesting and difficult problem of literature.

There are two problems about literature which it seems to be relevant to discuss. First, it has been part of the programme of this paper to make use of a distinction between temporal and atemporal works of art. But we have found some difficulty in applying this distinction to literary works, and this casts doubts on the validity of the distinction. Secondly, part of the thesis of the paper has been that when the identity of the work is philosophically problematic, at least part of the explanation will be that the art in question is a performing art, or executive art, in which the creator provides a recipe or set of instructions for performance or production by an executive artist. But works of literature seem to have the same abstract character as those of the performing arts; and yet it is hard to see the novel, for example, as falling into the field of the performing arts. This is the second difficulty for my thesis.

I believe that both these difficulties stem from the same root, which is the ambivalent relation of the written to the spoken word. The written word is sometimes merely a notation of the spoken word; sometimes it is clearly independent, as in the case of a typical work of logic, any oral version of which will be a second-best, makeshift affair.

If, in the case of literature, the written word can be regarded as the notation of the spoken word, as I have assumed throughout to be the case so far as the text of a drama for acting is concerned, our difficulties vanish. Literature will be essentially a temporal and performing art. The writer will provide a score for the performer who reads it, and the speech that we hear is essentially a set of events.

In the case of some literature this view is not merely arguable but immediately plausible. Much poetry, for example, is clearly intended to be read aloud, and Homer's poetry was recited long before and after it was committed to paper. But the case can also be strengthened where it is not so immediately plausible.

Music is clearly an audible art; music consists of sound. But a trained score-reader can imagine with great accuracy what the sounds would be as he reads the score. Very learned music may be written for the score-reader rather than for performance (some pieces in Bach's 'Musical Offering' are perhaps examples); the technical ingenuities can be better appreciated in the study than in the concert-hall. Now few of us are skilled in reading musical scores; but all who read these words are of necessity highly skilled in reading notated speech. Perhaps, then, we may assimilate the reading of literature to musical score-reading, with examples intended primarily for reading as predominant numerically in literature as they are rare in the case of music. Thus the temporality of literature will be concealed. Just as when the musician reads a score there is no performance and, *a fortiori*, no question how long the performance took, so, when we read a poem silently, there is no performance, and so no question how long it took. Of course it takes time to read a score; but the facile score-reader will take less time to read a slow movement than he imagines the music as taking; the time the reading takes is not the performance time; and so with the silent reading of poetry. Score-reading and silent book-reading are neither composition nor performance and so are irrelevant to the theses of this paper.

That much literature, if not all written communication, should be regarded in this way is further suggested by the kind of criticism we make of literature that would rarely be read aloud. We refer to the rhythm of the prose, but what sort of rhythm would this be if not the imagined rhythm of the sound? Johnson's prose has been called sonorous. We criticise the written word as being ugly if syllables are juxtaposed which would sound ugly if spoken aloud.

So in the case of much literature I think that this theoretically simplest line is also the right line to take. But it cannot be all that there is to say on this topic. To consider but two low-flying examples, the limerick-writer who rhymes *Cholmondeley* with *comely*, but spells the latter word 'colmondeley', is not merely providing a recipe for the essentially audible; again, the visual aspect of Carroll's mouse-tailed 'Mouse's Tale' is quite essential. Yet neither is an example of a work intended, like a painting, for purely visual contemplation. Perhaps such cases should not be regarded as novel art-forms but analysed as complex works containing different elements less puzzling in character. The beautifully engraved musical score may be a parallel. I cannot now show this to be so. But it is perhaps reasonable to leave the reader with a problem.

MAIN PUBLICATIONS

Philosophical Analysis: Its Development between the Two World Wars (OUP, 1956)
The Emotive Theory of Ethics (Hutchinson, 1968)
Encyclopaedia of Western Philosophy (ed.) (1960)

LOCKE AND WITTGENSTEIN ON LANGUAGE AND REALITY

by

Godfrey Vesey

Professor of Philosophy in The Open University,
Honorary Director of The Royal Institute of Philosophy

In his later philosophy Wittgenstein attacks the idea of a private language. Commentators frequently ascribe the idea he attacks to Locke.[1] Sometimes what they say suggests that a more far-reaching comparison of what Locke and Wittgenstein say about the relation of language and reality might be worth while. Anthony Manser, for instance, says that Wittgenstein's 'discussion is ultimately about a whole class of philosophical views, roughly to be characterised as sense-datum empiricism, the idea that our language must have a foundation in a certain special class of experiences, namely sensations'.[2] In the first part of this paper

[1] I shall use the abbreviation '*E*', followed by the book, chapter and section numbers, to refer to John Locke, *An Essay Concerning Human Understanding* (1690); and the following abbreviations to refer to works by Ludwig Wittgenstein:

BB: *The Blue and Brown Books* (Oxford, Blackwell, 1958), followed by page number.

OC: *On Certainty* (Oxford, Blackwell, 1969), followed by paragraph number.

PE: 'Wittgenstein's Notes for Lectures on "Private Experience" and "Sense Data" ', ed. R. Rhees, *Philosophical Review*, vol. lxxvii (1968), followed by page number.

PI: *Philosophical Investigations* (Oxford, Blackwell, 1953), followed by paragraph number in Part I, or 'II' and section number, and, if necessary, page number, in Part II.

RFM: *Remarks on the Foundations of Mathematics* (Oxford, Blackwell, 1956), followed by part and section numbers.

Z: *Zettel* (Oxford, Blackwell, 1967), followed by paragraph number.

[2] Peter Winch (ed.), *Studies in the Philosophy of Wittgenstein* (London, Routledge, 1969), p. 171.

I list the ingredients of Locke's version of what Manser calls 'sense-datum empiricism'. In the second part I examine what Wittgenstein says about *some* of these ingredients.

1. LOCKE

The Theory

There are seven ingredients in Locke's version of what Manser calls 'sense-datum empiricism'. The recipe may be represented in a diagram.

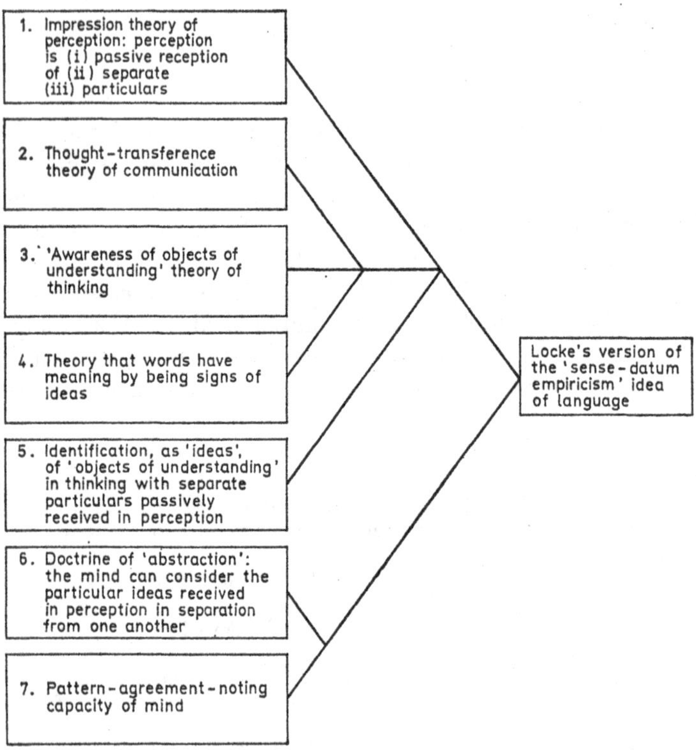

By way of exposition, rather than criticism, I shall say a little about each of these ingredients, in the order in which I have numbered them in the diagram.

1. 'The first capacity of human intellect', Locke says, is 'that the

mind is fitted to receive the impressions made on it; either through the senses by outward objects, or by its own operations when it reflects on them.'[3] By his talk of 'impressions made on the mind through the senses' – talk which reflects the assimilation by earlier philosophers[4] of the role of the mind in perception to that of wax receiving an impression from a seal – Locke means to convey three things. (*i*) The mind in perception – that is, in receiving the impressions – is *passive*. 'These simple ideas, when offered to the mind, the understanding can no more refuse to have, nor alter when they are imprinted, nor blot them out and make new ones itself, than a mirror can refuse, alter or obliterate the images or ideas which the objects set before it do therein produce.'[5] (*ii*) 'Though the qualities that affect our senses are, in the things themselves, so united and blended that there is no separation, no distance between them; yet it is plain the ideas they produce in the mind enter by the senses simple and unmixed.'[6] This, Locke holds, is as true of ideas that come in by the same sense as it is of ideas that come in by different senses.[7] Thus, if I look at something that is white and round I have two *separate* ideas, one of white and the other of round, not one, of something white and round. (*iii*) The things let in by the senses are *particulars.*[8] That is, to talk, in the terms of the impression theory of perception, of having an impression of white, is not the same as to talk, as we ordinarily do, of seeing the whiteness of something. Whiteness is a universal. An impression of white is not. Empiricists usually try to bridge the gap between their talk of 'impressions' and what we ordinarily say we perceive by invoking the notions of 'interpretation' or 'classification'.

2. 'The most noble and profitable invention of all other', wrote Hobbes,[9] 'was that of SPEECH, consisting of *names* or *appellations*, and their connexion; whereby men register their thoughts; recall them when they are past; and also declare them one to another for mutual utility and conversation.' 'The general use of speech', he went on, 'is to transfer our mental discourse, into verbal; or the train of our thoughts, into a train of words.'

[3] *E*, 2.1.24.

[4] E.g. Plato, *Theaetetus*, 191c; Descartes, *Rules for the Direction of the Mind*, Rule 12.

[5] *E*, 2.1.25.

[6] *E*, 2.2.1.

[7] ibid. See also *E*, 2.11.3.

[8] *E*, 1.2.15.

[9] *Leviathan* (1651), ch. IV.

The thought-transference theory of communication, as I shall call it, won general acceptance. Two hundred and thirty years after Hobbes' *Leviathan* was published, George Spencer Bower wrote:

'In order to communicate the trains of our thoughts to others, as well as to record for our own benefit and use our own past trains in the order in which the ideas composing them actually occurred, it was found absolutely necessary to employ sensible signs or marks. Mind cannot work upon mind directly. One person can only devise and use visible or audible signs, which shall impress themselves on the senses of another person, and, by means of predetermined associations, call up in his mind ideas in a certain order, and at the same time signify to him that those ideas are passing, or did at some previous time pass, in his (the first person's) mind.'[10]

Non-philosophers sometimes talk as if there could be no question of the truth of the thought-transference theory of communication. In Part Two of this paper I shall mention Wittgenstein's explanation of this. Cartesian philosophers may be predisposed to accept it by their commitment to the idea that the mind, the essence of which is thinking, can exist apart from everything material, including the 'visible or audible signs' to which Bower refers.

To grasp the full implications of the thought-transference theory of communication it is important to distinguish between three things: (*i*) what a person says out loud, (*ii*) what a person, soliloquising, says to himself, and (*iii*) what Hobbes calls 'mental discourse'.

Locke holds the thought-transference theory of communication.[11] Just as Hobbes distinguishes between mental discourse and verbal discourse, so Locke distinguishes between 'mental propositions' and 'verbal propositions'. If we wonder why it is not generally recognised that there are, besides verbal propositions, mental ones, an explanation is ready to hand: '. . . it is very difficult to treat of them asunder. Because it is unavoidable, in treating of mental propositions, to make use of words; and then the instances given

[10] *Hartley and James Mill* (London, 1881), p. 46.
[11] *E*, 3.1.1–2, 3.2.1.

of mental propositions cease immediately to be barely mental, and become verbal.'[12]

3. Thinking, according to Locke, is a matter of 'being employed' about certain '*objects* of the understanding'. He thinks that the word 'idea' is the term which serves best to stand for these objects, of which he holds everyone to be conscious in himself.[13]

4. Locke holds that words have meaning by signifying the objects of understanding in thinking, which he has called 'ideas'. Words stand as outward marks for these internal objects.[14]

5. Locke identifies the 'objects of understanding' in thinking with the separate particulars passively received in perception, calling both by the same name, 'ideas'. If there is an argument for this identification I have not been able to find it.

The product of 1–5 would be the theory that words have meaning by standing, like proper names, for sense-impressions (or 'ideas'). But if every idea had a word to itself, words would not be

'so useful as they ought to be. It is not enough for the perfection of language, that sounds can be made signs of ideas, unless those signs can be so made use of as to comprehend several particular things: for the multiplication of words would have perplexed their use, had every particular thing need of a distinct name to be signified by.'[15]

To show how 'signs can be so made use of as to comprehend several particular things' Locke adds, to 1–5 above, 6 and 7 below.

6. According to the impression theory of perception, the ideas produced in the mind 'enter by the senses simple and unmixed'. That is, they are separate. Moreover, they can be considered as separate. For instance, when I look at something that is white and round the idea of white enters my mind unmixed with the idea of round, and with any concomitant ideas, and I can consider it so. In what appears to be a definition of the term 'abstraction' Locke writes:

'. . . the mind makes the particular ideas received from particular objects to become general; which is done by considering them as

[12] *E*, 4.5.3.
[13] *E*, 1.1.8.
[14] *E*, 2.11.8–9, 3.1.1–2, 3.2.1–8.
[15] *E*, 3.1.3.

they are in the mind such appearances, – separate from all other existences, and the circumstances of real existence, as time, place, or any other concomitant ideas. This is called ABSTRACTION, . . .'[16]

Locke appears, here, to be saying that by the term 'abstraction' he means an act of considering a particular idea (for example, of white) in separation from other ideas (for example, of round) received at the same time.

Abstraction, so understood, will not by itself explain how 'the mind makes the particular ideas received from particular objects to become general'. To the mind's capacity for considering ideas in separation from concomitant ideas must be added a further capacity.

7. The further capacity is that of noticing that other ideas 'conform to', or 'agree with', the idea considered in separation (now called an 'abstract idea'). A later idea is said to conform to, or agree with, an earlier idea if, as we should ordinarily say, two things are seen to be the same colour, felt to be the same temperature, etc. The earlier idea, laid up in the memory, thus serves as a pattern or standard for later ideas. As such it may be called a 'general' idea, though it is still a particular. Its generality consists in the use to which it is put:

'Ideas are general when they are set up as the representatives of many particular things; but universality belongs not to things themselves, which are all of them particular in their existence, even those words and ideas which in their signification are general . . . their general nature being nothing but the capacity they are put into, by the understanding, of signifying or representing many particulars.'[17]

A different sense of 'abstraction'

Locke was not consistent in his use of the term 'abstraction'. In addition to what Berkeley called the 'proper acceptation' of the term, he used it in connection with the theory that abstract ideas are ideas of what a number of things have in common. On this

[16] *E*, 2.11.9. This is the section referred to in Berkeley, *Principles of Human Knowledge* (1710), introduction, § VII, 'Proper acceptation of abstraction'.

[17] *E*, 3.3.11. Cf. Berkeley, ibid, introduction, § XII: '. . . an idea, which considered in itself is particular, becomes general by being made to represent or stand for all other particular ideas of the same sort.'

theory, one observes what is common to Peter and James, Mary and Jane, and accordingly frames an abstract idea in which what is peculiar to each is left out and what is common to them all is retained. This, according to Locke, is the abstract idea signified by the name *man*.[18]

To the theory that we frame abstract ideas by observing what things have in common – for example, that different people have humanity in common – it may be objected that we could not recognise humanity in any one of them unless we already had the concept.[19] Can a similar objection be made to the other theory, the theory that an abstract idea (for example, an idea of white considered in separation from a concomitant idea of round) serves as a representative of other ideas that 'agree' with it? The objection would concern the 'agreement'. How, it would be asked, can we recognise the agreement without already having the concept? The answer would be that no particular kind of agreement need be recognised, since the kind is determined by the idea being the abstract one it is. Only ideas of white can agree with an abstract idea of white. The only concept presupposed is that of simple likeness.[20]

The problem of privacy

If words have meaning by standing for ideas, how can they have the *same* meaning for *different* people? In Locke's use of the term 'idea' different people cannot meaningfully be said to have the same idea. Or can they?

Locke says such things as that 'unless a man's words excite the same ideas in the hearer which he makes them stand for in speaking, he does not speak intelligibly'[21] and 'The chief end of language

[18] *E*, 3.3.7.

[19] Cf. D. W. Hamlyn, *The Theory of Knowledge* (London, Macmillan, 1971), p. 58.

[20] John Stuart Mill (*System of Logic*, 1843, book 1, ch. 5, § 6) says that in the case of words like 'white' 'though the predicate is the name of a class, yet in predicating it we affirm nothing but resemblance, the class being founded not on resemblance in any given particular, but on general resemblance . . . When, therefore, I say The colour I saw yesterday was a white colour, or, The sensation I feel is one of tightness, in both cases the attribute I affirm of the colour or of the other sensation is mere resemblance—simple *likeness* to sensations I have had before, and which have had those names bestowed upon them.'

[21] *E*, 3.2.8.

in communication being to be understood, words serve not well for that end . . . when any word does not excite in the hearer the same idea which it stands for in the mind of the speaker.'[22] This is near to being a truism in the ordinary use of the term 'idea'; but what does it mean in Locke's use of it? If the 'objects of understanding' in thinking are identical with separate particulars passively received in perception (5, above) how can talk of two people having the same idea have any meaning?

One way out of this is to say that 'same' means 'similar'. If it is then asked how it can be known that ideas in different minds are similar, it may be said that the supposition that they are not is of little use, or, alternatively, that it would not matter if they weren't similar. It would not matter, for example, if 'the idea that a violet produced in one man's mind by his eyes were the same that a marigold produced in another man's, and *vice versa*'.[23] It would not affect the ability of either of the men to distinguish between violets and marigolds.

Another way out of it is to suppose that provided we do not restrict ourselves to words which are proper names of particular ideas, but also have words for abstract ideas, the problem does not arise. For some reason, the names of abstract ideas cannot fail to be significant or intelligible to other people.[24]

Language and reality: the empiricist deduction

In his *Critique of Pure Reason* (1781), Kant remarked that 'many empirical concepts are employed without question from anyone. Since experience is always available for the proof of their objective reality, we believe ourselves, even without a deduction, to be justified in appropriating to them a meaning, an ascribed significance.'[25] (The term 'deduction' is one he had borrowed from the speech of jurists. Jurists distinguish between proof in questions of *fact* and proof in questions of *right*. The latter they call a 'deduction'. In the context of a discussion of language, a deduction is a proof of one's right to employ a certain concept.)

[22] *E*, 3.9.4. [23] *E*, 2.32.15.

[24] This supposition seems to me to be implicit in *E*, 3.3.3. The fact that I do not comment on these 'solutions' of the problem of privacy must not be taken as meaning that I think they work. I am restricting myself to exposition.

[25] *Immanuel Kant's Critique of Pure Reason*, trans. N. K. Smith (London, 1934), A84, B116–17.

Kant here distinguishes between a deduction, and a proof of the objective reality, of a concept. One can have the latter without the former – through experience. I think he must mean that in the face of the empirical *fact* that something is white (my experiencing it as white) the reality of whiteness is indisputable, and the question 'Have we the right to employ the *concept* white?' does not occur to us.

But suppose it does occur to us. How is it to be answered?

Locke's version of what Manser calls 'sense-datum empiricism, the idea that our language must have a foundation in a certain special class of experiences, namely sensations' is an answer to the question. It is the answer that we have a right to employ the concept *white* because our idea of white is an effect in us of a power in something real outside us:

'By *real ideas*, I mean such as have a foundation in nature; such as have a conformity with the real being and existence of things, or with their archetypes. *Fantastical* or *chimerical*, I call such as have no foundation in nature, nor have any conformity with that reality of being to which they are tacitly referred as to their archetypes. . . .

'Our *simple ideas are all real*, all agree to the reality of things. Not that they are all of them the images or representations of what does exist; the contrary whereof, in all but the primary qualities of bodies, hath been already showed. But though whiteness and coldness are no more in snow than pain is; yet those ideas of whiteness and coldness, pain, etc., being in us the effects of powers in things without us, ordained by our Maker to produce in us such sensations; they are real ideas in us, . . . the reality lying in that steady correspondence they have with the distinct constitutions of real beings. But whether they answer to those constitutions, as to causes or patterns, it matters not; it suffices that they are constantly produced by them.'[26]

In short, a simple idea is real – that is, agrees or conforms to the reality of things – because it is an impression on, or in, someone's mind, produced by a power in something real outside him. He is passive in the reception of simple ideas, so there is no danger

[26] *E*, 2.30.1–2. Kant had read Locke. Locke's 'fantastical or chimerical' ideas are Kant's 'usurpatory concepts'.

of their being altered, or blotted out and imaginary ones substituted (see 1 (*i*) above). An 'abstract' idea, moreover, is real, also; for it is no more than a simple idea put to a certain use. The use to which we put the simple idea, to be a representative of all of its kind, is dependent on the fact that 'nature, in the production of things, makes several of them alike'.[27] The likeness is in nature, not in us.[28] Thus abstract ideas are real on two counts: as simple ideas they are the product of real things outside us, and as abstract ideas their use reflects the real similitude of these things. Ideas being the objects of the understanding in thinking, and words standing for ideas, the agreement or conformity of language – at least in so far as it consists of words for simple and abstract ideas – to reality is guaranteed. It is guaranteed by 5 above: the identification, as 'ideas', of 'objects of understanding' in thinking with separate particulars passively received in perception. Once 5 is accepted it follows that we cannot fail to be justified in applying words like 'white' to the world. Since the mind is passive in perception there is simply no possibility of the ideas for which such words stand being fictitious. The language of words for simple qualities *must* agree with, in the sense of conforming to, reality. It must conform to reality because it is derived, without alteration, from it. This is the essence of Locke's version of what Manser calls 'sense-datum empiricism'.

2. WITTGENSTEIN

It is doubtful whether Wittgenstein ever read Locke.[29] He has other targets, including his earlier self, in mind in what he says in his later philosophy. Nevertheless, some of what he says has a bearing on what Locke says. I remarked earlier that commentators frequently relate what Wittgenstein says about private languages to Locke. But the privacy of language, for Locke, is not so much an ingredient in his account of language, as a consequence of it. It is a consequence of language being derived from reality via ex-

[27] *E*, 3.3.13.

[28] Contrast John Stuart Mill (*System of Logic*, book 1, ch. III, § 11): 'Resemblance is evidently a feeling; a state of the consciousness of the observer.'

[29] See P. M. S. Hacker, *Insight and Illusion* (Oxford, OUP, 1972), pp. 217–18.

perience, with experience conceived of according to the impression theory of perception. Judging from his treatment of the problem of privacy, Locke did not think it very important. Perhaps a comparison of Locke and Wittgenstein which is not confined to the privacy/non-privacy issue may bring to light something in what Wittgenstein says about language which is more important than its alleged non-privacy, something of which the non-privacy is a consequence. Let us see.

The impression theory of perception

According to this theory, perception is the (*i*) passive reception of (*ii*) separate (*iii*) particulars. Some things Wittgenstein says can be interpreted as a rejection of all three of these elements.

(*i*) Wittgenstein uses the term 'impression' himself, but his use of it is closer to Reid's than to Locke's. Thomas Reid criticised Aristotle, Locke and Hume for holding 'that, in perception, an impression is made upon the mind as well as upon the organs, nerves and brain', and said that 'if we conceive the mind to be immaterial we shall find it difficult to affix a meaning to *impressions upon it*' except in a figurative sense, in which we talk of being impressed by things that are interesting.[30] In this figurative sense, to talk of letting something make an impression on one is to talk of attending to it. The impression is something one produces, by attention. When Wittgenstein writes about 'impressions' in *BB* 127–85 and in *Z* 417–27, this is what he means, not something that figures in the impression theory of perception.[31] So, at least to the extent that he did not use 'impression' in the empiricists' sense, what Wittgenstein says can be interpreted as a rejection of the empiricists' sense of 'impression'.

(*ii*) Locke says that 'it is plain the ideas they [external objects] produce in the mind enter by the senses simple and unmixed'.[32] By being considered in separation from one another ('abstraction') they can serve as patterns for ideas that 'agree' with them. Berkeley denied that he could 'abstract one from another, or conceive separately, those qualities which it is impossible should exist so separated'.[33] Wittgenstein would have agreed with Berkeley. He

[30] *Essays on the Intellectual Powers of Man* (1785), essay II, ch. 4.
[31] See, especially, *BB*, p. 150, ll. 1–2; p. 176, ll. 35–6.
[32] *E*, 2.2.1.
[33] *Principles of Human Knowledge*, introduction, X.

remarks that 'if the word "red" summons up a colour in my memory, it must surely be in connexion with a shape'.[34]

(*iii*) If the things produced in us by external objects are, like the objects that produce them, particulars, then presumably they can be looked at, inwardly; and *must* be looked at, and 'interpreted', if perception is to yield knowledge by description. What Wittgenstein says in the *Brown Book*, II, 17 (*BB* 165–7) and *PI* 380, 604–5, and II, xi, constitutes a rejection of this as a false picture of what perceiving is. (Regrettably, I have not the space to expound his views on how it is false.)

The thought-transference theory of communication

Wittgenstein writes: 'Misleading parallels: the expression of pain is a cry – the expression of thought, a proposition. As if the purpose of the proposition were to convey to one person how it is with another: only, so to speak, in his thinking part and not in his stomach.'[35] He is particularly interested in *how* we come to be misled into thinking this. We think of understanding a spoken sentence as a matter of our hearing of it being accompanied by something that goes on in our minds.[36] Why? It is, he says, through misunderstanding our own forms of expression: 'established forms of expression' lead us 'to look for a peculiar act of thinking, independent of the act of expressing our thoughts and stowed away in some peculiar medium'.[37] 'We are like savages, primitive people, who hear the expressions of civilised men, put a false interpretation on them, and then draw the queerest conclusions from it.'[38]

One example of an expression on which we put a false interpretation is 'Now I understand!' or 'Now I can go on!'[39] Instead of asking 'What happens when a man suddenly understands?', which goes with thinking of 'sudden understanding' as the name of an inner process,[40] we should ask 'In what kind of case, under what circumstances do we say "Now I can go on," if the formula

[34] *Z*, 336.

[35] *PI*, 317.

[36] *BB*, 3, 5, 34–5, 42–3, 65, 157; *PI*, 154, 330, II, xi, 218; *Z*, 101, 139–40, 143, 163, 236; *PE*, 279.

[37] *BB*, 43.

[38] *PI*, 194. See also *PI*, 109, 339.

[39] *BB*, 112–18; *PI*, 151–5, 179–81, 195–6, 317–24, II, xi, 218; *Z*, 74, 193, 298, 446.

[40] *PI*, 321.

has occurred to us?'[41] The '*particular circumstances* which justify me in saying I can go on – when the formula occurs to me'[42] are such things as that I have learnt algebra.[43] The glad start 'Now I know how to go on'[44] is appropriate in these circumstances. It is no more a report on something observed internally than 'I hope . . .' is a description of a state of mind.[45]

Another example of an expression on which we put a false interpretation is 'I meant *X* when I said "*Y*" ' (for example, 'I meant the man who won at Austerlitz when I said "Napoleon" ').[46] It is our use of the past tense ('meant') that misleads us. Grammatically, 'I meant *X*' is like 'I kicked *X*' : the word 'meant' is used in the construction of the first sentence as 'kicked' is used in the construction of the second. And so we are led to think of meaning *X* as an activity, a 'mental' one, we performed at the time of saying '*Y*'. To see facts with unbiased eyes,[47] we need to attend to how such expressions as 'I meant . . .' are actually used, the grammar that lies below the surface.[48] We need to recognise that there is a use of language in which what happens later[49] is the criterion[50] of what, judging from the surface grammar, happened earlier.

'Ideas' and meaning

In the everyday, non-technical, use of the term 'idea' it is practically a truism that to talk of what a person is thinking is to talk of his ideas. But Locke's use of 'idea' is not the everyday, non-technical, one. Ideas are said to be '*objects* of understanding'. They are said to be what words signify.[51] And they are said to be the things passively received in perception.

Locke's notion is that for someone to have understood a sentence containing the word 'white', for instance, that word must have

[41] *Z*, 446.
[42] *PI*, 154.
[43] *PI*, 179.
[44] *PI*, 323.
[45] *Z*, 78.
[46] *BB*, 38–9. Cf. *PI*, 661–93, II, xi, 216–17; *Z*, 1–53.
[47] *BB*, 43.
[48] *PI*, 664.
[49] *Z*, 7–8, 14, etc.
[50] *Z*, 22.
[51] *E*, 3.2.7: 'So far as words are of use and signification, so far is there a constant connection between the sound and the idea, and a designation that the one stands for the other; without which application of them they are nothing but so much insignificant noise.'

excited in him, by the mechanism of association,[52] the idea it signifies. The idea is the *meaning* of the word.

Wittgenstein attacks a theory not very different from this, the theory that for the word to be understood it must have called up an image. He writes:

'If the meaning of the sign (roughly, that which is of importance about the sign) is an image built up in our minds when we see or hear the sign, then first let us adopt the method . . . of replacing this mental image by some outward object seen, e.g. a painted or modelled image. Then why should the written sign plus this painted image be alive if the written sign alone was dead? – In fact, as soon as you think of replacing the mental image by, say, a painted one, and as soon as the image thereby loses its occult character, it ceases to seem to impart any life to the sentence at all. (It was in fact just the occult character of the mental process which you needed for your purposes.)

'The mistake we are liable to make could be expressed thus: We are looking for the use of a sign, but we look for it as though it were an object *co-existing* with the sign.'[53]

Wittgenstein's alternative account

Wittgenstein talks of the *use* of signs (sentences, etc.) as being what gives them *life* (i.e. makes them different from the senseless utterances of a parrot).[54] He talks of *language-games*, to make the points (*i*) that the speaking of language is part of our life's activities,[55] (*ii*) that just as there are any number of games so there are any number of uses of signs,[56] and, presumably, (*iii*) that just as there are rules of games so there are *rules of language*.[57] He talks of there having to be a certain *agreement* between people for the language-game to work.[58] They must follow the same rules,[59] have the same *form of life*.[60] The agreement between people is the result of their having had the same *training*,[61] whereby they

[52] *E*, 2.33.6. The classical account of associationism is in David Hartley, *Observations on Man, his Frame, his Duty and his Expectations* (1749), part 1, ch. 3, section 1.

[53] *BB*, 5.

[54] *BB*, 3–5; *PI*, 432.

[55] *PI*, 23, 25; *RFM*, I, 4; *OC*, 559.

[56] *PI*, 23.

[57] *PI*, 31ff.

[58] *Z*, 428–30.

[59] *PI*, 224–5.

[60] *PI*, 241, II, xi, 226.

[61] *PI*, 206; *Z*, 318, 419.

mastered the *system of language* within which the sign has life.[62] People with a different *natural history*,[63] a different training, would have different concepts.[64]

If there is a key concept in Locke's theory it is that of an 'idea'. The fifth, unargued, ingredient in the recipe (the identification, as 'ideas', of the 'objects of understanding' in thinking with the impressions said to be made on the mind in perception) is the one which matters. It is the one which has, as its consequences, (*i*) the problem of privacy, and (*ii*) the empiricist deduction (language conforming to reality because derived from it).

The concept of a 'rule of language' (or 'rule of grammar') plays a comparable role in Wittgenstein's later philosophy of language. It is the one which matters. What Wittgenstein says about rules carries the implications (*i*) that language cannot be private, in the relevant sense, and (*ii*) that the agreement of language and reality is something other than a matter of the former 'conforming' to the latter.

The trouble with saying that just as there are rules of games so there are rules of language is that there seems to be an important difference between them. The rules which determine whether something – such as picking up a chess piece, rotating it, and replacing it where it was – is a move in a game are *expressed*. They are recorded in, say, a book of rules. So there are clearly *two* things: the rules, on the one hand, and the game-playing behaviour, on the other. But in the case of (natural) languages if any rules at all are expressed they are likely to be only those of what Wittgenstein calls 'surface grammar'. For example, one may find, in a school grammar book, a rule about saying 'I *am* here' and not 'I *is* here', but not a rule about not saying 'I am here' in answer to 'Where are you?' on the telephone, or in talking to oneself, when one is wondering where one is.[65]

But this difference is not as real as it seems. Disputes can arise

[62] *BB*, 5, 42; *Z*, 146.
[63] *PI*, II, xii.
[64] *Z*, 387.
[65] *BB*, 72. There is a story about Wittgenstein being challenged by some dons at Trinity to say what 'surface grammar' and 'depth grammar' have in common, and of his replying, after a few moments' thought, 'Is "Should one say 'Father, Son and Holy Ghost *is* one God' or 'Father, Son and Holy Ghost *are* one God'?" a question about surface grammar or about depth grammar?'

about how the expressed rules of games are to be interpreted. There may even be disputes about how rules for the interpretation of rules are to be interpreted. The successful rule-maker is the one who hits on a formulation which people, without thought of a further rule, will follow in the same way.[66] Realising that there could be, but is not, a further rule expressed lessens the temptation to think that when there are not rules expressed, as in the case of depth grammar, there are not rules.

The point of likening languages to games, by talking of 'rules of language' ('rules of grammar'), is that there are conditions of what Wittgenstein calls a 'language game' being played, these conditions always involving a commitment to a certain linguistic practice. An example, suggested by what Wittgenstein says about time on the sun,[67] may serve to illustrate the notion of there being conditions of a language game being played. Imagine someone on earth saying to someone in a spaceship halfway to the moon 'It's afternoon here in Houston, and night-time in London; what time of day is it where you are?' What this example brings out is the dependence of the time-of-day language game on two things: (*i*) the fact that the earth revolves on its axis so that the relation of a point on its surface to the sun varies, and (*ii*) the fact that we have an accepted practice of relating what we say (for example, 'It's early afternoon here') to these variations. Someone who wasn't at a point on the earth's surface, but was on a spaceship halfway to the moon, would (literally) not be in a position to say whether it was morning, noon, or night with him – unless, of course, he adopted some such convention as that it was night-time when he was due for a spell of sleep. But, equally, someone on earth who was not prepared to accept our practice relating what we say to our position on the earth's surface relative to the sun would not mean, by his time-of-day language, what we mean.

To talk of 'rules of language' is to talk of accepted practices which lie behind what we say and give it the meaning it has. Without implicitly accepting the practice with 'red' we would not, on uttering the word 'red' on seeing something, be describing it.[68] It is the rule, not an accompanying 'idea' as Locke supposed, which makes what we say meaningful. What we say makes a

[66] *Z*, 234.
[67] *PI*, 350.
[68] *PI*, II, ix, 187, ll. 18–26.

difference, is significant, in virtue of the rule,[69] just as moving a bishop along a diagonal – but not picking it up, rotating it, and replacing it where it was – makes a difference, is significant, in the game of chess, in virtue of the rules.

For someone to accept a practice, to follow a rule, is not for him to accept *that* the practice is what it is.[70] In the case of our time-of-day language one can describe the practice (for example, it is afternoon at some point on earth if the sun is past the zenith but not yet over the horizon). But one can accept a practice without being able to describe it other than vacuously ('We call red things "red", green things "green" '). 'There is a way of grasping a rule which is *not* an *interpretation*.'[71]

The role of an accepted practice is evident in the case of words like 'five'. To mean by 'five' what we mean (that is, to use 'five' as we use it) a person must have rote-learnt the sequence 'One, two, three, four, five', and have acquired the ability to match each item in it against one of a number of objects. In short, he must have learnt to count. Suppose someone invented a sequence of sounds to take the place of the 'One, two, three, four, five' sequence, and of written marks to correspond to the sounds, so that he could keep a secret record of numbers of things. We try to break the code, by comparing what he has written down with the numbers of things he has been seen 'counting'. We cannot break it, and ask him to tell us the sequence he is using. He tells us, but still the marks do not seem to fit. We ask him to tell us the sequence again. This time it is different, back to front. We say to him that it is no more the same sequence than the direction in which the arrows in the figure below are pointing is the same.

He may protest that the direction in which the arrows are pointing *is* the same, since they are both pointing at the same point, and challenge us to explain why we say that the following arrows are pointing in the same direction. (Is it because the point they are

[69] Cf. Rush Rhees, 'Can there be a private language?', *P.A.S.*, vol. xxviii (1954), pp. 77–94.

[70] *RFM*, II, 71.

[71] *PI*, 201. Cf. *PI*, 198, 217–19; *Z*, 301–3.

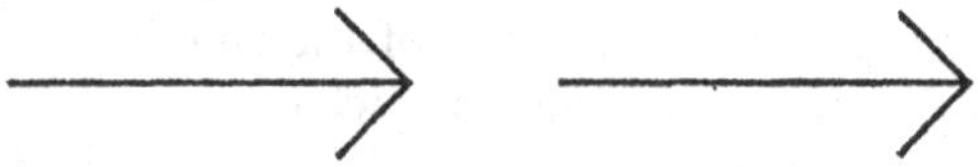

pointing at is at infinity?) If he then says that the following arrows, like the first pair, are pointing in the same direction,

since they are both pointing away from the same point, we may guess that what *he* calls 'the same sequence' is what *we* call 'the sequence reversed'. We then ask him to tell us the sequence a third time. But it is not a repetition of the first time, though he says it is.

If, despite this, we can at last reach agreement with him – I mean, in the sense of being able to produce a sequence he would say was 'the same', even if not in the sense of being able to say *why* it should be said to be the same[72] – we will grant that his marks are numerals. But suppose he says that it is not, in principle, possible for anyone to reach agreement with him. Now, to say this is to say (*i*) that his language is a private one, in the sense of 'private language' discussed by Wittgenstein, and (*ii*) that there is no rule of language involved (since, if there were, it would be, in principle, possible for someone else to reach agreement with him). But if there is no rule of language involved then what he says, or writes, is as meaningless as rotating the queen in a game of chess. Hence a 'private language' is not really a language. It is no more a language than pronouncing a word in front of an object is naming that object. In the absence of the use to which the word is put the pronouncing is merely an idle ceremony.[73] And to talk of a 'use' is to talk of 'rules'.[74]

Language and reality: Wittgenstein's alternative to the empiricist deduction.

Wittgenstein's attitude to the empiricist deduction (language conforming to reality because derived from it) is clear from a number of his remarks:

(*i*) Do not believe that you have the concept of colour within you because you look at a coloured object – however you look.[75]
(*ii*) We have a colour system as we have a number system.

[72] Cf. *OC*, 46.
[73] *BB*, 172–3.
[74] *OC*, 61–2.
[75] *Z*, 332. Cf. *PE*, 279, ll. 13–16.

Do the systems reside in *our* nature or in the nature of things? How are we to put it? – *Not* in the nature of numbers or colours.[76]
(*iii*) The agreement, the harmony, of thought and reality consists in this: if I say falsely that something is *red*, then for all that, it isn't *red*.[77]
(*iv*) Like everything metaphysical the harmony between thought and reality is to be found in the grammar of the language.[78]
(*v*) One is tempted to justify rules of grammar by sentences like 'But there really are four primary colours'. And the saying that the rules of grammar are arbitrary is directed against the possibility of this justification, which is constructed on the model of justifying a sentence by pointing to what verifies it.[79]
(*vi*) . . . the use of language is in a certain sense autonomous. . . . if you follow rules other than those of chess you are *playing another game*; and if you follow grammatical rules other than such-and-such ones, that does not mean you say something wrong, no, you are speaking of something else.[80]
(*vii*) I want to say: an education quite different from ours might also be the foundation for quite different concepts.
For here life would run on differently.[81]
(*viii*) What has to be accepted, the given, is – so one could say – *forms of life*.[82]

Earlier, I took Kant, in the passage about 'deduction',[83] to be saying that in the face of the empirical *fact* that something is white (my experiencing it as white) the question 'Have we the right to employ the *concept* white?' does not occur to us. (*i*) and (*ii*) above can be interpreted as a rejection of Locke's *answer* to the question about our right. (*iii*) can be interpreted as a rejection of the *question*: the only kind of agreement or disagreement between thought and reality is that of the correspondence, or lack of correspondence, of what we think to the facts. (*i*), (*ii*) and (*iii*) are negative, and anti-Lockean. (*iv*) is positive: a hint at an alternative account of agreement or harmony to that given by Locke. The harmony is to be found in the grammar of the language. (*v*) introduces us to a revolutionary feature of the alternative account:

76 *Z*, 357. 77 *PI*, 429. 78 *Z*, 55.
79 *Z*, 331. Cf. *RFM*, I, 4, re a truth corresponding to the sequence 'One, two, three, four, five'.
80 *Z*, 320. 81 *Z*, 387–8. 82 *PI*, II, xi, 226.
83 *Critique of Pure Reason*, A84, B116–17.

the rules of grammar are arbitrary. 'Language is in a certain sense autonomous' (*vi*). That is, it is not responsible to a reality which has to be accepted as given, and to which our rules of grammar must conform to be 'right'. A people can, *in* their language, say that something agrees with reality. But understanding this does not enable us to understand what could be meant by the statement that *their language* agrees, or does not agree, with reality.

There is, also, a sense in which the rules of grammar are *not* arbitrary. A person could no more change them at his whim than he could change his form of life – and for the same reason, since they have their foundation in his form of life. One cannot simply shrug off one's cultural heritage, and put on a new one at will. It is something one is brought up, trained, educated in; and one's upbringing is expressed as much, if not more, in one's instinctive behaviour as in one's consciously articulated views on life.[84]

The value of imagining different forms of life, and so making intelligible to ourselves the formation of concepts different from our own, is that it stops us believing 'that certain concepts are absolutely the correct ones'.[85] And that is a liberalisation which, if carried into practice in the relations between peoples, might help to promote their mutual tolerance.

[84] *OC*, 110, 204, 559; *Z*, 545.
[85] *PI*, II, xii.

MAIN PUBLICATIONS

The Embodied Mind (George Allen & Unwin, 1965)
Perception (Doubleday, 1971; Macmillan, 1972)
Personal Identity (Macmillan, 1974)

WORKS EDITED

Body and Mind (George Allen & Unwin, 1964; reprinted, 1970)
Philosophy in the Open (Open University Press, 1974)
and the following volumes of Royal Institute of Philosophy Lectures:
The Human Agent (Macmillan, 1968)
Talk of God (Macmillan, 1969)

Knowledge and Necessity (Macmillan, 1970)
The Proper Study (Macmillan, 1971)
Reason and Reality (Macmillan, 1972)
Philosophy and the Arts (Macmillan, 1973)
Understanding Wittgenstein (Macmillan, 1974)
Impressions of Empiricism (Macmillan, 1976)

THE CONSTANCY OF HUMAN NATURE

by

W. H. Walsh

Professor of Logic and Metaphysics, University of Edinburgh

To what extent do we need to presume the constancy of human nature in making judgements about the human past or present? I shall begin my discussion of this question with an extensive quotation from Hume, taken from the section on Liberty and Necessity in the *Enquiry Concerning Human Understanding.* Hume writes there as follows (pp. 83–4 in the Selby-Bigge edition):

'It is universally acknowledged that there is a great uniformity among the actions of men, in all nations and ages, and that human nature remains still the same, in its principles and operations. The same motives always produce the same actions: the same events follow the same causes. Ambition, avarice, self-love, vanity, friendship, generosity, public spirit: these passions, mixed in various degrees, and distributed throughout society, have been, from the beginning of the world, and still are, the source of all the actions and enterprises, which have ever been observed among mankind. Would you know the sentiments, inclinations and course of life of the Greeks and Romans? Study well the temper and actions of the French and English: you cannot be much mistaken in transferring to the former *most* [Hume's italics – W.H.W.] of the observations which you have made with regard to the latter. Mankind are so much the same, in all times and places, that history informs us of nothing new or strange in this particular. Its chief use is only to discover the constant and universal principles of human nature, by showing men in all varieties of circumstances and situations, and furnishing us with materials from which we may form our observations and become acquainted with the regular springs of human action and behaviour. These records of wars, intrigues, factions and revolutions are so many collections of experiments, by which the politician or moral philosopher fixes the principles of his science, in the same manner as the physician or natural philosopher becomes acquainted with the nature of plants, minerals or other external objects, by the experiments which he forms concerning them. Nor are the earth, water and other elements, examined by Aristotle and Hippocrates, more like to those which at present lie under our observation than the men described by Polybius and Tacitus are to those who now govern the world.'

In his subsequent discussion Hume adds a number of points to this trenchant declaration. He argues in particular that we not only in fact presume the constancy of human nature in thinking about these matters, but necessarily do so. We have to have a criterion by which to judge testimony, whether that of travellers from a far country or that produced in an historical context, and we find that criterion in our own experience of what men are like. 'If we would explode any forgery in history, we cannot make use of a more convincing argument, than to prove, that the actions ascribed to any person are directly contrary to the course of nature, and that no human motives, in such circumstances, could ever induce him to such a conduct' (p. 84). The knowledge of human nature in question here is, Hume adds, acquired by experience. A man of the world knows the ways of the world and is not deceived by 'pretexts and appearances'; his superiority is like that of the 'aged husbandman' over the 'young beginner'. But just as the husbandman can acquire skill in his calling only because there is what Hume calls 'a certain uniformity in the operation of the sun, rain and earth towards the production of vegetables', so the practical politician or moralist can profit from his experience only because human nature is constant. 'Were there no uniformity in human actions, and were every experiment which we could form of this kind irregular and anomalous, it were impossible to collect any general observations concerning mankind; and no experience, however accurately digested by reflection, would serve to any purpose' (p. 85).

Hume does not claim that human beings act in precisely the same manner in all times and places: we have, he says, to make allowance for 'the diversity of characters, prejudices and opinions'

(p. 85). The manners of men differ in different ages and countries, thanks to the operation of 'custom and education', which 'mould the human mind from its infancy and form it into a fixed and established character'. Different national and regional characteristics are thus possible, as are the differences between male and female, young and old. It is a fact of experience that different groups often react differently to the same stimulus. But Hume proposes to treat these differences as supervenient upon, or perhaps as specifications of, a common human nature which we all share. Similarly when he comes to deal with 'irregular and extraordinary actions', which 'have no regular connection with any known motives' (p. 86), he does not deny the surface diversity, but tries to show that it can nevertheless be accounted for in terms of fixed underlying principles. The vulgar are often surprised at the extraordinary character of natural events, but 'philosophers' know that their occurrence is not lawless, but due to 'the secret operation of contrary causes' (p. 87). A doctor who finds that a medicine fails to produce its usual effect on a particular patient will not conclude that the laws of nature are abrogated in this case; 'the philosopher, if he be consistent, must apply the same reasoning to the actions and volitions of intelligent agents' (p. 88). If men act out of character we must look for special circumstances to explain it, not put it down to a cause which is essentially arbitrary in its operation and thus no cause at all. Hume sums up his case in the following words (p. 90):

'What would become of *history*, had we not a dependence on the veracity of the historian according to the experience we have of mankind? How could *politics* be a science, if laws and forms of government had not a uniform influence upon society? Where would be the foundation of *morals*, if particular characters had no certain or determinate power to produce particular sentiments, and if these sentiments had no constant operation on actions? And with what pretence could we employ our *criticism* upon any poet or polite author, if we could not pronounce the conduct and sentiments of his actors either natural or unnatural to such characters and in such circumstances?'

Neither 'science' nor 'action of any kind' would, he concludes, be possible without the assumption for which he has argued.

The first and most obvious comment to make on this passage concerns its author's apparent lack of historical sense. Hume tells us that if we wish to find out what manner of men were the ancient Greeks and Romans, we must study our French and English contemporaries. No modern historian would repeat the advice, for he would insist that history shows not so much the uniformity as the diversity of human nature. The Greeks and Romans were, no doubt, in some respects men like ourselves. But they were also persons whose ways of acting and reacting differed notably not only from our own, but also among themselves: there was no such thing as a single Greco-Roman mind, any more than there is a single modern mind common to every adult in the world today. Historians and anthropologists know very well that one of the first lessons they must teach their pupils is not to assume that the agents they study are or were like themselves: to make that assumption is the surest way to gross misunderstanding. Hume displays his naïvete perhaps most obviously in the points he makes at the end. He asks how politics could be a science if laws and forms of government did not have a constant influence on society: the answer to this is first that laws and forms of government are not so easily comparable as he supposed, and second that in so far as they are comparable they do not necessarily have uniform effects. All men dislike tyranny, but what they count as tyranny varies enormously from age to age, society to society. Similarly the standard connections which Hume believed to lie at the foundation of a reasonable moral life may perhaps be more imaginary than real: agreement in moral reactions could well be a more local affair than men of the Enlightenment were apt to suppose. As for the remarks about criticism, we have only to think of modern literature and the modern stage to see how simple-minded is Hume's belief that experience will show what is 'natural' in stated conditions and so enable us to judge if literary works are acceptable or not.

I have put these points in a simple-minded way myself, without consideration of the arguments which lie behind Hume's bald questions, and must now attempt to state the case against him more seriously. First then let me suggest, following Collingwood, that Hume shows no proper awareness of the extent to which man can be described as an historical as opposed to a merely natural being. A being of the latter sort has a standing character which may be modified by external circumstances but can normally be counted on to remain unaltered, with the result that the behaviour of the thing in question is relatively constant; the human body would be an instance of such a natural existent. But the human mind is different from the human body in a number of important ways. In the first place it is not easy, if it is possible at all, to separate what it is from what it does; its underlying structure and its concrete performances are closely bound up together. Hume spoke as if each of us shares a basic human nature which is, in particular cases, overlaid with the accretions of custom; the difficulty, from his point of view, is that we have no means of getting at the supposed original, which accordingly begins to look as mythical as Rousseau's Noble Savage. We have only men's overt acts to go on, and these are so diverse as to belie the suggestion that they spring from a common source. But there is a further and more important difference. What I am calling a natural being is modified, if it is modified at all, mainly by circumstances outside itself; it changes typically as a result of environmental factors. An historical being is by contrast self-modifying: in taking account of what it has done or experienced it becomes something different from what it was. It is not just affected by its experiences, but transforms itself in the light of them. Nor is it necessary, for a transformation of this sort to ensue, that the man in question should personally have undergone the transforming experience; in many cases it will suffice if he has heard or read or been otherwise informed about it. His mind can be changed as a result of his taking account of what might be called the common experience, the experience, incidentally, with which historians and social enquirers are most generally concerned. If this is correct, the very fact that men are in a position to learn about the human past counts against Hume's comparison between the materials handled by Aristotle and the modern physicist on the one hand, and by Polybius and the modern student of politics on the other. In so far as those who now govern the world know any history, they cannot be said to have minds which are in principle identical with those of the rulers of ancient times.

A further point of difficulty in Hume turns on the ambiguities of his claim that 'the same motives always produce the same actions', with his subsequent talk of the natural or unnatural character of the conduct and sentiments of fictional persons. To say that someone acts naturally is to claim not that his actions conform to a regular pattern, but rather that they are in some sense appropriate; a natural action is one which is fitting, if you like rational, when seen from the agent's point of view. But when Hume speaks of motives 'producing' actions it is clear that he has something else than this in mind: as his gloss 'the same events follow the same causes' shows, he is thinking of what necessarily results when a certain combination of circumstances obtains. The whole context of his argument is an advocacy of what he himself calls 'the doctrine of necessity', the thesis that mental phenomena are subject to inexorable law in exactly the same way as physical phenomena. Hume is wanting to show that there are regularities in human behaviour just as there are regularities in the behaviour of physical objects; a large part of his case consists in pointing out that we take both sorts of regularity for granted, and could not act in the world if we did not. But he makes things easier for himself than he should by failing to notice that human behaviour is, in general, regular and predictable because it is governed by rule and so, in one sense of the term, rational. Men can be counted on to respond to situations in foreseeable ways not because they are determined to act by constant forces but because we can discover how they see the world and in what ways they think it appropriate to behave in this situation or that. Hume has a striking instance of a prisoner who

'when conducted to the scaffold, foresees his death as certainly from the constancy and fidelity of his guards, as from the operation of the axe or wheel. His mind runs along a certain train of ideas: the refusal of the soldiers to consent to his escape; the action of the executioner; the separation of the head and body; bleeding, convulsive motions, and death.'

He goes on:

'Here is a connected chain of natural causes and voluntary actions; but the mind feels no difference between them in passing from one link to another: nor is less certain of the future event than if it were connected with the objects present to the memory or senses, by a train of causes, cemented together by what we are pleased to call a *phsyical* necessity. The same experienced union has the same effect on the mind, whether the united objects be motives, volition or actions, or figure and motion. We may change the name of things, but their nature and their operation on the understanding never change.'[1]

One could agree with Hume that the prisoner could be as certain of the actions of his guards as he is of the coming severance of his head from his body, without having to grant that precisely the same sort of causal connection is present in the two cases. Motives such as 'constancy 'and 'fidelity' do not compel actions, but rather afford reasons for doing them, and we know in many cases that men will do what they think reasonable. Given that the soldiers feel loyal to their superiors, they will naturally refuse to let the prisoner escape. But this means only that they will see refusal as appropriate in the circumstances; it does not warrant the inference that their behaviour is caused as that of inanimate objects is caused.

Hume might reply that these comments misrepresent his position: they proceed on the assumption that human actions cannot be free if they are subject to causal determination. But this is a thesis which he expressly denies. Whatever comes about is caused to do so, on his view of the matter, but this is not to say that everything happens under constraint. For one thing, the necessity which binds cause to effect is not such that we can claim in any case that causes compel the production of their effects: it exists not in the world, but only in the mind of the observer who, when the impression of the cause appears, is conditioned by repeated experience into moving to the thought of its usual attendant. In one sense of the term, nothing in the Humean world happens of necessity. But there is a special way in which for Hume human actions are and have to be free of necessitation. They must be free in so far as the person who engages in them is not acting under constraint and hence would be at liberty to act otherwise had he chosen to do so. Like Hobbes, Hume sees no difficulty in claiming that men frequently are at liberty to do what they want.

[1] *Enquiry*, pp. 90–1, ed. Selby-Bigge; this passage is taken verbatim from *Treatise*, II, iii, 1, pp. 406–7 in Selby-Bigge's edition. Compare *Treatise*, I, iii, 14 (p. 171, SB), where Hume says that 'the common distinction betwixt *moral* and *physical* necessity is without any foundation'.

But, again like Hobbes, he argues that this has no bearing on whether or not what they do is caused.

Does this suffice to refute the thesis that the causation of actions is different in kind from that of natural events? I do not think it does. Hume speaks as if what he calls the 'passions' of ambition, avarice, self-love and the rest operate as causal determinants in the same way as the constituents of a body (a chemical substance, for instance) operate as causal determinants. What this leaves out is any account of how the influence is exerted, which in the case of the passions is through the medium of thought. That this fact is of crucial importance both for the assessment of Hume's account of human action and for the wider subject we are concerned with I shall now try to show.

According to Hume, the ultimate springs of human action are certain widely prevalent kinds of desire, a desire being a mental occurrence or, better, a persisting mental state. And desires have only to be felt to begin to have an influence on conduct, though the influence may be cancelled if the person concerned has a stronger desire for something of a different kind. It seems to me that this gives a very crude account of why men act as they do. Certainly they have wants of many different kinds, but wants are not mere feelings or even mere affective states. Wants are not independent of conceptions: I want what I do not just because I feel a certain impulse (in the case of many wants I *feel* nothing at all), but because I see the world and my situation in it under a certain description. My inclinations are coloured, indeed to some degree constituted, by my thoughts, which come in both at the stage of target-setting (when I am trying to get clear what it is I really want) and when it comes to finding the best means to the end sought. To think of 'desire' or 'the passions' as presenting the target and of 'reason' as concerned only with the means is to misrepresent the position grossly. Men are rarely, if ever, impelled by simple desire; even when they seek bodily satisfactions they mostly pursue them in a wider setting, one which involves, for instance, the thought of their own importance or the belief that things should be done in a certain style (normally, for example, I don't just want to eat, but to eat decently, without having the milk bottle on the table). To explain why they acted as they did we must hence take account not only of their basic conative drives, but also of how these found expression in a wider context of beliefs and conceptions, a context which in turn may have to be explained by reference to envisaged social conditions. It seems to me that Hume had little or no awareness of these points, with disastrous effects on his account of mental causation.

I pass now to the bearing of what has been said on the question with which this paper began, that of the extent to which we have to presume the constancy of human nature in making judgements about the human past or present. My claim here is that once we recognise the importance of thought in the determining of human action we can see that there is and must be something constant in human nature, without having to agree that men are fundamentally the same at all times and places. What is constant is not the principles which govern human action (these can and do vary widely), but the form of practical thinking itself. As an historian or an anthropologist I do not have to believe that men remote from me in time or space share or shared either my view of the world or my ideas about how to behave in it. But I do have to assume that they have or had some coherent conception of the world and their situation in it, together with some notion of what to do in the light of that conception. To put it crudely, they must think or have thought according to the general schema of the practical syllogism if I am to make any sense of their activities.

Let me try to elaborate these points. The first task in understanding a human action is to discover its rationale, which means recovering or reconstituting the thoughts which the agent had in mind when he did it. The thoughts in question were of two kinds: they had to do with the appreciation of fact on the one hand, i.e. with the nature of the situation as seen by the agent, and with practical principles on the other, i.e. with what to do in situations of this kind or that. Now it is clear that people differ widely both in their reading of the facts and in the way they respond to them, from one culture to another if not so obviously within a single culture. It is clear again that this circumstance does not constitute an insuperable barrier to mutual understanding, since it is possible to come to see how another man views the world and how he thinks it proper to deal with it, provided of course that one has sufficient information about him and sufficient skill in interpreting that information. Entering into the mind of another may not be an easy task; it may demand the abandoning of many assumptions that seem obvious and the acceptance for the purpose in hand of ways of thinking which are at first sight bizarre or even absurd. But once we see that it is one thing to *enter into* another's point of view and another to *share* it, it becomes clear that there is no objection of principle to the possibility of understanding others. I can in a certain sense leave myself behind when I put myself in another man's shoes: I can forget about my personal outlook, principles and prejudices, and appear on the scene in the capacity of an impersonal intelligence. Without this ability studies such as history and social anthropology would simply not be possible. With it men can come to understand, if not exactly to appreciate, actions which proceed from minds of many diverse kinds, actions which, in many cases, will have seemed to them at first sight to be wholly unnatural or quite irrational.

However, there is a limit on the amount of diversity allowable here. When I set myself the task of understanding another man's action I need not assume that he must think as I do, as far as the *content* of his thought is concerned. But I must presume that he and I share the same *formal apparatus* for thinking and deciding, that he is like me in having something like a connected and consistent view of things, in possessing a more or less intelligible set of rules for dealing with situations of this type or that, finally in having the ability to put together premises about what is the case and what should be done and draw particular practical conclusions from them. These may seem large assumptions, and clearly warrant some examination.

The first requirement is that the persons whose activities are to be made intelligible should possess a conceptual system and operate it in a consistent manner. Men need to see their situation under a certain description, and the view they take of one state of affairs must tally with the view they take of others. If similar data turn up they must offer similar descriptions; if conditions change descriptions must change too. But these requirements can be satisfied in relatively primitive circumstances; certainly without explicit possession of the vocabulary needed for talking about conceptual systems and their constituents, and perhaps without so much as a grasp of the distinction between general words and individuating expressions. Vico in some intriguing passages in *The New Science* conjectures that what he calls 'Poetic Man', man in the earliest stage of social development, thought in terms of 'imaginative universals'; such men, he explains, could not form abstract concepts, but would take individuals as types, letting 'Juno' stand for 'everything touching marriage' and 'Jupiter' for 'everything concerning the auspices'.[2] However this is supposed to work out, it is clear that the type of mind in question would be very different from the adult mind today. Even so, it would meet the requirement under discussion provided that it applied its imaginative vocabulary consistently. Suppose, for example, that in the presence of conditions which we should describe as eerie and thrilling Poetic Man was led to cry out that *Pan is here*: what he would need to do for us to make sense of his activities would be to cry out similarly in similar conditions, and not to do so where they were notably different. If he saw Pan everywhere, or nowhere in particular, we could make nothing of what he did. We might even doubt if he had a mind of any sort, poetic or prosaic.

The second requirement, that those whose behaviour we seek to understand have the power to frame rules for dealing with different sorts of situation, also seems at first sight to presuppose a degree of sophistication which we are not entitled to expect in every case. The distinction, familiar to modern philosophers, between a statement of what is the case and a rule which prescribes what is to be done is by no means obvious to less advanced minds, or even to some ordinary modern men; description for them more often than not carries with it an emotional charge which is itself an incitement to action. But just as we do not need the full conceptual apparatus of the present day in order to satisfy the first requirement, so we do not have to have explicitly formulated rules, recognised as distinct from descriptions, in order to satisfy the second. When Vico's Poetic Man cried out that Pan is here he perhaps at once stopped, fell on bended knee and bowed his head; the presence of Pan, for him, carried with it immediately the necessity for these actions. If it had been suggested to him that it was one thing for Pan to be present and quite another for a certain type of behaviour to be appropriate in his presence, he would have found it impossible to grasp the distinction. Pan was Pan and, as such, the proper object of a certain kind of fearful respect: description and evaluation were here inextricably mixed. But though Poetic Man could not separate

[2] *New Science*, § 933; see also § 34 and § 209 among other relevant passages (paragraph numbers as in the Bergin and Fisch translation).

them, the fact is that we can. We can reconstruct the thought of the characters with whom Vico was concerned in terms which they would not themselves have understood, but which connect clearly with aspects of their speech and general behaviour. As far as we are concerned Poetic Man not only knew in his own terms what particular situations were like; he also had rules for dealing with them. And it is a necessary condition of our making sense of his activities that he should have had such rules and used them with some consistency.

After these explanations it should not be necessary to spend much time on the third requirement, which concerns the need to put together descriptive and normative premises in a practical argument and draw the appropriate conclusion. It is clear when we come to think about it that possession of a conceptual system of any sort must carry with it ability to make at least some formal inferences: for someone to have concepts but know nothing of their interrelations would preclude him from using them properly. Even primitive man must recognise the most obvious implications of his beliefs, for example by seeing that Mars and Vulcan are antipathetic one to another. But if this so and if what was claimed in the last paragraph is true there will be no difficulty in ascribing to the less as well as the more sophisticated the power to draw practical inferences. It would admittedly be absurd to take it as literally true that men in all times and places think according to the canons of the practical syllogism, making a clear distinction between premises and conclusions in arguments and recognising in the case of action the need to include in their premises both statements of what is the case and injunctions about what to do in the type of situation specified. Poetic Man at least did not think along these lines. But we can allow that this is so and still claim that practical thinking is formally the same in all men provided that in all cases we can represent their thought in the form of a practical syllogism. They may well have put the matter in a different way, but stated in our terms what they were doing was advancing factual and evaluative premises from which a practical conclusion was meant to follow. My thesis is that we must assume that human nature is constant at least in this respect if we are to make sense of the actions of other people, above all those of members of remote societies in the present or of persons who lived in the past. Such persons need not see the world through eyes which are precisely like ours, nor need they accept our ways of dealing with it; on the side of material content they can differ from us indefinitely. But unless the formal apparatus by which they arrived at decisions was identical with our own to the extent described we could simply make nothing of what they said or did.

I come now to the question whether this formal identity in different minds is all that the student of human nature need presuppose as common. Hume as we saw was certainly not of this opinion. In his view the judging of testimony, whether about what was happening elsewhere or about what had happened in the past, proceeded on the assumption that men were everywhere actuated by the same motives, and indeed had to do so. In trying to decide whether some witness or historian was telling the truth we had nothing to appeal to but our own experience; our criteria for what was credible had to be drawn from ourselves. Hume argued that there was no difference in this respect in our attitudes to what was physically possible on the one hand and humanly possible on the other. A traveller from a far country who came back with stories of 'men who were entirely divested of avarice, ambition or revenge' and 'knew no pleasure but friendship, generosity and public spirit' would be disbelieved just as surely as if he had stuffed his narrative with stories of centaurs and dragons. And Quintus Curtius, the Roman historian of Alexander the Great, was suspect alike for ascribing supernatural courage to his hero and for crediting him with supernatural physical powers. 'So readily and universally do we acknowledge a uniformity in human motives and actions as well as in the operations of body.'[3]

Plausible as these examples sound, I suggest that Hume was wrong to treat the cases of physical and human possibility as identical. In deciding what is physically possible we do indeed judge by reference to physical nature as we know it today. We can of course be mistaken in particular cases, as was Hume's 'Indian' prince who refused to believe that water might freeze in winter : the bounds of what is really possible need not coincide with the bounds of our actual knowledge. But in general we are right to suppose that, at least as far as historical time is concerned, what holds in nature now is what has always held. Nature viewed

[3] *Enquiry*, p. 84, SB.

on this time-scale exhibits no development, and nature generally has no social dimension. As Hume himself puts it, the earth, water and other elements which scientists examine today may be taken as indistinguishable from their counterparts in ancient times.

The position is very different when we pass to the case of human possibility. Men, as already argued, are historical rather than merely natural beings; their minds change with the advance of their experience as well as with alterations in their social circumstances, and it is accordingly hazardous in the extreme to suppose that their behaviour is governed by the same principles always and everywhere. There is plenty of evidence to show that men in different societies, or in the same society at different times, do not always react to the same stimuli in the same ways. The reasons for this diversity are simple enough: men's reactions depend in part on their view of their situation and conception of themselves, and these in turn vary with social conditions and socially accepted beliefs. What seems natural and normal to a solid man of the Enlightenment like David Hume would not necessarily seem natural and normal to a Romantic of fifty years later. Regularities in the behaviour of, say, a band of Vikings need not be reproduced when we turn our attention to the activities of, say, a band of Mormons. In cases like this it would be rash to assume that we shall find more than a certain amount of local uniformity, and even this will be subject to variation in a greater or less degree.

There *is* a sense in which, in trying to decide what could have been the case with other men, we have to start from ourselves. If an anthropologist or an historian comes up with stories of actions and activities which at first hearing seem incredible, what I have to do is to try to think myself into the position of the subjects concerned, to discover their beliefs, aims and attitudes and through that to establish a rationale for their supposed acts. I must ask myself whether, had my situation been what they took theirs to be, and had their general outlook been mine, I could see myself doing what they are reported to have done. If I come up with a negative answer I might well decide that the acts in question could not have taken place, or at least could not be what they were said to be: because what is reported does not make sense I say that it cannot have happened. But it should be noticed that the 'I' in this experiment is not the personal 'I'. The self adduced is not the concrete self, the particular person possessed of particular beliefs, convictions, aims, principles and prejudices. To perform the test correctly I have to empty this self out and appear as an impersonal 'one' : I have to ask myself not whether *I* could have acted in the way suggested, but whether *a person* could have acted in that way, given those beliefs and attitudes. I necessarily do this by thinking myself into the situation described, and I may of course make mistakes by what is called a failure of imagination, that is by bringing too much of myself to bear. What I need to do, as is obvious, is to abstract from my particular self altogether. When this is recognised, to say that the judging of testimony about human behaviour involves an appeal to my own experience is to say something quite innocuous.

I am inclined for the reasons given to think that Hume is wrong when he claims that human nature must be constant not merely as regards the formal apparatus for thinking and deciding, but also from the material point of view. To demand that what is reported be true to life in the sense of conforming to human nature as we know it today is hardly justified, even supposing that the ambiguities of the latter notion could be overcome. Yet Hume's remarks about the 'passions' which constitute the 'regular springs of human action and behaviour' certainly sound convincing. We should think it very strange to be told of people who showed no awareness, in any circumstances, of the needs and interests of others, or who were totally lacking in any sense of themselves; we might even disbelieve the reports on the ground that their content was contrary to all experience. It is in fact true that we tend to suppose that men the world over are actuated by the same general motives, and thus that human nature is constant in more than form. It could be that over and above the variable character of man there is a natural endowment which remains unchanging and whose presence is felt, though no doubt in different ways, in every society and at every epoch. But if this is so Hume would be right in his main claims after all.

I believe myself that men do have certain purely natural impulses, but that these are neither identical with the 'motives' of which Hume spoke nor of very great importance for the explanation of human behaviour. What Plato called the 'necessary' appetites, for food, drink and sexual gratification, are in their basic forms natural rather than social; so perhaps is the love of a parent for its offspring. But, as has already been argued, hunger and thirst and sexual libido are seldom the sole determinants of action; we gratify such impulses in a social setting, and the setting often has an important bearing on the form the gratification takes. In consequence few significant generalisations can be made about the behaviour of hungry men. Moreover, our activities in this area are deeply affected by another factor which is quite distinct from the impulses so far mentioned: the sense of ourselves as opposed to others. Pride, shame and indignation often determine our behaviour, and it seems clear that the sense of self enters into each of them. It also seems clear that it is only in society that men acquire consciousness of their separate identities, as Hegel showed in the celebrated passage about Master and Slave. Without this consciousness most of the motives Hume lists would be quite impossible. Ambition, for example, is a peculiar form of self-gratification, aimed at doing justice to one's own importance, and not just desire for the satisfaction of a series of particular propensities.

It may be true, as a matter of empirical fact, that ambition, avarice and the rest function as 'springs of action' in all known human societies. But even if this is true it takes us very little way towards concrete knowledge of human nature. To know that men are liable to be influenced by ambition, greed, vanity or public spirit is to know nothing definite; for definite knowledge we need to know on what *objects* their ambition, greed, etc. will be directed. There is no law of nature making it necessary for an ambitious man to manifest his ambition in one way rather than another; how he will manifest it depends generally on what is in contention, or what is specially valued, in that particular society. In some communities men struggle most for honour, reputation or public esteem, in others for political power and influence, in others again for wealth. To find out the multifarious forms in which ambition, public spirit and vanity find expression we have to have recourse to empirical investigations. If only for that reason Hume cannot be right in saying that we judge what is humanly credible by reference to such motives.

Having made this declaration I am nevertheless left with a doubt, which I will set out briefly in conclusion.[4] Suppose there

[4] I am indebted to my colleague Dr Leon Pompa for pressing this point and refusing to let me get away with easy answers.

were to be a race of beings which shared the formal apparatus for thinking and deciding spoken of above, but whose normative premises were, to our minds, utterly bizarre: try as we would, we could make no sense of them. Could we be said to understand the actions of such beings? Given appropriate evidence, we could find out how they saw the world and discover the principles they followed in dealing with it, and that being so could establish the rationale of their actions. Nevertheless, those actions would remain in a real sense opaque to us, since *ex hypothesi* we cannot see the appeal of the normative premises concerned. To say that we cannot see their appeal is to say that we could not connect them with standard human impulses as experienced by ourselves.

I am not sure how, if at all, such doubts are to be silenced. One possible line to follow would be to argue that the notion of understanding is itself ambiguous. In one sense we could understand the behaviour of the beings in question, just because we could become masters of their thoughts; in another sense we could not, in so far as we could not see ourselves thinking as they do. In somewhat the same way we can understand the activities of Hitler from one point of view, though from another they remain unintelligible. There are many human situations in which we find behaviour baffling, even when we know that it was reasoned and can establish its rationale. But it is our hope, when such circumstances arise, to reduce the puzzlement by finding further facts which will help to explain how the persons concerned came to think as they did, and in this process we assume that they were like ourselves in having the same basic impulses. This is just what we cannot do in the case envisaged. It seems therefore that this line of defence cannot succeed, and that we must in consequence agree that there is more to the Humean case than has been allowed in this discussion. It must nevertheless be emphasised that Hume's account of the matter is seriously wrong at many points. Moral and physical necessity are not the same, it is not true that there is great uniformity among the actions of men, and even if it has to be allowed that human nature remains still the same in its principles it is certainly extremely varied in its operations.

MAIN PUBLICATIONS

Reason and Experience (Clarendon Press, 1947)
An Introduction to Philosophy of History (Hutchinson, 1951)
Metaphysics (Hutchinson, 1963)
Hegelian Ethics (Macmillan, 1969)
Kant's Criticism of Metaphysics (Edinburgh University Press, 1975)

IMPERATIVES AND MEANING

by

Geoffrey Warnock

The Principal, Hertford College, Oxford

I believe that the question of imperatives retains some interest – and even, if I am right, some power to surprise. I am not thinking, primarily anyway, of the large and heterogeneous class of utterances that could be said to function in an imperative way, but of the grammatically identifiable class of actual sentences in the imperative mood. One reasonably has, I think, the initial feeling that occurrences, in the use of natural languages, of sentences of this class are peculiar, perhaps problematic, in being more than usually intimately involved (vaguely) with particular speakers, addressees, and linguistic performances. That one speaker is addressing another person, or other persons, or just conceivably himself, seems in this case somehow to get into the sense of the sentence itself; and questions seem also insistently to arise as to what is going on between the parties, what the speaker is doing in speaking – imperatives seem 'practical'; and all this is connected no doubt with their inflexibility in the matter of persons and tenses. Considerations of this general kind form the main ground, I believe, of the uneasiness which philosophers have often felt about the notion of 'imperative logic'. I believe that this uneasiness is well founded; and in this paper, after sketching (for the record) some of the rather inconclusive, quite familiar perplexities about imperatives, I shall try to bring out what seems to me to be the basic awkwardness in the case. This looks paradoxical, but I think is quite literally sustainable : it is not possible to say what imperative sentences mean.

If there is to be such a thing as imperative logic, there has to be something for it to be the logic of. Presumably that would have to be 'imperative argument', or 'imperative inference'. It is not, however, by any means clear straight off what those would be. Take, for example, one of the little sequences apt to occur in discussions of this topic – 'Do *A* or *B*', 'Do not do *A*', 'Do *B*' – in which the third item is suggested to follow, to be a conclusion, from the other two. One would like this, I take it, to be understandable as a succinct representation of some possible process of discourse or thought; but what process of discourse or thought, and by whom? Are we to envisage someone reflecting 'I tell *X* to do *A* or *B*, and not to do *A*; so . . .' – but so *what*? So *X* is to do *B*? The speaker is entitled, nay required, to *tell X* to do *B*? Or is it that he has – 'in effect', 'implicitly', though not actually – already done so? Why, in any case, should any speaker tell any addressee to do one or other of two things, *and not* to do one of them? Perhaps he might first issue the disjunctive imperative, and later, on further reflection perhaps or in the light of new facts, the non-disjunctive negative one; but if so, is it important, and would we want it to be important, in imperative logic in what order imperative 'premises' are set out? With premises, it would not ordinarily occur to us that that could matter. Or are we to look at the matter from the addressee's point of view – to consider, perhaps, how someone, to whom has been addressed some set or sequence of imperatives, might try to work out what, taken collectively, they 'tell' him to do? If so, there seems liable to break in the very awkward question, by whom the imperatives were issued in the first place. A colonel's order 'overrides' a corporal's; but is it a tolerable thought that it should be a matter of logic that that is so? Alternatively, are we to make the general stipulation that imperative 'premises' are always to be taken as issued by one and the same speaker? But that looks pretty curious also, as a matter of logic; for we do not usually, in considering what follows from this or that, need to ask who said it.

It is perhaps only another way of saying the same thing to remind ourselves that imperative sentences do not as such fit syntactically into what one might call the apparatus of argument. Propositions can be argumentatively concatenated by *if* or *since*, *therefore* or *then*; but to follow *if* or *since*, imperatives must be transformed, and the question arises how that is to be done. 'If I tell you to . . .'? 'If you are told to . . .'? 'If I am told to . . .'? 'If I am to . . .', perhaps? Without transformation, imperative sentences stand, as it were, rigidly in mere adjacency to one another, so that, as we have said, what process of thought is intended does not luminously emerge; but exactly what transformations is one supposed to be allowed to make?

Further, imperative logic seems not well-defined, in that its scope cannot, it appears, be intelligibly limited to imperative sentences. 'Shut the door' is perhaps not in *logical* conflict with 'The door is shut' – in such a case it may be that one should speak rather of 'presupposition'; but 'Shut the door' at least appears to be flatly, directly contradicted by 'You may leave the door open', which latter is, of course, not an imperative at all. But if imperative logic does not treat only of imperatives, how are we to make the extent of its subject matter tidily clear?

These are all pretty familiar points, and they may well be manageable more or less. If, for example, it is conceded that it is not *clear* what process of thought, what progression of argument, is supposed to be represented by such a string as 'Do *A* or *B*', 'Do not do *A*', 'Do *B*', it might be said that what is called for is not despair, nor even clarification, but rather stipulation. Perhaps it can simply be laid down that, for this purpose, sets of imperatives are to be appraised in the light of the question 'when given a command, what other commands must necessarily be fulfilled if we are to fulfil the first command?';[1] or alternatively, and differently, in the light of the question 'what other things we are, implicitly, commanding when we give a certain command'.[2] Perhaps it is just a matter of making up our own minds as between various possibilities available to us. I do not quite see that all the snags can be negotiated in this way – what, for instance, of the question of logical *liaisons* with sentences that are not imperatives at all? – but perhaps many can be, and in any case, if I am right, there are less tractable difficulties yet to be mentioned.

There is, I believe, a difficulty at least *prima facie* with the notion, in this context, of inconsistency. It is obvious enough that, if we are to be in a position to apply any terms of logical appraisal to imperatives, we shall need to know what 'inconsistent' is to mean here; but it is not of course clear straight off what 'inconsistent' *could* mean here, since of course we cannot define it with direct reference to truth. We cannot say that imperatives are inconsistent if they cannot both be true, since it makes no sense

[1] R. M. Hare, *Practical Inferences* (Macmillan, 1971), p. 42.
[2] ibid., p. 43.

to call such things, or what is 'said' when such things are uttered, either true or false.

I believe that this has usually been regarded, however, as a minor, even an unreal, perplexity, on the ground that a usable sense of 'inconsistent' for imperatives is quite readily derivable from that of what we may call ordinary inconsistency. Somewhat as, we may say, propositions are inconsistent if they cannot both (or all) be true, imperatives may be said to be inconsistent if they cannot both (or all) be 'fulfilled'; and this looks like an intelligible derivative from ordinary inconsistency, since it amounts to saying that imperatives are inconsistent if it would be ordinarily inconsistent to affirm all those things actually to be done which they require should be done. 'Do *X*' would be thus inconsistent with 'Do *Y*', if the proposition that *A* does *X* is inconsistent with the proposition that *A* does *Y*. Imperatives are, in general, inconsistent if their conjunction amounts to requiring that to be done, the actual doing of which cannot be consistently described; the notion of contradictory imperatives is derivable from that of self-contradictory tasks, or performances.

But this manoeuvre, satisfactory so far as it goes, does not go far enough to leave the picture perfectly clear. It has been correctly pointed out by Bernard Williams that there remains a certain asymmetry between indicative and imperative inconsistency in that, whereas there is equally something wrong both in making inconsistent assertions and in silently accepting inconsistent beliefs, it appears that there is something wrong only in actually issuing inconsistent imperatives. It is not at all clear, in fact, what the silent analogue of that locutionary performance would be; but if it were, say, *wanting* someone to do inconsistent things, that state of mind may be an unfortunate one, but it is not of course impossible, nor does it involve any 'wrongness' or error – there is nothing in it to merit the professional censure of the logician.

I believe that this is correct; but there seems also something more to be said. There is, from a logical point of view, nothing 'wrong' in being, say, silently inclined to issue imperatives that would be inconsistent in the sense explained; but is it yet clear what would be wrong in actually issuing them? It is extremely important for this topic, I believe, not to be too quickly satisfied with an easy answer to this question.

One's immediate thought is, no doubt, that it must be wrong to tell someone to do something that it is actually – indeed, logically – not possible that he should do; one might want to say, indeed, that if the putative specification of what is to be done is itself self-contradictory, in such a case one has not really 'told' him to do anything at all – that one has in a sense, much as in the case of ordinary self-contradiction, said nothing, nothing that the addressee could even *try* to comply with. But there is a lurking over-simplification here. Presumably if I intend that you should do, and (say) order or purport to order you to do, everything that I say, then I have made a mess of it if that is not logically possible, if my orders are contradictory. But imperatives, of course, are neither necessarily nor exclusively used in giving orders – so that what is wrong with giving someone contradictory *orders* does not tell us in general what is wrong, or whether anything is, with issuing inconsistent imperatives. It may be objected that it *must* be wrong to 'tell' someone to do something logically impossible, inconsistent things; but may it not be that, in that objection, 'tell' is liable to be tacitly construed as 'order', so that the remark is still really about orders, rather than imperatives?

Consider the following cases. The commandant of a prisoner-of-war camp, on the losing side in a war that will foreseeably end very soon, receives the desperate instruction from higher authority that all his prisoners are to be shot. He receives this gloomily, not unmindful of possible indictments of the defeated before war-crimes tribunals. He sends for his subordinate officer currently on duty, outlines his warm regard for military duty and his ardent patriotism, and mentions also the foreseeable hazards that in these days may threaten the defeated. He says in conclusion, 'So my order is : shoot all the prisoners. My advice is : don't.'

Second, consulted perhaps in my capacity as your broker, attentive as such to your financial interests but acutely conscious also of my own, I advise you to withdraw the money I now hold on your behalf ('Withdraw the money') and go on to implore you not to ('Please don't withdraw it').

What is the right view to take of such cases as these? The commandant in the first case is not in the (I dare say) logically culpable position of having given his subordinate contradictory orders; for he has given him only one order, a perfectly coherent though no doubt ethically objectionable one, and he is, in general, entitled to give him orders. As your broker, in the second case, I do not give you inconsistent advice; for my advice to you is perfectly clear and intelligible, even though I go on to implore you, as a friend perhaps, not to take it. It might be said of course that the commandant has not unequivocally 'told' his subordinate to do things which, taken together and all round, it is actually possible that he should do – that, on the contrary, he has been 'told' to do something logically impossible. But it is quite clear that 'told' here simply conceals the problem. The subordinate was ordered to do one thing, and advised to do another; the commandant spoke first as a loyal officer, then as a prudent fellow; is *that* 'inconsistent'? It is even, one might think, quite clear what a subordinate so addressed is actually to do, even though what was said to him contained 'inconsistent' imperatives; having been given an order, and a piece of sagacious advice, he is to consider for himself whether to follow the advice or obey the order. In the second case the broker's proceedings might be thought not only intelligible but positively admirable. I cannot properly, as your financial counsellor, *advise* you to take a certain course of action just because, or mainly because, that would suit my book; my advice must be based on assessment of your financial interests, not mine. But there seems no reason why, after scrupulously giving you advice on that basis, I should not go on to implore you not to follow it. And again, is it at all unclear, really, what you are to do? You are to weigh my professional advice against my non-professional pleas, and make up your mind what you will actually do.

It may be said – and said, indeed, with obvious justice – that there is *something* a bit rum, unideal, about these cases. It may be true that in the normal, neat case of giving (say) an order, he who gives it is unperplexedly of a mind that the addressee should actually do the thing in question. It may be true (though it is not, in fact, at all clear why, even as a rule, it should be) that one who offers advice should want the person advised to act as he is advised to. But what if these tidy conditions do not hold? It is really quite clear that I may be positively obliged to give you an order to do something which I also think you would be most ill-advised to do; or that your interests may lead me to give you advice of a sort that my interests make me fervently want you not to follow. It is true that in such cases one is scarcely likely to say baldly 'Do it; and don't'; but one still might, in the course of a not much longer slice of discourse, actually say both.

Are such cases perhaps to be brought under the rubric 'unhappy'? Well, no doubt they could be. But it is again not perfectly clear what we are to make of that. Could it be held that, if I advise you not to do something, there is some sense in which I cannot also have ('really') ordered you to do it? That seems more than dubious. To be given an order and advised not to obey it may indeed be perplexing, but it seems that that *is* what is perplexing – to be actually given both the order and the advice. Both, though no doubt in odd circumstances, really are given; or at least it is not at all clear that that cannot be so.

The source of the uncertainty one feels about these cases is, as it appears to me, the fact that they are cases in which imperatives occur in what one might call different performative modes. It seems plain enough that there has to be something wrong with self-contradictory orders, self-contradictory instructions, self-contradictory advice, or prayers, or pleas; for in such cases, one might say, there ought to be, is supposed to be, some single upshot – what the addressee is, all-in, ordered, instructed, advised, implored to do – and things must be wrong if that one supposed upshot comes out in an incoherent, unintelligible form. But the case of an order-issuing imperative 'contradicted' by an advice-offering imperative is not bad in exactly that way; for in that case there is not in the same sense any purported, single, composite upshot – or if there is, it might be the *non*-contradictory one that the addressee is to weigh up his predicament and make up his own mind. So it is at least not clear that we have here a case of discourse that is logically reprehensible at all – so that either the imperatives in the case are, formal appearances notwithstanding, not 'really' inconsistent, or – which looks even stranger – inconsistency in imperative discourse is not necessarily logically reprehensible. If that were so, the prospect for logic would be indeed unpromising.

A line of thought here temptingly offers itself. Have we not, it may be said, been allowing the picture to become confused and unsatisfactory in consequence of involvement with considerations that, from a *logical* point of view, should be disregarded? For surely, from a logical point of view, it should not be held to matter what particular speakers might be doing in speaking. That all men are mortal, for instance, might be said in warning, by way of a reminder, as an objection, as consolation, purely informatively, and in many other styles, but one need not as a logician become confused by that consideration; one can simply ignore it. For the logical *liaisons* and incompatibilities of the proposition – that all men are mortal – are independent of who says it, why, in what circumstances, in doing what, and indeed of *whether* anyone has occasion to say it at all. 'All men are mortal' is inconsistent with 'Some men are not mortal'; and that is just so, whoever (if anyone) says either, or whatever he or they may be up to in saying so. So should we not, in order to clarify the logical consistencies and inconsistencies of imperatives, similarly abstract *what is said* – as it were the imperative 'proposition' – from these extraneous issues of illocutionary force? If we do this, it may be possible even in problematic cases to say that what is said, or what certain imperative sentences actually mean, constitutes a clear case of (say) inconsistency; and even if, for other purposes, there may remain a lot more to be said about speech acts and so forth, this may be enough to enable the logician to go professionally to work.

In pursuing this notion further I propose to make exploratory use of some of the things said on meaning and related topics in Stephen Schiffer's *Meaning* (1972). First, on the subject of illocutionary acts. It has often been remarked that, while, as Austin particularly insisted, the species of such acts are very numerous, the fundamental genera may well be much less so. Schiffer suggests (p. 95) that 'the class of kinds of illocutionary acts divides into two jointly exhaustive and mutually exclusive subclasses', which he calls 'the assertive class' and 'the imperative class'. Now this very neat dichotomy is perhaps liable to strike one as too good to be true; and one would certainly like to be able to say something, if there really are just these two fundamental sub-classes, as to why that should be so. There is, however, at the very least a certain plausibility in the suggestion that, fundamentally, there may be two sorts of objects for which speech occurs – to tell people things, or to get people to do things – and, though Schiffer is not of course making a grammatical point here, this suggestion seems to fit quite well with the grammatical phenomena of the indicative and imperative moods. So let us adopt it as the present basis for further discussion.

A speaker *S*, Schiffer says, performs an act of the assertive kind in uttering *x* only if, for some *p*, *S* means that *p* by uttering *x*. Let us leave that on one side for the present. Our present interest is in the other sub-class; and on this Schiffer says that *S* performs an act of the imperative kind in uttering *x* only if, for some *A* and some *V*, *S* means that *A* is to *V* by uttering *x*. (Schiffer uses some Greek letters here, but '*V*' will do.) Naturally enough, the *x* that is uttered in this latter case will often, though of course not necessarily or always, be a sentence in the imperative; and this is the case with which we are particularly concerned.

There is a possible objection to this account of which Schiffer takes brief notice at an earlier point (p. 60). The class of 'acts of the imperative kind' is clearly meant to be pretty wide and comprehensive; indeed, he himself instances, as examples of acts of this kind, the rather widely differing cases of ordering, requesting, entreating, and asking, and, later, advising; and one might add, for instance, suggesting. But if so, is not the phrase 'is to' (in '*A* is to *V*') much too strong? Have we not here a case of the rather common failing, all too pervasive in the literature, of construing all imperatives – or rather, in this case, acts of the imperative kind – on the model of *orders*? If the colonel orders the recruit to get his hair cut, no doubt he does therein mean that *A is to V* – the recruit, the recipient of the order, is to do just that. But if I respectfully advise you to get your hair cut, surely I do not mean that you *are to* – but perhaps rather (as indeed Schiffer tacitly notes, at p. 103, in his sketch of advising) that you *should*; and if I suggest taking the dog for a walk – say to a child at a loose end on a Sunday afternoon – I do not mean that the child *is to* do that thing.

One rather ramshackle way of dealing with this point would be, I suppose, to stipulate that the phrase 'is to', in the general account, is simply not to be understood as having any definite sense, but rather as marking a sort of imperative blank, to be differently filled accordingly as particular utterances from time to time are taken to be cases of ordering, advising, entreating, or whatever. That, however, would be to leave things rather painfully in the air; and it might well be thought more tempting (as Schiffer suggests) to advert to the point that, in the general account, we are given plenty of latitude in our choice of values of *V*. Perhaps we can represent the difference between, say, ordering and suggesting not as a difference in what *S* means by 'is to', but as a difference in what he means that *A* is to do – if, in saying 'Take the dog out', I am giving an order, I mean that *A* is to take the dog out; if making a suggestion, that he is, say, to *consider* taking the dog out. That does not look unpromising.

However, it does not make much difference to my particular argument which of these options one takes; for either device, we must note, has a certain important consequence – namely, that there is a certain question to which the offered account enables us to give only the misleading appearance of an answer. If in uttering *x* (a sentence, let us suppose, in the imperative mood) *S* performs an illocutionary act of the imperative kind, what does *S* mean by uttering *x*? The account here provides us with the form of an answer: *S* means that *A* is to *V*. But this, as we can see from the point just made, is not really an answer at all; for if the extent of our information is that *A* issued the utterance, say, 'Take the dog out', then, in interpreting the phrase '*A* is to *V*', either we have no way of determining the sense of 'is to', or we have no way of determining what value to assign to *V*. We have, that is to say, no way, on either view, of actually specifying what *S* means, until it is established whether he was giving an order, making a request or suggestion, offering advice, or what not. Of course that may not seem very surprising; for one may say, for that matter, of acts of the assertive kind as well that, if the question is what the speaker means, it will not in general be enough to be told merely what he says. If he utters *x*, and by uttering *x* means that *p*, then, if *x* is 'Cats don't eat fruit', it may not be that *S* means (only) that cats don't eat fruit.

It seems to me, however, that the point becomes a more serious matter when we turn to consider, not what speakers mean, but what sentences mean. This is of course a distinction which cannot be drawn for every utterance, nor even for every sentence. It may be, for example, that on a certain occasion a speaker (collapsing into a deckchair) utters 'Boof!', meaning thereby that he is hot and out of breath. It would not be correct, on the strength of such an occurrence, to say in general that that is what 'Boof!' means; indeed, it would be correct, so far as I know, to say that 'Boof!' does not mean anything, so that the question what *it* means can be given no answer at all. The reason for this is (stating briefly and coarsely considerations to which Schiffer and others have devoted much elegance and ingenuity) that, while a speaker on a certain occasion may by uttering 'Boof!' convey, intend to convey, mean that he is hot and out of breath, 'Boof!' is not in English in general, a standard (conventional) means of conveying that, or indeed of conveying anything else – as by contrast the sentence 'I am hot and out of breath' would be. Thus we cannot, as it were, detach 'Boof!' from the particular circumstances and occasion of its utterance, and say what *it* means.

Consider by contrast the case of an ordinary indicative sentence, say 'Cats don't eat fruit'. It is true, as we noted above, that when in uttering that sentence a speaker performs an act of the assertive kind, it may well not be the case that by uttering it he means *only* that cats don't eat fruit; he may mean ('objecting' – see Schiffer, p. 97) that the fact that cats don't eat fruit is a reason for abandoning my well-meant suggestion of buying apples for the cat. It seems, however, that in such a case we can distinguish what we may (coarsely) call the conventional and non-conventional components in what the speaker means. There is no convention of the language in virtue of which, in issuing his utterance, the speaker is objecting – means, that is, that in the light of what he says my suggestion should be abandoned, or at any rate modified. That he means *that* (and so does that) is a matter not of English, but of the particular circumstances in which, and intentions with which, he speaks. There is, however, also something which 'Cats don't eat fruit' is, in English, a standard, conventional means of meaning – namely, that cats don't eat fruit. We are thus in a position to say that, while this particular speaker means that the fact that cats don't eat fruit is a reason for abandoning my suggestion, he also means – and, more importantly for our purpose, 'Cats don't eat fruit' means – that cats don't eat fruit. In saying all this I am, I think and hope, agreeing (in coarse terms) with Schiffer's contention that, while what sentences and expressions mean (and so *in part* what speakers mean) is a matter of convention, the illocutionary force of utterances is, in general, not. For the most part at any rate, it is not in virtue of exploiting conventions of the language that speakers warn, object, remind, agree, and so on.

Turn now to the case of an ordinary imperative sentence. One might think (and Schiffer says, at p. 131 for instance, that he for his part does think) that the picture here would be '*mutatis mutandis* identical'; but in fact it appears to me that there are reasons why that cannot be so.

Take a case in which a speaker, in performing an act of the imperative kind, issues an actual imperative sentence, say 'Stay in London'. Now we know that, in such a case, he means by uttering 'Stay in London' something of the form that *A* is to *V*. But, as we saw above, until we know the illocutionary force of his utterance, we *either* do not know how 'is to' is to be understood, *or* we do not know what it is that *A* is to do. Does *S* mean that *A* is to stay in London? To stay in London if he likes? To consider the possibility of staying in London? (Is *S* ordering, requesting, suggesting?) One is tempted here of course, hopefully pursuing the analogy, to ask what it is that – as distinct from what particular speakers may from time to time be illocutionarily up to – 'Stay in London' is a *conventional means* of doing; but does it not now appear that that must be a question without an answer? One would like to say that to utter 'Stay in London' is, at any rate, a conventional means of meaning (something of the form) that *A* is to *V*; but we have already seen that that is not really an answer at all; for we can give no definite sense *on the basis of conventions* to 'is to *V*' as it occurs in that formula. That formula can be given a sense only when the illocutionary force of the utterance is identified; and we do not do that on the basis of conventions of English, but rather of the circumstances in which, and intentions with which, particular speakers speak. If we seriously said that to utter 'Stay in London' is a conventional means of meaning that some person therein addressed *is to* stay in London, we should merely be making what seems to be the sheer mistake of claiming that it is a matter of English usage that imperative sentences are used to give orders. This mistake is indeed, in varying degrees of explicitness, very frequently made, but it is none the better for that.

It is worth observing that I am not suggesting that imperative sentences are as such *ambiguous*; ambiguity is a quite different phenomenon. 'The cat is in the cupboard' is (as quite possibly most sentences, and many imperative sentences, are) an ambiguous sentence, in that what we are coarsely calling the conventions of English enable us to assign to it at least two distinct senses (or 'readings') – one concerning the whereabouts of a familiar kind of domestic animal, the other of a kind of instrument of corporal chastisement. What the sentence means in this or that particular occurrence is a question of *which* conventions are applicable, or are exploited, in particular cases. As distinct from this, my suggestion about imperative sentences is that the conventions of English do not suffice for us to assign to them readings *at all*, even numerous readings; we can indeed mention various things which, in the utterance of a given imperative sentence, a speaker might well mean by uttering it, but in no case would reference to conventions of English alone enable us to assign a determinate meaning to the sentence.

What it comes to is, in a nutshell, this. If we approve Schiffer's suggestion that, when a speaker in uttering *x* means that *A* is to *V*, the sense (or 'value') of 'is to V' depends upon the particular illocutionary force of his utterance; and if, further, we approve Schiffer's suggestion that illocutionary forces (except perhaps in the case of the fully explicit performative) are not constituted or determined by conventions; then, if we further agree that the assigning of meanings to words, phrases, and sentences *is* founded in conventions, we reach the conclusion that, while of course speakers mean something by uttering imperatives and we are normally able to grasp well enough what they mean, there is in general no answer to the question what *what they say* means. And thus the odd-looking thesis stated at the end of my first paragraph appears to come out true: it is not possible to say what imperative sentences mean.

Would it be proper to conclude that the notion of 'imperative logic' should be finally abandoned? It rather looks as if we are in a position to apply terms of logical appraisal to commands, pleas, requests, pieces of advice, and so on – specimens or tracts of discourse in which, *ex hypothesi,* the pertinent illocutionary forces are determinate; but not to imperatives, a class whose bond of union is nothing more than grammatical, and whose relations both internal and external are, in just those respects that might appear to be of logical interest, indefeasibly – if all that we have to go on is that they are imperatives – indeterminate. The imperative 'mood' has no determinate force, so that sentences *in* that mood have no determinate sense.

MAIN PUBLICATIONS

Berkeley (Penguin Books, 1953)
English Philosophy Since 1900 (OUP, 1958, 2nd edn, 1969)
Contemporary Moral Philosophy (Macmillan, 1967)
The Object of Morality (Methuen, 1971)

UTILITARIANISM AND MORAL SELF-INDULGENCE

by

Bernard Williams

Knightbridge Professor of Philosophy, University of Cambridge, and Fellow of King's College, Cambridge

My problem arises from the question of what one is to do in circumstances where there are strong reasons, particularly of a utilitarian kind, for doing something which one finds morally distasteful, and against which one has a strong personal commitment. It also of course involves questions of what one says and thinks about other people's actions in such situations. My concern is with a charge that can be brought against people who reject morally distasteful acts in such cases, namely that they are guilty of a certain kind of self-indulgence. When the agent's refusal takes the particular form of saying that while others, no doubt, will bring evil about, at least it will not come about through *him*, the charge may handily take the form of saying that the agent displays a possessive attitude towards his own virtue.[1]

The problem particularly comes up in relation to utilitarianism. If the reasons for the act are, from a utilitarian point of view, strong enough, then utilitarians will say that the fact that the act is morally distasteful is certainly not an adequate reason against doing it in this case; as a general characteristic of acts of this sort, it is largely irrelevant to questions of what to do here and now, though it may be relevant to other aspects of the situation – thus we may think well of the agent for finding this kind of act distasteful, his reaction being taken as a reassuring sign of good character. It is in the context of a critique of utilitarianism that I

[1] The phrase appears in a discussion of these issues by Jonathan Glover, *Proc. Arist. Soc.*, Supplementary Volume (1975).

have elsewhere[2] invoked the notion of *integrity* in this connexion, and it is in this context that I shall discuss the problem here, taking, that is to say, the reasons inviting one to the distasteful act as utilitarian reasons. However, the general structure of this problem for individual action is not confined to this sort of case, and I hope that my discussion will help, at least indirectly, to bring that out.

There is a set of problems very closely related to this one, which are problems of politics – taking this in a broad sense of action in a public capacity in a public domain, though the clearest and most important issues arise from matters of state. The clearest of all cases are actions by politicians in the exercise of their office in the context of international affairs, but similar issues can range down to such matters as rising politicians making deals to advance their careers, and their aspirations, and their supporters' moral hopes. These problems of political morality – the matter of 'dirty hands'[3] – I shall not try to discuss here. It is important that they are not just a special case of the issue I shall discuss, not just examples of that issue arising in the political domain. In the clearest examples of the political, we have two special features. First, the agent stands in a relation to others – citizens, supporters, electors, etc. – in which he is supposed to effect results which involve, and can be known to involve, such acts; and this relation itself can have a moral dimension, for instance of trust. I say 'is supposed to effect results which involve . . .' rather than 'is supposed to perform such acts' because the public sometimes do take, and the media often pretend to take, a moralised view by which politicians are supposed not to do the acts required for what they are supposed to achieve. This turns into some specially complex issues about the public image of politics. Second, the sphere of operation is itself less moralised and less structured by moralised expectations than at least a lot of other activities in at least settled communities: international relations are of course the prime example of this.

These two factors are different from one another. Issues of the second kind might arise even if there were no one you were

[2] In J. J. C. Smart and B. Williams, *Utilitarianism: For and Against* (CUP, 1973).

[3] See Michael Walzer's discussion in *Philosophy and Public Affairs* (Winter, 1973).

responsible to and for: some, though not all, traditional moralists have thought that there were restrictions on the extent to which moral considerations apply in the state of nature, and believed in the moral analogue to *silent leges inter arma*. The first feature, again, can arise without the second; but without the second factor, there would be greater doubt that the role being exercised by those responsible was a legitimate or acceptable role – the expectations people have of the leader are affected by their perception of the terrain over which he is leading them.

For these reasons, questions of dirty hands are not just a special case of the present problem: or rather, to assume that they are is to beg a major question about the answer to them. The present problem is about the nature and proper content of what is undoubtedly a person's individual moral judgement, and (leaving aside an outlook which actually *defined* moral considerations in terms of utilitarianism) concerns what is certainly a moral choice between moral solutions. The question of dirty hands, at least in its strongest form, concerns what role a person's individual moral judgement is supposed to play in the business at all. The present problem is interested in the individual's moral consciousness and how it should appreciate the situation; the question of dirty hands raises the issue of whether his moral consciousness, and how it appreciates the situation, is not just an irrelevance.

One issue that does notably arise with both these questions, but which, again, I shall not discuss, is the extent to which, and the ways in which, actions offensive to morality can be retrospectively justified – perhaps even morally justified – by success; and what, if they can, may count as success. In its least palatable form, this is the view that even political atrocities can be justified by history. However, neither the unpalatableness of that application, nor (still less) some supposed guarantee offered by the sense of the term 'moral', should lead us to underestimate this view in general: it has more to it than people like to admit. But it is a topic for another occasion.

Our problem arises with cases in which the agent is faced with a reliable choice between a detestable action and an outcome which will be utilitarianly worse: where 'a reliable choice' means that he has a choice between doing and not doing the action, and it is certain beyond reasonable doubt that if he does not do the action, then that outcome, or something yet worse than that outcome, will follow.[4] There are familiar arguments to suggest that no, or few, such choices are in fact reliable. On the one hand, utilitarians urge the importance of side-effects in calculating the balance of utility between acting and refraining : when side-effects are included, the detestable action will be said to possess less utility than at first appearance, and may have less utility than the alternative outcome. It is worth remarking that the level of probability attaching to these considerations is usually left quite indeterminate : some of these effects, on which great weight in the abstract is put by defenders of utilitarianism, are so problematical that in any actual case a consistent and clear-headed utilitarian would be bound very largely to discount them. In any case, we shall assume that we are dealing with a class of cases in which, when all these considerations are counted in, the balance of utilitarian advantage favours the (otherwise) detestable action. Clearly no utilitarian could say, and few would want to, that there could not be any such case.

An alternative tack for casting doubt on the reliability of such choices, used this time by anti-utilitarians, is to suggest that the efficacy of the detestable action (e.g. in preventing great harms which would otherwise occur) is more doubtful than the example supposes. This is a line often taken by those defending an absolutist position in cases of detestable actions extorted by threats made by hijackers and so forth, to the effect that the very character of the threat shows that one has reason to doubt the efficacy of giving in to it : why should one expect such threateners to keep their promises anyway? As a *general* line of argument, this seems to me, bluntly, a cop-out. Of course there are some cases in which it is a reasonable bet that nothing is to be gained by giving in to threats, but there are others in which it is not a reasonable bet, and it is merely an evasion to pretend that we have an *a priori* assurance, applicable to every case, that it is inadequately certain that the action will have its expected effect.[5]

[4] It can be accepted even, perhaps, by a utilitarian that the more horrible the action which is to be justified by the prospect of a given good outcome, the more probable it has to be that the outcome will indeed follow the action : suppose this already allowed for in the case. For two examples of the kind in question, see Smart and Williams, op. cit., pp. 97–9.

[5] The underlying idea seems to be the *unity of the vices*, a psychologically unsound principle. A bizarre application of much the same idea is an argument which I have heard advanced by P. T. Geach, to the effect that

In any case, there are only certain sorts of examples to which this line of reasoning can be relevantly applied at all, namely those in which, if the threateners fail to deliver, the all-round outcome is worse than if one had not done the detestable action. Not all cases which raise our problem – not even all that involve threateners – are of this structure. There is the case in which I am invited to kill one man, and told that if I refuse, someone else will shoot that man and several other men as well. If we think solely in terms of outcomes, then the only conceivable outcome actually better than those which involve my accepting, is that in which I refuse and they decide not to kill anyone; but there is absolutely no probability of that at all. If the other persons do what is analogous to promise-breaking in a hijacking case, namely that I accept and they nevertheless kill the rest, then the outcome, regarded as an outcome, is only the same as what it certainly will be if I refuse. So in terms of outcomes, we need only some non-zero probability that they will do what they say for my acceptance to be rational.

In general, arguments of this kind seem only too ready to confuse the idea that some factor ignored in the example is possible, with the idea that it has some indeterminately high probability. In this, they notably resemble some arguments brought forward by their utilitarian opponents. No doubt the reason is the same: each in its own way is trying to find a consequentialist argument for some sentiment which does not have its roots in consequentialist considerations at all.

Let us then grant a reliable choice of the kind in question. Someone who knowingly takes the anti-utilitarian course in such a case might be open to the charge of being concerned with his own integrity or purity or virtue at others' expense. To use one phrase as a general label, though it might not always be the best phrase, let us call this the charge of moral self-indulgence. The first things I want to discuss are certain necessary conditions of such a charge being appropriate. In doing this, I shall assume that this charge is not, and is not intended to be, just trivially *equivalent* to a disapproving claim that someone, for reasons of the moral kind, knowingly acted in an anti-utilitarian way. I take it that an

---

we could have no reason to believe in an unjust hell: the only ground for belief in hell being revelation, we should have no reason to regard as trustworthy the communications of a God wicked enough to run an unjust hell.

equivalence is not intended, since one who makes this charge in this connexion surely intends to commend the utilitarian solution to such cases, and hence indirectly the utilitarian system, by bringing non-utilitarian outlooks in certain of their applications under a charge which has some independent force, and which might already be recognised as an objection. It is this independent force which I shall try to uncover; and I shall, more particularly, assume that the charge of moral self-indulgence imputes a specific kind of *motive*.

It is, in fact, neither a sufficient nor a necessary condition of this charge's being appropriate that the agent knowingly does from a motive of the moral kind something which is counter-utilitarian. It is not sufficient, for consider the case of a man who, courageously doing what he takes to be his duty (or even just courageously), gets himself killed in the course of a counter-utilitarian project. He may be rash or foolish, but not, on the strength of this, morally self-indulgent: what contributes to this may possibly include the fact that he pays a high price himself. It is also not a necessary condition. It is possible for someone to be open to the charge of moral self-indulgence when the moral considerations which influence him are themselves utilitarian ones. Someone might incur this charge in certain cases (not all) who, for reasons of the general utilitarian welfare, left high and dry someone who depended on him. If the man who refused to shoot when invited to by the threateners was keeping his hands clean from what the utilitarian would regard as ultimately unreal dirt, *this* man is keeping his hands clean from what, for the utilitarian, is real dirt.

What would encourage one to bring this charge against this man? One feature might be that he did not really seem to care about any particular other beneficiaries very much. This cannot mean just that there were no particularly identified beneficiaries about which he cared – *that* would be the case with, for instance, a man who honourably acted in the interests of the unidentified inhabitants of an identified town, or, to take a more radical case, had to act in this way to prevent radiation hazard to future people. Nor will refinements on this thought get us to the nub of the charge; but the thought is suggestive of something which is much nearer the nub of the charge. One thing the thought can express is the suspicion that what the agent cares about is not so much other people, as himself caring about other people. He has an image of himself as a virtuous utilitarian, and this image is more important in his motivation than any concern for other persons, in particular that person for whom he is specially invited to show concern.

It is this type of *reflexive* concern which, I suggest, is significantly related to the charge of moral self-indulgence. It can arise with any moral motivation whatsoever. Thus a person may act from generosity or loyalty, and act in a counter-utilitarian way, and not attract the charge of moral self-indulgence; but that charge will be attracted if the suspicion is that his act is motivated by a concern for his own generosity or loyalty, the enhancement or preservation of his own self-image as a generous or loyal person. In the case of a man who acts in a counter-utilitarian way for reasons not of the moral kind, the charge of moral self-indulgence will not in any case stick, since 'moral' is not the sort of self-indulgence, if any, that he is going in for. But there are highly analogous contrasts in the matter of reflexivity. It is one thing for a man to act in a counter-utilitarian way out of his great love for Isolde, another for him to do so out of a concern for his image of himself as a great Tristan. The distinction applies even to the case of selfishness. One can act selfishly, that is to say, in a manner motivated by desire of things for oneself and indifferently to the welfare of others, but it would be different from that to act from a conception of oneself as a person who so acts. While the latter is unlikely to be nicer, it has a chance of being a bit grander.

I take it that there is in general a clear conceptual distinction between the first-order motivation in each of these cases, and its reflexive second-order substitute. After that very general recognition, however, there are many respects in which even at the analytical level, let alone in psychological reality, boundaries are quite unclear. I shall make one or two remarks on what is obviously a large set of questions.

One necessary condition of ascribing the second-order motivation to an agent is that we also take him to possess the concept of the first-order motivation in question; and a particularly clear distinction between the two types of motivation is available where it is possible to be motivated in a certain moral way without possessing the relevant concept of that motivation at all. Some types of virtuous motivation permit this, and it is one more mistaken consequence of Kantian moral theory that the only genuine moral motivation is taken to be one which essentially involves the agent's being conscious of that type of motivation. But even if an agent does possess the concept of a certain virtuous motivation, it may be that he does not apply it to his own case: in the space provided, with some virtues, by this possibility, there is room for such a thing as intelligent innocence. And even if, last, the concept is applied and the thought of his own disposition is present, that is not the same as his motivation being provided by that thought. It is a point worth further inquiry that in the case of some virtues (such as, perhaps, courage) the presence of such a thought may be encouraging to the first-order motivation, whereas with others it is not so, the presence of the thought tending to destroy the first-order motivation. To the extent that this latter is so, there will be a reason (there are others) why some virtues are only imperfectly accessible to highly self-conscious and reflective agents, as there are other virtues fully accessible only to them.

It may well be that the route to acquiring and sustaining the first-order virtuous motivations requires a kind of self-esteem which may involve to some degree and in some form second-order motivations: it is a question of psychological theory to what extent that is so, though that extent is certainly limited, for instance by the matters of concept-possession which have already been mentioned. It is a psychological matter also, less perhaps of theory than of common observation, to what extent what sort of motive actually operates. Nothing I say is meant to imply that it is in the least easy to tell to what degree what sort of motive is operating, in someone else's case or – what in the nature of this matter is a very different thing – one's own.

However, even if there is a difference between these sorts of motivations, there remains a question about what, if anything, is supposed to be wrong with the second-order motivation – in particular, what about it makes it self-indulgent. Indeed, some philosopher might argue that for at least some kinds of second-order motivation there could not be anything wrong with it. For on the account given so far, it looks as though a man would be motivated in some such second-order way if he were to ask himself 'What would I do if I acted as a generous man would act here?', and were motivated to act on the answer; and if he gave the right answer to the question, and acted on it, then it looks as though he would do just what a generous man would do, and for no worse reason. Is that moral self-indulgence?

No; though as a picture of moral deliberation the pattern is surely very distorted (whether the distortion is in the picture or in what is pictured). What is lacking from this for it to be, however odd in other ways, a matter of self-indulgence is some element of self-esteem – a point suggested by the fact that it is, after all, the generosity of some hypothetical ideally generous person that is invoked here, not the agent's own. Here we can be misled by phrases such as 'he is concerned with being generous'. This may mean merely that he is concerned to do the generous thing in a sense in which that is what any generous man is concerned to do; or that he is concerned to conform his conduct to some paradigm of a generous man, like the agent just mentioned (this kind of reflexivity looks, in fact, like a familiar example of a more primitive, rather than a fuller, moral development); or it may mean that he is concerned with his own generosity, where this implies that he has substituted for a thought about what is needed, a thought which focuses disproportionately upon the expression of his own disposition, and that he derives pleasure from the thought that his disposition will have been expressed – rather than deriving pleasure, as the agent who is not self-indulgent may, from the thought of how things will be if he acts in a certain way, that way being (though he need not think this) the expression of his disposition.

It is this sort of reflexivity which invites the name 'self-indulgence'. It involves a reversal at a line which I take to be fundamental to any morality or indeed sane life at all, between self-concern and other-concern; it involves a misdirection not just of attention, though that is true too, but genuinely of concern, and they both issue in differences in what actually gets done. Distortions which are due primarily to diverted attention, are familiar also with skills; those which come from diverted concern, the virtues share with the affections. These differences in what gets done fit in with something noted earlier in the matter of courage, the evidential weight attached in these questions to the agent's himself paying a price; he *can* do that in the course of reflexively regarding his own virtue, but the space for it becomes more constricted. These remarks about reflexivity and moral motivation do involve a claim, which I should make explicit, about a subject which is hard and important and has been inadequately studied, the question of how we are to picture the expression of moral dispositions in an agent's deliberative thought. We have some views in philosophy about the reference to dispositions in explaining and evaluating other people's conduct. We have some views about the occurrence of moral considerations in practical deliberation (though they are largely restricted to questions about the function in deliberation of 'moral judgements'). What we seem to lack is any coherent representation of something which is certainly true, that distinctive moral dispositions, such as generosity, are expressed in the content (and not just the occasions) of the agent's deliberations. The one claim that I make about that subject here is that the characteristic and basic expression of a moral disposition in deliberation is *not* a premise which refers to that disposition – it is not the basic characteristic of a generous man's deliberations that they use the premise 'I am a generous man'. Whatever one goes on to say about this subject, that negative claim is surely correct; though the generous man is partly characterised by what goes into his deliberations, it is not that what goes into them are reflections on his generosity.[6]

We are now in a position to see better the relations between utilitarianism and integrity in the matter of moral self-indulgence. If the objectionable feature of moral self-indulgence is identified with a certain kind of reflexive motivation, then it cannot stand in any simple contrast with utilitarian motivation. For, first, it can be contrasted with many things other than utilitarian motivation – as, in general, with first-order virtuous motivations. Further, utilitarian benevolence is itself open to this reflexive deformation. The reason why utilitarian motivation seems to many the unique enemy of moral self-indulgence is that it seems the purest expression of other-concern as opposed to self-concern – isn't utilitarianism just the devotion to other-concern? But in fact the

[6] Nor, we can add, is it merely thoughts such as 'he needs help'; the occurrence of such thoughts certainly marks out some men from others, but does little to mark out generous men from non-generous. Nor is it the 'moral judgement', 'I ought to help'; apart from well-known questions about the connexion of that with motivation, it is not specially the mark of a generous man to have or act on that thought. An answer will probably have to start from the idea that the basic representation in deliberation of such a disposition is in the form 'I want to help . . .'; this has the further advantage of not making it unintelligible how such moral considerations can be weighed in deliberation against quite different considerations.

distinction between other-concern and self-concern is in no way the same thing as the distinction between utilitarian and non-utilitarian; and in the sense in which other-concerned motivations which are not those of utilitarianism are capable of reflexive deformation into one kind of self-concern, so is utilitarian motivation itself.

What about concern with one's own *integrity*? The simplest thing to say about this would be that integrity is one case of a virtue, and that, like other virtues, it is subject to reflexive deformation. But I think that this would be wrong; rather, one should perhaps say that integrity is not a *virtue* at all. In saying that, I do not mean that there is not all that much to be said for it, as one might say that humility was not a virtue. I mean that while it is an admirable human property, it is not related to motivation as the virtues are. It is not a disposition which itself yields motivations, as generosity and benevolence do; nor is it a virtue of that type, sometimes called 'executive' virtues, which do not themselves yield a characteristic motive, but are necessary for that relation to oneself and the world which enables one to act from desirable motives in desirable ways – the type which includes courage and self-control. It is rather that one who displays integrity acts from those dispositions and motives which are most deeply his, and has also the virtues that enable him to do that: integrity does not enable him to do it, nor is it what he acts from when he does so.

If that is right, we can see why integrity, regarded as a virtue, can seem to smack of moral self-indulgence. For if it is regarded as a motive, it is hard to reconstruct its representation in thought except in the objectionable reflexive way: the thought would have to be about oneself and one's own character, and of the suspect kind. If integrity had to be provided with a characteristic thought, there would be nothing for the thought to be about except oneself – but there is no such characteristic thought, only the thoughts associated with the projects, in carrying out which a man may display his integrity. Relatedly, one cannot directly bring someone up to possess integrity, in the sense of teaching him to display or exercise it; rather one brings it about that he genuinely cares for something and has the characteristics necessary to live in the spirit of that.

But what of the thought 'not through me' – the thought that even if others are going to bring evil and injustice into the world, it will not be by my agency that it comes about?[7] This, certainly, is already a reflexive thought, and involves at least one step away from the simply unselfconscious expression of counter-utilitarian dispositions. The thought, however, is not in itself a motivating thought, and those words do not express any distinctive motivation. It is not merely that they do not on all occasions express some one motivation. Rather, they do not, in themselves, express any motivation at all: if one is motivated *not to do it oneself*, then there is some (other) motive one has for not doing it. One such motive is fear, and in the particular form, perhaps, of the fear of pollution, it can attract the accusation of cowardice to some agents in the sort of circumstances we are discussing. With the motivation of fear in general, it is often the case that the agent *would prefer to be able to do* whatever it is he fears doing. In relation to that, the fear of pollution is a special case, providing either an exception to it, or a peculiarly complex instance of it. But in any case, fear, of whatever kind, is by no means always the motive of agents who use those words.

A quite different, perhaps limiting, case of a motive lying behind those words would be one related to pride, the motive of one of whom it is not true that he would prefer to be able to do it – he could do it – but who does not want it done, and refuses to be made to do it by another's providing him with reasons for doing it. A bare, unsupported motive of this kind could hardly be adequate to the cases we have in mind: because the interests of innocent parties have been thrown into the reasons for acting, this would be, too much, arbitrary self-assertion. But a similar, though different, thought can be expressed by the agent in our case: similar, in that he registers a refusal to be coerced by the threats, inducements or example of others; different in that he is not just asserting his own independence and right to refuse, but expressing the other motivations he has for not doing the act in question.

Utilitarians will, of course, dispute his right to refuse, but the point is that the agent's affirmation 'not through me' does not, in such a case, express a motivation of the suspect, 'self-indulgent', kind. In itself, it does not represent any motivation at all, and

[7] Glover, op cit., has called this the 'Solzhenitsyn principle', after a passage in that writer's Nobel oration. The name is well invoked; but this thought should not be regarded as a *principle*.

the motivations which can lie behind it include some which are, for various reasons, suspect and some which are not. The reflexivity of the utterance does not represent in itself any suspect motive, but only the self-consciousness of the refusal, however the refusal is motivated.

There are many and various forms of dispositions, patterns of feeling and desire, which can motivate people to counter-utilitarian acts; some themselves virtues, some more particular projects, affections and commitments. The question I turn to last is the place that utilitarianism can allow to such dispositions. They can be variously admired or deplored, cultivated or discouraged. Some may indeed be admired and encouraged for what are, remotely and ultimately, utilitarian reasons, in the sense that human welfare is served indirectly by the presence of these dispositions in the world. I think it is wrong to try to reduce all questions of the assessment of such dispositions to utilitarian considerations, and indeed that it is incoherent, since there is no coherent view of human welfare itself which is independent of such issues as what people care for, in non-utilitarian spirit, with regard to such things as these dispositions. But that is not my concern here, and if the present argument goes through for those dispositions of this type which can be granted indirect utilitarian value, then it will presumably have some *ad hominem* force against utilitarianism.

The difficulty is that such dispositions are patterns of motivation, feeling and action, and one cannot have both the world containing these dispositions, and its actions regularly fulfilling the requirements of utilitarianism. If you are a person who wholeheartedly and genuinely possesses some of these admirable dispositions, you cannot also be someone in whose thought and action the requirements of utilitarianism are unfailingly mirrored, nor could you wish to be such a person. If you want the world to contain generous, affectionate, forceful, resolute, creative and actually happy people, you do not wish it to contain people who uniformly think in such a way that their actions will satisfy the requirements of utilitarianism.

The supposition that one might combine the dispositions one wants and admires in the world with actions that maximally satisfy the utilitarian criterion stems from a number of errors. One is an idea, which utilitarianism, though it denies it, is in fact disposed to share with other pictures of moral experience, and indeed of practical rationality in general, that the processes of practical thought are transcendental to experience and do not actually take up any psychological room. But in fact to think in one way rather than another about what to do is to be empirically different, to be a certain kind of person, and it is not possible to combine all kinds of reflection with all kinds of disposition. Utilitarians neglect this to some extent at the level of the individual, but they have made a speciality out of neglecting it at the social level, supposing for instance that there could be an élite of utilitarian thinkers who possess an esoteric doctrine unknown to others, without there being specified any form of social organisation to make this structure a social reality.

Second, there is the error, also shared with others, of dissociating moral thought and decision from moral feeling. It is a commonplace that there is a form of weakness which consists in being overcome by unstructured moral feeling; and there is another which consists in a kind of squeamishness. These are often failures of confusion, of lack of self-knowledge. But the cure for them cannot or should not consist in teaching people to discount their moral feelings, to dissociate themselves from them.[8] Theorists who encourage this are fond of such cases as that of the lapsed and now unbelieving Catholic who feels guilty when he does not go to Mass. But whatever is to be said about that case, it cannot be a paradigm of what the utilitarian needs. For the lapsed Catholic aims to dissociate himself entirely from the Mass and its claims, to reach a position from which no such feeling has any significance at all. But no such thing is true of the man involved in counter-utilitarian feelings in a case such as we are discussing; for these feelings represent something he in general stands by, and which the utilitarian, we are supposing, wants him to stand by.

No one is suggesting that moral feeling should express itself unmodified by thought (at the limit, this is not even a comprehen-

[8] A theory of the moral sentiments is needed here. One approach to the questions of dissociation from moral feeling might be suggested by a certain contrast between moral feeling and sense-perception. Those views, of rationalist type, which most strongly advocate dissociation from perceptual sensations, at least emphasise a truth, that the aim of objective knowledge is to dissociate thought about the world, certainly from what is distinctively oneself, and perhaps (on realist views) from anything that is distinctively human. But that cannot be the aim of moral thought and experience, which must primarily involve grasping the world in such a way that one can, as a particular human being, live in it.

sible idea). There are, further, some moral feelings, particularly concerned with the observance of rules, which can be formed by experience in ways which to some extent fit round and accommodate utilitarian thoughts: it is so, up to a point, with the rules of promise-keeping and truth-telling. But there is no reason at all to believe, for many dispositions of the kind that it is desirable to have in the world, that they can retain their position and significance and yet systematically make way, whenever required to, for the deliverances of utilitarian thought, the feelings associated with the disposition being made the objects of dissociation.

Relatedly, there is not much to be got out of a third line of thought, which can also encourage an oversimple view of these problems, the supposedly clear distinction between judging the act and judging the agent. For if a man has a disposition of a kind which it is good that he has; and if what he did was just what a man with such a disposition would be bound to do in such a case, but (as I claim must sometimes be the case) counter-utilitarian; what is the force of saying that what he did was as a matter of fact wrong? It is important that it does *not* have the force – which really would give some point to the distinction of act and agent – that, if he had been in a position to conduct his deliberations better, he would have acted differently. He conducted his deliberations as such a man does, and it is good that he is such a man. By the same token, it cannot mean that we ought to try to bring people up to be such that they do not make such mistakes. If there is any content to saying that this man did the wrong thing, it must be compatible with our thinking that it is a good thing that people do not always do the right thing; and not just in the very general sense in which we may reflect on the uncovenanted benefits which can flow even from dire acts, but in the more intimate sense that we want the world to contain people who when they ask themselves 'what is the right thing to do?' will, on definitely specifiable sorts of occasion, give the wrong answer.

The utilitarian's theory, once he admits the value of these dispositions, takes the question 'what is the right thing to do?' a long way away from the question 'what answers is it desirable that people should be disposed to give to the question "what is the right thing to do?"?' The tension created by this separation is very great, and there is very strong pressure, if utilitarianism is to retain any distinct identity *within* moral thought, for it to reject or hopelessly dilute the value of these other dispositions, regressing to that picture of man which early utilitarianism frankly offered, in which he has, ideally, only private or otherwise sacrificeable projects, together with the one moral disposition of utilitarian benevolence. I hope to have shown that that false picture cannot be commended to us by rejecting other moral motivations, in their counter-utilitarian appearances, as pieces of moral self-indulgence.

MAIN PUBLICATIONS

Morality: An Introduction to Ethics (Penguin, 1972; CUP, 1976)
Problems of the Self (CUP, 1973)
A Critique of Utilitarianism; in Smart and Williams, *Utilitarianism: For and Against* (CUP, 1973)

LANGUAGE, BELIEF AND RELATIVISM

by

Peter Winch

Professor of Philosophy, King's College, University of London

It is one thing for a man to think that something is so and quite another thing for what he thinks to be so. This simple truism is fundamental to what we understand thought to be; for a thought is a thought about something – it has an object – and the kind of relation it has to its object involves the possibility of assessing the truth or adequacy of the content of the thought by confronting it with its object. All this would disappear, apparently, if there were no distinction between truth and falsity of a kind which presupposed a distinction between what is the case and what is merely thought to be the case.

However, it is considerably easier to recognise this as a truism than it is to understand exactly how it is to be applied in different areas of human thinking. The attempt to win clarity about such issues is philosophy. And the controversy surrounding different forms of 'relativism' is one large complex of aspects of this attempt.

The crudest form of relativism, associated with the name of Protagoras, makes a frontal assult on the very possibility of evaluating beliefs as true or false by assimilating the truth of a belief to the fact that the belief is held by someone. This position originates partly in a confusion (connected with 'Moore's Paradox') about how the distinction between truth and falsity is related to the notion of belief. If one person, *A*, believes that *p*, he believes that *p* is true; and if *B* believes that *p* is false, he believes that not-*p*. People sometimes feel a temptation to express this position by saying that *p* is 'true for *A*' and 'false for *B*'. As long as this is understood as simply equivalent to saying that *A* believes that *p* and *B* believes that not-*p*, the only thing wrong with this way of speaking is its barbarity. But since – one may now be tempted to argue – to claim that *p* is true is merely to express one's belief that *p*, *A*'s utterance '*p* is true' may be re-expressed by *A* as 'I believe that *p*'; and this in its turn may be re-expressed by someone else as '*A* believes that *p*'. And since the two assertions, '*A* believes that *p*' and '*B* believes that not-*p*' are perfectly consistent with each other one seems at once led to the conclusion that *A*'s assertion '*p* is true' is perfectly compatible with *B*'s assertion '*p* is false'. One is now right in the middle of the relativist quagmire.

But, of course, in so far as *A*'s utterance 'I believe that *p*' *can* be taken to express the same as his utterance '*p* is true' it can *not* be expressed by *B* in the form '*A* believes that *p*'. It would merely be a poor joke if *B* were to respond to *A*'s question: 'I believe that *p*; do you agree with me?', by saying: 'Yes I agree; you do believe that *p*'. We cannot argue from the mutual consistency of '*A* believes that *p*' and '*B* believes that not-*p*' to the consistency of '*p* is true', said by *A*, and '*p* is false', said by *B*, even though these two utterances express respectively *A*'s belief and *B*'s disbelief in the truth of *p*. If '*p*' is interpreted as expressing a single proposition whose sense is unchanged by a change in the person who asserts it, it is evident that these latter two assertions are *not* consistent.

The interesting difficulties appear when we ask under what conditions two people can be said to believe the same thing. It seems to me a failure to appreciate the nature and extent of these difficulties which has led some critics of earlier publications of mine[1] to suppose that I was denying the simple truth which I have tried to state in my opening paragraph. They have taken a situation like that comprising the Zande 'belief in witchcraft' and the twentieth-century European 'rejection' of such a 'belief' as a case of two sets of people, who respectively assert that *p* and that not-*p*. And they have misinterpreted my argument against such an assumption as an espousal of a relativism which, if perhaps a little more sophisticated than that laid out above, is essentially open to the same kind of objection.

In 'Understanding a Primitive Society' I was discussing the conditions under which a European anthropologist can render the sense of what a Zande tribesman says when he talks of what

[1] Especially 'Understanding a Primitive Society' in Peter Winch, *Ethics and Action* (Routledge, 1972).

the anthropologist translates as 'witchcraft', 'oracle', etc. We may speak of 'Zande witchcraft beliefs' in such a discussion. But what is being referred to is not the sum of particular beliefs held by individual Azande that this or that tribesman has exerted witchcraft; we are discussing rather the language in which such beliefs are expressed and which makes them possible.

The issues raised by such a discussion differ from those raised by the sort of relativism concerning truth which I have so far considered. Roger Trigg's *Reason and Commitment* provides an instructive example of the confusions which result from failing to observe the distinction. Trigg thinks that the following remark in 'Understanding a Primitive Society' is evidence of objectionable relativist leanings: 'Reality is not what gives language sense. What is real and what is unreal shows itself *in* the sense that language has.'[2] Trigg comments that while a language certainly 'expresses a community's beliefs about reality', reality nevertheless exists 'apart from people's beliefs', which may be mistaken. 'An essential function of language . . . is to concern itself with what is actually the case. Its business is to attempt to communicate *truth*.' It follows from my quoted remark that 'different languages cannot be thought of as different attempts to describe the same reality. "Reality" is made relative to a language, and if different languages portray the "world" differently, then there must be different worlds.'[3]

Unlike Trigg, I did *not* speak of a language as expressing a community's *beliefs* about reality. On the contrary, my main objection to Evans-Pritchard's treatment[4] of Zande thought was precisely that he did so treat their language. The confusions involved are highlighted by Trigg's talk of *language* as concerned 'to attempt to communicate truth', to 'describe reality'. It may indeed be argued – I have done so myself[5] – that there could be no language whose speakers were not normally concerned to say what is true rather than what is false. But it is *speakers* of a language who attempt to say what is true, to describe how things are. They do so *in* the language they speak; and this language

[2] ibid., pp. 12–13.

[3] Roger Trigg, *Reason and Commitment* (CUP, 1973), p. 15.

[4] E. E. Evans-Pritchard, *Witchcraft, Oracles and Magic among the Azande* (OUP, 1937).

[5] Cf. 'Nature and Convention' (*Ethics and Action*, pp. 50–72).

attempts no such thing, either successfully or unsuccessfully. Trigg is right to say that, on my view, 'different languages cannot be thought of as different attempts to describe the same reality', but wrong to suppose that the alternative which I must accept is that different languages attempt to describe different realities: they do not attempt to describe anything at all. If we do want to speak of a 'relation between language and reality', this is not a relation between a set of descriptions and what is described; although, no doubt, an account of this latter relation would have to form part of any account of the relation between language and reality.

The point may be brought out by the following consideration. If Tom believes that Harry is in pain and Dick that he is not, then, in the ordinary sense of the word 'belief', Tom and Dick have different beliefs. But according to Trigg's way of speaking, Tom and Dick, because they both speak the same language and mean the same thing by the word 'pain', share a common belief: even though their descriptions of Harry are mutually contradictory – indeed, precisely because they are – they in a sense share a common belief about reality: perhaps that it contains such a thing as pain. But if it is possible to affirm that there is such a thing as pain, it ought to be possible to deny it too. The language in which the denial is couched must be meaningful; and it must mean the same as the language in which what is denied might be affirmed, else the denial would not contradict the affirmation. So to deny that there is such a thing as pain, I must mean by 'pain' just what someone who affirms that there is such a thing means by 'pain'. Hence we are still both speaking the same language and still, according to Trigg's way of thinking, offering the same 'description of reality'. This incoherence illustrates how important it is to recognise that the grammar of a language is not a theory about the nature of reality, even though new factual discoveries and theoretical developments may lead to grammatical changes. What is difficult in particular cases, like that of Zande notions of witchcraft, is to understand clearly what belongs to grammar and what belongs to theory or 'belief'. I will return to this point later.

But first I should like to comment on another way in which we may be confused when we speak in this context about the relation of one 'language' to another.[6] On the one hand we speak of 'the

[6] Cf., for instance, Martin Hollis, 'Reason and Ritual', in B. R. Wilson (ed.) *Rationality* (Blackwell, 1970); especially on p. 236.

English (French, German) language'; and on the other hand philosophers frequently use such expressions as 'the language of science (of religion, of morals, etc.)'. These two different ways of distinguishing between 'languages' raise different issues; but the two kinds of distinction overlap in certain cases, as they do for instance, very confusingly, when we compare the English language with the language of the Azande.

An Englishman who wants to learn French will have to master a new vocabulary having varying degrees of equivalence with the vocabulary of English, new grammatical rules of sentence-construction, declension, conjugation of verbs, and the like. All this takes place within the broad context of a shared culture. French and English life differ at various points of course and at such points there may indeed be difficulties concerning the translatability of sentences from one language into the other. How relevant such considerations are will depend on the kind of material to be translated and the purpose of the translation. A report of scientific experiments, for instance, will not raise the same kind of problem as a serious work of literature. But by and large such differences are marginal: there is so much common ground in respect of, for example, political ideas and practices, economic institutions, religious tradition, etc., etc., that learning French does not consist for the most part in learning to express radically new ideas, but in learning to express in a different medium of vocabulary and syntax the kind of thing which an Englishman is already perfectly well able to express in his own language.

Learning the language of mathematics on the other hand can hardly be distinguished from learning mathematics. To learn how to express commands in French is not to learn how to command or what it is to command. But if I learn how to formulate a mathematical proof (as distinct from how to operate with a particular notation), I am not acquiring a new way of expressing something I already grasp (viz. mathematical proof). I am learning how to prove something – even: *what it is* to 'prove' something mathematically. Correspondingly, while one would speak of a translation from English into French, one would hardly speak of a translation from mathematics into . . . well, what? There is no such thing as a translation into non-mathematical terms of the phrase 'solution of a differential equation'. The concept of a differential equation belongs to mathematics and has to be expressed in 'the language of mathematics'.

When we are considering the 'translatability' of Zande into English these ways of distinguishing 'different languages' overlap. There would be little difficulty, over a wide area, in agreeing that certain expressions in the one language 'mean the same' (roughly) as certain expressions in the other. But in other areas, to demand a translation from the Zande into English would be like asking for a translation of something mathematical into something non-mathematical. Someone from a tribe with no knowledge of mathematics who wants to learn English will be able to find equivalents in his own language to much of what he learns. But if he happens upon an English textbook of mathematics he will not be able to proceed in the same way. If he does want to learn what is written there he will have to learn mathematics. In so doing he will not merely be learning new ways of expressing himself; he will also be learning new things to express. The English anthropologist is in a somewhat similar position when he tries to understand Zande talk of the poison oracle, of witches and of magic medicines. He has to learn not merely how the Azande express what they are doing when they consult the oracle, but what they are doing, *what it is* to consult the poison oracle. There is no more reason to suppose that the English language which he speaks will, without extension, provide expressions into which what the Azande say about this subject may be translated than there is for supposing that the language of a tribe with no mathematics will provide a means of translating expressions for differential equations.

However, an Englishman who wishes to understand the poison oracle will face additional difficulties. Even if I know little mathematics I have grown up with and live in a community which cultivates mathematics and I am familiar with the position it occupies in our cultural landscape. The poison oracle on the other hand is a feature of a cultural landscape which is itself alien to me. Our own culture provides a well-established and well-understood route by which a non-mathematician can learn mathematics. When learned, mathematics has a multitude of well-established applications in the lives people lead in this culture. But there is no place for any 'application' of Zande magical beliefs and practices in the life which it is open to anyone to lead in contemporary England. And the interest of an English anthropologist in learning about and trying to understand such beliefs and practices will not be directed towards any such practical application. Correspondingly, to raise the question whether we have properly 'understood' Zande ways of thinking will be to apply different criteria of understanding from those appropriate to the question whether we have properly 'understood' a certain branch of mathematics. The point is not that a 'greater or less degree' of understanding is possible in the one case as compared with the other. It is rather that 'understanding' takes different forms in the two cases (though there will be many points of connection). Moreover, though there is no room for a direct application in our own lives of what we may learn when we study Zande magical practices, this does not mean that we shall find no points of contact at all with elements familiar to us in our own cultural tradition. In 'Understanding a Primitive Society' I wanted to indicate that we are in danger of missing the useful points of contact if we concentrate too exclusively on the relation of Zande magical thought to our own scientific theories. This particular comparison is one which forces itself on our attention not merely because of the dominant position occupied by science in our culture, but also because of certain general ideas about the relation between thought and reality which we may find philosophically attractive and of which we may think (mistakenly) science provides a clear paradigm.

This brings me back to a point I raised earlier in discussing Trigg: that the grammar of a language does not constitute a theory about the nature of reality. Questions about the relation between language, thought and reality, as they are raised in philosophy, are characteristically connected with sceptical worries: worries about whether the world can be known to be such as our forms of thought seem to presuppose. But sceptical worries may have diverse sources and, according to the diversity of the sources, scepticism itself will take different forms which it is not always easy to distinguish. The scepticism which belongs to the stock in trade of Western philosophy is usually directed at ways of thinking which are fundamental to the way we live: for instance, our ways of thinking about time, about causality, about physical things in relation to our perception of them. Augustine fails to see how we can distinguish between a shorter and a longer period of time; Hume how we can say that one event is necessarily connected with another which we call its effect; Berkeley how we can speak of a physical object as existing when it is not being perceived. Much of the difficulty in all these cases springs from the fact that the forms in which we speak and think seem, on a certain sort of examination, to suggest a kind of application to the world which is not the application they in fact have. When we do, in the course of our lives, apply them in the appropriate way, the sceptical worries strike us, in Hume's phrase, as 'strain'd and ridiculous', but the worries are not laid to rest until we have succeeded in the surprisingly difficult tasks of attaining a clear view of the *actual* application of our ways of thinking and of the nature of the obstacles which stood in the way of our taking proper stock of these.

Such sceptical difficulties do not concern doubts about whether someone is right on a particular occasion in the claim he makes about how much time has passed, what caused such and such an event, what kind of object he is perceiving. They concern rather the possibility of making *any* such claims; they tend to undermine confidence in there being any genuine distinction between truth and falsity in such judgements; they attack, that is, the possibility of making any sense of them at all.

The scepticism to which we are likely to feel inclined when we contemplate the forms of thought of alien cultures is in many ways similar in form. We find a Zande tribesman asking whether such and such a man is a witch, or consulting an oracle to determine whether a proposed marriage would be propitious. We want to ask not whether he is right in the particular answers he arrives at, but whether he is asking questions to which there could be a right and a wrong answer, or whether the methods he customarily uses to answer his questions could conceivably serve to distinguish right from wrong answers. But, in contrast with the former cases, our scepticism here does not conflict with our settled thought habits. Like Augustine, we feel that we know what time is as long as we are not asked; but this is not what we feel about witches and oracles. Whereas, like Hume, we find sceptical arguments strain'd and ridiculous as long as we are actually investigating the cause of something or establishing by observation the characteristics of some physical thing, we are never in the position of inquiring whether someone is a witch or of asking the advice of an oracle. Our scepticism does not evaporate over a game of backgammon. The arguments which will appear strain'd and ridiculous are not those of the sceptic, but those of a philosopher who suggests that perhaps questions about witches, or inquiries of oracles, could be interpreted as logically perfectly in order.

Not only do we have no use, in the lives we lead, for notions like witchcraft and oracles but, more strongly, those lives seem to exclude the possibility of any such use. If I came across an Englishman in Richmond Park administering poison to a chicken while asking questions, I should not think that he was consulting the poison oracle as a Zande tribesman might do; I should be at a loss as to what was going on – I might think him deranged, or perhaps perpetrating some bizarre 'happening'. Culture sets limits to what an individual can intelligibly be said to be doing. This is not to say that there cannot be new cultural developments ('happenings' constituted a new cultural development); but what can count as a new development is also limited by the cultural framework.

I have already said that the mere fact that we can find no application in our lives for a way of thinking which has an application in other cultural contexts is no good reason for arguing that it is 'in principle impossible to understand' it. That would be to employ criteria of 'understanding' inappropriate to the case in hand. It would be equally wrong to suppose that we are necessarily faced with the question who is 'right', we or the Azande. There is certainly *conflict* between European and Zande modes of thinking and even a sort of mutual exclusion; but this is not so far to say that they logically 'contradict' each other. It could be that people who interest themselves in cricket find it impossible to take baseball seriously, and *vice versa*: there would be conflict here too, but no contradiction. It would make little sense to ask, in the abstract, which game it was 'right' to support (though of course in particular circumstances a man might have reasons for supporting the one rather than the other).

Philosophical scepticism about such notions as time, cause and physical objects often represents these notions as 'incoherent'. I have suggested (and space precludes more than the suggestion) that the appearance of incoherence springs from our substituting for the actual application of such concepts another application, suggested by misleading grammatical analogies, which will not permit them to retain their original sense. When we are dealing with such notions as witchcraft and oracles among the Azande, we do not even have a first hand unreflective mastery of their application and are the more easily misled into seeking analogies with concepts more familiar to us. Seeking such an application, we may well run into incoherencies; but this is so far no argument for the conclusion that their proper application in their native setting has anything incoherent about it.

I shall try to develop this by considering some points in H. O. Mounce's interesting paper 'Understanding a Primitive Society'.[7] Mounce agrees with me that the notion of reality which Evans-Pritchard appeals to in his criticism of Zande thought cannot be given a sense independently of the practices of science and that, therefore, it can serve as a standard for criticising magic only if magic is first shown to be a sort of science. He differs from me about how we are to determine whether Zande magical thought does 'make sense', i.e. involves an appeal to an independently intelligible notion of reality.

The philosophically important point here is not the correctness or otherwise of any particular suggested interpretation of Zande thought so much as the kind of reasoning needed to support an interpretation. Mounce's main criticism of me is that I argue from the established acceptance of a set of practices to the impossibility of questioning their sense, when the only premise which would support such a conclusion is one concerning the established use of a set of *concepts*. He goes on to argue that Zande beliefs about witchcraft and oracles are not fully intelligible in themselves, but can only be understood as a confused application of concepts having their proper home in other contexts, generated by a sort of conceptual bemusement similar to that found in certain kinds of metaphysics. I shall not here examine Mounce's interpretation of my original argument, but try to identify a confusion about the relation between beliefs and concepts which Mounce's own discussion betrays.

In identifying superstitions, Mounce argues, we must distinguish between men's spontaneous reactions to certain situations and the beliefs which they may come to hold associated with those reactions. For instance, a married couple may be upset over the loss of a wedding ring; and there is nothing absurd or irrational in this. 'It is just the way many people, at least, happen to feel.'[8]

[7] In *Philosophy* (October 1973), vol. 48, no. 186.
[8] ibid., p. 353.

But if they come to feel that the loss is a sign that their marriage will founder, this 'is just as absurd as anything held by the Azande'. Again, a man is distressed when induced to stick a pin into the eyes in a picture of his mother. This again is just a natural reaction, 'neither rational nor irrational'. But if, on his mother's eyes subsequently becoming diseased, he finds himself believing that this is somehow due to his action, then this *is* absurd.

Mounce rightly claims that such beliefs cannot be interpreted as simply 'mistaken'; rather, 'there is a certain craziness about this whole way of thinking'.[9] It is like the thinking characteristic of some forms of metaphysics, where we try to apply certain forms of expression in ways which the sense which we want them to retain will not admit. He suggests that Zande beliefs about witchcraft and oracles can be similarly diagnosed: they too apply notions like 'causal influence' and 'prediction' in situations where the conditions needed for making the sort of sense desired for them are lacking.

Mounce does not suggest any determinate aetiology for beliefs in witchcraft and oracles comparable to those he offers for his examples of superstitions. Neither does he consider whether any difference is made by the central position occupied in Zande life and thought by their magical notions, for which there is no analogy in his examples. Yet he does think that the reason why, in our society, a superstitious belief can be met with the rejoinder, 'Come now. Don't be stupid', is that 'such a belief will not fit into the network of beliefs about the physical world which has been developed by western science and which has been taught to us since childhood; or, rather, it does not even qualify as something which could possibly fit into such a network of beliefs'.[10] Such a resource is not obviously available within the context of Zande life.

A man who is distressed at having treated his mother's picture in the way described, and even more distressed when her eyes subsequently become afflicted, may express his distress in the words 'I have injured her'. That he does so *may* be a symptom of superstitious confusion, but need not be. This will depend not on the fact that he uses that particular expression, but on *how* he uses it; it depends on the *kind* of 'connection' he sees between his

[9] ibid., p. 354.
[10] ibid., p. 354.

action and his mother's affliction. He is not confused, but perfectly right, in thinking that there is *some* connection. He stuck pins into a picture of his mother, not any old sheet of paper; and he aimed for the eyes. If his mother had seen him do that she might well have been distressed and that would have been an injury to her. She did not as a matter of fact see him do it, but still, he is aware that if she had, . . . And he may also, not at all absurdly, feel that his action was anyway a betrayal of the respect and affection he owes her. Why should he not see that as an injury to her? And why should not his sense of that injury be heightened by her subsequent physical affliction?

We might speak here of the primitive reaction, which Mounce describes, as the basis for a new *concept* of 'injury', a concept the particular articulation of which may depend on the fact that the word 'injury' also has that other ('causal') use; but this latter use is not simply being taken over and applied in a situation where it does not belong. Its use is *modified* in the new circumstances and it thereby comes to bear a different sense. The point I want to make here is that though the thought 'I have injured her' *may* be a confused one, the mere fact that it is expressed in that way is not enough to show that it is. We need to see what other thoughts it is connected with, and how; we need to understand what role it is playing.[11]

Something similar may happen to the notion of 'prediction' when it is applied in the context of oracles. Mounce insists rather emphatically that the Azande's attitude to the poison oracle shows them to regard it as a source of 'true statements about the future'; he thereby misses the variety of forms 'statements about the future' may take – even with us. (Compare, for instance, 'I will meet you at 4 o'clock'; 'the government will be defeated at the election'; 'Harold Wilson will go down in history as a successful Prime Minister'.) To understand precisely what sort of relation to the future these statements have (and hence what truth and falsity comes to in the various cases), we have to attend to, amongst other things, the kind of reaction which is appropriate to various eventualities; and this of course may be a complicated and unperspicuous matter.

[11] There is a more extended discussion of analogous ways in which a concept may receive new applications, and thereby develop a modified sense, in my 'Ethical Reward and Punishment' (*Ethics and Action,* pp. 210–28).

The same goes for the poison oracle. Mounce himself claims that we must attend to the details of the Zande attitudes to the oracle. But when he comes to attempt this, he constantly appeals to analogies from other contexts. Thus he says that the Zande practice of asking the same question twice in the oracle's presence, interpreting the fowl's death as a 'yes' and a 'no' respectively on the two occasions, is analogous to the procedure of checking on the reliability of a witness. But we have to remember that though the oracle is consulted by administering poison to chickens, it is not the chickens that are being consulted, but the oracle. So the grammar of the consultation is not that one *chicken*'s answer is being checked against another's. It is of one and the same oracle that the same question is asked twice; and what sort of 'check on its reliability' is that? What we must say is that two posings of the same question while *benge* is administered to two fowls constitutes *one* complete consultation of the oracle. And there is an obvious rationale for this procedure quite different from the (confused) one suggested by Mounce. Given the importance of the *benge*'s being neither too weak nor too strong a poison – since this would predetermine the outcome and make the consultation nugatory – a good way of *checking on the goodness of the* benge is to do precisely what the Azande do do. This illustrates the importance of what I have wanted to emphasise: that we should view any particular utterance or procedure in the context of the other utterances and procedures to which it belongs.

The grammar of oracular pronouncements is determined by various factors: by, for instance, the procedure of consultation, the kind of question it is generally regarded as proper to ask, the kind of reaction considered appropriate to various kinds of outcome in relation to what the oracle has said. All this, and much else besides, constitutes a language in which certain kinds of thing can be said, certain kinds of question raised. A person *using* such a language may of course fall into confusion and into superstitiously expecting results which reflection would show it to be irrational to expect. But this would not show that there was anything confused, irrational or superstitious in the language itself.

There are consequences here for the methodology of ethnographic fieldwork. If the investigator interrogates native informants about the use of the poison oracle, he must be alive to the possibility that some of the answers he gets will betray such confusions. He must also be wary of reading such confusions back into the grammar of the mode of thinking he is trying to understand for it is only against the background of that grammar that what is confused can be distinguished from what is not. Evans-Pritchard cites a consultation of the oracle to determine who was responsible for performing some specific act (placing magic medicines in the roof of a hut). Mounce comments, plausibly, that in this case what the consultants 'hope will be revealed is exactly what might have been revealed by adopting other, and to us, more normal procedures, if these procedures had been available'.[12] And, he clearly wishes us to conclude, this can only be regarded as an absurd superstition. Such behaviour *may* indeed be a case of superstition. This is a question that could only be settled in the light of much more information than Evans-Pritchard supplies: about the surrounding circumstances of the consultation, about what, if anything, is taken as 'independent evidence' concerning the same allegation, about the kind of use to which the oracle's answer is put – and much else besides. But even if, in the light of such information, we do conclude that there is a confusion of thought here, this is certainly not enough to show that 'the Zande belief in oracles' is confused.

As I read Evans-Pritchard's account, oracles are mainly consulted to determine whether it is propitious to undertake some important and potentially hazardous enterprise. Now though to say that circumstances are 'propitious' is in a way to make a kind of prediction, the relation of what is said to the future is very complex and indeterminate. For instance, that it is propitious to act in a certain way is no guarantee that so doing will be successful or turn out well: there are endless opportunities for explaining failure which do not conflict with the act's propitiousness. Again, there is ample room for debate as to what is to count as an action's 'turning out well'. The literature of oracular consultation in other cultures, the Greek for example, is full of cases in which an agent misreads the oracle's pronouncements because his ideas of what is and is not advantageous are distorted or blinkered; indeed it seems clear that one important role of oracles has been precisely to raise probing questions on this sort of issue. Such a literature is essential to our understanding of what the oracle was

[12] Mounce, op. cit., p. 352.

for the Greeks, for example, to our understanding of what sort of pronouncements the oracle issued. Any analogue to this literature in Zande folklore would be an essential feature of the grammar of the Zande poison oracle; essential, therefore, too to the possibility of distinguishing between what is and what is not superstitious in the thinking of individual Azande.

I have wanted, in the foregoing discussion, to distinguish between the beliefs people hold and the language in which those beliefs are expressed and which makes them possible. And I have tried to undermine the seductive idea that the grammar of our language is itself the expression of a set of beliefs or theories about how the world is, which might in principle be justified or refuted by an examination of how the world *actually* is. This temptation is hard enough to resist in the case of our own language; so much the harder when we are dealing with a language the forms of which are alien, and even perhaps repugnant, to us. A large part of the difficulty springs from the fact that the distinction is not a clear cut or stable one (as is brought out, probably more forcefully than anywhere else, in Wittgenstein's *On Certainty*). Furthermore, the grammar of a language has its concrete realisation *in* the expression of particular beliefs (though not only there). The grammar of the word 'pain' finds expression in what we say about the pains (or absence of pains) of particular people. The grammar of the Zande word we translate as 'oracle' finds expression in what individual Azande say and do in connection with particular oracular consultations. But what we mean by 'pain' is not the sum of our particular beliefs about the pains (or absence of pains) of particular people; and what the Azande mean by their word for 'oracle' is not the sum of their particular beliefs about oracles. Indeed, the whole notion of a 'sum of beliefs' in this connection is highly suspect.

Of course, the influence of modern industrial civilisation may (and does) tend to squeeze out the practices and judgements in which talk of oracles and witches find its expression. But this is not to say that 'belief in oracles and witches' has been *refuted* – perhaps by showing that the world does not contain such things. Any more than the decline in religious faith in industrial society is the result of its having been demonstrated that reality does not contain such a thing as a God. None of this is to say that belief in oracles and witches (or in God) cannot be criticised – there are more kinds of criticism than one. Though when we engage in such criticism we might do well to remember the parable of the mote and the beam. 'For with what judgement ye judge, ye shall be judged : and with what measure ye mete, it shall be measured to you again.'[13]

[13] *Matthew*, vii, 3.

MAIN PUBLICATIONS

The Idea of a Social Science and its Relation to Philosophy (Routledge & Kegan Paul, 1958)

Ethics and Action (Routledge & Kegan Paul, 1972)

Studies in the Philosophy of Wittgenstein (ed.) (Routledge & Kegan Paul, 1969)

BIOGRAPHICAL NOTES

G. E. M. Anscombe was born in 1919 and studied philosophy initially at Oxford, and held research studentships at Oxford and Cambridge before becoming a Research Fellow and subsequently Fellow at Somerville College. She was made an Honorary Fellow of Somerville College on her appointment to the Chair of Philosophy at Cambridge which she has held since 1970. She has also become since an Honorary Fellow of St Hugh's College, Oxford, and a Fellow of New Hall, Cambridge. She was a prominent member of Wittgenstein's circle at Cambridge and remained one of his closest friends. She has been much involved in translation and posthumous publication of some of Wittgenstein's writings and in the exposition and discussion of his work. She is married to another contributor to the volume, Peter Geach, who is also a noted interpreter of Wittgenstein. She has contributed extensively to various philosophical symposia and taken a lively part at philosophical conferences in Britain and abroad. She was made a Fellow of the British Academy in 1967.

Renford Bambrough was born in 1926 and entered St John's College, Cambridge, with a Major Scholarship in classics in 1945, upon his release from war service as a coal miner. He read classics, but also attended philosophy lectures and meetings of the Moral Sciences Club, where he heard Russell, Wittgenstein, Broad and Wisdom. He has been a Fellow of St John's College since 1950 and Dean since 1964. In 1966 he moved from a University Lectureship in Classics to a similar appointment in the Faculty of Philosophy. He was Stanton Lecturer in the Philosophy of Religion from 1962 to 1965. He has held visiting appointments at Cornell University, the University of California, Berkeley, the University of Oregon and the University of Melbourne. Since 1972 he has been Editor of *Philosophy*, the journal of the Royal Institute of Philosophy. He was distinguished Visiting Scholar at Melbourne in 1975 and he gave the first H. B. Acton lectures at the Royal Institute of Philosophy.

Michael Dummett was born in 1925 and came as a scholar to Christ Church College, Oxford, in 1942. He served in the army, in the Royal Artillery and later the Intelligence Corps, from 1943 to 1947, when he resumed his studies at Oxford. He was Assistant Lecturer in Philosophy at Birmingham from 1950 to 1951 and became a Fellow by Examination at All Souls College, Oxford, from 1950 to 1957, and a Junior Research Fellow from 1957 to 1962 when he became a Reader in the Philosophy of Mathematics at Oxford, a post which he relinquished in 1974. He remained a Fellow of All Souls during this period and has lately become Senior Research Fellow. He has been on several occasions Visiting Professor at Stanford University and other major American universities. He became a Fellow of the British Academy in 1969. Mr Dummett has taken a prominent part in work for racial integration and the welfare of immigrants, his wife contributing materially, in organisation and writing, to the same cause.

Antony Flew was born in 1923 and brought up in Cambridge, where his father was Principal of Wesley House. He studied at St John's College, Oxford, and won the John Locke Scholarship at Oxford where he was also Lecturer in Philosophy at Christ Church. He later became a Lecturer in Philosophy at Aberdeen and was appointed to the Chair of Philosophy at Keele in 1954. In 1973 he became Professor of Philosophy at Reading. He combines with his main philosophical concerns a considerable interest in the problems of psychical research and in the critical examination of religious claims. In addition to his own books he has been the Editor of various other studies. In recent years he has shown much interest in social and political questions. He has been a visitor at many universities abroad.

Peter Geach was born in 1916 and studied at Balliol College. Oxford, from where he proceeded, via a Research Studentship at St Deiniol's Library, Hawarden, to philosophical research at Cambridge from 1945 to 1951, when he became Assistant Lecturer in Philosophy at Birmingham and subsequently Senior Lecturer and Reader. He was appointed to the Chair of Logic at Leeds in 1966. Like his wife, Professor Anscombe, Geach has been a very close student of Wittgenstein and has helped in making his work better known and more fully available. He has interested himself extensively in the philosophy of religion as well as in logic and general philosophy. He was made a Fellow of the British Academy in 1965.

D. W. Hamlyn was born in 1924 in Plymouth where he was brought up. He went to Exeter College, Oxford, in 1942. After a year there he served for three years in the army (RAC and Hodson's Horse, IAC), returning to Oxford in 1946 where he read first *literae humaniores* and then philosophy and psychology. In 1950 he was appointed Junior Research Fellow at Corpus Christi College, Oxford, and from 1953 to 1954 was Lecturer in Philosophy at Jesus College, Oxford. In 1954 he was appointed Lecturer in Philosophy at Birkbeck College, University of London, being promoted to Reader in 1963 and Professor and Head of the Department in 1964. He has occupied this position since that date. He has been Editor of *Mind* since 1972. Professor Hamlyn has continued his interest in psychology and in Greek philosophy along with his main philosophical concerns.

R. M. Hare was born in 1919 and served as an officer in the Royal Artillery in the war of 1939–45. He was a prisoner of war at Singapore and Siam, after which he resumed his place as a scholar at Balliol College, Oxford, where he became Fellow and Tutor in Philosophy in 1947. He was appointed to the White's Chair of Moral Philosophy at Oxford in 1966 and is now a Fellow of Corpus Christi College. He has been Visiting Professor at Michigan and Delaware, and Visiting Fellow at Princeton and

Canberra. From 1963 to 1966 he gave the Wilde Lectures in Natural Religion at Oxford. He became a Fellow of the British Academy in 1964. Professor Hare's interest in problems of practice is reflected, not only in his writings on Moral Philosophy but also in his work on bodies such as the National Road Safety Advisory Council, and the Church of England's Working Party on euthanasia.

Jonathan Harrison was born in 1924 and began his university education as a scholar of Corpus Christi College, Oxford, where he took his degree in PPE in 1945. He became a Lecturer in Philosophy in the Durham Division of the University of Durham in 1947. He moved to Edinburgh as a Lecturer in Philosophy in 1959, becoming later Senior Lecturer, and in 1964 he was appointed to his present post of Professor of Philosophy in the University of Nottingham. He was a Visiting Professor at North Western University in 1968. In addition to his general interest in Philosophy Professor Harrison has paid special attention to some of the problems presented by the claims of paranormal psychology. He was President of the Mind Association in 1971.

R. W. Hepburn was born in 1927 and brought up and educated at Aberdeen, except for a brief spell, during the war, at Oxford. He taught in the Department of Moral Philosophy at Aberdeen from 1952 to 1959, when he became Visiting Professor, New York University, for 1959–60. He was appointed to the Chair of Philosophy, University of Nottingham in 1960, then to a Chair of Philosophy at the University of Edinburgh in 1964. In 1975 he became Professor of Moral Philosophy at Edinburgh. He has taken a special interest in the philosophy of art and aesthetics and in the critical investigation of religious claims. The latter interest is reflected in his appointment to deliver the Stanton Lectures at Cambridge from 1965 to 1968 and the Margaret Harris Lectures on Religion in the University of Dundee in 1974. He also gave one of the Heslington Lectures in the University of York in 1970.

Stephan Körner was born at Ostrava, Czechoslovakia, in 1913 and had his university education, first at Charles University, Prague, and then at Trinity Hall, Cambridge. After a period of Army service he started his academic career as a Lecturer in Philosophy at Bristol where he also became Professor of Philosophy in 1952 and served later as Dean of the Faculty of Arts and Pro-Vice-Chancellor. He has held Visiting Professorships at many American universities and been President of the Mind Association, the Aristotelian Society, and the International Union of History and Philosophy of Science. He combines his present post with a Professorship at Yale University where he resides for part of the academic session. Professor Körner has been Editor of *Ratio* since 1961 and was made a Fellow of the British Academy in 1967.

P. F. Strawson was born in 1919. He was a scholar of St John's College, Oxford, from 1937 to 1940 and served in the RA and REME from 1940 to 1946, attaining the rank of Captain. He became Assistant Lecturer in Philosophy at the University College of North Wales in 1946 and won the John Locke Scholarship at Oxford in that year. In 1947 he returned to Oxford as Lecturer in Philosophy, and subsequently as Fellow and Praelector, at University College. He became a Reader in Philosophy at Oxford in 1966 and was appointed to the Waynflete Professorship of Metaphysical Philosophy at Oxford and a Fellowship at Magdalen College in 1968. He has lectured much in American universities, including a period as Visiting Professor at North Carolina and on two occasions at Princeton. He was President of the Aristotelian Society from 1969 to 1970 and has been a Fellow of the British Academy since 1960. He is an Honorary Fellow of St John's College, Oxford.

Richard Swinburne was born in 1934. After national service he went up to Exeter College, Oxford, on a classical scholarship in 1954. After graduating, he read for a B.Phil. in philosophy, and then spent the next four years studying theology, certain branches of science, and the history of philosophy and science. In 1958 he was appointed Fereday Fellow of St John's College, Oxford, and three years later, Leverhulme Research Fellow in the History and Philosophy of Science at the University of Leeds. In 1963 he became a Lecturer in Philosophy at the University of Hull, where, apart from a year teaching at the University of Maryland, he remained until 1972, when he took up his present appointment as Professor of Philosophy at the University of Keele. He is Wilde Lecturer in Natural and Comparative Religion at the University of Oxford from 1975 to 1978. He is also Secretary of the *Analysis* Committee.

J. O. Urmson was born in 1915 and entered Corpus Christi College, Oxford, in 1934. He became a Senior Demy of Magdalen College in 1938. He was a Fellow by Examination of Magdalen from 1939 to 1945, rather nominally since he served in the Army throughout this period. He became a Lecturer of Christ Church in 1945, and was a Student of Christ Church from 1946 to 1955. He was Professor of Philosophy in St Andrews University from 1955 to 1959 when he returned to Corpus Christi College, Oxford. He has been a visiting Professor at Princeton University and, three times, at the University of Michigan. He has taken part in the publication of some of the papers of the late Professor J. L. Austin.

Godfrey Vesey was born in Yorkshire in 1923 and brought up in Cheshire. After five years in the Army he read moral science at St Catharine's College, Cambridge. From 1952 to 1969 he was successively Assistant Lecturer, Lecturer and Reader in Philosophy at King's College, London. He has been Visiting Professor of Philosophy at Carleton College, Minnesota, and at the University of Oregon. He was elected Honorary Director of the Royal Institute of Philosophy in 1965, and instituted the publication of the Annual Lectures and the holding of conferences every other year. He has edited the Proceedings of these conferences. In 1969 he was appointed to the Chair of Philosophy at the Open University, where his work includes the writing of correspondence texts for single-discipline and inter-disciplinary courses, and the making of radio and television programmes.

W. H. Walsh was born in 1913 and received his university education at Oxford. He won the Gaisford Greek Prose Prize and became a Junior Research Fellow at Merton College in 1936. He served in the war of 1939–45 in the Royal Corps of Signals and was later employed in a branch of the Foreign Office. He became Lecturer in Philosophy at Dundee in 1946, but returned to Oxford in 1947 to become Philosophy Tutor at Merton College. In 1960 he was appointed Professor of Logic and Metaphysics at Edinburgh, where he is now a Vice-Principal of the University. He has been a Visiting Professor at Ohio State University, Dartmouth College and the University of Maryland. Professor Walsh's main philosophical work has been on Kant, but he has also shown special interest in philosophy of history and again in the renewed study of Hegel. He was President of the Aristotelian Society from 1964 to 1965 and has been a Fellow of the British Academy since 1969.

Geoffrey Warnock was born in 1923 and served in the war of 1939–45 becoming a Captain in the Irish Guards. He entered New College, Oxford, in 1945 and in 1949 became a Fellow by Examination at Magdalen College, Oxford, where, after a period as Fellow and Tutor at Brasenose College, he became Fellow and Tutor in 1953. He became Principal of Hertford College, Oxford, in 1971. He has been Visiting Professor at Princeton and the University of Wisconsin. He has helped to edit papers of J. L. Austin for posthumous publication.

Bernard Williams was born in 1929 and studied classics and philosophy at Oxford. He spent his National Service as a pilot in the RAF. He was elected to an Examination Fellowship at All Souls College, Oxford, in 1951, and to a Tutorial Fellowship at New College in 1954. Between 1959 and 1967 he taught in the University of London, first as a Lecturer at University College and then as Professor at Bedford College. He was elected Knightbridge Professor of Philosophy at Cambridge and a Fellow of King's College in 1967. He has held Visiting Appointments at the University College of Ghana (now Legon University), Princeton, and Harvard. He has been a Fellow of the British Academy since 1971.

Peter Winch was born in London in 1926. On leaving school he served in the Royal Navy from 1944 to 1947. From 1947 to 1951 he studied at St Edmund Hall, Oxford. His university teaching career began in 1951 in the University of Wales at the University College of Swansea, where he held successive appointments of Assistant Lecturer, Lecturer, and Senior Lecturer until 1964. From 1961 to 1962 he was Visiting Professor at the University of Rochester in New York State. In 1964 he was appointed to a Readership in Philosophy in the University of London at Birkbeck College, a post he held until his appointment to the Chair of Philosophy at the

University of Arizona in 1970. From 1965 to 1971 he edited *Analysis*, subsequently becoming a member of the *Analysis* Committee. He is a member of the Editorial Board of Blackwell's *Library of Philosophy and Logic*. Like some other contributors to this volume Professor Winch has taken a close interest in Wittgenstein and made this in part the basis of his approach to other subjects, for example in problems of social science and of religion.

INDEX